CALVERT-HENDERSON
QUALITY OF LIFE INDICATORS

HAZEL HENDERSON, JON LICKERMAN, AND PATRICE FLYNN, EDITORS

Calvert Group®

A member of The Acacia Group®

Table of Contents

All over the country, citizens are demonstrating a desire to engage in serious discussions about how to measure quality of life and livable communities in the United States. For the past five years, Calvert Group has been preparing for this exciting debate. We are pleased to release in this initial volume the Calvert-Henderson Quality of Life Indicators, the first national, comprehensive assessment of the quality of life in the United States using a systems approach. The deep insights, illuminating findings, and bold explorations into historical and contemporary environmental, economic and social conditions of the country are our contributions to this important debate. We hope its messages and many lessons will empower people from all walks of life who are equally concerned about our future together on this planet.

Barbara Krumsiek

President and CEO

Calvert Group

December 1999

Chapter 1

Foreword

by Hazel Henderson

This book, which launches and explains the ongoing Calvert-Henderson Quality of Life Indicators, is about change. It is no surprise to anyone today that our society and economy and the very fabric of our daily lives are undergoing rapid restructuring. The twin forces of globalizing technology and markets are accelerating these changes in all countries as they move us toward a seamless global economy.

Many see these changes as ushering in a "New Economy." *Business Week* editorializes that technological productivity and globalization can continue to deliver low inflation and full employment with budget surpluses and lower interest rates as well. Others are more cautious, including U.S. Federal Reserve Board Chairman Alan Greenspan, London's *The Economist*, and others who see the current U.S. economy quite differently. They worry about over-valued stocks leading to an asset bubble, record trade deficits, heavy consumer and corporate debt, and other potential threats, leading to a lower dollar that's already giving ground to the euro as a global reserve currency. The debate concerns appropriate methods for measuring productivity and inflation.

How can there be two such diametrically opposite views of the same market data and official national statistics? The answer relates to differing world views and assumptions underlying both the statistics and the mindsets of the analysts on whose interpretations we rely. What kind of mental models, or paradigms inform their judgements? These paradigms (or different pairs of "spectacles" through which they see the data) are key to understanding why so many brilliant people disagree, even those who spend their careers studying market and social trends in our globalized economy.

This book and our ongoing Calvert-Henderson Quality of Life Indicators will enable the reader to peek into the minds of a wide range of experts on trends in our economy, society, and environment. The reader will understand how statistics, which always lag the real world, have fallen further behind as global change has accelerated. I hope that the reader will find it easier to interpret the proliferating debates about indicators and indexes of our national wealth, progress, health, and well-being. The reader can join the debates about whether the Consumer Price Index (CPI) overstates inflation (by up to 1.5 percent as the Boskin Commission reported) or if the CPI is understated (because it omits energy, food, and assets such as houses). This volume provides a statistical bedrock assessment of a wide range of key factors affecting the overall quality of our lives and our children's future.

The 12 Calvert-Henderson Quality of Life Indicators range far beyond the traditional national accounts of Gross National Product (GNP) and its narrower form Gross Domestic Product (GDP) and other money-denominated indexes on inflation (CPI), incomes, interest rates, trade deficits, and the national budget. Our indicators dig deeper, going behind the national statistics on employment, health, education, and the state of our infrastructure and national security. We are not trying to offer reweighted and recalculated versions of macroeconomic statistics, as many other worthy efforts have attempted. Our approach is to paint a broader picture of quality of life to complement current statistics and identify statistical "blind spots" where new data collection is needed.

The study shows that current "statistical cameras" are pointed at areas where conditions are rapidly restructuring our institutions, whether business, government, academic, or civic society. For example, the composition of our GNP has been changing from goods you can drop on your foot to services. Statisticians are reformulating GNP to reflect these new realities, but still lag in recategorizing software and many other services, which together now represent the largest sector of our "Information Age" economy. Indeed in November 1999, the Bureau of Economic Analysis recategorized software as investment rather than consumption in the GDP, which revised average productivity since 1990 from 1.5 percent up to 2 percent.

All the world's industrializing societies are undergoing similar changes and restructuring, as they move from the earlier to the later stages of the Industrial Revolution. Part of this great transition is toward information-based economies. Here knowledge, intellectual capital, and the more intangible human and social assets replace manual labor and some of the tangible capital earlier economic textbooks called the "factors of production." This transition is often accompanied by a deeper knowledge of natural processes and ecological assets and the services nature provides. We slowly shift to recycling our industrial materials in closed-loop production, waste-reduction, re-manufacturing, and re-use. An industrial design revolution is quietly under way.

How was it that macro-economic statistics fell so far behind in mapping these fundamental shifts? A large part of the problem is that conventional economics and accounting considered air, water and nature's purifying cycles to be "free" goods. Only recently have textbooks begun to embrace "full-cost" prices, which account for all the social and environmental costs of production. Only in the past decade, have we seen the rise of environmental and ecological economics, full-cost accounting, and life cycle costing for investment purposes. All this, together with the rise of social and environmental auditing – accounting for "intangibles" and intellectual property – and the many attempts to overhaul GNP and GDP represent a potential revolution in accounting and statistics.

On the conceptual foundations of these early economic innovators, a host of new efforts to redefine human development, wealth and progress emerged in the 1980s and 1990s. David Morris of the Institute for Local Self-Reliance produced the Physical Quality of Life Index (PQLI) for the Overseas Development Council; Herman Daly and John Cobb created the Index of Sustainable Economic Welfare (ISEW) with Clifford Cobb in 1989. These indices deduct from GNP many environmental and social costs, arriving at a significantly lower "net GNP." They have been adapted widely in Europe, Australia, and the United States as the Genuine Progress Index (GPI) by 1995. Other approaches include the Fordham University Index of Social Health devised by Marque-Luisa and Marc Miringoff, also a consultant on our Calvert-Henderson Quality of Life Indicators.

To mixed reviews, the Clinton Administration attempted to "green" the GDP by means of an Integrated Environmental and Economic Satellite Account (IEESA) developed by the Bureau of Economic Analysis (BEA) of the Department of Commerce in 1994. The Congress directed the BEA to halt this work and charged the National Research Council to review the entire issue. In late 1999, the Council issued its report, *Nature's Numbers*, urging that the BEA be funded to re-start this effort. The World Bank in 1995 issued its own Wealth Index, which redefined "the wealth of nations" in significant ways. The World Bank now defines 60 percent of this wealth of nations as "human capital" (social organization and human skills and knowledge), 20 percent as environmental capital (nature's contribution), and 20 percent as "built capital" (factories, finance, capital). This caused a major change in the economics profession, with many of its best minds embracing pieces of the new thinking including Joseph Stiglitz, now the bank's chief economist, Harvard University's Jeffrey Sachs, and the Massachusetts Institute of Technology's Paul Krugman.

Perhaps the most influential, widely used and quoted new formula is the United Nations Human Development Index (HDI), produced by the UN Development Programme every year since 1990. The HDI began by weighting per capita income (in terms of Purchase Power Parity), education, and life expectancy to produce a rank for every one of the 187 member countries of the United Nations. The HDI updates and enhances its methodologies regularly, to include military vs. civilian budget ratios, environmental factors, poverty gaps, gender, and human rights data. The HDI has become a world benchmark on government performance and has given rise to some 50 national HDI versions.

The most pressing methodological debate over new measures of wealth, progress, and human development has concerned the extent to which money coefficients and macroeconomic models can capture broad new areas of concern: human rights, health, education, environmental, and overall quality of life. Such methods currently weight all data from different economic sectors into one index. Many believe, as we do with the Calvert-

Henderson Quality of Life Indicators, that aggregating all these "apples and oranges" into one index is inappropriate and often confusing. Another issue concerns the use of "satellite accounts" for such environmental and social data. This designation indicates lesser value for such data.

We further believe that the diverse areas of quality of life covered in the Calvert-Henderson approach deserve their own metrics, specifically metrics that are most appropriate within the diverse disciplines that study such fields. For example, money coefficients cannot quantify human rights, air and water quality, recreational satisfaction, education, health, public safety, or national security. Money measures and percentages of national budgets can give clues about quality of life but are often simply input data. Composite indices do not measure outcomes or results.

In all the indicators we created, with the help of our experts in each area, we present a model linking the major factors and processes, providing a roadmap of how decisions flow through various institutional structures to create outcomes. These systems models help identify why in each area, our country has succeeded or fallen short in achieving its stated policy goals.

In examining each area or domain of quality of life, we have been in a process of discovery. Surprises came as we rethought how each indicator contributed to or, in some cases, diminished our overall quality of life. We identified the "holes" in the statistical pictures and where data-gathering needs new focus.

Most of all, in this five-year research project, we all came to appreciate each others' expertise and began to see a bigger picture. Thus, our 12 unbundled indicators came together as a broader pattern represented on our cover, while at the same time, retaining the richness and detail of each of the 12 domains. This systems approach allows us to display the wealth of diverse data rigorously without the loss of detail, which plagues any single index approach.

In each indicator, the domain it covers is related to all the other indicators. The 12 indicators were selected using many sources. Firstly, they are major areas of public concern as reflected in public opinion polls, the media, political campaigns, and debates over decades. Secondly, these domains are most often covered in many of the existing sets of local state, national, and international statistics we reviewed. However, few integrate so many diverse elements as in the Calvert-Henderson Quality of Life Indicators or include such groundbreaking approaches. Each one of our indicators is grounded in current demographic data, allowing revealing insights often invisible in highly averaged indices. Furthermore, in two separate polls on governmental reform by the highly respected Americans Talk Issues Foundation, Americans were asked if they approved or disapproved of the following proposal:

"In the same way we've developed and use the Gross National Product to measure the growth of the economy, [we should] develop and use a scorecard of new indicators for holding politicians responsible for progress toward other national goals, like improving education, extending health care, preserving the environment, and making the military meet today's needs."

In these two surveys in March of 1993, 72 percent of the American people agreed that such quality of life indicators were needed. These results were verified in a debate format where an opposing view was offered in the second survey in January of 1994:

"Opponents say that eventually economists will be able to calculate a single indicator of progress, a kind of enlarged GNP, that bundles into this money-based statistic our progress in all major areas including the economy, health, education, the environment, and so forth. This single number would be easier for everyone to use to rank ourselves against other nations and to judge the performance of our political leaders."

Only 22 percent of respondents found this opposing view to be convincing, and when the original question was asked again, support went up to 79 percent (Kay 1998).

Now, a word about each of our indicators, regarding the rapid transformation our society is experiencing, and how each indicator may evolve to capture such changes in our world. The indicators are presented in alphabetical order to reflect our belief that each domain is equally important in understanding quality of life in a holistic manner.

Education

Our Education Indicator gives an overview of current educational issues. Swirling around the debates over educational reform, school vouchers, "charter" schools, and home schooling are those on the shift to today's globalized information-based economy. Knowledge is now widely recognized as a key factor of production.

The World Bank and other multilateral institutions now agree that investments in education (particularly at preschool and K through 12 levels) are the new keys, along with investments in health, to economic development. Nothing is changing our business and academic institutions faster than the new definitions of human and intellectual capital. As many new Internet-based, e-commerce businesses know, a company cannot "own" the part of its knowledge base that resides in the heads of its employees. The rise of generous stock options, partnerships, and Employee Stock Ownership Plans are all related to this new evaluation of intellectual capital on which all technical and social innovation is based. Today, more than ever, education is a basic human right in many other countries as well as in the United States. Furthermore, levels of education will drive all the world's economies toward development, depending on how they structure and invest in educating our most precious resource: our children.

Employment

The field of employment and work has changed immensely in the past decade. We have come from a recession in the early 1990s to the lowest (4.1 percent) unemployment recorded since the 1950s. This has caused a rethink of the Non-Inflation Accelerating Rate of Unemployment (NAIRU) used by the Federal Reserve Board in setting interest rates. A NAIRU under 5.5 percent was thought to be inflationary. Today, our economy is running at higher levels of employment without this expected rise in inflation due, many say, to the "New Economy" factors mentioned earlier. Our Employment Indicator reminds us that a large but not well measured percentage of productive work is unpaid. This unpaid work in caring for elders, the sick, and children in home or volunteer organization settings is unaccounted for in the GNP. Many organizations in the nonprofit, civic sector of our society now call for full recognition of the value of this caring work. Some call for housework and parenting to be paid, through statutory pension benefits or in marriage contracts. This area of concern will likely grow as both parents in families are in the paid work force. The "family values" debate encodes many new dilemmas faced by parents as they juggle two jobs plus child care and elder care as our population ages. Worldwide, the United Nations HDI in 1995 estimated unpaid work by the world's women at $11 trillion and by men another $5 trillion. This $16 trillion total was simply missing from the 1995 World GDP of $24 trillion. In addition, our indicator tracks the growing ranks of the self-employed, part-timers, and the composition by gender, ethnicity and age of the U.S. workforce.

And whatever happened to the promise of the Industrial Age for more leisure, as machines and automation took over production tasks? Today, Americans work longer hours than their counterparts in Europe and Japan. Yet, there is much debate over the statistics on work and leisure, as we learn in our Re-Creation Indicator.

Energy

This indicator is a key to the overall efficiency of our economy. Our GNP has been growing with less energy input in the past 25 years, since the first OPEC oil embargo in 1973. But the United States still lags Japan and Europe, using almost twice the energy they use per unit of GNP. This puts the United States in an uncompetitive position in our older manufacturing sectors even as our Internet-based "New Economy" grows. Our reliance on low-fuel efficiency cars and fossil fuels decreases our flexibility. All these issues of restructuring our economy came to a head in the debate over climate change. The fossil fuel industry lobbied hard and spent millions on ad campaigns to oppose the 1997 Kyoto Agreements to reduce fossil fuel carbon emissions. Yet the scientific evidence now overwhelmingly points to the need to reduce such emissions. Many analysts, including Amory Lovins of the Rocky Mountain Institute in Colorado, believe that the fossil-industrial transition to the Information Age and what I have called the Solar Age will usher in a prosperous, profitable economy based on renewable resource use and deeper knowledge. Thus energy-efficiency can mean less waste, higher, cleaner profits, more comfortable homes, communities, and travel with less pollution. The transition from here to there is illuminated in the Energy Indicator.

Environment

This indicator seeks to embrace the interactions between human society and our economic processes and the natural world, its resources, and other species. Naturally, such a task is too enormous to do more than find within the model some key "surrogate" indicators as proxies for such a vast area. We are learning more about our environments locally and about planetary ecosystems, the crucial role of biodiversity, and human effects on the ozone layer and climate.

While our Environment Indicator recognizes these broad concerns, we focus attention on indicators closest to the lives of a majority of U.S. citizens. Air and water quality became our focus, since people cannot survive without acceptable air and water quality. The National Research Council's 1999 report, *Nature's Numbers,* also notes "Greater emphasis should be placed…on measuring actual human exposures to air and water pollution" (Recommendations 4.3 and 5.9). Through these lenses we can understand better the causes of degradation and pollution and the many steps needed to reverse these threats. As our systems approach reveals, many other domains of quality of life, such as infrastructure design, energy use, shelter, health, employment, public safety, and national security, all impinge on our environment for better or worse.

Sheer population increases show by most forecasts a rise of between 8 to 10 billion people on our planet early in the new millennium. However, the huge global gap between rich and poor still shows that per capita consumption of energy and resources in the United States is some 50 times greater than that of 2 billion of the world's poor and undernourished. Thus, the most potent threat to the environment is waste and over-consumption, with the United States as the world's chief polluter. As we see in our other indicators, the potential for redesigning our infrastructures and production methods using better information and "greener technologies" can also benefit the world's climate and ecology as well as our own quality of life.

Health

Our Health Indicator begins by explaining that the United States provides more health care services at higher costs per capita than any other country in the world. This enormous sector of our economy is becoming a top focus of national concern since it delivers only modest improvements in health status in some areas and none in others. Of growing concern are the some 50 million Americans who have no health insurance and the debate over a "Patient's Bill of Rights" to hold health maintenance organizations and insurance companies more accountable for decisions over patient treatment.

This indicator offers a model of our current system that helps to clarify the situation as a systemic set of issues. Health is being redefined beyond the medical intervention model. Today, Americans are focusing on prevention, stress-reduction, and life-style choices. Tobacco and alcohol use and even the availability of guns are issues entering the public health debate. More Americans now consult "complementary" and "alternative" health providers than visit conventional medical doctors and facilities. This is a paradigm shift that is restructuring the entire medical-industrial complex and its technocratic, bureaucratic approach, which represents more than 13 percent of our GNP.

How will we integrate these two very different approaches to health? How will we provide for those left out of the current system, especially children? An October 1999 study in the Federal Reserve Bank of New York's *Economic Policy Review* cites the effects of urban poverty. Fifteen-year-old black and white males life expectancy rates were compared in several cities. In areas of New York City that were predominantly low-income and African American, only 37 percent of the population was expected to live to age 65. In Detroit, the figure was 50 percent. White fifteen-year-olds in poverty areas of Detroit and Cleveland did a little better. In Detroit, 60 percent were found likely to live to age 65 with 64 percent likely in Cleveland. Average life expectancy for all U.S. whites is 77 years compared to 62 years for blacks. Our indicator allows us to see such gaps, which, of course, relate to similar data in our Income, Shelter, Safety, Education, and Human Rights Indicators.

Human Rights

This indicator views the state of human rights in the United States in broad areas: fundamental rights to the security of person and the U.S. Bill of Rights and Amendments to the Constitution, including freedom of expression, religious freedom, right of assembly, and voting rights. Beyond these basic rights, the model embraces an evolving international view embodied in the Universal Declaration of Human Rights.

These and other human rights issues are of great concern in Europe, Japan, and Canada and serve as a cornerstone of U.S. foreign policy. Today a crucial issue is to what extent the sovereignty of a nation must be balanced with the human rights of its citizens. Many other countries include in human rights economic, cultural, and social rights (to education, social participation, health care, leisure time, and to social security). Another evolution concerns the embracing of women and children in the definition of human rights –

now widely recognized – if not fully achieved. This indicator is crucial to quality of life in the United States and worldwide.

Income

Our indicator dissects conventional macro-statistics to reveal important information concealed by the averages. Although U.S. incomes at the low end have been essentially flat for over a decade, there are now signs of increase due to the "New Economy" phenomenon. Yet the gap between rich and poor Americans is still historically high, an issue that does not bode well for any democracy. Other issues include the extent to which technology and globalization are squeezing the incomes of less skilled Americans. These issues also relate to our Employment and Education Indicators. And what are we to make of the 1995 national survey by the Merck Foundation and the Harwood Group that found 28 percent of Americans had opted for lower incomes and moved to rural communities in order to improve their quality of life? Clearly, values are changing and new trade-offs are being made between more money and more time, tranquil and less-polluted environments.

Infrastructure

This indicator unpacks macro-statistics to reveal an ongoing debate: to what extent has our country been overlooking the vital role its infrastructure plays in undergirding our economy. Historically, infrastructure referred to highways, railroads, harbors, bridges, aqueducts, public buildings, dams, and the like. As our industrial societies evolved, we added airports, communications systems, energy supplies, water, and other utilities. Today, we think of infrastructure as including education, research and development, computerized "backbone" systems, and all taxpayer-supported systems that we use in commerce and on which large sectors of our economy rely. A recent trend picked up by our indicator is that of the privatization of growing areas of our formerly publicly owned infrastructure, including electric utilities, phone, water, and other services. Such publicly-funded investments used to be "expensed" items in our GDP accounts. As of 1996, a more realistic asset budget in GNP now accounts for such investments as "assets" since they often have a useful lifetime of 50 to 100 years or more. This accounting change has contributed to the budget surplus. This indicator is related to most other indicators, as infrastructure is the key to energy-efficiency, whether our cities sprawl over virgin lands and farms, or whether we infill older or vacant land in our cities. These factors, in turn relate to environmental protection, pollution, housing , education, public health, and safety.

National Security

The U.S. public's view of national security has been changing for over a decade. Even before the end of the Cold War, Americans were identifying global economic competitiveness and environmental pollution as issues of national security beyond traditional military views of defense.

Our National Security Indicator reveals how Americans, Congress, the Executive Branch, and a host of institutional players actually shape our current national security policy. This inside view from a retired military officer, identifies other potential lags in the military view of national security. These relate to prevention of threats and conflicts. These must be addressed via intelligence, diplomacy, treaty-making, surveillance, and verification most often involving allies and multilateral agencies including the United Nations.

Short-changing such anticipatory, preventive policies inevitably leads to more drastic, expensive military interventions such as those that might have been prevented in Bosnia, Kosovo, East Timor, and other trouble spots. Yet our indicator shows an alarming drop-off in such preventive activities, including deteriorating U.S. embassy facilities, cuts to State Department diplomatic activities, pull-backs from international peace-keeping and surveillance operations with our allies and the United Nations. As this volume goes to press, the Congress voted to pay some of our now $1.6 billion arrears owed to the UN. The public debate about a "new isolationism," the changing meaning of "national sovereignty," and globalization will continue for years to come. Our National Security Indicator will provide an ongoing roadmap to clarify these issues, which are fundamentally linked to all other areas and indicators of our national life.

Public Safety

Our indicator maps the rapid evolution in the debate about this aspect of our quality of life. As our society became more complex, the views that safety was a personal affair and risk-taking a private choice evolved. While individuals are still largely responsible for their behavior, today we live in an interdependent world. Many risks of daily life (e.g., exposure to toxic wastes, gun violence in schools, car and highway design, and risks in foods and other products) are involuntary and often unavoidable. Thus our indicator also captures these new concerns in public safety and links today's risks to health, education, and cultural factors. Crime statistics and the tragedies of gun violence are seen in this larger setting. This systemic view provides insights for individual risk-reduction and may help us rethink our views on improving public safety.

Re-Creation

This indicator goes beyond the material aspects of our existence and our focus on healthy bodies and well-educated minds to our spirits and how we re-create ourselves. Of course body, mind, and spirit are all integrated within our lives. We all have diverse ways of expressing these aspects of our being and personal development.

Our indicator embraces all these aspects in mapping our extraordinarily diverse forms of recreation from volunteering in community projects, helping preserve wildlife, and serving the poor to attending concerts, museums, or just enjoying bowling, hunting, and fishing. The model traces how we organize and spend our private and public resources on such recreational activities. The indicator embraces self-improving experience (from religious, spiritual pursuits to other forms of self-development); patronizing the arts; physical sports and fitness; do-it-yourself crafts; gardening; home-improvement; hobbies; vicarious experience (TV, video games, and the Internet); socializing and home entertaining; travel and tourism (now the world's biggest industry); games of chance and betting; and chemical escape (alcohol, tobacco and drugs).

This indicator is a fascinating panorama of these evolving activities of Americans, which together form the largest and fastest-growing sector of our services-dominated economy. Statistical and methodological debates abound on the size and shape of this emerging "Attention Economy" (Henderson 1996). How can we resolve the debates about work and leisure time? As in all our indicators, we become vividly aware of the crucial nature of statistics and the assumptions and paradigms driving their collection.

The rapid evolution of the entire field of self-development and re-creation augurs additional social and political change. Today's drive for self-development-an essentially spiritual need-is now spilling over into our material lives through the growth of socially responsible investment and in communities opting to honor their local past and culture by building museums and art galleries, as LORD Cultural Resources Principal, Kathleen Brown continues to document. Over 109 million Americans volunteer at least 3.5 hours a week in their communities, and the nonprofit, voluntary sector contributes between 7 percent and 10 percent of the GNP (Independent Sector 1999). A 1999 poll cited in *Business Week,* found that 78 percent of Americans say that they feel the need in their lives to experience spiritual growth, up from 20 percent in 1994. Our Re-Creation Indicator will keep us aware of such changes.

Shelter

This indicator dissects the macro-economic data to reveal a "good news, bad news" picture. The American dream of home ownership has never been so fulfilled, with a record 66.3 percent now owning homes. A majority of Americans are well-housed with over two-thirds in affordable, physically adequate, uncrowded housing. The bad news is that shelter deprivation still exists in spite of our economic expansion. Some 5.3 million low-income renters are in distress and an additional half to three quarters of a million Americans are homeless at any given time. These statistics seem to be a reflection of our national poverty gap shown in our Income Indicator. The state of shelter in the United States also affects opportunities for social mobility, education, and energy efficiency, and thus is related to many other indicators, including Employment, Health, Energy, and Environment.

In summary, I hope that this brief overview of our Calvert-Henderson Quality of Life Indicators will whet your appetite to delve deeper into this volume. Perhaps you will keep it as a desk reference as your interest in some or all of these aspects of quality of life is deepened. We will continue tracking this holistic view of our lives, society, and the economy with the help of FLYNN RESEARCH and Patrice Flynn, our co-editor.

It only remains for me to thank Patrice and our co-editor Jon Lickerman, Director of Calvert Social Investment Research Department, and all his colleagues, including Bruce Kenney, Shannon Pearce, and Adrienne Fitch-Frankel, for their thoughtful and dedicated contributions to this project. I am deeply grateful to both Jon Lickerman and Patrice Flynn for their wisdom and tenacity in wrestling with the mountains of data that we sifted and sorted into our indicators. I salute all of our experts in each area for their insights, academic rigor, and willingness to work together with us on this lengthy project. I salute our CEO, Barbara Krumsiek, who recognized the value of this project in the first weeks of her tenure and gave us all wholehearted support. My deepest gratitude goes to my dear colleague of 20 years, D. Wayne Silby, co-founder of Calvert Group who quietly encouraged me to introduce it to our Calvert Social Investment Fund Advisory Council almost 10 years ago. Chaired by Tim Smith of the Interfaith Center on Corporate Responsibility, this Council, on which I have served since 1982, has been "family" to me. The Council embraced the Calvert-Henderson Quality of Life Indicators and recommended the project to the Calvert Group. The results are in your hands.

REFERENCES

Henderson, Hazel. 1996. *Building a Win-Win World: Life Beyond Global Economic Warfare*. San Francisco, CA: Berrett-Koehler Publishers.

Henderson, Hazel. 1988. *The Politics of the Solar Age: Alternatives to Economics*. Indianapolis, IN: Knowledge Systems, Inc. and New York, NY: TOES Books.

Independent Sector. 1999. *Giving and Volunteering in the United States Executive Summary*. Washington, DC.

Kay, Alan F. 1998. *Locating Consensus for Democracy: A Ten-Year U.S. Experiment*. St. Augustine, FL: Americans Talk Issues Foundation.

National Research Council. 1999. *Nature's Numbers*. Washington, DC: National Academy Press.

Chapter 2

Introduction

by Jon Lickerman and Patrice Flynn

This volume is the culmination of a five-year research effort to paint a broad picture of the quality of life in the United States. It was created jointly by a multi-disciplinary group of practitioners and scholars from government agencies, for-profit firms, and nonprofit organizations who see the need for more practical and sophisticated metrics of societal conditions. The Calvert-Henderson Quality of Life Indicators allow individuals and/or groups to access in one place a comprehensive picture of the overall well-being of the nation in a manner that is easy to understand and use, statistically verifiable, grounded in theoretical and empirical knowledge about each domain, and rigorous in its treatment of the subject matter. The study offers a primer on the deeper trends and complexities that underlie oft quoted national statistics on quality of life. It is our hope that the Calvert-Henderson Indicators will be used to educate the public; broaden the national debate about our social, economic and environmental conditions; hold government and business accountable; and clarify the multiple choices we make as individuals in our work, education, leisure, and civic commitments.

The Calvert-Henderson Quality of Life Indicators represent the first national, comprehensive effort to redefine overall quality of life using a systems approach. The variables included in our definition of national quality of life are diverse, complex, and wide ranging. The indicators include traditional economic measures of employment, income distribution, and housing, along with assessments of infrastructure, health, and education. Our approach reviews aspects of public safety and energy consumption and their relation to quality of life while tackling complex issues related to national security, the environment, human rights, and re-creation. We believe that all of these measurements are necessary to attempt a comprehensive view of national well-being.

This report is a public education tool by which to distill and assess national trends. We report in-depth on major issues, some of which may be generally familiar to the readers and others unique to our work. We present comprehensive and complex views on each indicator, yet we do not offer a critique of what is working or what is not. The indicators suggest, for example, a growing divide in national incomes, significant improvements in national air quality, historically high home ownership rates, and a long-term decline in public infrastructure investment. We do not pass judgment on these trends, nor do we offer solutions or policy recommendations to some of the major challenges of our time. Our goal is more basic: to inform and

The Calvert-Henderson Quality of Life Indicators represent the first national, comprehensive effort to redefine overall quality of life using a systems approach.

present a framework through which to understand and assess salient national trends, using rigorous empirical techniques and reliable data.

In this era of information overload, the availability of reliable information, accompanied by an analysis of how to make sense of national data, is more critical than ever. The old adage that in a democracy "information is power" remains. An informed citizenry that has the intellectual tools and critical judgment to make sense of a complex picture exponentially increases its influence. To be understood, statistics must be placed in context to enhance its meaning. The Calvert-Henderson approach was designed as a response to this observation. We dedicate a chapter to each of the 12 Calvert-Henderson Indicators to bring the readers up to speed on the state of each indicator. We describe in detail the cutting-edge thinking on the topic from the perspective of scholars and practitioners well-versed in the respective fields of study. Complex issues are deconstructed by each author; underlying elements driving outcomes are revealed and discussed. We intend for this report to inform the public debates within government, business, and communities on our national well-being.

Although this study is not prescriptive, we are not impartial to national trends. We share a deep concern, accompanied by optimism, regarding the many findings that come out of this report. We believe that a broader, deeper, and more inclusive national debate about "what matters" is essential. As Hazel Henderson says, "we measure what we treasure." Therefore understanding the complexities of income distribution, environmental quality, and the status of education, among other issues, is essential to drawing a clearer picture of the health of the nation.

I. Origins of the Report

This study grew out of an 18-year relationship between an international futurist and an asset management firm. Calvert Group is a 23-year-old asset management company that is a leading specialist in the field of socially responsible investing. Hazel Henderson is an independent futurist, author, and pioneer in the field of sustainable development. Dr. Henderson authored and helped steer the quality of life conceptual approach for this project, which is based on her Country Futures Indicators©, and Calvert Group lead the research effort.

So it might be asked, why is an asset management firm toiling in the field of quality of life indicators? The answer lies in Calvert's specialty in socially responsible investing (SRI). At its core, SRI is about assessing the societal impacts of investments. Calvert and its cohorts apply an investment strategy that integrates portfolio management with the promotion of a healthy, equitable, and sustainable society. Simply put, we invest in companies that treat their workers well, minimize their environmental impact, contribute to their communities, and make healthy and socially useful products.

Over the course of our practice in socially responsible investing, it became evident that there were no broad indicators by which to guide our unique investment strategy. Yes, our portfolio managers had traditional economic indicators to help guide their financial investment decisions. Routine releases of the Consumer Price Index, housing starts, consumer credit, manufacturing orders and capacity utilization, job vacancies, growth in average earnings, productivity, and unit labor costs all provide information to navigate the direction of economic cycles and investment strategies.

Yet no such measurements existed to assess how a specific company contributes to or is affected by broader societal and environmental trends. While Calvert analysts had developed sophisticated tools to analyze a specific company's environmental impact, for example, there were no reliable indicators to determine the larger environmental trends. How was it that we could analyze the environmental impact of a major chemical company, yet we could not ascertain the overall quality of the environment in which it operates? Company management typically insists that it is improving its overall environmental record. We did not have the tools to assess whether indeed environmental quality was improving or worsening as a result of a company's behavior.

In a similar vein, when reviewing how to invest in the fast food industry, analysts had no indicators that would elucidate how further investments in an inherently low wage industry might impact broader socio-economic trends. What were the trends in national income distribution? What were the demographics of this traditionally low wage segment of the workforce? Was this growth industry contributing to increased national income disparities or simply providing a low rung step in the ladder of economic development for workers?

As a leading practitioner in the field of socially responsible investing, Calvert analysts did not have tools similar to those available to traditional investment professionals. We understood the need for a broader array of socio-economic indicators. We also began to understand that there was little information available to understand the relationships between economic forces and societal or environmental impacts. This dilemma led Calvert into the field of quality of life indicators.

Calvert analysts had a hard time separating their professional responsibilities from their roles as citizens. We saw that there was a broader audience who might benefit from analytical tools that take a comprehensive view of societal trends. Within the asset management business there are many proprietary tools, but very few are shared with the public. Calvert eventually decided to open up the process of developing quality of life indicators, work with a group of independent experts, and take our findings public. As this project unfolded, we at Calvert eventually understood our work as one of public education.

On a personal note, the editors of this volume individually received their introduction to the subject of quality of life indicators in various ways. Hazel Henderson's alarm in having to wash off pollutants from her daughter Ali's tiny body resulted in her leading a group of citizens to develop the now well-known air quality index in New York City in the 1960s. Hazel went on to dissect the problems of macroeconomic indexes and lend her support to Marian Chambers' Jacksonville Quality of Life Indicators in the mid-1980s, setting a precedent for community indicators project. Jon Lickerman received his introduction to the subject while working as a researcher and manager at Working Assets (now Citizens Trust) in San Francisco in the 1980s. Patrice Flynn became involved with quality of life indicators at the Urban Institute while working on the National Neighborhood Indicators Project in the 1990s. We have all watched the quality of life movement ripen and provide essential information for scholars, practitioners, funders, policy makers, and leaders in the United States and abroad.

II. Quality of Life Indicators Studies

The Calvert-Henderson Quality of Life Indicators deal with the application of statistics to the measurement of environmental, social and economic conditions over time. The project rests on the wealth of knowledge gained from four major fields of research. The first is the field of sustainable development or environmental indicators, which began in the 1950s in the United States, and has gained increasing attention among scholars, advocates, and elected and appointed leaders. A December 1998 report, spearheaded by David Berry with the U.S. Interagency Working Group on Sustainable Development Indicators, entitled *Sustainable Development in the United States*, provides a valuable reference point on the state of sustainable development research.

The Calvert-Henderson study also builds on the vast literature on social indicators. In the United States, the social indicators movement began in the 1960s with the well-known study by the American Academy of Arts and Sciences study for the National Aeronautics and Space Administration (NASA) from which Raymond Bauer coined the term "social indicators." The field of social indicators involves "issues related to variables and organizations that have an effect on the subjective and/or physical well-being of individuals, groups, communities, and/or society" (International Society for Quality of Life Studies). Kenneth Land's forthcoming article in the *Encyclopedia of Sociology* is a seminal treatise on the origins and state of social indicators in the United States as we cross into the 21st century (Land 2000). The collaborators in the Calvert-Henderson project learned a great deal from the pioneers in the field of social indicators.

The authors of the Calvert-Henderson Indicators also relied upon the solid research and analysis on economic indicators in the United States, mainly through the vast Federal government statistical system put in place in the 1910s and further developed in the mid-1940s. Scholars, business people, and citizens have come to rely upon these economic statistics, which are reported on a consistent basis. The monthly *Economic Indicators*, prepared by the Council of Economic Advisors for the Joint Economic Committee, provides a summary of these data.

The fourth source of knowledge upon which the Calvert-Henderson Indicators grew was the growing body of information on socially responsible investing (SRI), which now represents an estimated $2 trillion in the United States alone. Over the past 15 years, SRI analysts have struggled to develop reliable metrics on company performance. The annual review by the Environmental Information Service, a unit of the Investor Responsibility Research Center, is a good source of information on measuring company social performance.

Historical and contemporary efforts to assess the nation's progress and well-being thus informed the design and development of the Calvert-Henderson Indicators. We believe the results provide a well-developed next step in the collective effort to measure quality of life from a holistic perspective. It is now common to describe the GDP as a less-than optimal measure of the progress of a nation or community. Numerous groups are developing alternative measures of progress and collecting many bytes of data. Missing at this junction, however, is a methodology for organizing, synthesizing, and analyzing these myriad statistics in ways that allow the bytes of data to be transformed into meaningful "indicators" to help citizens understand and influence complex socio-economic phenomena. The Calvert-Henderson Quality of Life Indicators provide such a methodology to add transparency and traction to the current efforts and advance the thinking about quality of life indicators.

III. The Calvert-Henderson Approach

There is no existing indicators project that rivals or duplicates the Calvert-Henderson approach, which is unique in several ways. First, the approach was designed and implemented by a multi-disciplinary group of researchers, scholars, and practitioners with considerable expertise in creating and using indicators in their respective fields of study. The 15 authors who contributed to this study worked intensively with the editors to design the conceptual models and concurrently frame the issues. This process greatly informed the rigor and innovation of this study.

Second, the indicators unbundle central social, economic, and environmental issues into 12 distinctive domains of quality of life. This contrasts with macro-economic indicators or recent "green GDP" analogues that collapse the elements into a single composite index, mask how figures are calculated, and cancel out countervailing forces. Third, the indicators reveal the underlying trends and deeper processes that accompany the daily reported news events. Fourth, all of the indicators identify interfaces with

Calvert-Henderson Quality of Life Indicators

Education

Employment

Energy

Environment

Health

Human Rights

Income

Infrastructure

National Security

Public Safety

Re-Creation

Shelter

Missing in the quality of life literature, however, is a methodology for organizing, synthesizing, and analyzing myriad statistics in ways that allow the bytes of data to be transformed into meaningful "indicators" to help citizens understand and influence complex socio-economic phenomena.

other domains, allowing a systemic overview of our society often concealed by aggregation of traditional indices.

The Calvert-Henderson Indicators include traditional components of macro-economic indicators that directly affect Americans' quality of life, including Employment, Incomes, Shelter, and Infrastructure. We include an indicator on the natural Environment, which has emerged as a separate field of indicator research and strongly influences overall quality of life. Energy use is included as a focus, since it has a major impact on environmental and economic quality. Traditional socio-economic domains include Health, Education, and Public Safety. We expanded our purview to include Re-creation, as leisure activities, art, culture, and humanities can also contribute to a high quality of life. Finally, we include the domains of Human Rights and National Security, which address fundamental rights we enjoy as Americans. They incorporate our basic political rights and our collective need to secure and maintain our way of life in a changing world of complex, geopolitical forces.

Each indicator provides a road map into its subject, explaining leading concepts, and detailing national trends through time series data. National statistical information is presented on a host of variables included in each indicator. Data are primarily from the federal statistical system. Where federal data gathering is lacking, the authors make note and, in some cases, input data from private sources. The information is presented in a language that is accessible to those not necessarily schooled in the respective fields examined.

Also unique to this project is the development of a model for each indicator that serves as a frame through which the underlying phenomena can be clearly organized, examined, and understood. The model outlines and prioritizes key concepts and relationships that are central to understanding each domain. The models immediately reveal to the reader what is and is not in the indicator, the type of data presented, and how to expand upon the information. As described in more detail in Chapter 3, the models provide the cornerstones through which time series data can be viewed and analyzed in order to provide meaning and context when dealing with complex issues.

For example, assessing the quality of the environment is a huge task given its all encompassing domain. The Calvert-Henderson Environment model focuses on economic and industrial processes and their contributions to environmental quality through the lens of two key indicators – air and water quality – that can be monitored over time. Similarly, within the Income and Employment domains, there is a plethora of data and categories available for measuring economic activity. Thus the challenge was to develop conceptual models that would limit the purview and quickly identify what the respective authors viewed as key to understanding the phenomena today. In contrast, data on National Security and Re-Creation were not as readily available, thus the models are more theoretical, whereas the Human Rights Indicator is grounded in the U.S. Constitution and case law. In these ways, the Calvert-Henderson models reflect the unique nature of scholarly research and data collection in each field of study.

IV. The Calvert-Henderson Indicators

Brief descriptions of the 12 Calvert-Henderson Quality of Life Indicators are as follows:

- **Education Indicator** summarizes the quantity, quality and distribution of education in the U.S. defined as life-long learning and contributes to the broader dialogue on who learns what, where, when, and how throughout the life cycle.

- **Employment Indicator** describes the structure of employment in the U.S. as developed by the government and amended by private research efforts and helps clarify basic questions as to what constitutes "employment" and "unemployment" and what it means when figures fluctuate over time.

- **Energy Indicator** describes how much and how efficiently energy is consumed in the U.S. and provides feedback to the public on what can be done to reduce the environmental impact of energy consumption.

- **Environment Indicator** presents detailed information on the health of our environment with a special emphasis on the production-consumption process. A research focus on water and air quality offers data of primary interest to the general public.

- **Health Indicator** initiates a discussion on what constitutes "health" and examines the overall state of health of the people in America by age, race and gender.

- **Human Rights** Indicator examines the degree to which the Bill of Rights is protecting U.S. citizens and the level of citizen participation in the electoral process.

- **Income Indicator** focuses on changes in the standard of living as reflected in monetary measures of family income. The indicator examines and explains trends in the level and distribution of family income and wealth along with stagnant and unequal wage growth over the past 25 years.

- **Infrastructure Indicator** explains the importance of the physical infrastructure to our economy and provides an example of how to supplement our national accounts with an improved asset account to monitor our physical stock.

The Calvert-Henderson Quality of Life Indicators provide such a methodology to add transparency and traction to current indicators projects and advance the thinking about quality of life indicators.

- **National Security Indicator** explains the process our nation takes to achieve a state of national military security beginning with the President's National Security Strategy through the Congressional Budget Process. This includes both a diplomatic strategy and a military strategy, all of which are affected by public opinion and the perceived threat to security.

- **Public Safety Indicator** examines how effectively our society promotes private and public safety when faced with complex interrelationships between personal decisions, public actions, risks, and hazards in the environment that result in deaths from injuries.

- **Re-creation Indicator** provides a novel approach to identifying the myriad ways that Americans chose to re-create the self, to be revitalized in body and mind, and to reestablish social contacts through leisure and/or recreational activities.

- **Shelter Indicator** explores the type of housing Americans have access to, the level of affordability of that housing, and how housing in turn affects broader social outcomes.

In sum, each quality of life indicator includes a unique conceptual model, national statistical trends, and analysis to bring the reader up to speed on the subject. Our intent is that the indicators serve as sophisticated primers on the respective topics. We do not attempt to unify the information or devise a new theory to measure or explain how society is doing overall. Further research will explore the relationships across domains and build on the foundation we have laid to define what constitutes quality of life for the core indicators and provide reliable, consistent, and verifiable statistics from which the reader can come to their own conclusions about quality of life.

We envision multiple audiences using and benefiting from the Calvert-Henderson Quality of Life Indicators and the underlying models and data. For example, we hope that the models can become a starting point for community groups who want to quickly get a handle on an important issue and do not have the resources to fund such research locally. We invite groups to customize the models by adding components that are unique to a given community and/or deleting elements that are not applicable to the situation at hand. We offer the findings to professional journalists and reporters who are searching for reliable, consistent and verifiable data on key issues of concern to Americans coupled with a story to put the data in context. We envision this volume serving as a desk reference for social scientists and practitioners who are seeking in-depth analysis and statistics on a given topic. We also invite elected and appointed leaders to use the indicators to help reframe debates about what constitutes growth and quality of life in a locality, state, or the nation. We expect to continue researching and updating the indicators, and we welcome participation by other research institutes and foundations in this work.

REFERENCES

Council of Economic Advisors. *Economic Indicators*. Washington, DC: United States Government Printing Office (monthly).

Land, Kenneth. 2000. "Social Indicators." In *Encyclopedia of Sociology*. Edgar F. Borgatta and Rhonda V. Montgomery (eds.). Revised Edition. New York: Macmillian (forthcoming).

U.S. Working Group on Sustainable Development Indicators. 1998. *Sustainable Development in the United States: An Experimental Set of Indicators*. Washington, DC (December).

Chapter 3

Research Methodology

by Patrice Flynn, Ph.D.

The American public has become accustomed to social scientists disagreeing with each other about the condition of the nation. The print and broadcast media presents information on the social, economic, and environmental state of the country in a "cross-fire" format. This pits individuals with different research findings against each other in public debate. Social scientists invited to participate in such media events are trained to ask beforehand on which side of an issue they will be positioned.

As a result, public faith that scientists somehow cooperate with each other in enlarging and advancing our collective understanding of the world is giving way to doubt – as new knowledge assaults existing knowledge. We are challenged to ask whether science is indeed progressive and cumulative. Are forays into the unknown characterized by researchers adding a modicum of new and better data to advance a more complete explanation of reality? Or does science advance when scientists modify or even discard previously established truths and disagree vehemently with each other?

The research methodology developed for the Calvert-Henderson Quality of Life Indicators seeks to shed light on when and where social scientists agree and disagree with each other about the overall conditions in the United States. The approach builds on the knowledge of scholars who have devoted their entire careers to the fields of study (i.e., domains) examined in this volume. Each author was presented with the challenge of: (a) identifying and rectifying apparent clashes in our public discussions about the respective domain; (b) educating the readers about the state of the field; and (c) taking us to the cutting-edge of thinking about the topic as it fits into the whole. Methodologically, the challenge was to condense complex issues into discrete components to be understood and used by the broad public. The aim was to provide meaning and context for an information driven society, using rigorous empirical techniques.

The Calvert-Henderson Quality of Life Indicators research methodology combines reliable and verifiable numerical results with new research methods that provide an antidote to the increasingly chaotic output of contemporary research on well-being. The methodology may also serve to renew the public's belief in and support for nonpartisan, rigorous scientific research to inform practitioners, policymakers, funders, scholars, and leaders about what is happening in the nation.

Below is a summary of the research methodology developed for the Calvert-Henderson Quality of Life Indicators. The methodology is grounded in the seminal work of Thomas Kuhn, described in Section I, which provides a theoretical framework for the systems approach we adopted. Section II discusses how this approach adds transparency and traction to current measurement efforts (e.g., index analyses and community-based indicators projects) while advancing the rigor with which we develop quality of life indicators. Section III identifies the institutional structure within which the research was conducted and the experts who created the indicators. Section IV describes the Calvert-Henderson models and underlying data and their utility in developing rigorous measures of well-being.

I. Transitions in Science

The research methodology designed for the Calvert-Henderson Quality of Life Indicators is grounded in the seminal work of Thomas S. Kuhn as articulated in *The Structure of Scientific Revolutions* (1962). Dr. Kuhn, the Laurance S. Rockefeller Professor of Philosophy at the Massachusetts Institute of Technology and later a Fellow of the Institute for Advanced Study at Princeton University, examined the process of transitions in science and how new theories emerge to explain the evolving world. Struck by the number and extent of overt disagreements between social scientists about the nature of legitimate scientific problems and methods, Kuhn attempted to discover the source of such differences. He came to recognize the role of scientific research in the development of new paradigms, defined as "universally recognized scientific achievements that for a time provide model problems and solutions to a community of practitioners" (1962:viii).

Kuhn advocated a reorientation in the evaluation of familiar scientific data as they continually are impacted by changing external intellectual and economic conditions. Along with fellow historians of science, he posited that perhaps science does not develop through the accumulation of individual discoveries and inventions. Rather, research will reveal fundamental novelties or anomalies that challenge substantive conclusions to key scientific questions. When this occurs, the natural tendency is for the scientific community to defend its preconceived assumptions. However, the anomalies will not be suppressed for long. At some point scientists begin the "extraordinary investigations" that lead to a new basis for the practice of science.

Each famous episode in scientific development necessitated the research community's rejection of a time-honored theory. New theories imply a change in the rules governing the prior practice of science. Such paradigms or theories add value by drawing from an existing body of concepts, phenomena, and techniques to help explain new facts or information. Kuhn writes that "in the absence of a paradigm or some candidate for paradigm, all the facts that could possibly pertain to the development of a given science are likely to seem equally relevant" (p. 15).

This initial volume sets the stage for further scientific developments in the field of rigorous empirical measurement of quality of life. The Calvert-

Henderson Indicators put forth a new model (or pattern) to organize our thinking about quality of life. We have not yet achieved a paradigm that will guide subsequent scientific research in the field. However, efforts to re-define quality of life are at sufficiently high levels to suggest that the development of new models and theories about quality of life is timely and useful to fellow researchers and practitioners in the field. Ours is one of many contributions to this emerging field of scientific inquiry. It allows us to investigate some parts of society in detail and depth that would otherwise be unimaginable.

II. Measuring Quality of Life

There are two standard approaches to measuring well-being employed by social scientists today. The first is the *index number*, which tracks changes in a selected phenomena over time. Indices are common in economic analysis. The Gross Domestic Product index, for example, measures production; the Consumer Price Index measures inflation. In the language of economists, the fundamental problem upon which the index analysis rests "is that of determining merely from price and quantity data which of two situations is higher up on an individual's preference scale" (Samuelson 1947:146-147).

Index number theory is limited in that we assume an individual's tastes do not change in the period under consideration or if more than one person is considered, that their tastes are identical. Another limitation is that unless the reader is thoroughly familiar with the model employed to develop the index, it is not transparent what variables are included and excluded or the relative weights assigned to each variable. Scholars in the field of quality of life have documented these and other methodological difficulties over the past few decades in such journals as *Social Indicators Research* and *Social Indicators Network News*. While powerful when fully understood and well-fitted to the data, index numbers can be very limiting when trying to understand a topic about which a person is not familiar.

The second approach to measuring quality of life comes from the field of community indicators, currently involving over 200 groups in the United States. During the 1980s and 1990s, the quality of life movement re-gained the attention of citizen groups, scholars, practitioners, policymakers, and private foundations interested in alternative measures of well-being beyond those created by economists and other social scientists (Sawicki and Flynn 1996). An increasing number of groups began redefining well-being – at the neighborhood, community, or city levels – in ways that expand the traditional parameters of the National Income and Product Accounts (NIPA). A host of new and innovative data sets are being identified, collected, and analyzed. The quality of life literature is expanding rapidly as the concept is integrated into the mainstream of life in America and as the growing movement for livable communities intersects further with local, state, and national policy-making.

The Calvert-Henderson Indicators put forth a new model to organize our thinking about quality of life. They allow us to investigate some parts of society in detail and depth that would otherwise be unimaginable.

A certain level of frustration occurs in the process of pooling information on quality of life in this manner. In the absence of a theory or reason for seeking more recondite information, early fact-gathering is usually restricted to data that are readily accessible. Groups end up with a morass of facts that juxtaposed may or may not illuminate a situation. Kuhn writes that "only very occasionally…do facts collected with so little guidance from pre-established theory speak with sufficient clarity to permit the emergence of a first paradigm" (1962:16).

Hence, participants in the quality of life movement may be ready for the next phase of "measuring what we treasure," as Hazel Henderson noted in *Paradigms in Progress* (1995). It is common parlance among participants in local community indicators projects to describe the GDP as a less-than optimal measure of the progress of the nation or community. Alternative measures are in abundance; many bytes of data are collected and stored. Missing at this junction, however, is a methodology for organizing, synthesizing, and analyzing these myriad statistics in ways that allow the bytes of data to be transformed into meaningful "indicators" that can help citizens understand and influence complex social, economic, and environmental phenomena. The Calvert-Henderson models offer a solution to this problem.

Systems Theory

The Calvert-Henderson Quality of Life Indicators provide a methodology to add transparency and traction to current measurement efforts and at the same time advance the rigor with which to develop quality of life indicators. We adopted a systems approach, whereby all 12 dimensions of quality of life were viewed as integral to defining a broad picture of national well-being. It becomes clear to the reader where and how each indicator relates to the other indicators included in the Calvert-Henderson system.

Transparency is also created in the "unbundling" of the 12 Calvert-Henderson Indicators. As noted above, the reader will not find a single index or simple answer to the question: How well are we doing in a given domain? Rather, the approach unpacks the existing warehouse of information about a given dimension and presents the information or data in an organized fashion. Our intent is to make data on the various indicators accessible to people who have an interest in the topic, but are not necessarily experts in the field of study. This step in the methodology assumes that the general public not only wants more information about what is happening in the country, but can digest complex data when presented in a thoughtful, organized manner.

A systems approach that adds transparency to current discussions about quality of life is by necessity nonlinear. The connections that each author makes between components they have identified as critical within each domain do not follow a linear pattern in all instances. Rather, the information is presented in a circular, iterative fashion, which we believe characterizes the human phenomena in the long-term more accurately than a linear approach. As such, this book was not designed to be read from front to back. Readers are invited to jump into the volume wherever their interests are greatest. The algorithm for ordering the indicators is simply alphabetical.

III. Institutional Home and Authors

Another critical step in designing the Calvert-Henderson Indicators was to house the project in the Social Investment Research Department of the Calvert Group under the leadership of Jon Lickerman. Historically, quality of life research projects have been conducted by either social scientists at a nonprofit think tank or academics at a university. One unique aspect of this project is that is was co-created by Hazel Henderson, an independent author and futurist in St. Augustine, Florida; the Calvert Group, an asset management firm in Bethesda, Maryland; and a group of scholars and practitioners located in various universities, government agencies, think tanks, and research firms across the county. In essence a new, virtual research institution was created to develop the Calvert-Henderson Indicators under the auspices of Calvert Group, which provided talented human capital and a strong research base from which to design and implement the project.

The scientists who took on the challenge of designing the Calvert-Henderson Indicators have devoted their careers to the study of the respective domains. They represent part of the nation's brain trust on these issues. The authors are attracted to scientific inquiry for all sorts of reasons. Some desire to show that social science research is useful and relevant to real world events. Others are excited about the prospects of exploring new territory. Some hope to find order in the complexity of the human and environmental condition. Others are driven to test established knowledge and beliefs in their respective disciplines. Each person rose to the challenge of making explicit the connections of their field of specialty with the greater social-economic-environmental whole as articulated by Hazel Henderson. While often frustrated and tested in the five year process, we were able to work together to solve a new puzzle that no one has explored so thoroughly before. For this, each author is to be commended.

IV. Calvert-Henderson Models

How do social science discoveries come about? Kuhn says that discoveries are not isolated events, but extended episodes with a regularly recurrent anomaly. The emergence of a new theory is generally preceded by a period of pronounced professional insecurity generated by the persistent failure of the puzzles of normal science to come out as they should. For example, economists debate anew when low unemployment persistently accompanies low inflation in defiance of the Phillips curve. Kuhn suggests that the failure of existing rules is the prelude to a search for new ones.

Hence, we began the search for better metrics to define quality of life by designing a conceptual model for each of the 12 domains. The Calvert-Henderson models serve as a framework through which a complex issue can be condensed into discrete components and understood by people who are not necessarily well-versed in the topic. Each model presents both a systematic method of capturing the relationships among the variables of interest and a technique for handling a host of statistical data on the topic.

When presented with one of the Calvert-Henderson models, the reader will be able to identify immediately what is and is not in the indicator. This is not the case with index numbers, which must be read in light of its construction. We have developed models that are easy to grasp and help tell a concise story about what is happening in the given domain. It is our intention to inform the reader of the state of knowledge about the indicator, not to ask why things are the way they are or how we got here. In this regard, the aim is positive not normative. We leave it to the readers to reach their own conclusions and come to judgment about how well we are doing in each domain.

Econometricians who conduct statistical analysis of economic data, learned to develop sophisticated models the hard way. Henri Theil (1971) reminds us that too often in the academy students wanting to conduct empirical research plunge into regression analysis with only a vague notion of what the technique is supposed to perform theoretically. Computer output forces the students to work backwards in order to interpret test statistics by studying general statistics and matrix algebra. The easier way would have been to first study econometric theories and devote attention to models and techniques before fast-forwarding to problem-solving.

The Calvert-Henderson models were thus specified at the beginning of the research process to reflect a theoretical understanding of each domain, albeit a simplified version of a complex reality. Only then were appropriate and relevant data assembled to enable the reader to determine the joint and simultaneous relationships between a number of variables of interest and come to judgment about our nation's progress. In the future, it may well be that different specifications need to be estimated as our world continues to evolve.

The principles guiding the collection of data presented in the Calvert-Henderson models include the following:

National Data:
The unit of analysis is the United States. Users are encouraged to extend the unit of analysis to the international arena and/or disaggregate to the local, state, or regional levels.

Annual Data:
The indicators track changes on a yearly basis for simplicity and to avoid seasonal biases.

Federal Government Data:

The United States statistical system provides a wealth of reliable, consistent, and verifiable data for most of the indicators. Wherever possible, authors used federal government data from public use files. Where gaps in federal data were identified, private data were used.

Time Series Data:

Data streams begin and end at periods specified by the authors to reflect salient moments in history for the respective domains. Most of the indicators include the most recent year of data provided by the United States statistical system.

Data and Values:

The data employed in this analysis are not value free. We emphasize that the selection of data draws attention to what each author deemed important to understand the state of the respective domain.

Data and Theory:

Scientific facts or data do not speak for themselves, they are read in light of theory. Hence the teachings that emerge from each indicator are captured in the respective models that represent a theoretical construct through which data can be easily conveyed and perhaps tested in the future.

Scientific facts or data do not speak for themselves, they are read in light of theory.

Stratification of Information:

The Calvert-Henderson models have prioritized information on a given subject based on each author's theoretical understanding of the topic. The authors made critical and often difficult decisions about what to include in the initial model and what could be added in subsequent editions. Recognizing the constraints of developing the first national, comprehensive effort to redefine quality of life using a systems approach, it was understood that there are many layers underneath each model for future exploration.

V. End Result

It is our hope that the Calvert-Henderson Indicators will provide the readers with a solid body of empirical work to articulate a new theory and/or understanding of quality of life. We strived to resolve some residual ambiguities about these 12 aspects of life to permit citizens to solve problems related to key issues of concern. We hope to see this approach applied in various arenas and further articulated under new and more stringent conditions.

Kuhn's closing thoughts on scientific transitions are both hopeful and cautionary. The introduction of new theories and anomalies, in this case systemically measuring quality of life, is a sign of maturity in the development of any given scientific field. However, he predicts that there will be resistance when scientists are introduced to the new type of research. Kuhn warns that scientists wed to old schools of thought will devise numerous articulations and ad hoc modifications of their theory in order to eliminate any apparent conflict with the new research. This we have seen in the 1990s with the introduction of satellite accounts to the National Income and Product Accounts; chain-weighted productivity indices; calculating government expenditures on infrastructure as investments in the Gross Domestic Product; and "green GDP" analogues to redefine progress. Second, we can expect to see new and different analyses of science within which anomalies are no longer a source of dissonance (e.g., new theories of scientific knowledge). Third, more and more attention will be devoted to the anomalies by the field's most eminent people, demonstrated by the RAND Corporation and other mainstream firms' current interest in quality of life indicators.

We welcome such interest in improving the way we articulate and measure quality of life in the United States. The door is open to continually improve our methods, laws, and facts that constitute scientific techniques and theories. We believe the Calvert-Henderson Quality of Life Indicators provide a fruitful, rigorous methodology to help us come to grips with the central issues captured in the respective 12 domains. The significance of the indicators lies not in the numbers themselves, but in the larger reality toward which they point.

Retooling social science research methodologies is a luxury reserved for special occasions. For this, the brain trust behind the effort is indebted to Hazel Henderson and the Calvert Group for moving us toward a perceptual transformation in our collective thinking about quality of life.

REFERENCES

Hazel, Henderson. 1995. *Paradigms in Progress: Life Beyond Economics.* San Francisco, CA: Berrett-Koehler Publishers

Kuhn, Thomas S. 1962. *The Structure of Scientific Revolutions.* Chicago, IL: The University of Chicago Press.

Samuelson, Paul A. 1947. *Foundations of Economic Analysis.* Cambridge, MA: Harvard University Press.

Sawicki, David S. and Patrice Flynn. 1996. "Neighborhood Indicators: A Review of the Literature and an Assessment of Conceptual and Methodological Issues." *Journal of the American Planning Association,* Vol. 62, No.2 (Spring).

Theil, Henri. 1971. *Principles of Econometrics.* New York, NY: John Wiley & Sons, Inc.

Chapter 4

Biographical Sketches of the Authors

Constance Battle
Executive Director
Foundation for the National Institutes of Health
Health Indicator

Constance Battle is a medical doctor who served as the first Fellow of the Healthier Communities Program of the Healthcare Forum. She is currently Executive Director of the Foundation for the National Institutes of Health, which develops private and public sector partnerships to support the goals of the National Institutes for Health and meet the challenges of the many diseases that affect society.

Before joining the Foundation, Dr. Battle was Executive Director of the National Museum of Women in the Arts for nearly two years. Dr. Battle served as the Chief Executive Officer and Medical Director of the Hospital for Sick Children in Washington, D.C. from 1973 to 1995. Dr. Battle is currently a professor in the Department of Pediatrics at the George Washington University School of Medicine where she is president of the Medical School Alumni Association. She is also a member of the academic staff at Children's National Medical Center.

Dr. Battle received a B.S. in chemistry from Trinity College and an M.D. from the George Washington University School of Medicine.

Riane Eisler
President
Center for Partnership Studies
Human Rights Indicator

Riane Eisler is the author of *The Chalice and the Blade: Our History, Our Future*, which was hailed by Princeton anthropologist Ashley Montagu as "the most important book since Darwin's *Origin of Species*" and translated into 16 languages. Her other books, *Sacred Pleasure: Sex, Myth, and the Politics of the Body*, *The Partnership Way, Women, Men, and the Global Quality of Life* (based on a study of statistical data from 89 nations), *Dissolution and the Equal Rights Handbook*, have also received wide use and critical praise. Her forthcoming book, *Tomorrow's Children*, applies the partnership model to education, providing guidelines for Partnership Education from kindergarten to 12th grade and beyond.

Dr. Eisler is President of the Center for Partnership Studies. She has been a consultant to corporations such as Stentor International, Disney, and Paramount and is a fellow of the World Business Academy and the World Academy of Art and Science. She has addressed corporations such as DuPont and Volkswagen, lectured at universities such as Yale and UCLA, appeared on television, and keynoted conferences worldwide.

Ms. Eisler obtained degrees in sociology and law at the University of California at Los Angeles. She has taught at the University of California and Immaculate Heart College in Los Angeles and is a member of the General Evolution Research Group and the Club of Budapest. She founded the Los Angeles Women's Center Legal Program (the first in the United States) and has performed pioneering work in human rights, expanding the vision of international organizations to include the rights of women and children.

Patrice Flynn

Economist and Co-Founder
FLYNN RESEARCH
Employment Indicator

Patrice Flynn is a labor economist and a social worker who has taught, provided program assistance, and conducted research on economic and social issues in the United States and abroad. She has worked broadly in the field of measurement with a particular focus on developing models and indicators to assess quality of life, designing survey instruments, fielding national surveys, and analyzing large databases. Related work focuses on the phenomenology of changes in work and workplaces in both formal and informal markets. She has produced a strong publication record from her research.

In 1997, Dr. Flynn co-founded FLYNN RESEARCH, a basic and applied research institute that meets the custom measurement and reporting needs of organizations that plan, fund, evaluate and/or deliver programs that impact quality of life. Dr. Flynn previously worked as Vice President of Research at Independent Sector – the national leadership forum that encourages giving, volunteering, and not-for-profit initiatives – and as a labor economist for the Urban Institute in Washington, D.C.

Dr. Flynn is an adjunct economics professor at George Washington University in Washington, D.C. She holds a Ph.D. in Economics from the University of Texas, an M.A. in Economics from the University of Chicago, and an M.S.W. in Social Work from the Catholic University of America.

Hazel Henderson

Hazel Henderson is an independent futurist, author, worldwide syndicated columnist, and consultant on sustainable development. She conceived the Country Futures Indicators (CFI), an alternative to the Gross National Product in 1989. The first version of the CFI is the Calvert-Henderson Quality of Life Indicators, a co-venture with the Calvert Group.

Dr. Henderson's editorials are syndicated by InterPress Service to some 400 newspapers in 27 languages. She has published articles in over 250 journals, including *The Harvard Business Review, The New York Times, The Christian Science Monitor, Challenge* (United States), *Mainichi* (Japan), *El Dario* (Venezuela), *Australian Financial Review,* and *World Economic Herald* (China). Her books have been translated into German, Spanish, Japanese, Dutch, Swedish, Korean, Portuguese, and Chinese. Dr. Henderson is a board member of Worldwatch Institute and serves on the advisory boards of the Calvert Social Investment Fund, the Cousteau Society, the Council on Economic Priorities, the New Economics Foundation (London), and WETV, the global network based in Ottawa, Canada, and on the editorial boards of several publications, including *WorldPaper* (distributed in 25 newspapers throughout Asia, Latin America, China, Japan, Russia, Africa, and the Middle East), *Futures Research Quarterly, World Business Academy Perspectives* (United States), *E: The Environmental Magazine* (United States), *Resurgence* (United Kingdom), and *Futures* (United Kingdom). She served on the Global Commission to Fund the United Nations and co-edited its report, *The United Nations: Policy and Financing Alternatives* (with Harlan Cleveland and Inge Kaul, 1995).

She is a Fellow of the World Business Academy, has been a Regent's Lecturer at the University of California at Santa Barbara, held the Horace Albright Chair in Conservation at the University of California at Berkeley, and advised the U.S. Office of Technology Assessment and the National Science Foundation from 1974-1980. She is an active member of the National Press Club (Washington, D.C.), the Social Venture Network, the World Future Society (United States), and the World Futures Studies Federation (Australia). Dr. Henderson shared the 1996 Global Citizen Award with Nobel Laureate A. Perez Esquivel of Argentina.

Information on the Country Future Indicators as well as related work by Dr. Henderson can be found in the following publications: *Building a Win-Win World: Life Beyond Global Economic Warfare* (1996); *Paradigms in Progress: Life Beyond Economics* (1991, 1995); *Creating Alternative Futures: The End of Economics* (1978, 1996); *The Politics of the Solar Age: Alternatives to Economics* (1981, 1988); and *Redefining Wealth & Progress: The Caracas Report on Alternative Development Indicators* (1990).

Mary Jenifer
George Washington University
Health Indicator

Mary Jenifer holds a Master's in Health Care Administration from the George Washington University. She completed her administrative residency with Dr. Constance Battle at the Hospital for Sick Children. She currently works for Georgetown University in Washington, D.C.

Trudy A. Karlson
Senior Scientist
University of Wisconsin-Madison
Public Safety Indicator

Trudy A. Karlson is a senior scientist at the University of Wisconsin-Madison. She has joint appointments in the School of Medicine and the College of Engineering. Dr. Karlson has a Ph.D. in injury epidemiology from the University of Wisconsin-Madison and has done research on motor vehicle crashes, gun violence, emergency medical services, and other areas related to injury prevention and control. She is the author, with Stephen Hargarten, M.D., of a book on gun violence, *Reducing Firearm Injuries and Death: A Public Health Sourcebook on Guns* published by Rutgers University Press in 1997.

She is a senior scientist with the Center for Health Systems Research and Analysis at the University of Wisconsin. Her activities in this position include the development of an outpatient data system for the State of Wisconsin, linkage of motor vehicle crash and health data for the National Highway Traffic Safety Administration, and consulting on health care quality measures for employer's coalitions.

Since 1998, Dr. Karlson has been the Deputy Director of the Wisconsin Network for Health Policy Research with Dr. David Kindig, the Director. The Network is housed in the Department of Preventive Medicine. Its mission is to translate health policy research into practice and bring health policy issues to the attention of the research community. From 1994 to 1996, she was the Director of the Office of Health Care Information, an agency that housed the state's hospital discharge data system. In addition to injury control, she has taught program evaluation and research methods to engineering students, medical residents, and public health workers. She has additional expertise in state health data systems, health care evaluation, quality measurement, and probablistic data linkage methods.

Alya Z. Kayal
Social Research Analyst
Calvert Group
Human Rights Indicator

Alya Kayal joined Calvert Group's Social Research Department in 1994 as an International/Human Rights Analyst. Ms. Kayal was previously employed as a research assistant by the U.S. Department of Labor's International Labor Affairs Bureau to work on an International Child Labor Report. Ms. Kayal worked on a special project of the U.S. Information Agency and the Soros Foundation on the status of independent media in Eastern Europe and the states of the former Soviet Union. In 1992, Ms. Kayal worked as an aide to the U.S. expert member of the United Nations Sub-Commission on Prevention of Discrimination and Protection of Minorities. While there, she drafted several human rights resolutions and assisted in the negotiations on complex political and human rights issues with representatives from various countries.

Ms. Kayal is an active member of the American Bar Association's international law division. She is a co-author of *The Forty-Fourth Session of the United Nations Sub-Commission on Prevention of Discrimination and Protection of Minorities* and *The Special Session of the Commission on Human Rights on the Situation in the Former Yugoslavia* (1993). She is also a contributor to the annual *International Legal Developments Review of the International Lawyer,* American Bar Association. Ms. Kayal holds a law degree from the University of Minnesota and a B.A. in Sociology and International Communications from the University of New Jersey.

John A. "Skip" Laitner
Senior Economist
EPA Office of Atmospheric Programs
Energy Indicator

Skip Laitner is a resource economist with nearly 30 years of experience in public policy analysis, economic impact studies, and economic development planning. He currently serves as the Senior Economist for Technology Policy within the EPA's Office of Atmospheric Programs. In that capacity, Mr. Laitner was awarded the EPA's 1998 Gold Medal for his work with a team of economists that helped lay the foundation for the recent Kyoto Protocol on Greenhouse Gas Emissions.

With more than 100 articles, reports, and studies to his credit, Mr. Laitner is best known for his many studies on the employment, economic development, and productivity benefits of a more energy-efficient future. He is a frequent lecturer and has appeared as an expert witness in more than four dozen legal hearings and adjudicatory proceedings throughout the country. He has testified on a variety of issues before legislative committees in Congress and in numerous states. He has conducted technical seminars in such diverse places as Germany, Canada, and Korea. In addition to his expert testimony, Mr. Laitner has written a large number of papers and reports in the fields of community and economic development, decision sciences, energy and utility costs, and natural resource issues. He has a master's degree in resource economics.

Carrie Y. Lee
Vanderbilt University
Re-Creation Indicator

Carrie Lee is a graduate student in sociology at Vanderbilt University. She holds a B.A. degree from the University of California at Santa Cruz. Her interests are in stratification, gender studies, culture, and policy.

Jon Lickerman
Director
Social Investment Research Department
Calvert Group

Jon Lickerman is Director of the Social Investment Research Department at Calvert Group, a leading asset management firm specializing in socially responsible investment (SRI). Mr. Lickerman directed and contributed to the research development of the Calvert-Henderson Quality of Life Indicators Project throughout its entire development from 1994 to 1999.

Jon Lickerman is a practitioner in the field of evaluating corporate social responsibility practices within an investment context. He was one of the first professional analysts in the field of SRI research. He has co-developed analytical techniques for evaluating company, social, and environmental performance. Mr. Lickerman has led the development of numerous investment policies that has placed Calvert at the forefront of the SRI field. His work includes a focus on international SRI, working extensively with colleagues in the U.K. Mr. Lickerman also focuses on working directly with corporations, with an emphasis on human rights and environmental practices. He has co-developed a number of public education initiatives as an extension of Calvert's investment policies.

Jon Lickerman was the first researcher and later Manager of Social Research at Working Assets (now Citizens Trust) from 1986 to 1992. In this capacity he specialized in environmental analysis. He is active in the fields of international labor rights and community reinvestment and sits on several boards of nonprofit organizations. Mr. Lickerman holds a B.S. in Political Science from the University of Oregon.

William J. Mallett

Research Analyst
U.S. Department of Transportation,
Bureau of Transportation Statistics
Infrastructure Indicator

Will Mallett currently works with the Bureau of Transportation Statistics (BTS) in the U.S. Department of Transportation on the condition, use, and performance of the U.S. transportation system. He has been a major contributor to several BTS publications including the Transportation Statistics Annual Report and American Travel Survey research reports. Before joining BTS, he worked as consultant to Congress's Office of Technology Assessment. Dr. Mallett has taught geography at George Mason University and is currently an adjunct assistant professor in the Department of Geography at George Washington University where he teaches courses on urban geography and statistics. He holds geography degrees from the University of Bristol in Britain and West Virginia University, and a Ph.D. in City and Regional Planning from Cornell University. He lives with his wife, Cathy, an urban planner, in Arlington, Virginia.

Lawrence Mishel

Vice President
Economic Policy Institute
Income Indicator

Lawrence Mishel is the Vice President of the Economic Policy Institute and specializes in the field of productivity, competitiveness, income distribution, labor markets, education, and industrial relations. He is the co-author of *The State of Working America*, a comprehensive review of incomes, wages, employment, and other dimensions of living standards published biennially.

He holds a Ph.D. in economics from the University of Wisconsin, an M.A. in economics from the American University, a B.S. (Magna Cum Laude) from Pennsylvania State University and has been published in a variety of academic and non-academic journals.

Richard A. Peterson
Professor of Sociology
Vanderbilt University
Re-Creation Indicator

Richard Peterson is a Professor of Sociology at Vanderbilt University. He has also served at the University of Wisconsin, the University of Leeds, and the National Endowment for the Arts. A participant in six professional societies, he was the founding Chair of the Culture Section of the American Sociological Association.

Peterson has authored or edited eight books, the most recent of which are *Age and Arts Participation* for the National Endowment for the Arts and *Creating Country Music: Fabricating Authenticity* for the University of Chicago Press. Both were widely reviewed by the national press and the latter has received several awards. Dr. Peterson's numerous articles have focused on the production and consumption of culture, patterns of leisure, and the working of the media industry.

With colleagues, Dr. Peterson is currently researching the impact of Internet transmission of music on the music industry and on the nature of popular music itself; the changing patterns of recreation among Internet users; long-standing fascination of whites with African-American music; and the Internet-driven coalescence of alternative country music.

Kenneth P. Scott
Social Research Analyst
United States Trust Company of Boston
Environment Indicator

Kenneth P. Scott is a Social Research Analyst at United States Trust Company of Boston (USTC). He evaluates the social and environmental performance of client portfolio holdings and participates in shareholder activism initiatives. Mr. Scott is also co-portfolio manager of the USTC Small-cap Innovations Fund. From 1993 through 1998, he served as senior environmental analyst at Calvert Group, where he evaluated the social performance of mutual fund investments and initiated shareholder dialogue activities. He served previously for three years at the Council on Economic Priorities where he co-authored company-specific environmental reports. Mr. Scott earned a B.A. (with Honors) at Boston College.

Patrick A. Simmons

Director of Housing Demography
Fannie Mae Foundation
Shelter Indicator

Patrick Simmons is Director of Housing Demography at the Fannie Mae Foundation. Prior to joining the Fannie Mae Foundation, he held several positions in the Office of Housing Research at the Fannie Mae corporation, including Manager of Housing Policy Research.

Dr. Simmons is currently managing a multiyear research program on the effects of immigration on U.S. housing markets. He is also editor of a statistical compendium titled *Housing Statistics of the United States*, and is Associate Editor of the Foundation's two research journals, *Housing Policy Debate* and *Journal of Housing Research.* While at the Fannie Mae corporation, Dr. Simmons managed research projects in the areas of housing and mortgage market discrimination, homelessness, and urban housing policy.

Colonel Daniel M. Smith, Ret.

Chief of Research
Center for Defense Information
National Security Indicator

Colonel Daniel M. Smith graduated from the United States Military Academy at West Point in 1966. Commissioned as a 2nd Lieutenant of Infantry, Colonel Smith's initial assignment was as an infantry and heavy weapons platoon leader with the 3rd Armor Division in Germany. Following language training, he then served as an intelligence advisor in Vietnam before returning to the United States to do graduate work at Cornell University and teach philosophy and English at West Point.

Subsequent intelligence and public affairs assignments took him to Fort Hood, Texas; the Army Material Research and Development Command, where he was the speech writer for the Commanding General; the Defense Intelligence Agency; and Headquarters, Department of the Army. Six of his years with the Defense Intelligence Agency were spent in London working in the British Ministry of Defense and then as Military Attache in the U.S. Embassy. Colonel Smith retired from the Army in 1992 after 26 years of service.

Colonel Smith is a graduate of the Army Command and General Staff College, the Armed Forces Staff College, and the Army War College. He joined the Center for Defense Information in April 1993 as Director of the Center's Arms Trade Project. He became an Associate Director in 1994 and is now the Center's Chief of Research.

Jill Dianne Swenson
Professor of Journalism and Media Studies
Ithaca College
Education Indicator

Jill Swenson is a tenured associate professor of journalism and media studies with more than 15 years of teaching experience and research related to media ethics, public deliberation, community development, and the role of news in a mass-mediated democracy. She has taught in the Roy H. Park School of Communications at Ithaca College since 1992. Previously she has held faculty positions at the University of Georgia-Athens, University of Wisconsin-Green Bay, Roosevelt University, and the University of Chicago. She has contributed chapters to seven books, authored six refereed academic journal articles, co-authored an additional six academic articles, and presented 45 conference papers. Her work as a scholar reflects a commitment to creating an informed citizenry, fostering public deliberation, investigating socioeconomic and environmental issues from interdisciplinary approaches, cultivating critical thinking skills, and developing new rigorous research and reporting methods.

Dr. Swenson earned her Ph.D. in 1989 from the Committee on Human Development and her Master of Arts in the Social Sciences in 1981 at the University of Chicago. She graduated from Lawrence University, Appleton, Wisconsin, with a Bachelor of Arts in 1980. She has received previous recognition and support for teaching, research, and service from Lilly, the Poynter Institute, Annenberg Washington Program, International Radio-Television Society Industry/Faculty Seminars, the Freedom Forum Leadership Institute, Kettering Foundation Public Policy Workshops and National Issues Forums, Cox Center, Kellogg, and the Roy H. Park Foundation.

Chapter 5

Education Indicator

by Jill Dianne Swenson, Ph.D.

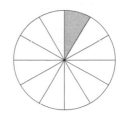

I. Introduction

In the broadest terms, education can be defined as the active acquisition of information and skills and the construction of knowledge across the lifespan. From nursery school and kindergarten to college and workplace training, education directly involves most Americans. Education is becoming increasingly central to an "Information Age" economy: "...[T]he acquisition and distribution of formal knowledge may come to occupy the place in...which the acquisition and distribution of property and income... occupied...over the two or three centuries that we have come to call the Age of Capitalism" (Drucker 1994:66).

Education is a key national resource for our country's economic strength and growth, but preparing individuals for the workforce is only one goal of education. Enabling individuals to live lives of dignity and purpose, to construct knowledge and put it toward humane ends, and to participate as informed citizens in democracy are also important goals of education (Boyer 1990). Of course the acquisition of knowledge has a cost, but the benefits to self and society exceed the price.

The Calvert-Henderson Education Indicator will consider how education contributes to the socioeconomic welfare of our nation. In some respects, education is an enigma to economists. Unlike the traditional resources considered by the economist – land, labor, capital – knowledge is assumed instead of assessed. Market economic models simply assert that behaviors are rational and based on the best information available. Rational economic behavior, however, is learned and not innate. To get rigorous results in free market models one must specify who knows what when. Plugging such specifics into economists' formulas requires we account for the effects of learning and the costs of information. Determining who knows what when becomes an overwhelming, if not impossible, task in a complex system.

A relatively new economic perspective suggests we consider education an investment in human capital rather than an expense (Patrinos 1995, Becker 1993, Marshall 1992, and Reich 1991). Education is a resource for America's economic performance and a dominant source of comparative and competitive advantage in the world economy.

This Calvert-Henderson Quality of Life Indicator presents summary statistics on education in the United States to answer fundamental questions: Who is involved in education? Where do people learn and when does it happen? What do students learn and how? And, finally, why invest in education?

These deceptively simple questions require empirical answers. Most of the data used in this report are from the U.S. Department of Education's National Center for Education Statistics (NCES), drawn primarily from the publications *The Condition of Education (1998, 1996a)*, *The Digest of Education Statistics (1999, 1996b)*, and *Projections of Education Statistics to 2005 (1995)*, unless otherwise noted. Since 1867, the U.S. Department of Education has collected, analyzed and disseminated statistics and other data related to education. Nationwide in scope, data come from federal and state agencies, private research organizations, and professional associations and are carefully reviewed by NCES. Department of Education reports are explicit and detailed regarding sources and comparability of data. This indicator will consider pre-primary, K-12 and post-secondary schooling because reliable data sets and statistical significance allow some confidence in these numbers.

The Education Indicator is presented as follows. The education model is introduced with supporting information presented in three parts. The first part reports educational attainment levels and educational expenditures. The second part provides literacy rates, access, and distribution of education. The third part explores mitigating factors that affect the quality of education. The final section summarizes the findings and presents some of the key policy challenges.

II. Education Model: A Metaphorical Pie Recipe

The model for education as a quality of life indicator takes the metaphorical form of a pie. The model puts statistical measures of American education into a meaningful framework and operationalizes the indicator as one measure of quality of life. Pie charts are familiar to most Americans as popular visual representations of numerical data. The metaphor of a pie – not just the way it's sliced but the way it's made – can help explain this model for assessing education.

Pie charts are icons in our public discourse of demographic and economic statistics. This report provides a recipe for understanding the demographic pie chart's answers to questions about American education. Talk about pie charts typically involves issues of distribution and access. The size of the total pie is not debated nearly as often as the size of each slice.

Social scientists – economists, statisticians, demographers – measure the pie slices but don't always tell us how the pie tastes. Anyone who has ever enjoyed a piece of French silk, pecan, or key lime pie knows the size of one's slice isn't always the best measure of a pie's quality. So goes it with assessing the quantity and quality of education in the United States. If we can think about education in terms of baking a pie instead of a pie chart perhaps we can get a more sensitive measure of education as a quality of life

Calvert-Henderson Education Model

Crust
Educational Attainment Levels
Educational Expenditures

Filling
Literacy Rates
Access to Education
Distribution

Spices
Segregation
Discrimination
Lifelong Learning
Alternative Forms of Education

indicator. So what kind of a pie is American education? Peach, pecan, or pizza pie?

Education, when it happens, is like baker's magic: a pie red as raspberry, blue as berry, and American as apple. If you've ever learned from a master baker or witnessed any transformative learning moment between student and teacher, you know the magic of education. In so many ways, measures of education defy numbers. When the magic happens in classrooms it is easy to recognize although too often instructional effectiveness eludes statistical measures.

Education – like shoofly, shepherd's, and soda cracker pie – pulls us through tough economic times; and in good times education is served à la mode. There are all kinds of pies imaginable – custard, meat, fruit, meringue – just as there are diverse pedagogies and a wide range of learning styles. What kind of pie we make depends on the ingredients, how we mix them together, and on baking conditions.

The Education Indicator deploys the metaphor of a pie to present three sets of summary statistics on the status of American education. First, the model examines the piecrust of American education in terms of educational attainment levels and educational expenditures. Second, the pie filling looks at literacy rates, access, and distribution of educational resources in America. Finally, key factors that add seasoning by stirring in policy issues are examined.

As the numbers presented below illustrate, the size of the pie keeps increasing as enrollments in American schools continue to rise. Educational attainment and expenditures also keep going up. The upper crust is rich and delicious but the pastry underneath is getting mealy and the filling still tastes quite tart. Poverty and race remain critical variables in access and distribution of education. There are shifts occurring in funding for education with significant and potentially negative ramifications for the future welfare of the nation.

The Piecrust

The pastry – the foundation underneath and the delicate upper crust – has a couple basic ingredients. The pie dough of American education is made from levels of educational attainment and expenditures on education. Like flour and shortening, these two ingredients need to be carefully measured before mixing.

Educational Attainment Levels

Evidence of educational attainment in the United States is readily available from the U.S. Department of Education in several statistical forms. The number of children enrolled in public and private elementary and secondary schools in fall 1998 was 52.7 million. Across all levels of educational institutions from K-12 to professional and graduate students, more

…what kind of a pie is American education?

than 67 million students are enrolled in America's schools. The amount of three-, four-, and five-year-old children enrolled in pre-primary programs climbed to 65 percent in 1997 compared to 27 percent in 1965. Almost 60 million people or 40 percent of the adult population participated in adult education during the previous 12 months (NCES 1999, 1995).

Consider that in 1910 only 13.5 percent of Americans 25 years and older completed four years of high school. In 1997, 82 percent had a high school diploma. Now, more than 1.76 million Americans hold a doctoral degree and more than 11 million hold a master's or professional degree. An estimated 2.4 million students graduated from high school in June 1998, and the Department of Education estimates more than 3 million will graduate from high school in 2005.

Sixty-seven percent of 1997 high school graduates enrolled in college for the following academic year. The percentage of high school graduates going on to college has continued to increase steadily throughout American history. There was a significant increase in the percentage of men going to college during the buildup of the Vietnam War and then a decline before rising again after 1980. The percentage of women going to college increased dramatically and steadily from 1965 on, virtually closing the gender gap in education.

The overall number and percentage of high school graduates pursuing post-secondary education continues to grow (Appendix 1). The numbers of nontraditional-age college students also continues to expand. The educational attainment levels of the adult population continues to rise as they have done since 1947 when the government began collecting these data.

Educational Expenditures

Educational expenditures are ingredients as basic to pie dough as levels of educational attainment. Like educational attainment, there are a variety of ways to measure expenditures: total current dollars, per student, and as a percent of the Gross Domestic Product (GDP).

Annual current expenditures in public elementary and secondary education continue to increase to more than $250 billion a year (NCES 1999). For public and private institutions of higher education, current-fund expenditures increased from $96 million in school year (SY) 1970-71 to almost $190 billion in SY 1995-96 (in constant dollars adjusted by the Higher Education Price Index). While spending has risen substantially, increases can be explained in part by the greater inflation rate for school costs and the disproportionate growth in spending for programs serving special populations, expansion of school lunch and breakfast programs, dropout prevention, alternative instruction, counseling, transportation, after-school athletics, and security and violence prevention efforts (Rothstein and Miles 1995).

Another way to measure educational expenditures is to look at the dollars spent per student. In public primary and secondary education, dollars spent per pupil have increased over the last three decades (Appendix 2). Expenditures per pupil in public elementary and secondary schools for SY 1995-1996 averaged $6,146, ranging from a low of $3,867 in Utah to a high of $9,955 in New Jersey.

Expenditures on post-secondary education have also increased over time. In constant SY 1995-96 dollars, average spending per student rose from $14,281 in SY 1970-71 to $18,383 in SY 1995-96. Levels of spending per student are highest at private universities ($28,623) and lowest at public two-year colleges ($7,180).

Total educational expenditures represented 7.2 percent of GDP in 1997, the same as 25 years ago at the peak of baby boomers' enrollment in American schools. Elementary and secondary schools' total expenditures comprised 4.3 percent of GDP, colleges and universities the remaining 2.9 percent.

When we cut the shortening (expenditures) into the flour (attainment levels) we can begin to see the dynamic interaction between costs and benefits in education. The relationship between average family income by educational attainment levels of head of household is positive: the higher the level of educational attainment the greater the family income and the less likely an individual will be unemployed or receiving welfare benefits (NCES 1999). Educational attainment is also strongly related to voting behavior, community service, attending public meetings, participating in civic activities, organizational memberships, reading a newspaper, and health-related behaviors (NCES 1998, 1996a).

Metaphorically, a good crust is about more than measuring the ingredients. The techniques of blending and rolling out the pastry are just as important. In other words, we need to consider how and where dollars are expended on education, not just how many dollars. There are no money-back guarantees that increased spending on education will improve attainment or literacy levels, although historical trends suggest a strong positive relationship. What is evident, however, is that when we fail to invest economic resources in education, levels of attainment do not improve. Jonathan Kozol (1995, 1991) documents this economic fact more poignantly than numbers ever can with his descriptive assessments of the educational experiences of children in low-income neighborhoods.

The Pie Filling

So what goes into the pie? Literacy rates, access, and distribution of education go into the mix. Indicators of what students learn in school are important measures of the outcomes of education, and literacy rates in the adult population are key indicators of the educational level of the citizenry. Literacy rates, while ubiquitous and widely country comparable, have not been assessed nationally until recently. The National Assessment of Educational Progress – a federal survey that assessed students for reading, writing, science, mathematics, and other subjects for more than 20 years – provides evidence that overall proficiency test scores of America's school children have not improved at a statistically significant level in the last two decades (NCES 1998). The data reveal the largest gains in student proficiency scores in elementary and secondary schools between 1972 and 1992 were made by minority students. The academic gap between whites and blacks has narrowed by 40 percent (Grissmer, Kirby, Berends, and Williamson 1994).

The percentage of high school graduates who took the Scholastic Aptitude Test (SAT) remained at 42 percent from 1992 to 1995, up from 35 percent in 1984. Again, the greatest gains in achievement scores were made by minority students. The combined math and verbal average SAT scores in 1995 was 910, down from 937 in 1972 (NCES 1998). Recently, SAT scores were reported to have risen; however, these increases can be attributed to a change in the standardized scoring system.

Elliot Eisner (1985) notes there are more modes of knowing than through verbal and mathematical skills as assessed by the Educational Testing Service on the SAT. Eisner, a Stanford University educator, argues for the recognition of "aesthetic" modes of knowledge and advocates a theory based on multiple dimensions of intelligence beyond the standardized two. His work provides a more inclusive and holistic measure of "literacy." A musical or artistic genius may perform marginally on standardized tests of verbal and mathematical skills yet score high on tests of aesthetic or physical abilities.

Literacy Rates

Assessing the lessons learned by Americans in everyday life is virtually impossible. We know people learn in schools, but learning also takes place at work, at home, at the public library, through continuing education and professional training programs, and by working through the problems of modern life. For the first time in our history, the U.S. Congress called on the Department of Education in 1988 to address the need for better information on the nature and extent of literacy in America's adult population. Plans are under way to conduct a second wave of data collection on adult literacy; however, data are not yet available. Previous reports (Kirsch 1992, 1986; National Center on Education and the Economy 1990; Chisman 1989; U.S. Departments of Education and Labor 1988; Hudson Institute 1987; Venezky 1987; National Commission on Excellence in Education 1983) indicated the lack of adequate literacy is a serious national problem. However, these reports defined illiteracy as a condition an individual has or does not have. The National Adult Literacy Survey (NALS), acknowledging the complexity of literacy issues, followed a different approach. The NALS assessed levels of literacy based on performance across an array of tasks adults encounter in everyday life. Adult literacy proficiency rates were assessed at five levels in three areas: prose, document, and quantitative.

The 1992 NALS survey completed by Educational Testing Services under contract with NCES indicated that one in five Americans scored in the lowest level of proficiency and one in five scored in the top two levels of proficiency (NCES 1994). Half of college graduates can't understand a bus timetable, determine the cost per ounce of creamy peanut butter from two unit price labels, or write a theme contrasting two opposing views reported in a newspaper feature article, all tasks required for Level 3 proficiency.

Individuals with higher levels of literacy were more likely to vote, be employed, earn higher wages, attain higher levels of education, and read a newspaper. Fifty percent of college graduates score in the top two levels of the quantitative and prose literacy scales.

What should be noted is the steady rise over time in average literacy proficiencies across the entire range of education levels. Literacy proficiency increases with educational attainment levels: 75 to 80 percent of adults with zero to eight years of education scored in Level 1 while only 4 percent of adults with four-year college degrees scored in Level 1.

If we think of literacy as social currency, adults on a limited literacy budget have more difficulty meeting their basic needs, solving problems of modern life, and pursuing their goals. Adults who function in society at the lowest levels of literacy may be at increasing risk as our economy and culture continue to change rapidly in ways that directly affect literacy needs.

Access to Education

Access to education continues to expand and projections estimate the overall size of the pie will increase. The Department of Education projects public and private elementary and secondary school enrollments will climb to 55.9 million students in 2005. There is also no foreseeable downturn in the numbers of students enrolling in higher education through 2005.

Moreover, enrollment rates in pre-primary education increased throughout the 1970s and 1980s. In 1996, 36.7 percent of three-year-olds, 57.7 percent of four-year-olds, and 90.2 percent of five-year-olds were enrolled in center-based programs or kindergarten (NCES 1998). Access to pre-primary education is largely affected by family income level. The gap between enroll- ment rates for children from low-income and high-income families persists. This gap in enrollment rates closes by age five because access to kinder- garten is provided by public school systems and almost all children attend kindergarten before starting primary school.

High school completion rates continue to rise for those who make it to the tenth grade. Ninety-five percent of students who were in grades 10-12 in the fall of 1996 had reenrolled or graduated by the fall of 1997. Between 1972 and 1996, the drop-out rates for whites and blacks decreased while the drop-out rate for Hispanics was not significantly different. Although the drop-out rate decreased at a faster rate for blacks than whites, blacks and

Hispanics were still more likely to drop out of school than white students (NCES 1998, 1994). Drop-out rates before tenth grade, however, increased between 1972 and 1992. One quarter of Native American students, 8.3 percent of Hispanic students, and 14.5 percent of black students in the class of 1992 had dropped out by the 10th grade. For black male students, the persistence rate increased from 90 to 97 percent between 1972 and 1992. In 1996, the drop-out rate for high school students from high-income families was about 2.1 percent compared to 11.1 percent for students from low-income families.

Distribution

Although access to education continues to expand (including access for students with disabilities and students with limited English proficiency), distribution of educational resources remains a function of demographic variables including age, race, residence, and household income.

Percentages of adults with four years of high school or more are increasing generationally: 86 percent in the 25- to 34-year-old age group compared with 63.5 percent in the 65- to 74-year-old age group (Kominski and Adams 1992). Comparisons by race and Hispanic origin reveal sizeable differences in educational attainment levels. The percentage of persons ages 25- to 29-years-old who completed four years of high school or more was 93 percent for whites compared with 87 percent for blacks and 62 percent for Hispanics.

The implications of educational access and distribution for the workforce are significant. Adults with higher levels of education are also more likely to participate in the labor force than those with less education. In 1999, the Department of Education reported that 83.9 percent of adults with a bachelor's degree or more participated in the labor force compared with 58.6 percent of high school graduates. The unemployment rate in 1997 for adults 25 years or older with less than a high school degree was 8.1 percent compared with 2 percent for those with a bachelor's degree or more.

Workers with more formal education continue to earn higher wages than those with a high school education or less (see Appendix 3). In 1997, the median annual income for men with less than a ninth grade education was $19,291 and $14,161 for comparable women. For men with a bachelor's degree or more, median annual income in 1997 was $53,450 and for women $38,038. Women's incomes are much lower than men's, even after adjusting for level of education.

These ingredients – measures of the quality of education – are as important to the pie filling as the cornstarch or tapioca needed for thickening.

Seasonings

In assessing the quality of the pie we make of American education there are a variety of factors that are not easily measured but critical to the taste. Some recipes call for lemon juice, melted butter, or vanilla depending on the variety and ripeness of fruit. Cinnamon and sugar, nutmeg and allspice, salt and orange rind are all spices that determine how good the pie will taste. Alternative schools and home schooling add a dash of ginger and anise to the pie. Public libraries, continuing adult education programs, cooperative extension services, community study circles and public forums, museums, health and fitness classes, book clubs, public broadcasting, freenets, and other educational resources in our communities certainly sweeten the pie.

In many states, increased numbers of students are completing tougher course requirements in English, math, science, and social studies for high school graduation, as advocated more than ten years ago in *A Nation At Risk* (National Commission on Excellence in Education [NCEE] 1983). The percentage of public high school districts that have graduation requirements meeting or exceeding NCEE recommendations for the four core subject areas increased from 12 percent to 20 percent between school years 1987-88 and 1993-94 (NCES 1998).

A great deal of work remains to be done on producing reliable and rigorous measures of educational quality and its distribution. We need to consider who else is involved in education besides students, including teachers, families, communities, taxpayers, politicians, and school administrators. It is difficult to measure safe and supportive learning environments and the quality of teachers, textbooks, and instructional technology. The increasing numbers of children in poverty mitigates the impact of improvements in school curriculum.

The legacy of discrimination continues to flavor education. The bitter taste lingers, and seasoning is still needed. While great strides have been made to narrow learning gaps, poverty and race remain key factors in American educational systems. In 1996, 19.8 percent of all children lived in poverty, and both black and Hispanic children were more than twice as likely as white children to live in poverty (U.S. Bureau of the Census 1997). The effects of poverty and race on child education are well documented.

While the emphasis remains on the "three Rs" – reading, writing, and arithmetic – art and music, field trips, and class plays are important seasonings to a child's educational experience. National statistics on curricular offerings are not readily available, nor are they available for extra-curricular programs – from athletics to the school newspaper. Despite the globalization of information and the economy, enrollment in foreign-language instruction for grades 9 to 12 dropped 13.5 percent between 1978 and 1985 and dropped another 8.5 percent between 1985 and 1990 (NCES 1996b).

In SY 1990-91, 96 percent of public schools had libraries or media centers, however, there was an average 931 students per librarian at public elementary schools and 1,052 students per librarian at secondary schools. Computer use by students at school increased from 27 percent in 1984 to 69 percent in 1997. By 1995, 50 percent of all public schools had access to the Internet, however, only 9 percent of classrooms had access. The proportion of schools with Internet access increased rapidly from 35 percent in 1997 to 98 percent in 1998. In 1998, about 50 percent of instructional rooms had access to the Internet. In higher education, technology is increasingly important, although it is not yet clear how it can keep down tuition and expenses while reaching more students.

What is clear from the research literature on instructional technology is that machines can not replace caring and attentive teachers. A computer is a tool – like chalk, pencils, overheads, and video – and can enhance the lessons prepared by an instructor, but cannot itself teach.

While teachers' salaries increased during the 1980s, they reached a peak in 1991 and have decreased slightly each year since. In SY 1997-98 the average annual salary of public elementary and secondary school teachers was $39,385. In higher education, faculty salaries, adjusted for inflation, decreased over the past two decades (NCES 1998, 1999).

As the costs for higher education continue to rise, borrowing to pay for college and university education has also increased dramatically. The number of loans provided through the Federal Family Education Loan Program reached an all-time high of $5.5 billion in 1993, dropping to $2.37 billion in 1996. The amount of federal dollars budgeted for post-secondary education programs rose from $1.2 billion in 1965 to $16 billion in 1998. As tuition increases outpace inflation rates, students and their parents are losing ground in their ability to afford college, especially families with low incomes.

The basic research community anchored in U.S. colleges and universities has been undergoing a quiet but radical transformation in financing the last decade. A new relationship between business and institutions of higher education allows corporations to take advantage of federal investments in university-based research. Not surprisingly, corporate dollars going to institutions of higher education more than doubled between 1980 and 1986 to $600 million and doubled again to $1.2 billion in 1991 (Soley 1995). Soley argues that the educational costs of increased corporate funding are the reduced importance of classroom instruction, degraded academic freedom by setting research agendas, and shifting patent revenues from institutions of higher education to the private sector. Proposed federal cuts in university research funding will likely exacerbate the trend toward privatization of public goods derived from education. We need education not only to serve industry but also to reshape it.

As educational expenditures continue to rise for elementary and secondary education, partnerships between businesses and schools may be misperceived to be a new panacea. Corporations seek such partnerships as a win-win-win scenario: tax write-offs, positive public relations, and greater influence in the mission and methods of instruction. Training for workplace skills is not a good substitute for an educational foundation; students need to learn how to learn as the workplace and the nature of work itself is transformed. Students may lose if industrial interests supersede national interests of educating Americans for the future. Education, not training, offers new possibilities to invent new industries that create new jobs.

Training employees, however, yields higher productivity and profits and is a wise investment. To examine this relationship, the Labor Department commissioned a study from Harvard University, the Wharton School of Business, and Ernst and Young LLP (Mavrinac, Jones and Meyer 1995). They reported that Motorola earns $30 for every dollar spent on training. "Motorola U" found treating employees as an asset is more successful than looking at workers first for layoffs when cutting costs. The report also claims Xerox's strategy of empowering workers in research, development, and production lowered the firm's manufacturing costs by 30 percent. The report is important evidence of the return on investments in human capital.

Educational reform initiatives in recent years have taken several forms: charter schools that circumvent district bureaucracies, schools privately managed with public funds, magnet schools, pilot schools, parental subsidies, mayoral control of school systems, budget cuts, voucher programs, and others. The exasperation with large spending gaps between schools in wealthy and poor communities, with district and school board bureaucracies unable to bring about financial solvency and public accountability, and with property taxpayers' fatigue have created a demand for reform.

However, there has been little or no assessment of the effectiveness of these school reforms to date. Some say the answer isn't going to be found in new schools but in adequately funding the current system. In its 1995 report, "Using What We Have to Get the Schools We Need," the Consortium on Productivity in the Schools calls for better evaluation of educational reforms. Sue E. Berryman, senior education specialist at the World Bank and chair of the Consortium, said reform efforts have failed to improve education because they have been designed to overhaul parts of the system and not the system in its entirety. As the competition for decreasing public funds heats up and educational expenditures continue to increase, we will have to define the quality and productivity of education if we want to measure and improve both.

III. Key Policy Challenges

As data show, enrollment and expenditures in American schools will increase, and the tide of educational attainment levels will rise, lifting all boats. Education ratchets up economic opportunities and social mobility. Yet there are shifts occurring in funding for education. The questions about cost increases have significant and potentially counterproductive ramifications for the future welfare of the nation.

Poverty and race remain critical factors in access and distribution of education in the United States. Education and its byproducts are key to eradicating racism and alleviating poverty. The price of admission to today's labor force may be too high for those without adequate education and literacy skills.

Education is interrelated with other Quality of Life Indicators, particularly income, employment, and human rights. Education is a form of social capital and empowers because it instills liberty, especially intellectual liberty. Educational expenditures remain more cost effective than the expenses of ignorance.

Appendix 1   College Enrollment Rates of High School Graduates, 1960-1997
(numbers in thousands)

Year	Total High School Graduates[1]	Enrolled in College[2]	
		Number	Percent
1960	1,679	758	45.1
1961	1,763	847	48.0
1962	1,838	900	49.0
1963	1,741	784	45.0
1964	2,145	1,037	48.3
1965	2,659	1,354	50.9
1966	2,612	1,309	50.1
1967	2,525	1,311	51.9
1968	2,606	1,444	55.4
1969	2,842	1,516	53.3
1970	2,757	1,427	51.8
1971	2,872	1,535	53.4
1972	2,961	1,457	49.2
1973	3,059	1,425	46.6
1974	3,101	1,474	47.5
1975	3,186	1,615	50.7
1976	2,987	1,458	48.8
1977	3,140	1,590	50.6
1978	3,161	1,584	50.1
1979	3,160	1,559	49.3
1980	3,089	1,524	49.3
1981	3,035	1,646	53.9
1982	3,100	1,568	50.6
1983	2,964	1,562	52.7
1984	3,012	1,662	55.2
1985	2,666	1,539	57.7
1986	2,786	1,499	53.8
1987	2,647	1,503	56.8
1988	2,673	1,575	58.9
1989	2,454	1,463	59.6
1990	2,355	1,410	59.9
1991	2,276	1,420	62.4
1992	2,398	1,479	61.7
1993	2,338	1,464	62.6
1994	2,517	1,559	61.9
1995	2,599	1,610	61.9
1996	2,660	1,729	65.0
1997	2,769	1,856	67.0

[1] Individuals age 16 to 24 who graduated from high school during the preceding 12 months.

[2] Enrollment in college as of October of each year for individuals age 16 to 24 who graduated from high school during the preceding 12 months.

Source: NCES 1999:184.

Average Current Expenditure Per Pupil in Average Daily Attendance in U.S. Public Elementary and Secondary Schools, 1959-60 to 1995-96

Appendix 2

(in current dollars)

School Year	Current Expenditures Per Pupil
1959-60	$375
1969-70	$816
1979-80	$2,272
1989-90	$4,980
1995-96	$6,146

Source: NCES 1996b:184.

Median Annual Income of Year-Round Full-Time Workers 25 Years Old and Over by Level of Education Completed and Sex, 1997

Appendix 3

(in 1997 current dollars)

Educational Attainment	Men Median Income	Women Median Income
All ages, 25 and over	$36,678	$26,974
Less than 9th grade	$19,291	$14,161
9th to 12th grade (no diploma)	$22,048	$15,113
High School graduate (includes equivalency)	$31,215	$22,067
Some college, no degree	$35,945	$26,067
Associate degree	$38,022	$28,812
Bachelor's degree or more	$53,450	$38,038
- Bachelor's degree	$48,616	$35,379
- Master's degree	$61,690	$44,949
- Professional degree	$85,011	$61,051
- Doctor's degree	$76,234	$53,037

Source: NCES 1999:380.

REFERENCES

Becker, Gary. 1993. *Human Capital: A Theoretical and Empirical Analysis with Special Reference to Education.* Chicago: University of Chicago Press.

Boyer, Ernest L. 1990. *Scholarship Reconsidered: Priorities of the Professoriate.* Princeton, NJ: The Carnegie Foundation for the Advancement of Teaching.

Chisman, Forrest P. 1989. *Jump Start: The Federal Role in Adult Education.* Southport, CT: The Southport Institute for Policy Analysis.

Consortium on Productivity in the Schools. 1995. *Using What We Have to Get the Schools We Need: A Productivity Focus for American Education.* New York: Institute on Education and Economics, Teacher's College, Columbia University.

Drucker, Peter. 1994. "The Age of Social Transformation." *Atlantic Monthly* (November), pp. 53-80.

Eisner, Elliot. 1985. "Aesthetic Modes of Knowing." pp. 23-36 in Eisner, Elliot (ed.), *Learning and Teaching the Ways of Knowing.* Eighty-fourth Yearbook of the National Society for the Study of Education, Part II. Chicago: University of Chicago Press.

Grissmer, David W., Sheila Natarj Kirby, Mark Berends, and Stephanie Williamson. 1994. "Student Achievement and the Changing American Family." Santa Monica, CA: Rand, MR-488-LE.

Hudson Institute. 1987. *Workforce 2000: Work and Workers for the 21st Century.* Indianapolis, IN.

Kirsch, Irwin. 1992. *Beyond the School Doors: The Literacy Needs of Job Seekers Served by the U.S. Dept. of Labor.* Princeton, NJ: Educational Testing Service.

_____. 1986. *Literacy: Profiles of America's Young Adults.* Princeton, NJ: Educational Testing Service.

Kominski, Robert and Andrea Adams. 1992. *Educational Attainment in the United States: March 1991 and 1990.* Washington, D.C.: U.S. Government Printing Office.

Kozol, Jonathan. 1995. *Amazing Grace.* New York: Crown Publishers.

_____. 1991. *Savage Inequities.* New York: Crown Publishers.

Marshall, Ray. 1992. *Thinking for a Living: Education and the Wealth of Nations.* New York: Basic Books.

Mavrinac, Sarah C., Neil R. Jones, and Marshall W. Meyer. 1995. *The Financial and Nonfinancial Returns to Innovative Workplace Practices: A Critical Review.* Boston: Center for Business Innovation.

National Center on Education and the Economy. 1990. *America's Choice: High Skills or Low Wages.* The Report of the Commission on the Skills of the American Workforce. Rochester, NY.

National Center for Education Statistics. U.S. Department of Education. Office of Educational Research and Improvement. 1993. *Adult Literacy in America.* Washington, D.C.: U.S. Government Printing Office.

National Center for Education Statistics. U.S. Department of Education. Office of Educational Research and Improvement. 1999. *Digest of Education Statistics 1999.* Washington, D.C.: U.S. Government Printing Office.

National Center for Education Statistics. U.S. Department of Education. Office of Educational Research and Improvement. 1998. *The Condition of Education 1998.* Washington, D.C.: U.S. Government Printing Office.

National Center for Education Statistics. U.S. Department of Education. Office of Educational Research and Improvement. 1996a. *The Condition of Education 1996.* Washington, D.C.: U.S. Government Printing Office.

National Center for Education Statistics. U.S. Department of Education. Office of Educational Research and Improvement. 1996b. *Digest of Education Statistics 1996*. Washington, D.C.: U.S. Government Printing Office.

National Center for Education Statistics. U.S. Department of Education. Office of Educational Research and Improvement. 1994. *The Condition of Education 1994*. Washington, D.C.: U.S. Government Printing Office.

National Center for Education Statistics. U.S. Department of Education. Office of Educational Research and Improvement. 1995. *Projections of Education Statistics to 2005*. Washington, D.C.: U.S. Government Printing Office.

National Commission on Excellence in Education. 1983. *A Nation at Risk: The Imperative for Educational Reform*. Washington, D.C.: U.S. Government Printing Office.

Patrinos, Harry Anthony. 1995. "Economics of Education: New Approaches and Empirics." Paper presentation for session, "Priorities for Education in the Next Century: The World Bank and the Delors Commission." Comparative and International Education Society, March 29-April 1, Boston.

Reich, Robert B. 1991. *The Work of Nations: Preparing Ourselves for 21st Century Capitalism*. New York: Random House Inc.

Rothstein, Richard with Karen Hawley Miles. 1995. *Where's the Money Gone? Changes in the Level and Composition of Education Spending*. Washington, D.C.: Economic Policy Institute.

Soley, Lawrence. 1995. *Leasing the Ivory Tower: The Corporate Takeover of Academia*. Boston: South End Press.

U.S. Bureau of the Census. 1997. Current Population Reports P60-198, Washington, D.C.: U.S. Government Printing Office.

U.S. Department of Education and U.S. Department of Labor. 1988. *The Bottom Line: Basic Skills in the Workplace*. Washington, D.C.

Venezky, Richard L. 1987. *The Subtle Danger: Reflections of the Literacy Abilities of America's Young Adults*. Princeton, NJ: Educational Testing Service.

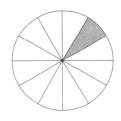

Chapter 6

Employment Indicator

by Patrice Flynn, Ph.D.

I. Introduction

On January 22, 1930, the front page of the *New York Times* and the *Herald Tribune* announced that the depression had turned a corner; for the first time since the stock market crash in October 1929, employment was up. Secretary of Labor James J. Davis predicted that 1930 "should see us well on the way to complete recovery" (Martin 1976:213).

Frances Perkins, Industrial Commissioner of New York and later Roosevelt's Secretary of Labor from 1933 through 1945, challenged the statistics. She noted that Secretary Davis had by-passed the Department of Labor's Bureau of Labor Statistics data, which showed a steady decline in employment, in favor of the U.S. Employment Service (ES) figures. Perkins pointed out that the ES figures were up because every Christmas season big department stores hired extra help. Comparing the December figures to those of November was meaningless; the figures had to be compared to a previous December, or "seasonally adjusted" in the lexicon of statisticians. Indeed, December 1929 proved to be the worst month of unemployment since 1927 in New York, the country's largest commercial state, and the worst December since the government began recording monthly national unemployment figures in 1914.

Five months later, Secretary of Commerce R.P. Lamont announced that unemployment was only 3 percent. Again, Perkins pointed out the fallacy: the government used population rather than labor force figures. When the number of unemployed was divided by the number of adults in the labor force, the unemployment rate was 13 percent. Children, retirees, the handicapped, and institutionalized were not expected to be employed.

These cases illustrate both the power of statistics and the ease with which statistics can be used to tell very different stories. Perkins's attention to detail was not an effort to expose the Hoover Administration. Rather, she believed that if presented with the facts of working conditions, the American people would want to correct what was wrong and public officials could enact constructive reform. Soon, whenever a statement on unemployment was issued in Washington, D.C., labor leaders, public officials, and newspaper editors would call Frances Perkins to check the figures against those in New York.

The desire for uniformity in reporting and interpreting employment-related statistics prompted the U.S. Department of Labor to develop our national labor market statistical system, put in place over 50 years ago. The objective of the Calvert-Henderson Employment Indicator is to describe the structure of the U.S. labor market and how the government defines and counts those who are employed, unemployed, and not in the labor force. Questions to be explored include the following. Who is in the labor force? What is the difference between voluntary and involuntary employment? What are the definitions of unemployment and underemployment? How are part-time, temporary, and other contingent workers counted? How does the statistical system account for those who work for no pay? What does "jobless economic growth" mean and is it something to be concerned about? What are the central labor market concerns of workers and employers today?

The Employment Indicator is divided in 4 parts. Section II describes the structure of the U.S. labor market and identifies those who are employed and unemployed by demographic and work characteristics. The focus is on nonwage dimensions of the labor market. Section III describes workers excluded from the labor market statistics including unpaid and discouraged workers. Section IV discusses the implications.

Like the other Calvert-Henderson Quality of Life Indicators, the Employment Indicator condenses a broad body of literature familiar to a small group of professionals into a straightforward presentation of an important dimension of life: our jobs. Moreover, the indicator examines employment from a holistic perspective in that it pieces together various aspects of work that are normally examined in isolation, such as paid employment, volunteering, hours worked, and gender. Finally, through the close examination of data on labor markets, the indicator reveals what we do not know about employment and unemployment. Growing concerns with a burgeoning labor force, downsizing, rising hours worked, falling wages, moonlighting, underemployment, and the growing competition for jobs highlight the need to understand more fully the changing nature of work and workplaces.

II. The Labor Market

Each month, the U.S. Bureau of Labor Statistics (BLS) releases employment-related data. The basic information reveals the number and characteristics of people who are employed and unemployed. To appreciate the meaning of these statistics requires an understanding of how the labor market is structured and how the government enumerates employment-related activities.

On the next page is a model of the U.S. labor market that serves as a framework through which employment-related statistics can be conveyed. The model shows the relationships between employment, unemployment, and nonmarket work. It reveals the kinds of data collected by the government and how the data streams fit together to describe overall labor market activities. For simplicity, the data presented in the model reflect activities in 1998. Time series data are presented in the text and appendix.

Calvert-Henderson Employment Model

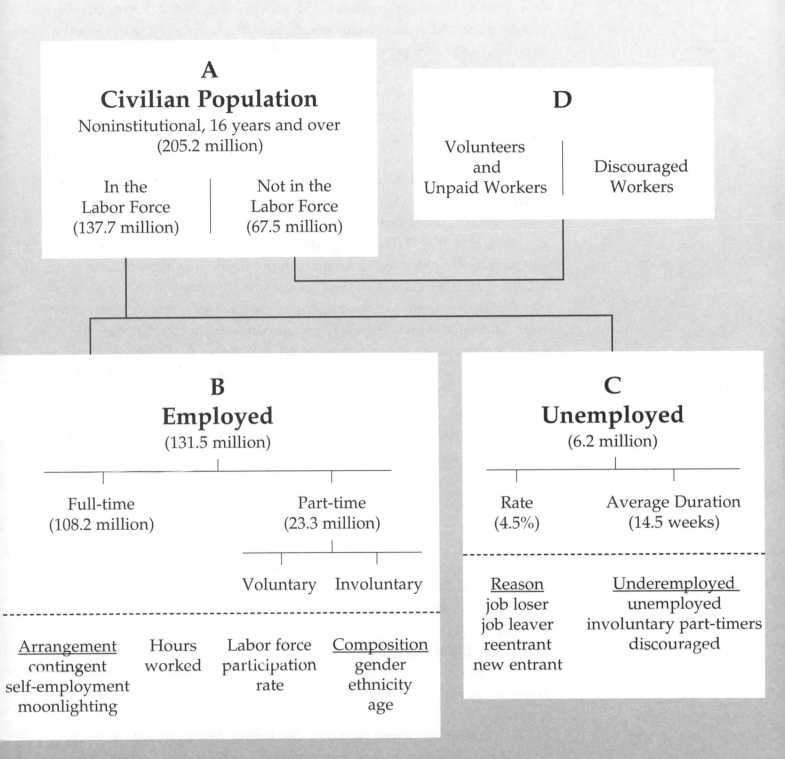

A
Civilian Population
Noninstitutional, 16 years and over
(205.2 million)

| In the Labor Force (137.7 million) | Not in the Labor Force (67.5 million) |

D

| Volunteers and Unpaid Workers | Discouraged Workers |

B
Employed
(131.5 million)

Full-time
(108.2 million)

Part-time
(23.3 million)

Voluntary   Involuntary

Arrangement
contingent
self-employment
moonlighting

Hours
worked

Labor force
participation
rate

Composition
gender
ethnicity
age

C
Unemployed
(6.2 million)

Rate
(4.5%)

Average Duration
(14.5 weeks)

Reason
job loser
job leaver
reentrant
new entrant

Underemployed
unemployed
involuntary part-timers
discouraged

Note: 1998 data.

The starting point of the model is the civilian, noninstitutionalized adult population of 205.2 million in 1998 (box A). This population is divided into two groups: those in the labor force (137.7 million) and those not in the labor force (67.5 million). To be considered part of the labor force a person must be either gainfully employed in the formal economy or unemployed. Out of the 137.7 million persons in the labor force in 1998, 131.5 million were employed and 6.2 million were unemployed. The unemployment rate is the ratio of unemployed persons to the total civilian labor force, or 4.5 percent in 1998.

Various employment arrangements within the civilian labor force are listed in box B. Individuals are employed on a full-time or part-time basis, as contingent and self-employed workers, and in multiple jobs. Unemployed workers, noted in box C, include those who are temporary or permanent job losers, voluntarily job leavers, labor market reentrants, and new entrants, all of whom are looking for work.

Finally, box D includes individuals not in the labor force who totaled 67.5 million in 1998. These adults either do not want to work, work for no pay, and/or have stopped looking for work because they have become discouraged at the prospects of successfully finding jobs.

The data in the Calvert-Henderson Employment Indicator are drawn from the federal statistical system, primarily information gathered by the U.S. Department of Labor's Bureau of Labor Statistics (BLS). The BLS has developed a complex methodology to survey individuals and employers on a regular basis. (See Appendix 1 for details on the BLS employment-related data.) We acknowledge that the federal statistical system is not complete; however, the data provide consistent and reliable baseline information on labor market activities.

Who is in the Labor Market?

In 1998, over 205 million persons were in the civilian population. The civilian population includes adults, ages 16 and over, not living in institutions such as penal facilities, mental facilities, and homes for the aged. The government examines military personnel separately from the civilian population under the assumption that all members of the armed services are employed.

The BLS divides the civilian population into two groups: those who are in the labor force and those not in the labor force. Table 1 identifies the labor force status of the civilian population for selected years, beginning in 1950.

The number of people in the labor force has risen steadily since the federal government began recording labor market statistics. Moreover, an increasing proportion of the population is engaged in market work. Over the period 1950 to 1998, the civilian adult population nearly doubled while the

Civilian Population by Labor Force Status
Noninstitutional Population, 16 years and over
(thousands)

Table 1

| Year | Noninstitutional Population | Labor Force | | Not in the Labor Force |
		Total	Percent of Population	
1950	104,995	62,208	59.2	42,787
1960	117,245	69,628	59.4	47,617
1970	137,085	82,771	60.4	54,314
1980	167,745	106,940	63.8	60,806
1990	189,164	125,840	66.5	63,324
1998	205,220	137,673	67.1	67,547

Source: U.S. Bureau of Labor Statistics 1999. Post January 1994 data are not strictly comparable to prior years due to a redesign of the CPS (see BLS 1994).

labor force grew by 121 percent (from 62 million to 137 million). The total labor market participation rate among the noninstitutionalized adult population rose from 59.2 percent in 1950 to 67.1 percent in 1998. A record high number of Americans are now in the labor market.

Labor force participation rates vary considerably by gender (see Table 2). Women's participation in the labor force has increased steadily over the past three decades from 37.7 percent in 1960 to 59.8 percent in 1998. During the same period, men's participation rate dropped from 83.8 to 74.9 percent, largely due to early retirements, expansion of the Social Security disability program, higher school enrollments, and an increase in wives' employment. Currently men comprise 54 percent of the civilian labor force. By the start of the next millennium, the BLS estimates that the labor force will be half men and half women.

A record high number of Americans are now in the labor market.

Selected Civilian Labor Force Participation Rates
by Gender and Ethnicity
(percent)

Table 2

Category	1960	1970	1980	1990	1998
Total	59.4	60.4	63.8	66.5	67.1
Women	37.7	43.3	51.5	57.5	59.8
Men	83.3	79.7	77.4	76.4	74.9
Blacks	-	-	61.0	64.0	65.6

Source: U.S. Bureau of Labor Statistics 1999. Dash indicates data were not collected.

Who is Employed?

Out of the 137.7 million persons in the labor force in 1998, 131.5 million were employed. The BLS defines as employed those persons who, during the reference week of the survey: (a) did any work at all (at least one hour) as paid employees, in their own business, profession or on their own farm, or who worked 15 hours or more as unpaid workers in an enterprise operated by a member of the family, and (b) all those who were not working but who had jobs or businesses from which they were temporarily absent because of vacation, illness, bad weather, child-care problems, maternity or paternity leave, labor-management dispute, job training, or other family or personal reasons, whether or not they were paid for the time off or were seeking other jobs (BLS 1995).

Employers and employees negotiate various types of employment arrangements to include full- and part-time work, independent contracting, temporary help, self-employment, and moonlighting. Workers in each group are described below.

Full-time Workers

Full-time workers are those who usually worked 35 hours or more a week. Hours are counted for all jobs a person holds. Thus, if a person has two part-time jobs that together provide employment of at least 35 hours a week, the person is counted as a full-time worker. An estimated 82 percent of employed workers were categorized as full-time in 1998, representing over 108 million workers. The same year, 60.8 million women held jobs, of whom 74 percent worked year round on a full-time schedule. The number of working men was 70.7 million, of whom 89 percent were employed year round, full time (see Table 3).

The average year-round, full-time male wage and salary worker earned $31,096 in 1998; comparable female workers earned $23,712. Between 1973 and 1998, hourly earnings of private, nonagricultural workers fell an average of 9 percent to $12.77 an hour. Acute is the growth in wage inequality over the past two decades, with the college-educated (22 percent of the adult population) experiencing income gains and most others experiencing wage losses. Economists point to a host of factors to explain the shift in earnings, including the trade deficit, low-wage competition from other countries, immigration, foreign direct-investment, growth in low-paid service sector jobs and contingent employment, the erosion of the minimum wage, and a weakening of union bargaining power.[1]

The period of growth in wage disparity has been accompanied by a rise in the number of persons working. To maintain family standards of living, women's labor force participation has risen considerably, especially among married women and mothers of young children. By the 1990s, nearly three-fourths of married mothers were gainfully employed outside the

Distribution of Full-time and Part-time Workers in 1998 by Age and Gender
(thousands)

Table 3

Age and Gender	Employed Workers	Full-time Workers		Part-time Workers	
		Total	Percent of Employment	Total	Percent of Employment
Total, 16 and over	131,463	108,202	82	23,261	18
16-19	7,051	2,320	33	4,731	67
20 and over	124,412	105,882	85	18,530	15
55 and over	16,597	12,336	74	4,261	26
Women, 16 and over	60,771	45,014	74	15,757	26
Men, 16 and over	70,693	63,189	89	7,504	11

Source: U.S. Bureau of Labor Statistics 1999. Numbers may not sum to totals due to rounding.

home, up from half in 1970 (Hayghe and Bianchi 1994). The proportion of employed married mothers with children under a year old was 56 percent in 1998. The BLS reports that year round, full-time working mothers provide as much as 40 percent to family income while remaining the primary caretakers of children, older persons, and households.

Two other notable changes are the increases in the share of people who work very long workweeks and the total number of hours Americans work during the year, especially women. BLS economists Rones, Ilg, and Gardner provide the following analysis (1997). The average workweek for full-time employees is 43 hours: men average 45 hours a week and women average 41 hours. Many workers have benefited from the Fair Labor Standards Act of 1938 that set the legal workweek maximum at 40 hours – beyond which hourly workers must be paid time-and-a half. Over the past 25 years, however, an increasing number of people work extended hours (defined by the BLS as 49 hours or more). Those working long workweeks tend to be professionals and/or managers and are among the highest paid people in the country. Hence there is some self-selection into jobs that require long hours of work.

The other major trend in work activities is the dramatic increase in the total number of hours workers in America spend on the job over the course of the year, in contrast to within the typical workweek. The BLS reports that employed women worked an average of 15 percent more in 1993 than 1976, after age-adjustments, and men worked 3 percent more (Rones, Ilg, and Gardner 1997). Women added 193 hours to their average work year over this period, while men added 62 hours.

Part-time Workers

Part-time workers include persons who normally work between 1 and 34 hours a week in all jobs held. In 1998, over 23 million persons were employed on a part-time basis representing 18 percent of total employment. Table 3 shows that part-time employment occurs most often among teenagers, women, and older workers.

Government surveys ask workers if they are employed on a part-time basis for economic or noneconomic reasons. Economic reasons include slack work or unfavorable business conditions, inability to find full-time work, and seasonal declines in labor demand. As of January 1994, those who usually work part-time must also indicate that they want and are available to work full-time in order to be classified under part-time for economic reasons. These persons are also referred to as involuntary part-time workers.[2]

Noneconomic reasons for usually working less than 35 hours a week include illness or other medical limitations, personal obligations, school or training, retirement or Social Security limits on earnings, and being in a job where full-time work is less than 35 hours. The group also includes those who gave an economic reason for usually working 1 to 34 hours but said they do not want to work full time or were unavailable for such work. These workers are referred to as voluntary part-time employees.

In 1998, there were approximately 2.5 million involuntary part-time workers: 1.4 million women and 1.1 million men. Voluntary part-time workers totaled 19.2 million, of whom 13.2 million were women and 6 million were men.

Employers have become reliant upon part-time workers. From 1973 to 1997, the share of employment in part-time jobs rose from 16.6 to 17.8 percent while full-time employment fell from 83.4 percent to 82.2 percent (see Table 4). Moreover, weekly hours of part-time workers have increased more rapidly than hours of full-time workers. From 1976 to 1990, average

Table 4 **Composition of Employment, 1973-1997**
(percent)

Year	Part Time			Full Time
	Total	Involuntary	Voluntary	
1973	16.6	3.1	13.5	83.4
1979	17.6	3.8	13.8	82.4
1989	18.1	4.3	13.8	81.9
1997	17.8	3.2	14.5	82.2

Source: Mishel, Bernstein, and Schmitt 1999. Table 4.17. Post January 1994 data are not strictly comparable to earlier figures due to changes in the CPS.

weekly hours of full-time workers rose 2.1 percent (42.6 to 43.5) while weekly hours of part-time workers rose 6.8 percent (19.1 to 20.4) (Callaghan and Hartmann 1991).

The reliance on part-time employment arrangements is not unique to the United States. According to the International Labor Organization (ILO), by 1993, part-time workers accounted for between 10 percent and 20 percent of all workers in the United States, Germany, Belgium, Canada, France, and Japan; more than 20 percent in Australia, Denmark, New Zealand, and Britain; 26 percent in Norway; and 33 percent in the Netherlands (ILO 1993). Approximately two-thirds of part-time workers in OECD (Organization for Economic Co-Operation and Development) countries are women and over one-third would prefer full-time jobs.

Alternative Employment Arrangements

Alternative employment arrangements are becoming more common. The government reports that 21 million persons do job-related work at home (3.6 million for pay), and 12 million are on flexible schedules (i.e., able to vary the time they begin and end their work day), up from 9 million in 1985 (BLS 1998). New contractual arrangements are emerging as well, such as subcontracting out basic functions of a business through employee leasing and temporary help. Much less is known about these alternative arrangements, the workers employed, and reasons why nontraditional jobs are growing. In an effort to collect better data on contingent, temporary, and contract work, the BLS administered special surveys in February of 1995 and 1997. The findings indicate the following.

Contingent Workers

In February 1997, between 2.4 million and 5.6 million workers were in contingent jobs. There were 2.4 million wage and salary workers in their jobs for no more than a year who expected their jobs to continue for no more than another year. This group represented 1.9 percent of total employment in 1997. When the definition of contingent was broadened to include all workers whose jobs were temporary or not expected to continue, the BLS found that 5.6 million workers were in contingent jobs, 4.4 percent of total employment. Table 5 presents characteristics of these contingent workers

The 1997 survey also showed that 8.5 million workers (6.7 percent of the total employed) said they were independent contractors, 2 million (1.6 percent) worked "on call" or as day laborers, 1.3 million (1 percent) worked for temporary help agencies, and 800,000 (0.6 percent) worked for contract firms that provided the worker's services to one customer at that customer's worksite (see Table 6).

Temporary employment is a relatively recent phenomenon, hence, government statistics are only available since 1982. The evidence points to a growing number of temporary jobs in the economy, defined as jobs of

Table 5 **Employed Contingent and Noncontingent Workers in 1997
by Selected Characteristics**

(thousands)

Characteristics	Employed Workers	Contingent Workers		Noncontingent Workers	
		Total	Percent	Total	Percent
Total					
Women	58,811	2,828	50.7	55,983	46.2
Men	67,931	2,746	49.3	65,185	53.8
Full-time	102,813	3,205	57.5	99,608	82.2
Part-time	23,929	2,368	42.5	21,560	17.8

Source: U.S. Bureau of Labor Statistics 1997. Contingent workers include all workers whose jobs were temporary or not expected to continue.

Table 6 **Employed Workers with Alternative Work Arrangements in 1997**

(thousands)

Characteristics	Independent contractors	On-call and day laborers	Temporary help agency workers	Workers provided by contract firms
Total, 16 years and over	8,456	1,996	1,300	809
Women	2,824	1,017	719	244
Men	5,633	979	581	565
Full-time	6,221	947	1,044	670
Part-time	2,235	1,049	256	139

Source: U.S. Bureau of Labor Statistics 1997.

limited duration (some of which are through temporary help agencies). The number of temporary jobs quadrupled from 417,000 in 1982 to 1,668,000 in 1993. As with part-time employment, employers are using temporary workers for more hours of the work week. Weekly hours of temporary workers rose from 27.1 in 1982 to an average of 30.8 hours in 1990.

For some workers, contingent and alternative employment arrangements provide desirable work schedules. For others, nontraditional arrangements result in a feeling of job insecurity and/or an insufficient number of paid hours of work. To assess worker preferences, the BLS asked whether respondents prefer traditional or nontraditional work arrangements. With the exception of independent contractors, most persons in contingent work arrangements would prefer traditional employment. Among the 5.6 million contingent workers, only 36 percent preferred their current arrangements. Opinions varied across workers, with 34 percent of temporary help agency workers and 84 percent of independent contractors expressing satisfaction with their work arrangements.

Self-Employed

Another type of alternative work arrangement is self-employment, which includes those who work in their own business, farm, craft, or profession. In 1996, there were 10.5 million self-employed persons or 8 percent of total employment, up from 7 percent in 1979. The BLS expects the number of self-employed to top 11.6 million people by 2006 (Silvestri 1999). Striking is the increased number of women among the self-employed. Women represented one out of four self-employed workers in 1975 and one out of three in 1990 (Devine 1994).

Moonlighters

The last group of alternative workers in the Employment Indicator are those who hold more than one job, or moonlighters. The BLS estimated that in 1996 there were 7.8 million multiple-job holders in the United States or 6.2 percent of those employed (Stinson 1997). The rate of multiple job holding has fluctuated from 4.9 percent in 1980 to 5.4 percent in 1985 and 5.9 percent in 1994. An increasing number of workers took second jobs during the 1985-1989 recovery, during which time multiple-job holders rose from 5.7 million to 7.2 million people. Moonlighters work an average of 48 hours per week, almost 5 hours more than the average full-time worker.

The BLS reports that an increasing number of persons take second jobs to pay regular household expenses or to pay off debts. Almost half of workers permanently displaced from their jobs during the recession between January 1991 and December 1993 were reemployed in jobs paying less than their last jobs. Some of these workers have taken two jobs at lower pay to make ends meet.

Who is Unemployed?

The labor force also includes all persons who want to work but are unable to find jobs. In 1998, 6.2 million persons were unemployed, 4.5 percent of the civilian labor force. Statistics on unemployment are drawn from the monthly Current Population Survey (CPS). The CPS does not directly ask if a person is unemployed. Rather, a worker is counted as unemployed if the person: (1) has not worked during the survey week, (2) is available for work, and (3) has looked for work during the preceding four weeks.

This basic definition, developed about 50 years ago by a group of survey statisticians working for the Works Progress Administration, is based on job search activity (Norwood 1994). Unemployment statistics do not

Table 7   **The Employed and Unemployed in the Labor Force**
Selected Years
(thousands)

Year	Labor Force	Employed	Unemployed	
			Number	Rate
1973	89,429	85,064	4,365	4.9
1975	93,775	85,846	7,929	8.5
1979	104,962	98,824	6,137	5.8
1982	110,204	99,526	10,678	9.7
1989	123,869	117,342	6,528	5.3
1992	128,105	118,492	9,613	7.5
1998	137,673	131,463	6,210	4.5

Source: U.S. Bureau of Labor Statistics 1999.

measure economic hardship. Falling unemployment statistics indicate that many people have either been successful in their job search or stopped looking for work altogether and are no longer in the labor force numbers. Thus, the current relatively low rate of unemployment does not necessarily signify a strong recovery from the recession of the early 1990s.

Table 7 lists the number of civilian workers who were employed and unemployed in selected peak years (1973, 1979, 1989, 1998) and trough years (1975, 1982, 1992).[3] During the past two decades, unemployment reached a peak of 9.7 percent in 1982 and a low of 4.5 percent in 1998. Despite the official end to the 1990-1991 recession in the second quarter of 1991, unemployment did not stop rising until the second quarter of 1992. The unemployment rate rose steadily in 1990, 1991, and 1992 to a high of 7.5 percent and began declining thereafter. It took the economy almost two years to fully recover from the recession of the early 1990s, more than twice the normal length of recovery in terms of employment. This phenomenon is referred to as "jobless economic growth."

Unemployment varies considerably by age, gender, and race. In 1998, for example, the overall unemployment rate was 4.5 percent. However, as noted in Table 8, unemployment was 14.6 percent for teens, 3.9 percent for white workers and 8.9 percent for black workers; and 7.2 percent for women with children. The disparate pattern of unemployment across workers has remained fairly consistent over time.

Interpreting Unemployment Statistics

The aggregate rate of unemployment has fallen considerably since the recession of 1990-1991 to a rate of 4.5 percent in 1998. Presidential hopefuls breath a sigh of relief, while economists fear rising inflation, and

Selected Civilian Unemployment Rates, 1975-1998   *Table 8*

Characteristics	1975	1982	1992	1998
Total	8.5	9.7	7.5	4.5
Females, 20 and over	8.0	8.3	6.3	4.1
Males, 20 and over	6.8	8.8	7.1	3.7
Teenagers, 16-19	19.9	23.2	20.1	14.6
White, total	7.8	8.6	6.6	3.9
Females, 20 and over	7.5	7.3	5.5	3.4
Males, 20 and over	6.2	7.8	6.4	3.2
Black, total	14.8	18.9	14.2	8.9
Females, 20 and over	12.2	15.4	11.8	7.9
Males, 20 and over	12.5	17.8	13.5	7.4
Experienced wage and salary workers	8.2	9.3	7.2	4.3
Women with children	10.0	11.7	10.0	7.2

Source: U.S. Bureau of Labor Statistics 1999.

the Federal Reserve hesitates to lower interest rates. While much stock is put in the monthly unemployment rate, the figure tells us little about the quality of life of individuals throughout the nation. Our well-being is better reflected in the numbers underlying the unemployment rate, including the duration of unemployment, the reason for being unemployed, the extent of possible underemployment, and compensation paid during spells of unemployment discussed below.

Duration of Unemployment

In 1998, the average duration of unemployment was 14.5 weeks, up from 11.9 weeks in 1989. Contrary to other post-recessionary periods, the duration of unemployment kept lengthening in 1992, 1993, and 1994. Moreover, the number of persons who experience long-term unemployment – lasting 27 weeks or more – is now 875,000 or 14 percent of the unemployed, up from 10 percent in 1989. The permanent loss of many jobs in the 1980s and early 1990s has made it difficult for some groups of unemployed people to find work quickly during nonrecessionary times.

Reasons for Unemployment

The BLS asks workers why they are unemployed. Responses are grouped into four categories: (1) job losers, comprising persons on temporary layoff, permanent (involuntary) job losers, and persons who completed temporary jobs, (2) job leavers who voluntarily quit, (3) reentrants who previously worked but were out of the labor force prior to beginning their job search, and (4) new entrants who never worked. In 1998, job losers comprised over 45 percent of the unemployed, job leavers 12 percent, reentrants 34 percent, and new entrants 8 percent.

The number of people who voluntarily leave their jobs fluctuated in the 1990s. In 1990, 15 percent of the unemployed reported voluntarily leaving their jobs to search for another job. By 1994, job leavers comprised only 10 percent of total unemployment. Perhaps the lengthening duration of unemployment, growing involuntary contingent employment arrangements, and falling real wages in the early part of the decade signaled growing uncertainty about employment opportunities and a reticence to leave a secure job. As employment grew in the latter part of the decade, the percentage of voluntary job leavers slowly began to rise again, as did the proportion of unemployed who are reentrants to the labor market.

Underemployment

Another indicator of opportunity in the labor market is the measure of underemployment, referred to as the real rate of unemployment by some economists. Those commonly included among the underemployed are: (1) the unemployed, (2) those who want but cannot find full-time work (i.e., involuntary part-timers), and (3) those who want work but have become discouraged at the prospects of finding a job (i.e., discouraged workers). Underemployment, which grew from 8.2 percent in 1973 to 12.6 percent in 1993, reached 8.9 percent in 1997. While many people in the labor force are able to find employment – as represented in the relatively low unemployment rate of 4.9 percent in 1997 – employment prospects are less encouraging for the 12.2 million underemployed people in the nation.

Unemployment Insurance

A fourth means of unbundling the unemployment rate to assess the well-being of workers is to consider the compensation paid to unemployed workers. According to the Advisory Council on Unemployment Compensation (ACUC), the percentage of unemployed workers that received unemployment insurance benefits dropped from over 80 percent in the 1940s (when the program began) to less than 40 percent in 1994 (ACUC 1996). Most unemployment insurance programs provide eligible unemployed workers with about one-half of their previous wages. Hence, the unemployment insurance system no longer fulfills its intended role of alleviating hardship caused by short-term unemployment for the majority of workers.

In sum, the past two decades have witnessed: (1) a rise in the number and proportion of people employed in market work in the United States, (2) a shift in the demographic composition of the labor force to include more women and people of color, (3) an increase in the incidence of alternative work arrangements, such as involuntary part-time, temporary, contract labor, self-employment, and moonlighting, and (4) a drop in aggregate unemployment accompanied by lengthening spells of unemployment and dwindling unemployment insurance coverage.

III. Nonmarket Work

We now turn to the segment of the population not in the labor market statistics presented above. This group includes children, retirees, volunteers, unpaid workers, discouraged workers, and others.

In 1998, there were 68 million adults not in the labor force: 43 million women and 25 million men. Over half were individuals 55 years of age and older. The BLS asked these individuals about their desire to work. Almost 60 million people indicated that they were out of the labor market because they did not want a job. Of the remaining 8 million, half did not look for work in the previous year and half searched but were unsuccessful in finding a job.

There are two primary groups of "workers" who are not in the official labor market statistics described above: discouraged and unpaid workers. Discouraged workers are individuals who would like to find employment but have stopped searching specifically because they believe no jobs are available to them. These workers are not counted as unemployed because they have not looked for work in the past four weeks. According to the new BLS guidelines, effective January 1994, discouraged workers must also indicate their willingness to take a job if offered and that they have searched for work sometime in the past 12 months (or since the end of their last job if they held one within the past 12 months). After one year of unsuccessful search, a discouraged worker is no longer part of the government statistics even if the person still wants to work. In October 1995, the BLS estimated there to be at least 412,000 discouraged workers, 1.1 million less than would be counted under the pre-1994 survey (BLS 1995).

Unpaid workers include any person who works outside the formal economy and for no pay or profit (also called nonmarket work). These individuals include homemakers, caretakers of children and other dependent persons, volunteers, and others providing pro bono services.

A longstanding debate continues among economists on whether to include nonmarket work in the U.S. national wealth accounts. The Gross Domestic Product (GDP), the most heavily relied upon measure of economic performance, enumerates only activities for which a person is paid. Any and all home production, caring, and volunteer work is excluded. Only when those services are formally exchanged in the labor market are they added to wealth and productivity figures.

Hence, in the 1960s and 1970s when increasing numbers of middle- and upper-middle class wives entered the paid labor market, the GDP grew commensurately. Not only were these women doing paid work, but many

What the numbers do not reveal is what we are doing all day, the skills we employ, and the level of satisfaction with our work.

were paying others to do jobs that were once done for no money. The reported increase in GDP was to some degree an illusion. Overall production did not grow, but rather moved from the nonmarket to the market sectors.[4] This phenomenon has caused economists to question the way in which work is valued. Some argue that national wealth should include the value of unpaid work; others argue that only market activities should be included in national accounts.

The challenge of assessing the worth of unpaid work is a major obstacle to its inclusion in the GDP. Two common methods are the "replacement cost" approach (i.e., setting the value of household or community work at what it would cost to hire others to take over the work) and the "opportunity cost" approach (i.e., setting the value equal to the foregone salary that a person who stays at home could command in the market place). Neither method is ideal, and formal valuation will not ensure that society values nonmarket work. As explained by Henderson (1995) and Waring (1988), our system values monetary flows rather than natural and human resources.

Rough estimates of the value and magnitude of unpaid work are not trivial, however. The 1995 Human Development Report by the United Nations' Development Program (UNDP) estimated that if unpaid work were calculated at prevailing market wages, it would increase global output by $16 trillion, $11 trillion of which is women's work (UNDP 1996). The total represents two-thirds of the current estimated global output of $23 trillion. Independent Sector estimated that in 1998, 108 million adults in the United States (56 percent of adults 18 years of age and older) volunteered an average of 3.5 hours a week (IS 1999).

IV. Implications for Workers and Employers

Dramatic changes have taken place in employment this century, especially since the early 1970s. The main trends include:
- increases in the number of women in the labor force;
- increases in hours worked;
- decreases in wages;
- increases in contingent employment; and
- increases in long-term unemployment.

As the U.S. Department of Labor developed new statistical measurements in the 1940s to more accurately reflect "real life" employment situations, so today we see the need for a more in-depth inquiry into the nature of jobs in America. Several issues become apparent in reviewing the numbers. First, we need to know more about the content of work. The data indicate how many of us are employed, how many hours we work, our compensation, and so on. What the numbers do not reveal is what we are doing all day, the skills we employ, and the level of satisfaction with our work. We could examine whether longer hours is better for the economy and workers.

Such an inquiry might explore the ramifications of a work-and-spend tread-mill that consumes our energy, time, and resources and takes us away from other "work" for the betterment of our neighborhood, the earth, and civil society.

Second, our traditional data and economic analyses do not reveal why certain people cannot find work and whether they suffer economic hardship. Our current definition only indicates the pattern of job search and the success or failure of that search. To be explored is how the 6.2 million unemployed people make ends meet today. Further information on the economic condition of people who are unemployed would bring to life the employment statistics.

Third, the statistics do not reveal the ramifications of the subcon-tracting-out of work. Individuals are less likely to stay with one company for the duration of their working lives, and employers are investing less in maintaining a stable workforce. Increasingly, employers are maintaining only a core of traditional, full-time employees and contracting out much of the work that used to be performed in-house. It is not clear whether this is a healthy phenomenon for workers, firms, and the nation. Questions arise as to whether we might be losing part of our knowledge base as we veer toward short-run employment strategies in the interest of flexibility and saving money. Perhaps more independence by employees in negotiating contracts is a healthy response to globalization of labor and capital markets. Given the size and rate of growth of the contract industry, further exploration into the short- and long-term ramifications seems worthwhile and timely.

Fourth, the current labor market statistical system excludes the contributions made by unpaid workers. It is only when parents employ day-care workers to help raise their children that child care is officially valued. The necessity to take a second job is recorded as an economic gain in the GDP even though it may be a social loss to the workers and their friends and families. While spending time monetizing nonmarket work will not ensure that society values these efforts, the fact that more of our time is spent in paid employment suggests that there may be a substantial loss in other aspects of life that is important to understand.

While the Calvert-Henderson Employment Indicator is based on official statistics about the labor market, we intend to keep gathering statis-tics on these overlooked aspects of employment. As such data become avail-able, the Employment Indicator will be expanded and updated to reflect the changing picture of work in our society.

Meanwhile, when the government releases the employment and unemployment statistics next month, challenge yourself to ask what the numbers mean. Think about what the trends suggest on the surface. Then look deeper into the more subtle indicators and the implications for society. Relate the numbers to your community. Challenge economists to unbundle the aggregate statistics and connect the numbers to other aspects of the economy so that you get the information needed to assess your well-being and that of your family and community.

ENDNOTES

[1] For a fuller description of income trends since 1973, see the Calvert-Henderson Income Indicator in this volume.

[2] In January 1994, there were 5 million workers employed on a part-time basis for economic reasons, over a million fewer than would have been counted using the previous design (Norwood 1994).

[3] It is important to note that due to changes in the Current Population Survey, the statistics on unemployment since January 1994 are not strictly comparable with previous figures. The unemployment rate in January 1994 was 6.7 percent – 0.3 percentage points higher than the rate reported in December 1993. The increase is due to changes in measurement. On the pre-1994 survey, the first question was "What were you doing most of last week?" Available options for men were "working or something else" and for women "keeping house or something else." The new survey asks all adults "Last week, did you do any work for (either) pay (or profit)?" The change added about 950,000 people to civilian employment figures and 200,000 to unemployment (BLS 1995).

[4] On average, women spent five weeks more in market work in 1989 than in 1969, while the amount of time spent in nonmarket work (e.g., home repairs, child care, shopping, cleaning) dropped by two weeks. The opposite trend occurred among men, whose time in market work dropped four weeks a year between 1969 and 1989 while time in nonmarket work rose by 2.4 weeks a year (Leete-Guy and Schor 1992).

Appendix 1

Official labor market statistics on employment and unemployment are collected and prepared each month by the U.S. Department of Labor's Bureau of Labor Statistics (BLS). Information is gathered from several household and employer surveys administered at various increments. The primary sources of data on labor markets are the Current Population Survey (CPS), the Current Employment Survey (CES), and the Occupational Employment Statistics (OES) described below. (For more details, see the *BLS Handbook of Methods,* 1992.)

The CPS is a monthly survey of the working age population, 16 years and over. Children are excluded from the official definition of the workforce because child labor laws, compulsory school attendance, and general social customs prevent most children from working. The CPS is administered each month to a probability sample of approximately 50,000 households representing the civilian noninstitutionalized population in the United States, down from 60,000 prior to 1994. Statistics are gathered on the labor force, employment, unemployment, and persons not in the labor force by demographic, social, and economic conditions. Information is collected on both wage and salary workers and the self-employed. The survey response rate is 97.5 percent.

While named the Current Population Survey in 1948, the government has collected labor market information from households since the 1930s when the threat of high unemployment during the Depression called for unproved methods of data collection. In 1959, responsibility for analyzing and publishing the CPS was transferred to the BLS, with the Bureau of the Census continuing to collect and tabulate the statistics. The core set of information collected has remained fairly consistent over time. However, due to changes in women's labor force patterns and adjustment for the known Census undercount of minority populations, the BLS instituted a major redesign of the CPS survey in January 1994. Data from 1994 forward are therefore not strictly comparable with earlier data. (For details on changes to the 1994 CPS, see *BLS Employment and Earnings,* February 1994.)

CPS data are augmented with data from two BLS employer surveys: the Current Employment Survey (CES) and the Occupational Employment Statistics (OES). The CES collects monthly payroll data from over 350,000 establishments. Employers provide information on employment, hours worked, and earnings by industry on a national, state, and area basis. About 98 percent of all employees on nonfarm payrolls are covered by the CES survey.

The OES survey collects employment data on workers in approximately 725,000 establishments in 400 detailed industries with over 750 occupational categories. The survey follows a three-year cycle: manufac-

Appendix 1
continued

turing firms are surveyed in year one, nonmanufacturing in year two, and the balance of nonmanufacturing industries in year three. Information is collected on the occupational composition of different industries. The overall response rate is 79 percent.

The BLS releases key employment-related statistics each month. Supplemental information is collected through periodic surveys and released accordingly (e.g., discouraged workers, moonlighters). Wherever possible, annual data are presented in the Calvert-Henderson Employment Indicator. While not complete, government statistics provide reliable baseline information on labor market activities both at a point in time and longitudinally.

Civilian Labor Force, 1929-1998

(thousands; percent)

Year	Total	Employed	Unemployed	Rate
1929	49,180	47,630	1,550	3.2
1933	51,590	38,760	12,830	24.9
1939	55,230	45,750	9,480	17.2
1940	55,640	47,520	8,120	14.6
1941	55,910	50,350	5,560	9.9
1942	56,410	53,750	2,660	4.7
1943	55,540	54,470	1,070	1.9
1944	54,630	53,960	670	1.2
1945	53,860	52,820	1,040	1.9
1946	57,520	55,250	2,270	3.9
1947 *	59,350	57,038	2,311	3.9
1948	60,621	58,343	2,276	3.8
1949	61,286	57,651	3,637	5.9
1950	62,208	58,918	3,288	5.3
1951	62,017	59,961	2,055	3.3
1952	62,138	60,250	1,883	3.0
1953	63,015	61,179	1,834	2.9
1954	63,643	60,109	3,532	5.5
1955	65,023	62,170	2,852	4.4
1956	66,552	63,799	2,750	4.1
1957	66,929	64,071	2,859	4.3
1958	67,639	63,036	4,602	6.8
1959	68,369	64,630	3,740	5.5
1960	69,628	65,778	3,852	5.5
1961	70,459	65,746	4,714	6.7
1962	70,614	66,702	3,911	5.5
1963	71,833	67,762	4,070	5.7
1964	73,091	69,305	3,786	5.2
1965	74,455	71,088	3,366	4.5
1966	75,770	72,895	2,875	3.8
1967	77,347	74,372	2,975	3.8
1968	78,737	75,920	2,817	3.6
1969	80,734	77,902	2,832	3.5

Continued

	Year	Total	Employed	Unemployed	Rate
Appendix 2 *continued*	1970	82,771	78,678	4,093	4.9
	1971	84,382	79,367	5,016	5.9
	1972	87,034	82,153	4,882	5.6
	1973	89,429	85,064	4,365	4.9
	1974	91,949	86,794	5,156	5.6
	1975	93,775	85,846	7,929	8.5
	1976	96,158	88,752	7,406	7.7
	1977	99,009	92,017	6,991	7.1
	1978	102,251	96,048	6,202	6.1
	1979	104,962	98,824	6,137	5.8
	1980	106,940	99,303	7,637	7.1
	1981	108,670	100,397	8,273	7.6
	1982	110,204	99,526	10,678	9.7
	1983	111,550	100,834	10,717	9.6
	1984	113,544	105,005	8,539	7.5
	1985	115,461	107,150	8,312	7.2
	1986	117,834	109,597	8,237	7.0
	1987	119,865	112,440	7,425	6.2
	1988	121,669	114,968	6,701	5.5
	1989	123,869	117,342	6,528	5.3
	1990	125,840	118,793	7,047	5.6
	1991	126,346	117,718	8,628	6.8
	1992	128,105	118,492	9,613	7.5
	1993	129,200	120,259	8,940	6.9
	1994 **	131,056	123,060	7,996	6.1
	1995	132,304	124,900	7,404	5.6
	1996	133,943	126,708	7,236	5.4
	1997	136,297	129,558	6,739	4.9
	1998	137,673	131,463	6,210	4.5

* 1929-1946 persons 14 years and older; thereafter 16 and older.

** Not strictly comparable with earlier data due to population adjustments and a major redesign of the CPS household survey.

Source: U.S. Department of Labor, Bureau of Labor Statistics.

Labor Force Participation Rate and Employment-to-Population Ratio
Females and Males, 1948-1998
(percent)

Appendix 3

Year	Participation Rate			Employment-Population Ratio		
	Total	Female	Male	Total	Female	Male
1948	58.8	32.7	86.6	56.6	31.3	83.5
1949	58.9	33.1	86.4	55.4	31.2	81.3
1950	59.2	33.9	86.4	56.1	32.0	82.0
1951	59.2	34.6	86.3	57.3	33.1	84.0
1952	59.0	34.7	86.3	57.3	33.4	83.9
1953	58.9	34.4	86.0	57.1	33.3	83.6
1954	58.8	34.6	85.5	55.5	32.5	81.0
1955	59.3	35.7	85.4	56.7	34.0	81.8
1956	60.0	36.9	85.5	57.5	35.1	82.3
1957	59.6	36.9	84.8	57.1	35.1	81.3
1958	59.5	37.1	84.2	55.4	34.5	78.5
1959	59.3	37.1	83.7	56.0	35.0	79.3
1960	59.4	37.7	83.3	56.1	35.5	78.9
1961	59.3	38.1	82.9	55.4	35.4	77.6
1962	58.8	37.9	82.0	55.5	35.6	77.7
1963	58.7	38.3	81.4	55.4	35.8	77.1
1964	58.7	38.7	81.0	55.7	36.3	77.3
1965	58.9	39.3	80.7	56.2	37.1	77.5
1966	59.2	40.3	80.4	56.9	38.3	77.9
1967	59.6	41.1	80.4	57.3	39.0	78.0
1968	59.6	41.6	80.1	57.5	39.6	77.8
1969	60.1	42.7	79.8	58.0	40.7	77.6
1970	60.4	43.3	79.7	57.4	40.8	76.2
1971	60.2	43.4	79.1	56.6	40.4	74.9
1972	60.4	43.9	78.9	57.0	41.0	75.0
1973	60.8	44.7	78.8	57.8	42.0	75.5
1974	61.3	45.7	78.7	57.8	42.6	74.9
1975	61.2	46.3	77.9	56.1	42.0	71.7
1976	61.6	47.3	77.5	56.8	43.2	72.0
1977	62.3	48.4	77.7	57.9	44.5	72.8
1978	63.2	50.0	77.9	59.3	46.4	73.8
1979	63.7	50.9	77.8	59.9	47.5	73.8

Continued

		Participation Rate			Employment-Population Ratio		
Appendix 3 *continued*	Year	Total	Female	Male	Total	Female	Male
	1980	63.8	51.5	77.4	59.2	47.7	72.0
	1981	63.9	52.1	77.0	59.0	48.0	71.3
	1982	64.0	52.6	76.6	57.8	47.4	69.0
	1983	64.0	52.9	76.4	57.9	48.0	68.8
	1984	64.4	53.6	76.4	59.5	49.5	70.7
	1985	64.8	54.5	76.3	60.1	50.4	70.9
	1986	65.3	55.3	76.3	60.7	51.4	71.0
	1987	65.6	56.0	76.2	61.5	52.5	71.5
	1988	65.9	56.6	76.2	62.3	53.4	72.0
	1989	66.5	57.4	76.4	63.0	54.3	72.5
	1990	66.5	57.5	76.4	62.8	54.3	72.0
	1991	66.2	57.4	75.8	61.7	53.7	70.4
	1992	66.4	57.8	75.8	61.5	53.8	69.8
	1993	66.3	57.9	75.4	61.7	54.1	70.0
	1994	66.6	58.8	75.1	62.5	55.3	70.4
	1995	66.6	58.9	75.0	62.9	55.6	70.8
	1996	66.8	59.3	74.9	63.2	56.0	70.9
	1997	67.1	59.8	75.0	63.8	56.8	71.3
	1998	67.1	59.8	74.9	64.1	57.1	71.6

Source: U.S. Department of Labor, Bureau of Labor Statistics.

Duration of Unemployment, 1948-1998
(weeks)

Year	Mean	Median
1948	8.6	n/a
1949	10.0	
1950	12.1	
1951	9.7	
1952	8.4	
1953	8.0	
1954	11.8	
1955	13.0	
1956	11.3	
1957	10.5	
1958	13.9	
1959	14.4	
1960	12.8	
1961	15.6	
1962	14.7	
1963	14.0	
1964	13.3	
1965	11.8	
1966	10.4	
1967	8.7	
1968	8.4	4.5
1969	7.8	4.4
1970	8.6	4.9
1971	11.3	6.3
1972	12.0	6.2
1973	10.0	5.2
1974	9.8	5.2
1975	14.2	8.4
1976	15.8	8.2
1977	14.3	7.0
1978	11.9	5.9
1979	10.8	5.4

Continued

	Year	Mean	Median
Appendix 4 *continued*	1980	11.9	6.5
	1981	13.7	6.9
	1982	15.6	8.7
	1983	20.0	10.1
	1984	18.2	7.9
	1985	15.6	6.8
	1986	15.0	6.9
	1987	14.5	6.5
	1988	13.5	5.9
	1989	11.9	4.8
	1990	12.0	5.3
	1991	13.7	6.8
	1992	17.7	8.7
	1993	18.0	8.3
	1994	18.8	9.2
	1995	16.6	8.3
	1996	16.7	8.3
	1997	15.8	8.0
	1998	14.5	6.7

Note: n/a indicates data are not available.

Source: U.S. Department of Labor, Bureau of Labor Statistics.

Reason for Unemployment, 1968-1998
(percent distribution)

Year	Job Losers	Job Leavers	Reentrants	New Entrants
1968	0.380	0.153	0.323	0.144
1969	0.359	0.154	0.341	0.146
1970	0.442	0.134	0.300	0.123
1971	0.463	0.118	0.293	0.126
1972	0.432	0.131	0.298	0.139
1973	0.388	0.156	0.307	0.149
1974	0.435	0.149	0.284	0.132
1975	0.553	0.104	0.239	0.104
1976	0.497	0.122	0.260	0.121
1977	0.453	0.130	0.281	0.136
1978	0.417	0.141	0.299	0.143
1979	0.429	0.143	0.294	0.133
1980	0.517	0.117	0.252	0.114
1981	0.516	0.112	0.254	0.119
1982	0.587	0.079	0.223	0.111
1983	0.584	0.077	0.225	0.113
1984	0.518	0.096	0.256	0.130
1985	0.498	0.106	0.271	0.125
1986	0.490	0.123	0.262	0.125
1987	0.480	0.130	0.266	0.124
1988	0.461	0.147	0.270	0.122
1989	0.457	0.157	0.282	0.104
1990	0.481	0.148	0.274	0.097
1991	0.544	0.116	0.248	0.092
1992	0.561	0.104	0.238	0.097
1993	0.542	0.109	0.246	0.103
1994 *	0.477	0.099	0.348	0.076
1995	0.470	0.111	0.341	0.078
1996	0.466	0.107	0.347	0.080
1997	0.451	0.118	0.347	0.084
1998	0.454	0.118	0.343	0.084

* Beginning January 1994, job losers also includes persons who completed temporary jobs.

Source: U.S. Department of Labor, Bureau of Labor Statistics.

REFERENCES

Advisory Council on Unemployment Compensation. 1996. *Defining Federal and State Roles in Unemployment Insurance.* Washington, DC: ACUC (January).

Callaghan, Polly and Heidi Hartmann. 1991. "Contingent Work: A Chart Book on Part-time and Temporary Employment." Washington, DC: Economic Policy Institute.

Devine, Theresa J. 1994. "Characteristics of Self-Employed Women in the United States." *Monthly Labor Review* (March).

Hayghe, Howard V. and Suzanne M. Bianchi. 1994. "Married Mothers' Work Patterns: The Job-Family Compromise." *Monthly Labor Review* (June).

Henderson, Hazel. 1995. *Paradigms in Progress: Life Beyond Economics.* San Francisco: Berrett-Koehler.

Independent Sector. 1999. *Giving and Volunteering in the United States Executive Summary.* Washington, DC: Independent Sector.

International Labor Organization. 1993. "Part-Time Employment Reaches 60 Million." *ILO Washington Focus* (Fall).

Leete-Guy, Laura and Juliet B. Schor. 1992. *The Great American Time Squeeze: Trends in Work and Leisure, 1969-89.* Washington, DC: Economic Policy Institute.

Martin, George. 1976. *Madame Secretary Frances Perkins.* Boston: Houghton Mifflin Co.

Mishel, Lawrence, Jared Bernstein, and John Schmitt. 1999. *The State of Working America, 1998-99 Edition.* Armonk, NY: Cornell University Press.

Norwood, Janet L. 1994. "Measuring Unemployment: A Change in the Yardstick." *Policy Bites,* No. 21. Washington, DC: The Urban Institute (March).

Rones, Philip L., Randy E. Ilg, and Jennifer M. Gardner. 1997. "Trends in Hours of Work Since the Mid-1970s." *Monthly Labor Review* (April).

Schor, Juliet B. 1991. *The Overworked American: The Unexpected Decline of Leisure.* New York: Basic Books.

Silvestri, George T. 1999. "Considering Self-Employment." *Occupational Outlook Quarterly.* Washington, DC: U.S. Department of Labor (Summer).

Stinson, John F. 1997. "New Data on Multiple Jobholders Available from CPS." *Monthly Labor Review,* Vol. 120, No. 3.

United Nations. 1996. *Human Development Report 1995.* New York: Oxford University Press.

U.S. Department of Labor, Bureau of Labor Statistics. 1999. <www.bls.gov>.

U.S. Department of Labor, Bureau of Labor Statistics. 1998. "Work at Home in 1997." USDL 98-93. Washington, DC (March).

U.S. Department of Labor, Bureau of Labor Statistics. 1997. "Contingent and Alternative Employment Arrangements." USDL 97-422. Washington, DC (December).

U.S. Department of Labor, Bureau of Labor Statistics. 1995. *Employment and Earnings.* Vol. 42, No. 1. Washington, DC (January).

U.S. Department of Labor, Bureau of Labor Statistics. 1994. "Revisions in the Current Population Survey Effective January 1994." *Employment and Earnings.* Washington, DC (February).

U.S. Department of Labor, Bureau of Labor Statistics. 1992. *BLS Handbook of Methods.* Bulletin 2414. Washington, DC (September).

Waring, Marilyn. 1988. *If Women Counted: A New Feminist Economics.* San Francisco: Harper & Row.

Chapter 7

Energy Indicator

by John A. "Skip" Laitner

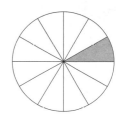

I. Introduction

Energy is the lifeblood of the economic process. It provides light, heat and air conditioning for homes, schools and businesses. It powers office equipment and production machinery, and it transports both people and freight. Energy, especially in the form of petroleum resources, is also a critical ingredient in a diverse mix of consumer goods ranging from medicine and children's toys to food and clothing.

With 4.3 percent of the world's population, the United States consumes 25 percent of the world's energy resources to maintain its current standard of living.[1] In 1998, the nation used an average 350.4 million British Thermal Units (Btus) of energy per capita. If we converted all energy resources to an equivalent amount of gasoline per capita, the United States would consume about 2,800 gallons of gasoline equivalent for every man, woman, and child that resides in the country. When multiplied by each of the 270.3 million persons who lived in the United States, total energy consumption was 94.7 quadrillion Btus in 1998.[2]

Most of the nation's energy needs are met with fossil fuels, including petroleum (39.1 percent), natural gas (23.2 percent) and coal (23.0 percent). The balance is provided largely by nuclear resources (7.3 percent), and other resources such as wood, wood waste, municipal solid waste, landfill gases, and solar and wind technologies (7.4 percent). The United States imports about one-fourth of its total energy requirement from other nations.[3]

While the United States has access to an adequate supply of energy resources, energy that is inefficiently or inappropriately used can constrain the economic activity of a nation. The inefficient use of energy contributes to environmental degradation and limits the job creation process. From an environmental perspective, the incomplete combustion of energy releases a wide variety of contaminants such as carbon emissions, widely believed to contribute to global climate change, and nitrogen oxide and sulfur dioxide emissions believed to contribute to deteriorating air quality. From an economic perspective, the inefficient use of energy means fewer goods and services that can be produced.

II. Energy Efficiency

When viewed from a materials and energy perspective, the American economy is perhaps only 10 to 15 percent efficient.[4] Electricity – typically thought of as 100 percent efficient at the end use – is a case in point. It takes energy to explore, mine and produce the coal, natural gas and oil needed to power electrical turbines. It takes energy to build transmission lines and power plants. And, of course, there are huge losses of energy in the power generation, transmission, and distribution systems of an electric utility.

Once the electricity reaches a building or factory, other losses occur in the end use or manufacturing process. Electric motors that power pumps and fabrication equipment all dissipate large amounts of energy – particularly under variable loads. Steam, water, and other forms of process heat are lost to the air. And inefficient heating, air-conditioning, and ventilation systems in the factory use even more energy, partly to compensate for the process losses. In homes and office buildings, inefficient lighting generates more heat than useful light while appliances consume much more electricity than is necessary. Toting up each of these inefficiencies yields the very small net energy gain that was noted above.

By itself, the inefficient production and use of electricity or other forms of energy does not necessarily pose a problem for the United States. Some observers suggest, however, that this high level of energy inefficiency constrains the effective use of both capital and labor resources in the economic process. The result is a weaker economy and greater environmental degradation. There are several reasons for this result. First, substantial amounts of capital must be devoted to energy supply investments compared to other forms of economic activity. For example, a review of the thirty-five gas and electric utility companies that appear on the list of the Fortune 500 shows that the utility industry required about $2.60 of capital assets for each dollar of sales or revenue in 1994. Other members of the Fortune 500 typically required only $1.00 to $1.25 of assets for each dollar of revenue.[5]

Second, net energy imports – totaling $61 billion as of 1997 – are already a major contributor to our trade deficit. They are expected to increase substantially with "business-as-usual" policies during the next twenty years.[6] Finally, it takes energy to produce energy. In 1960 the share of energy consumed by the energy sectors themselves was just under 24 percent of the total energy consumed in the United States. This rose to about 32 percent in 1993.[7] The increase suggests that the net return on energy supplies are declining even as we increase the overall use of energy. In effect, inefficiency begets further inefficiency.

For these and other reasons, the inefficient use of energy diverts dollars from other productive investments and from the U.S. economy as a whole. Thus, it is important to track how efficiently the nation uses its energy resources with respect to the total economic activity of the country. In this case, efficiency is measured as the level of energy intensity, or in other words, the number of Btus consumed per dollar of Gross Domestic Product (GDP). Hence, the balance of this chapter explores relevant indicators of energy intensity. It also examines how positive changes in energy intensity

Calvert-Henderson Energy Model

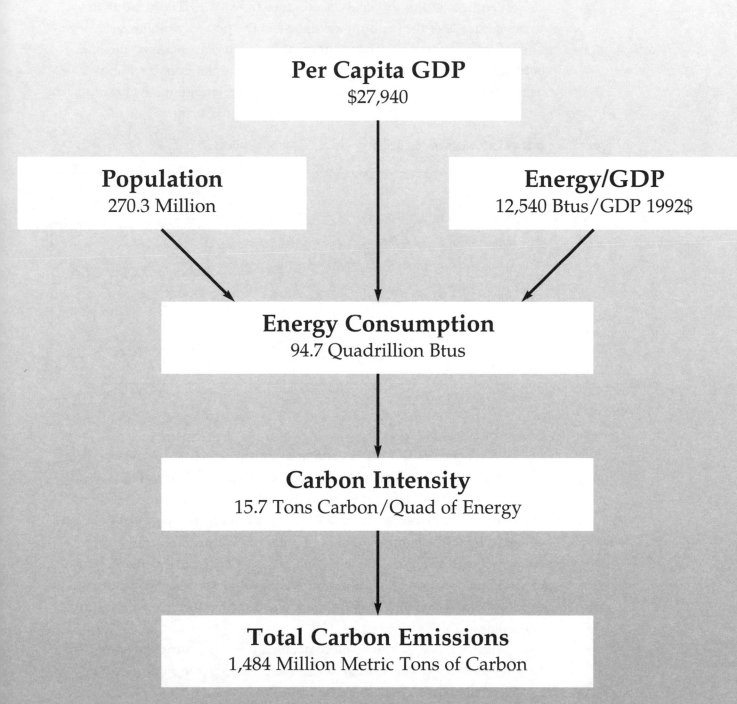

Per Capita GDP
$27,940

Population
270.3 Million

Energy/GDP
12,540 Btus/GDP 1992$

Energy Consumption
94.7 Quadrillion Btus

Carbon Intensity
15.7 Tons Carbon/Quad of Energy

Total Carbon Emissions
1,484 Million Metric Tons of Carbon

Note: 1998 data.

(i.e., a declining energy intensity) can positively contribute to the nation's economic and environmental well-being.[8]

Tracking the Nation's Energy Intensity

Appendix 1 of this chapter provides time series data relating to various aspects of the nation's energy use in the period 1960 through 1998. The information will be used in different forms to help examine the link between energy use and economic and environmental impacts. Figure 1 begins the review by charting the nation's overall energy intensity since 1972.

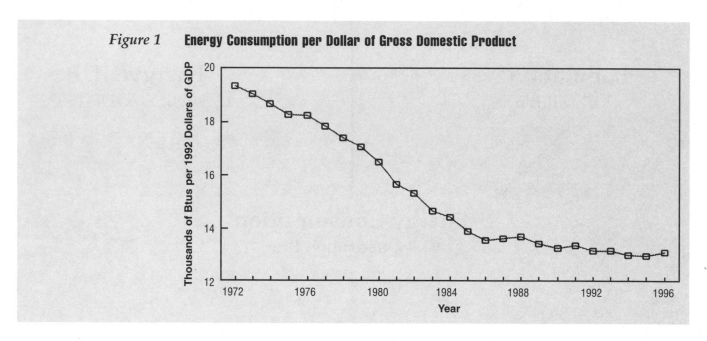

Figure 1 **Energy Consumption per Dollar of Gross Domestic Product**

Energy intensity is a benchmark that compares the number of Btus consumed per dollar of real Gross Domestic Product (GDP). It is currently measured in 1992 dollars. The indicator is often referred to as E/GDP (pronounced "E" over "GDP"). In 1972, for example, the year just before the embargo by the Organization of Petroleum Exporting Countries (OPEC) which opened much of the current interest in energy policy, the economy required an estimated 19.2 thousand Btus (kBtus) of energy consumption to support a dollar of GDP. By 1998 the intensity ratio declined to 12.5 kBtus per dollar.

Table 1, below, shows more detailed data regarding the energy consumption per dollar of GDP for selected years. As in Figure 1, the E/GDP ratio declines – in this case from 19.2 kBtus in 1973 to 12.5 kBtus in 1998. In reviewing the full time series data from the Appendix, however, there are actually four distinct periods in the annual rate of decline. In the period 1960 to 1973, the E/GDP ratio fluctuated slightly but remained largely unchanged.

In the years 1973-1986 the E/GDP ratio dropped by an average annual rate of 2.6 percent. This sharp decline in energy intensity allowed the nation's GDP (measured in constant 1992 dollars) to expand 40 percent

Energy and GDP Data for Selected Years   *Table 1*

Year	GDP		Energy		E/GDP	
	Billions of 1992$	Index (1960=1.00)	Quadrillion Btus	Index (1960=1.00)	Thousand Btus per GDP	Index (1960=1.00)
1960	2,263	1.00	43.8	1.00	19.4	1.00
1970	3,398	1.50	66.4	1.52	19.6	1.01
1973	3,916	1.73	74.3	1.70	19.0	0.98
1986	5,488	2.43	74.3	1.70	13.5	0.70
1996	6,995	3.09	93.9	2.14	13.4	0.69
1998	7,552	3.34	94.7	2.16	12.5	0.64
1998 Alt	7,552	3.34	74.0	1.69	9.8	0.51

without an increase in total energy use.

From 1986 through 1996, the change in energy intensity largely flattened. As a result, energy consumption grew almost in lockstep with the growth of GDP. In the last two-year period of 1996 through 1998, however, the nation's energy intensity dropped by 3.3 percent annually – a sharp contrast with the previous 10-year period.

Most analysts attribute the sharp decline in energy intensity from 1973 through 1986 as a response to the significant price hikes in the late-1970s through the mid-1980s. Other factors which contributed to this change were concerns about petroleum supply disruptions in the middle east and a variety of state and national legislation enacted within this period. In contrast, as energy prices and concerns about supply disruptions began to moderate after 1986, the level of energy intensity dropped from 13.5 kBtus to only 13.4 kBtus in 1996. In the period 1996 through 1998, a process of accelerated capital investment and increased international competition, as well as the growing influence of computers and electronic commerce, increased the rate of efficiency improvement. However, with only two years of data available to us at the time of this writing, it is too early to determine whether a significant shift is occurring within the nation's ongoing efficiency improvements.[9]

To illustrate the importance of this change in E/GDP in the nation's energy use, Table 1 also provides (in the row identified as 1998 Alt) an estimate of what consumption levels might be today if the United States had sustained its early trend toward fewer energy-intensive economic activities. Continuing a 2.6 percent drop in the annual energy intensity from 1986 implies that by 1998, the E/GDP ratio might have been as low as 9.8 kBtus per dollar of GDP. Total energy consumption, therefore, would have been about 74 quads – 22 percent less than otherwise indicated for 1998.

Continuing the 1973-86 trend in declining energy intensity would again have allowed the economy to grow without increasing energy consumption over the 1973 totals shown in Table 1. In thinking about this indicator, it is important to understand that it has long been possible to economically continue a 2.6 percent rate of decline in the nation's E/GDP ratio.[10] As a nation, however, we have not actively pursued that opportunity.

Yet, developing a series of energy intensity indicators is not an end in itself. Rather, we should be more interested in how the change in energy intensity can positively affect things we really care about. These include more income and employment opportunities and enhancement to our overall quality of life. For that reason it is important to provide complementary benchmarks that provide insights into the links between energy consumption and the resulting economic and environmental impacts.

Population, Energy Intensity, Carbon Emissions, and Employment

Despite growing worldwide concern about the link between carbon emissions and global climate change,[11] there is little discussion of how changes in population, per capita income, and energy intensity can affect the overall level of carbon emissions. This section explores the impact each of these influences can have on carbon emissions. It then continues with a review of how changes in energy intensity can also affect the nation's employment.

Fossil-fuel related carbon emissions have increased by 82 percent since 1960 to a record high of 1,484 million metric tons in 1998. From the data in Table 1 we can divide the growth of carbon emission into four separate influences: (1) population growth, (2) growth in per capita income, (3) changes in energy intensity, and (4) changes in the carbon intensities of the nation's energy resources. The key data for each of these influences are summarized in Table 2. This concept is also illustrated in the Energy model (on page 91).

The analysis of how each of the four major influences can affect carbon emissions stems from a straightforward relationship, calculated as follows:

$$Carbon = \frac{Population * GDPpcap * E/GDP * C/E}{10^9}$$

In this formula, *Carbon* refers to fossil-fuel related carbon emissions (measured in million metric tons), *Population* is the U.S. population (in millions of persons), *GDPpcap* refers to per capita Gross Domestic Product (or GDP, as measured in constant 1992 dollars), *E/GDP* is the energy intensity of the U.S. economy (in Btus per dollar of GDP), and finally, *C/E* is the carbon emissions rate (measured as tons per Quad, or 10^{15} Btus, of energy).

Energy and Economic Data for Selected Years

Table 2

Indicator Data	1960	1973	1998
Population (millions)	180.7	211.9	270.3
GDP Per Capita (1992$)	$12,525	$18,482	$27,940
Energy Intensity (Btus/GDP 1992$)	19,360	18,970	12,540
Carbon Intensity (tons/quad)	18.08	17.02	15.67
Total Carbon (MMT)	792	1,265	1,484

Using the formula with the summary data shown in Table 2, the growth in carbon emissions largely stems from a 49.6 percent population increase and a 123.1 percent increase in per capita GDP (measured in 1992 dollars) in the period 1960 through 1998.

While the population and income pressures have increased, a decline in both energy and carbon intensities offset these two upward pressures. The energy and carbon intensity factors showed a decline of 35.2 percent and 13.3 percent, respectively. The interaction of these four factors – population, per capita income, energy intensity, and carbon intensity – resulted in an 87 percent increase in energy-related carbon emissions as noted in Table 2.

With the methodology now established to estimate carbon emissions, the indicator data can be used to explore the changes needed to achieve a specific policy objective. For example, policy makers and business leaders have convened a series of discussions aimed at stabilizing the year 2010 energy-related carbon emissions to no more than current levels. What is more important, the intent is to reduce carbon emissions and still allow growth in the overall level of economic activity.[12]

To illustrate how we might adapt this information for policy analysis, let us assume that we are interested in reducing projected carbon emissions in the year 2010 to 1998 levels. The question becomes: "How much of a change in energy intensity would be needed to accomplish this purpose?" At this point we can adapt published information shown in Table 3 to provide annual growth rates that are specific to each of the four variables.

Here we turn to data taken from the reference in the *Annual Energy Outlook 1999* (AEO 1999). In that document, the annual growth rates through the year 2010 are: Population, 0.82 percent; Per Capita GDP, 1.44 percent; Energy Intensity (E/GDP), -0.94 percent; and Carbon Intensity (C/E), 0.25 percent.[13] The influence of these growth trends on the year 2010 carbon emissions is shown in Table 3.

With these assumptions, fossil-fuel related carbon emissions are projected to increase 20.6 percent to 1,790 MMT in the year 2010. If U.S. energy policy has little control over population growth, and if we assume that increased GDP is desirable, this means that the energy and carbon inten-

| Table 3 | Projected Carbon Emissions in the Year 2010 | | | |

Indicator Data	1998	Annual Change	2010
Population (millions)	270.3	0.82%	298.3
GDP Per Capita (1992$)	$27,940	1.44%	$33,170
Energy Intensity (Btus/GDP 92$)	12,540	-0.94%	11,200
Carbon Intensity (tons/quad)	15.67	0.25%	16.15
Total Carbon (MMT)	1,484	n/a	1,790

sities will need to decline by a greater degree than baseline forecasts. To achieve the goal of stabilizing carbon emissions to 1998 levels, the formula implies that energy intensity will need to decline by 2.47 percent annually through the year 2010 as discussed further below. This compares to the projected decline of only 0.96 percent shown in Table 3. Nevertheless, it is still slightly less than the 2.6 percent rate of decline that occurred in the period 1973-1986.

As an alternative to the use of what might be the unwieldy numbers associated with the various indicators data, policy makers might apply an index of those values instead. This would lead to an easier computation of "what-if" analyses. For example, in Table 3 the 1998 index of carbon emissions (where, here, 1998 = 1.000) might be found simply by multiplying the values associated with each of the four critical variables, or:

$$1.1036 * 1.1872 * 0.8931 * 1.0306 = 1.2062$$

Thus, carbon emissions in 2010 will be up by 20.6 percent over 1998 levels. Or, to find what the Energy Intensity Index would have to be to achieve a 1998 carbon level in the year 2010 – with all else held constant, we can work through the following calculation from the data in Table 3:

$$1.0000 / (1.1036 * 1.1872 * 1.0306) = 0.7406$$

Or, the energy intensity index for the year 2010 would need to be 0.7406 (where 1998=1.000) if energy policy were unable to affect any of the other three variables. To determine the annual rate of change in the 12-year period from 1998 to the year 2010, we would apply the following information:

$$[0.7406^{(1/12)} - 1] * 100 = -2.47\%$$

This calculation then provides the previously referenced 2.47 percent annual decline in the nation's overall energy intensity needed to bring energy carbon emissions down to the 1998 levels. Carrying out the mathematics a step further shows that the E/GDP ratio would need to drop from the projected level of 11,200 Btus in the year 2010 (see the result in Table 3) to 9,287 Btus. This is a 17.1 percent decline over baseline projections.

But what will be the economic benefit of this lower level of energy intensity? Can we have both a lower environmental impact and a healthier economy? To answer this question we can use the time series data in the Appendix to estimate a relationship between the change in energy intensity and employment. It turns out that for each percentage drop in the E/GDP ratio, employment can be expected to increase about 0.034 percent. This provides the first step in estimating the employment impact in the year 2010 from a lower energy intensity. To complete the process, however, we need one additional piece of information – the projected employment growth rate under a business-as-usual scenario. This is provided by AEO 1999 that suggests a 1.2 percent annual growth rate. Based upon the 1998 employment of 131.46 million jobs, the year 2010 employment can be expected to grow by 15.6 percent to 151.97 million jobs.

If we apply a 17.1 percent decline in E/GDP, then employment might be expected to rise by 0.64 percent over baseline projections, or 151.97 million times 0.64 percent for a gain of about 973,000 jobs. So, with a lower energy intensity in the year 2010, the indicators suggest that carbon emissions will decrease by 306 million metric tons while employment will increase by almost one million jobs.[14]

III. Findings and Implications

The United States now consumes about 95 quadrillion Btus of energy annually. As a measure of its "energy intensity," the nation requires about 12,540 Btus of energy for each dollar of GDP required to support its current standard of living and quality of life. Yet much of this energy is wasted. The waste is the result of large inefficiencies in the production and use of energy. These inefficiencies, in turn, limit the job creation process. The inefficient use of energy is also the single largest source of carbon emissions and other air pollutants.

Energy intensity in the nation's economy can be measured and evaluated for its impact by using the energy intensity or E/GDP indicator. As this ratio declines, employment can be expected to rise with respect to baseline levels. This is true up to the point where the cost of efficiency improvements is less than the cost of energy. And as E/GDP declines at a rate that is greater than the increase in GDP, carbon emissions will also be reduced. Thus, measuring the change in the energy intensity can become one of several key indicators to track the economic and environmental health of the nation.

ENDNOTES

[1] The figures are based upon 1998 data which is the most recent available for this comparison. See, U.S. Department of Energy, Energy Information Administration, International Energy Outlook 1998, Report Number DOE/EIA-0484(98), Washington, DC, April 1998, Table A1. Also, U.S. Department of Energy, Energy Information Administration, *International Energy Annual 1998*, DOE/EIA-0219(98), Washington, DC, December 1998, Table B1.

[2] U.S. Department of Energy, Energy Information Administration, Monthly Energy Review, DOE/EIA- 0035(99/08), Washington, DC, August 1998, Table 1.4. A Btu is the amount of energy needed to raise the temperature of one pound of water by one degree Fahrenheit, or about the heat contained in one wooden kitchen match. There are about 125,000 Btus in a gallon of gasoline, and 3,412 Btus in a kilowatt-hour of electricity used in a home or factory. Because of inefficiencies in the generation of electricity, however, it takes about 10,600 Btus of primary energy (such as coal or petroleum fuels) to generate a single kilowatt-hour of electricity used by the consumer.

[3] See, for example, U.S. Department of Energy, Energy Information Administration, *Annual Energy Outlook 1999*, DOE/EIA-0383(98), Washington, DC, December 1998, Table A2.

[4] Richard S. Claassen and Louis A. Girifalco, "Materials for Energy Utilization," *Scientific American*, October 1986, pages 103-117.

[5] "The 40th Anniversary Edition of the Fortune 500," *Fortune*, May 15, 1995, pages F-1 to F-68.

[6] Data from the U.S. Department of Energy indicate that net petroleum imports will cost the United States $54 billion in the year 2000 and $108 billion in 2010. These figures, in constant 1997 dollars, assume a stable increase in petroleum prices throughout that period. See, U.S. Department of Energy, Energy Information Administration, *Annual Energy Outlook 1999*, DOE/EIA-0383(99), December 1998, Table A11.

[7] These figures are calculated by the author based upon a structural analysis of how energy use has changed in the period 1960 through 1993 as a result of the growth of the economy, the changing structure of the economy, and changing energy intensities within the major economic sectors of the economy.

[8] For a more complete review of energy indicators and economic and environmental impacts, see, Skip Laitner, *Energy Efficiency and Economic Indicators: Charting Improvements in the Economy and the Environment*, American Council for an Energy-Efficient Economy, Report Number ED952, Washington, DC, February 1995.

[9] A preliminary analysis by the author indicates a significant drop in the nation's energy inensity may already be occurring as a result of a increased reliance on information and communication technologies. See, Skip Laitner, "The Information and Communication Technology Revolution: Can It Be Good for Both the Economy and the Climate?" U.S. Environmental Protection Agency, Office of Atmospheric Programs, Washington, DC, December 1999.

[10] This is the major insight in the nationally recognized study, *Energy Innovations*. In the alternative energy efficiency scenario of that 1997 analysis, it was shown to be economically possible to lower E/GDP by an average annual rate of 2.2 percent in the period 2000 through 2030. While such a trend was projected to cost $0.6 trillion over that period, it would save homes and businesses $1.0 trillion (with all values in 1993 constant dollars). Hence the benefit-cost ratio of the market efficiency scenario is a positive 1.70. See, *Energy Innovations: A Prosperous Path to a Clean Environment* (Washington, DC: Alliance to Save Energy, American Council for an Energy-Efficient Economy, Natural Resources Defense Council, Tellus Institute, and Union of Concerned Scientists, 1997), page 5.

[11] See, for example, Thomas R. Karl, Richard W. Knight, David R. Easterling, and Robert G. Quayle, "Trends in U.S. Climate During the Twentieth Century," *Consequences*, Spring 1995, pages 3-12.

[12] For example, the United States Climate Change Action Plan (CCAP) is a policy statement

Energy and Related Time Series Data for the United States

Appendix 1

Year	Population (1,000s)	Gross Domestic Product (Billion 1992$)	Employment (1,000s)	Energy Use (Quadrillion Btus)	Carbon Emissions (Million Metric Tons)	E/GDP Ratio
1960	180,671	2,261.7	65,778	43.8	791.9	19.37
1961	183,691	2,309.8	65,746	44.5	794.2	19.25
1962	186,538	2,449.1	66,702	46.5	823.5	19.00
1963	189,242	2,554.0	67,762	48.3	867.2	18.92
1964	191,889	2,702.9	69,305	50.5	904.1	18.68
1965	194,303	2,874.8	71,088	52.7	939.4	18.32
1966	196,560	3,060.2	72,895	55.7	990.6	18.19
1967	198,712	3,140.2	74,372	57.6	1,030.4	18.33
1968	200,706	3,288.6	75,920	61.0	1,071.6	18.55
1969	202,677	3,388.0	77,902	64.2	1,122.5	18.95
1970	205,052	3,388.2	78,678	66.4	1,156.5	19.61
1971	207,661	3,500.1	79,367	67.9	1,163.5	19.39
1972	209,896	3,690.3	82,153	71.3	1,217.1	19.31
1973	211,909	3,902.3	85,064	74.3	1,264.8	19.03
1974	213,854	3,888.2	86,794	72.6	1,221.1	18.66
1975	215,973	3,865.1	85,846	70.6	1,170.6	18.25
1976	218,035	4,081.1	88,752	74.4	1,253.7	18.22
1977	220,239	4,279.3	92,017	76.3	1,260.8	17.83
1978	222,585	4,493.7	96,048	78.1	1,283.5	17.38
1979	225,055	4,624.0	98,824	78.9	1,293.4	17.06
1980	227,726	4,611.9	99,303	76.0	1,252.5	16.47
1981	229,966	4,724.9	100,397	74.0	1,204.5	15.66
1982	232,188	4,623.6	99,526	70.9	1,144.6	15.32
1983	234,307	4,810.0	100,834	70.5	1,149.1	14.66
1984	236,348	5,138.2	105,005	74.1	1,184.6	14.43
1985	238,466	5,329.5	107,150	74.0	1,208.0	13.88
1986	240,651	5,489.9	109,597	74.3	1,227.7	13.53
1987	242,804	5,648.4	112,440	76.9	1,273.8	13.61
1988	245,021	5,862.9	114,968	80.2	1,347.6	13.68
1989	247,342	6,060.4	117,342	81.3	1,360.4	13.42
1990	249,913	6,138.7	117,914	81.3	1,344.2	13.24
1991	252,650	6,079.0	119,877	81.1	1,324.6	13.34
1992	255,419	6,244.4	117,598	82.1	1,346.3	13.15
1993	258,137	6,383.8	119,306	83.9	1,372.5	13.14
1994	260,660	6,604.2	123,060	85.6	1,397.0	12.96
1995	263,257	6,740.8	124,900	87.3	1,424.0	12.95
1996	265,753	6,883.0	126,729	89.9	1,444.0	13.06
d1960-96	1.471	3.043	1.927	2.053	1.823	0.674

Sources: (1) Population, Table B-32, Appendix, 1996 Economic Report of the President.

(2) GDP, Table B-2 ERP (for 1959-1994); Appendix E, Annual Energy Review 1994 (July 1995) for 1950-1959, MER 1-9 for 1995.

(3) Quads, Annual Energy Review and Monthly Energy Review.

(4) Carbon, '93 Carbon Trends through 1991, 1991 estimated by Score.wk1.

(5) Jobs, from Economic Report of the President, Table B-33.

(6) All data updated using the Energy Information Administration's Annual Energy Outlook 1997.

and initiative designed to reduce the year 2000 carbon emissions in the U.S. to 1990 levels. See, *Climate Action Report: Submission of the United States of America Under the United Nations Framework Convention on Climate Change,* Government Printing Office, Washington, DC, 1994.

[13] U.S. Department of Energy, Energy Information Administration, *Annual Energy Outlook 1999,* DOE/EIA-0383(99), Washington, DC, December 1998, Appendix A.

[14] This "rule of thumb" produces the same level of net benefit as found in more detailed econometric studies about the link between energy intensity and employment. See, for example, *Energy Innovations,* supra. See also, Howard Geller, John DeCicco, and Skip Laitner, *Energy Efficiency and Job Creation: The Employment and Income Benefits from Investing in Energy Conserving Technologies,* Report Number ED 922, American Council for an Energy-Efficient Economy, Washington, DC, October 1992. It should be noted that the estimate of a net employment benefit represents only a "potential" gain for the economy. It assumes that cost-effective investments in energy efficient technologies are made over a reasonable period of time.

REFERENCES

Claassen, Richard S., and Louis A. Girifalco. 1986. "Materials for Energy Utilization." *Scientific American* (October): 103-117.

Climate Action Report: Submission of the United States of America Under the United Nations Framework Convention on Climate Change. 1994. Washington, DC: Government Printing Office.

Council of Economic Advisers. 1999. *Economic Report of the President.* Washington, DC: Government Printing Office.

Energy Information Administration. *Annual Energy Outlook 1999,* DOE/EIA-0383(99). Washington, DC: U.S. Department of Energy.

Energy Information Administration. *International Energy Outlook 1998,* DOE/EIA- 0484(98). Washington, DC: U.S. Department of Energy.

Energy Information Administration. *International Energy Annual 1998,* DOE/EIA- 0219(98). Washington, DC: U.S. Department of Energy.

Energy Information Administration. *Monthly Energy Review,* DOE/EIA-0035(99/05). Washington, DC: U.S. Department of Energy.

Energy Innovations, 1997. *Energy Innovations: A Prosperous Path to a Clean Environment,* Washington, DC: Alliance to Save Energy, American Council for an Energy-Efficient Economy, Natural Resources Defense Council, Tellus Institute, and Union of Concerned Scientists.

Geller, Howard, John DeCicco, and Skip Laitner. 1992. *Energy Efficiency and Job Creation: The Employment and Income Benefits from Investing in Energy Conserving Technologies.* Washington, DC: American Council for an Energy-Efficient Economy.

Karl, Thomas R., Richard W. Knight, David R. Easterling, and Robert G. Quayle. 1995. "Trends in U.S. Climate during the Twentieth Century." *Consequences* (Spring): 3-12.

Laitner, Skip. 1995. *Energy Efficiency and Economic Indicators: Charting Improvements in the Economy and the Environment.* Washington, DC: American Council for an Energy- Efficient Economy.

Laitner, Skip. 1999. "The Information and Communication Technology Revolution: Can It Be Good for Both the Economy and the Climate?" Washington, DC: U.S. Environmental Protection Agency, Office of Atmospheric Programs, Washington, DC (December) 1999.

"The 40th Anniversary Edition of the Fortune 500." *Fortune,* May 15, 1995, pp. F-1 to F-68.

Chapter 8

Environment Indicator

by Kenneth P. Scott

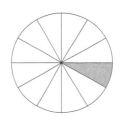

I. Introduction

The natural environment sustains human, animal and plant life. We need clean air to breathe; clean water to drink, fish, and swim in; fertile soil for food; and natural resources to manufacture products. Despite the significant value Americans attribute to nature, our nation faces major environmental challenges. Forty percent of Americans are living in areas with polluted air. One-third of rivers, lakes, and estuaries do not support important uses, such as fishing and swimming. Hundreds of endemic animal and plant species are endangered.

The environmental challenges we face have not escaped notice. In a 1996 report, the Organization for Economic Cooperation and Development (OECD) called upon the United States to review its consumption patterns and federal government financial assistance "that might lead to overuse of resources." The report highlighted the large population living in areas with poor air quality, the unsuitability of many lakes and rivers for fishing and swimming, loss of biodiversity, and the decline in wetland acreage. The OECD attributed America's problems to low-density housing, extensive use of automobiles facilitated by low gasoline prices and employers providing free parking, and high resource use. This included the highest per-capita water use rate among industrialized countries, and the highest per-capita waste generation rate in the OECD countries.

While the report praised the United States in other areas, such as enforcement and public access to environmental information, the OECD recommended strongly that we adopt performance-based programs, expand the use of the "polluter pays" principle, integrate transportation and land use policies to increase housing density in suburban areas, integrate our environmental policies into agriculture and forestry, and expand interagency development of environmental goals and indicators.

The jury is still out on whether or not the United States is making progress on the issues identified by the OECD. However, the United States Environmental Protection Agency (EPA) recently created a set of national environmental performance indicators. These indicators are forward-looking, whereby each indicator is established with a current base year and a future goal. For example, the EPA aims to reduce to five percent by the year 2005 the population served by community drinking water systems that violate health-based requirements. While we applaud this new effort, clearly additional information is needed to understand more fully the quality of our physical environment. In contrast to the EPA indicators, the Calvert-Henderson Environment Indicator presents historical trends in key environment indicators as well as an environmental model that serves as a framework to identify the causes of major environmental concerns. Four questions are answered: How clean is our air? How clean is our water? What improvements have been made in U.S. environmental quality? What questions remain unanswered?

Environmental science is a new and rapidly evolving, multidisciplinary field – far too complex for the scope of a single indicator. The Calvert-Henderson Environment Indicator incorporates only a portion of the data that represent U.S. environmental quality. The indicator does not present the summation of all resources extracted, all industries that use resources, all industrial and industrial product wastes, or all impacts of these wastes. The indicator fits within the vast literature on environmental quality and serves as a readily understandable measure of two environmental resources, air and water.

The indicator focuses on air and water quality for two reasons. First, air and water are crucial to human life and the pollution of these two resources affects our health. Knowing the quality of our air and water, and the kinds of pollutants that degrade them, helps focus our efforts in finding solutions. Second, the best available data deal with air and water quality. In order to implement its legal and regulatory mandates, the EPA has been tracking a range of air and water pollution data for nearly three decades. We can readily measure many, though not all, of the pollutants created by industrial operations and consumer products.

The Environment Indicator is presented in four sections. Section II describes the environment model. Sections III and IV explore U.S. air and water quality, respectively, with a reduced-scale icon of the environment model guiding the reader to the specific model component being described. Section V describes the role of population and economic activity. Section VI discusses the challenges for policymakers in addressing environmental quality concerns.

II. Environment Model

Because Earth's ecosystem is so complex, any evaluation of its health is a daunting challenge. The Calvert-Henderson Environment Indicator presents a conceptual model to illustrate how human populations and processes interact with the environment. It is our premise that air and water quality are key indicators of the overall health of the environment. The Calvert-Henderson environment model shows that use of natural resources by industry and industry's products leads to the generation of wastes that in turn affect environment quality. The environment model presents a linear relationship between these components: Resource Use, Industry Products, Waste, and Environment Quality. We are careful to acknowledge that this

Calvert-Henderson Environment Model

How Human Populations and Processes Interact with the Environment

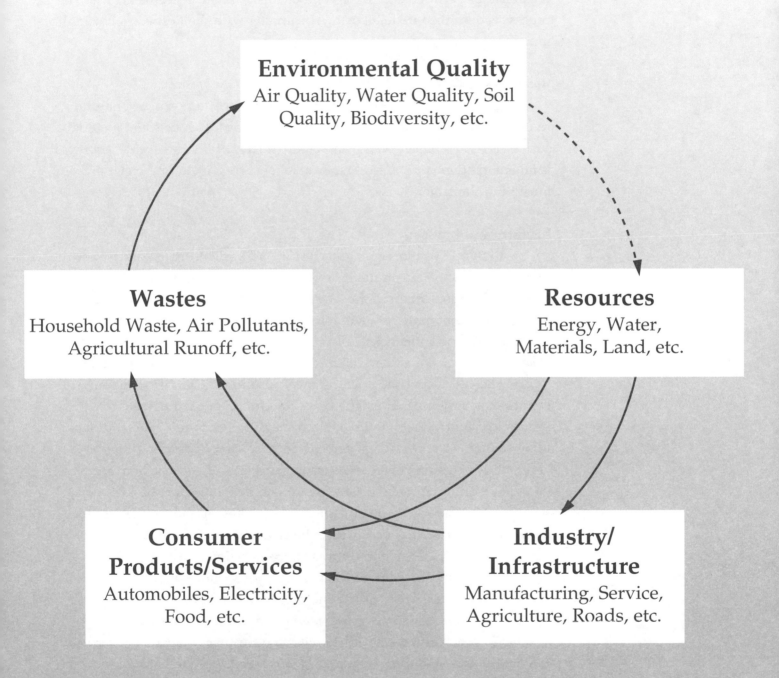

Environmental Quality
Air Quality, Water Quality, Soil Quality, Biodiversity, etc.

Wastes
Household Waste, Air Pollutants, Agricultural Runoff, etc.

Resources
Energy, Water, Materials, Land, etc.

Consumer Products/Services
Automobiles, Electricity, Food, etc.

Industry/ Infrastructure
Manufacturing, Service, Agriculture, Roads, etc.

model belies a complex set of environmental and economic relationships. While the strongest relationships in this model are linear, a more detailed model would convey a web of relationships between each of the components. For this reason, the model suggests direct relationships and feedback relationships between each of its components as noted with the arrows. The process is described in detail below, beginning with the Resources box in the model.

Resources

The industrial economy relies on the extraction and use of natural resources. These resources include energy such as fossil fuels and materials such as forest products, water, and land. The use of nonrenewable resources is inherently depleting. Use of renewable resources, including water and soil, must be sustainable.

Industry and Products

Industry, including manufacturing and agriculture as well as service sectors, uses the resources identified above to create products and services demanded by consumers. For example, automakers use metals, plastics, rubber, and other materials, and rely on the use of energy and water to manufacture cars and trucks. Pulp companies use trees, recycled materials, bleaching agents, water, and other resources to make pulp for papermakers.

The U.S. Department of Commerce estimated that the service and finance sectors of the U.S. economy account for 37 percent of the Gross Domestic Product (GDP) in 1996. Manufacturing accounts for an additional 18 percent, government for 13 percent, and all other industries (transportation, utilities, retail and wholesale trade, mining, and construction) account for the remaining 32 percent. Given differences among industries in efficiency and in reliance on other factor inputs (labor and capital), these ratios do not necessarily correlate to the environmental impact associated with each industry's use of resources and generation of waste.

Certain industrial products require additional resource use. For example, automakers use electric and boiler/furnace energy in vehicle production, while consumers must then use gasoline, or other energy resources, to power the vehicles. Similarly, computer makers use electricity at their factories, while individuals and businesses use electricity to power their desktop computers. The situation is similar for waste generation. A food company may generate waste in the field and in the factory while making a product. The "finished" product and any packaging will ultimately be disposed, composted, or recycled by the consumer.

Wastes

Industrial operations generate significant waste by-products. These wastes include air emissions, such as sulfur dioxide, nitrogen oxides, and volatile organic compounds; water pollutants, such as effluent with elevated biological oxygen demand; and solid wastes, such as municipal solid waste and industrial hazardous/toxic wastes.

Environmental Quality

The wastes, identified above, concentrate in the environment. At certain levels, they adversely impact the health of all species, including humans. Environmental quality can be broadly sub-divided into air quality, water quality, soil quality, and habitat quality or biodiversity. In 1997, approximately 40 percent of Americans lived in counties with unhealthy levels of air pollution – 107 million people lived in counties not meeting federal air quality standards. Nevertheless, EPA data indicate a significant improvement in air quality since 1988. Ground-level ozone, the primary constituent of smog, has accounted for most of the problem. There are also concerns with water quality. At least 6 percent of the U.S. population was provided drinking water that violated federal standards at least once during 1996. The data for recreational water use is more disturbing. More than one-third of the nation's surveyed waters are not clean enough for fishing or swimming, worse than in the mid-1980s.

There are tangible health concerns associated with environmental quality. Ozone pollution may be responsible for as many as 50,000 hospitalizations in the United States every year, according to a recent study by the Harvard School of Public Health and the American Lung Association (1996). An estimated 900 Americans die each year and an additional one million become ill from water-related illnesses. Land use patterns and other causes have led to severe impacts on wildlife and fish. The U.S. Fish and Wildlife Service (USFWS) lists 220 large animal species as endangered, and faces a backlog of listing petitions for other species that are potentially endangered.

Environmental quality concerns also have financial consequences. For example, clean water is of paramount importance to the U.S. economy. The EPA estimated that clean-water dependent industries contributed more than $1 trillion to the U.S. economy in 1996 (EPA 1996).

III. Air Quality

Humans breathe in approximately 15,000 quarts of air every day to stay alive. Air quality has a considerable impact on human health and the environment, as well as our wallets. This section reviews the percentage of U.S. population exposed to major air pollutants. It also discusses air pollutant concentrations, and their underlying emissions.

Air emissions have a variety of sources. The EPA uses direct monitoring and engineering calculations to measure the levels of such emissions. In addition, the EPA measures the concentrations of these pollutants, or the portion of air volume containing such pollutants. In this section, the environment model is traced counter-clockwise from environmental quality to waste to products to industry to natural resources. Thus, air quality is explained first, and is followed by key sources of air pollution. Ozone, the most problematic pollutant, is discussed in detail, and attention is given to the significant role of electric utilities and vehicle transportation in ozone pollution concerns.

U.S. air quality has improved significantly since measurements (in terms of affected population) began in 1987. This has been achieved through reduced emissions of major air pollutants. Emissions of major air pollutants peaked around 1970 – the year the Clean Air Act was passed. Since then, with greater monitoring and regulation, emissions have declined. Nevertheless, airborne concentration of ozone remains a significant environmental concern. Nitrogen oxides, a key contributor to ozone, is the only air pollutant for which emissions have increased since 1970.

Figure 1 **Percent of U.S. Population Living in Counties with Unhealthful Levels of Air Pollution, 1985-1997**

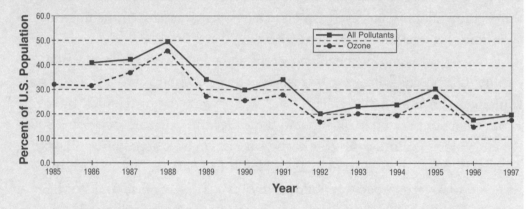

Source: U.S. Environmental Protection Agency.

Population Breathing Unhealthful Air

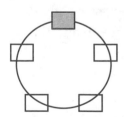

In 1997, the percent of Americans living in counties with unhealthful levels of air pollution would have increased from 17.6 percent to 19.6 percent (see Figure 1). However, EPA revised air quality standards for ozone and particulate matter. Thus, the portion of the U.S. population living in counties with air quality concentrations above the level of the revised standards in 1997 was 107 million – or 40 percent of the U.S. population (EPA 1998). In 1996, there were 46.6 million people living in counties not meeting federal air quality standards. This follows a decrease from 20.2 percent in 1992 to 17.6 percent in 1996. These values continue a longer-term improvement in air quality. In 1988, under pre-existing standards, nearly one-half of all Americans lived in counties with unhealthful levels of air pollution, as measured by the pre-existing standards (EPA 1997). The improvements in air quality have also had financial benefits, with the EPA estimating the net financial benefit resulting from the Clean Air Act to be $6.8 trillion from 1970 to 1990.

The EPA directly measures airborne concentrations of major air pollutants through a network of monitoring devices, determining whether air pollutant concentrations exceed the National Ambient Air Quality Standards. These standards are designed to protect human health. The EPA analyzes this pollutant concentration data, county by county, on an annual basis. This chapter's primary indicator of air quality measures the portion of the population exposed to unhealthful concentrations of such pollutants. The percentage is determined by dividing the number of people living in counties with unhealthful levels of air pollution by the total U.S. population. It is equivalent to the portion of the U.S. population living in counties not meeting national standards.

The improvements in the air quality indicator, and the reduction in air pollutant concentrations, are attributable to reductions in emissions of major air pollutants. The EPA attributes the latter to "effective implementation of clean air laws and regulations." Analysis of short-term trends is impractical due to several factors, especially variability in meteorological conditions. Certain weather/climate conditions are more conducive to ozone formation.

Ozone

During the past three decades, ground-level ozone has accounted for most of the air pollution problems reflected in Figure 1. The environmental effects of ozone, an oxygen compound, are different in the troposphere – ground level – than in the stratosphere. In the stratosphere, ozone forms a protective shield that blocks harmful ultraviolet (UV) rays, while tropospheric ozone contributes to respiratory-related and other illnesses. Volatile organic compounds and nitrogen oxides combine to form photochemical smog, of which the primary constituent is ozone. Volatile organic compounds are a class of chemicals that escape easily or evaporate readily into the air. They are the primary ingredients in solvents and by-products of combustion. Ozone can cause lung inflammation and eye irritation, increases susceptibility to infections and exacerbates asthma and allergies. Children and the elderly are particularly vulnerable to ozone (EPA 1997). As mentioned earlier, ozone pollution may be responsible for as many as 50,000 hospitalizations in the U.S. every year.

Regional Impact of Excess Ozone

The regulatory, public health, and environmental impacts of air pollution are strongest at the local level. As of January 1998, there were 57 metropolitan nonattainment areas – areas that were out of compliance for ozone. Appendix 2 lists the metropolitan areas most affected by ozone pollution. The metropolitan areas are classified by the degree to which airborne ozone concentrations exceed federal standards. Not surprisingly, large cities such as Los Angeles, Chicago, and New York are most severely affected (EPA 1997a). According to the Harvard study mentioned above, Los Angeles had the highest percentage, at 8.5 percent, of respiratory-related hospital admissions linked to ozone pollution. Ozone levels generally peak on hot, summer days. The topography and geography of Los Angeles were contributing factors.

In 1997, the EPA revised the ozone standard from the 1-hour 0.12 parts per million (ppm) standard to an 8-hour 0.08 ppm standard. In the year 2000, areas that do not meet the 8-hour standard will be designated as nonattainment.

Air Emissions Trends

Trends in air quality (as measured by concentrations of major air pollutants) are driven by trends in emissions, with some variability due to 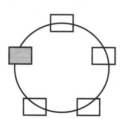 atmospheric conditions. Pursuant to the 1970 Clean Air Act, the EPA identified six major or "criteria" air pollutants to be targeted for reduction: ozone, carbon monoxide, sulfur dioxide, nitrogen oxides, lead, and particulate matter less than or equal to 10 microns in diameter (PM-10). The Clean Air Act requires the EPA to identify emissions, from mobile and stationary sources, that "cause or contribute to air pollution which may reasonably be anticipated to endanger public health or welfare."

Emissions of criteria air pollutants reached a peak in 1970 – the year the Clean Air Act was passed. Since then, emissions of most criteria pollutants have dropped significantly (see Appendix 3). These reductions have occurred despite a population increase between 1970 and 1996 and an increase in economic growth, as measured by GDP, of 103 percent. Between 1996 and 1997 (the year for which the most recent data are available), emissions of sulfur dioxide, lead, and volatile organic compounds increased, while emissions of nitrogen oxides, carbon monoxide, and particulate matter decreased (EPA 1998).

The EPA estimates emissions data based on engineering calculations that incorporate level of industrial activity, changes in technology, fuel consumption, vehicle-miles traveled, and other air-polluting activities.

Emissions of VOCs and NO$_X$

The two primary precursors of ozone are volatile organic compounds (VOCs) and nitrogen oxides (NO$_X$). VOC emissions increased 0.5 percent to 19.2 million tons in 1997, a decline of 37.7 percent from 1970. Most of this drop occurred in the 1970s and 1980s (see Figure 2). NO$_X$ emissions decreased to 22.9 million tons in 1997, a level 2.1 percent lower than in 1996, but still 5.8 percent higher than in 1970 (EPA 1998).

National Air Pollutant Emissions, U.S.: 1970-1997

Figure 2

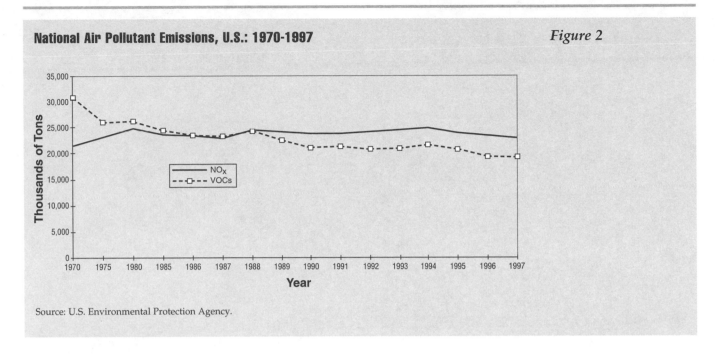

Source: U.S. Environmental Protection Agency.

NO_x is the only criteria pollutant that has increased since 1970. This is unfortunate since it is a precursor to ozone. It is important to note that increases in NO_x would have been substantively higher over the past two decades, had automobiles not been required to install catalytic converters.

There is no national ambient air quality standard for VOCs. However, regulations exist at both the state and local level. The Clean Air Act regulates some VOCs. Automobile controls, such as regulations governing fuel volatility, have lowered VOC emissions (EPA 1997).

International Comparisons

Adjusting for economic activity, the U.S. had the third highest level of air pollution among industrialized countries – members of the OECD – when ranked by emissions of four air pollutants per unit of GDP. The pollutants were sulfur oxides, nitrogen oxides, carbon monoxide, and particulate matter. Although U.S. pollution levels were worse than the average of industrialized countries, the U.S. levels were better than global averages, according to the OECD. For example, the U.S. standard for suspended particulate matter is an annual maximum average of 50 micrograms per cubic meter (mg/m^3). Several U.S. cities, such as Chicago, New York, Los Angeles, and Houston, exceed these levels by up to 100 percent. The World Bank reports that the annual mean level from 1987-1990 in Beijing was 370 mg/m^3, while in Calcutta it was 393 mg/m^3 during that period (World Bank 1994).

Below is a description of the role electric utilities and transportation play in the emission of the air pollutants discussed above.

Role of Electric Utilities

Wastes are emitted by industrial products and processes. Electric power plants emit major air pollutants, including those that form ozone.

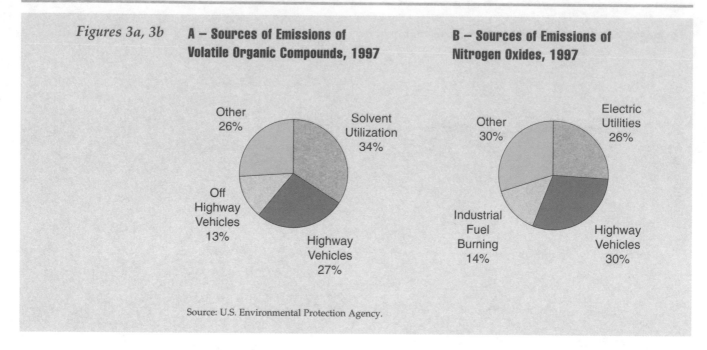

Figures 3a, 3b

A – Sources of Emissions of Volatile Organic Compounds, 1997

Other 26%
Solvent Utilization 34%
Off Highway Vehicles 13%
Highway Vehicles 27%

B – Sources of Emissions of Nitrogen Oxides, 1997

Other 30%
Electric Utilities 26%
Industrial Fuel Burning 14%
Highway Vehicles 30%

Source: U.S. Environmental Protection Agency.

Power plants are a large source of NO_x and a lesser source of VOCs (Figures 3a, 3b). Electric generators emitted 6.2 million tons of NO_x in 1997, or 26 percent of the United States total. Electric generators in the U.S. also emitted 13.1 million tons of sulfur dioxide, or 64 percent of the national total (EPA 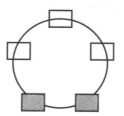 1998). Due to the associated concerns of acid rain, the Clean Air Act Amendments of 1990 sought further reductions in SO_2.

Electric generating plants provided 3.1 billion megawatt-hours of electricity to customers in 1997. These plants powered residential, commercial and industrial establishments. Electricity generation has climbed steadily over the past 25 years paralleling growth in population and GDP (Energy Information Administration [EIA] 1998a).

The decrease in electric power plant emissions of major air pollutants is associated with changes in energy sources and installation of pollution control devices and technological upgrades (such as combined cycle turbines) that permit more efficient use of energy by generators.

Continued large-scale emissions of nitrogen oxides (and sulfur dioxide) by power plants is associated with continued reliance on fossil fuels. In 1998, fossil fuels accounted for 70 percent of energy sources for electric generation (EIA 1998a). Coal alone provided 51 percent of generators' energy in 1998 (Figure 4).

Compared to 1973, 1998 data from the EIA indicate a significant increase in the use of nuclear power, a modest increase in the use of coal, and a significant decrease in the proportion of petroleum and natural gas. As the electric utility industry restructures, it is expected that coal plants will continue to be the primary energy source for most domestic electricity (EIA 1998a).

U.S. Electric Utility Generation by Source, 1998

Figure 4

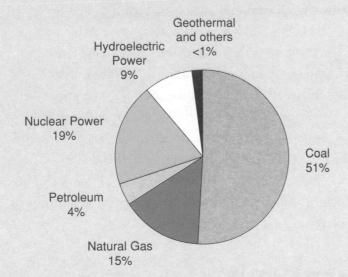

Source: U.S. Department of Energy.

Emissions Credit Trading

The Clean Air Act Amendments of 1990 implemented an emissions credit trading program for sulfur dioxide. Credits (or allowances) were distributed to electric utilities based on past emissions. The national cap for electric utility sulfur dioxide emissions was set for 8.95 million tons for the year 2000, requiring many power plants to reduce emissions or to purchase additional credits from plants that had reduced pollution enough to accumulate "excess" credits. The 110 most polluting plants were required to reduce emissions by 1995. The system aims to achieve emissions reductions in the most cost-effective manner. The stiff penalty ($2,000 per ton) for non-compliance serves as the theoretical maximum cost. As of 1999, emissions credits were trading at about $200 per ton. According to EPA, costs are lower than expected, emissions reductions are greater than required, and actual emissions are 40 percent less than allowed. In states with power plants covered by Phase I of the Acid Rain Program, EPA notes that sulfur dioxide emissions decreased 50 percent from 9.4 million tons in 1980 to 4.7 million tons in 1998 (EPA 1999). National and regional emissions credit trading programs have been proposed to cost-effectively reduce nitrogen oxides emissions.

Critics contend that: 1) rather than giving credits to polluters, credits could be auctioned with proceeds going to the U.S. Treasury; 2) emissions credit trading discourages industrial process innovation toward inherently less polluting technologies; and 3) historically innovative ("greener") companies are disadvantaged, in not receiving financial benefits equivalent to those making reductions from a more polluting baseline (Hawken 1986, Henderson 1991).

Role of Vehicle Transportation

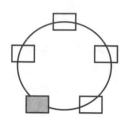

Power plants are the largest stationary – or "point" – sources of ozone-forming NO_x. However, automobiles account for an even greater share of domestic NO_x emissions. Automotive vehicles also account for a major share of VOC emissions. Highway vehicles accounted for 27 percent of VOC emissions in 1997 and 30 percent of NO_x (Figures 3a, 3b).

Since 1970, emissions of NO_x from highway vehicles (cars, motorcycles, and trucks) have increased from 7.4 million tons in 1970 to 7.6 million tons in 1995 (EPA 1997). This is associated with the doubling of vehicle use over the past 25 years (Figure 5): domestic highway vehicle use has gone from 1.11 trillion vehicle-miles in 1970 to 2.48 trillion vehicle-miles in 1996 (EIA 1998b).

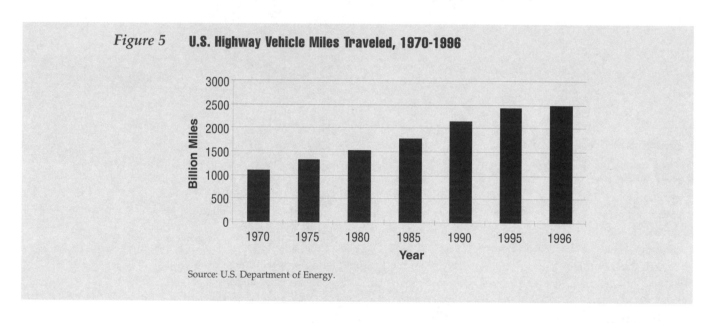

Figure 5   **U.S. Highway Vehicle Miles Traveled, 1970-1996**

Source: U.S. Department of Energy.

Tailpipe Emissions Limits

Clean Air Act regulations have lowered the permissible emissions of nitrogen oxides from autos and light trucks. In 1971, there was no such standard for automobiles. The standard was 3.6 grams per mile (g/mi) for light trucks. From 1972 through 1974, the standard was 3.1 g/mi for automobiles, and 3.6 g/mi for light trucks. This level of emissions was achieved through large-scale introduction of catalytic converters in automobiles. The Clean Air Act Amendments of 1990 lowered the tailpipe emissions standard for the year 1995, and after, to 0.4 g/mi for autos and some nondiesel light trucks (EIA 1998b). In February 1998, several automakers agreed with the EPA to voluntarily reduce tailpipe emissions for model year 1999 autos, in return for leniency on the requirement to introduce electric vehicles outside California. In early 1999, the EPA proposed a fleet tailpipe emissions average of 0.07 g/mi starting in 2004; this will be accompanied by mandatory introduction of lower-sulfur fuels that will facilitate reductions of tailpipe emissions.

The Stricter California Tailpipe Emission Standard

The California Air Resources Board has established regulations that require automakers to offer California consumers a defined percentage of vehicles with reduced emissions of nitrogen oxides, hydrocarbons, and carbon monoxide. Vehicles that emit 50 percent less NOx (so-called Low-Emission and Ultra-Low-Emission Vehicles) must account for at least 50 percent of a manufacturer's fleet from 1998 through 2000, and for 95 percent or more of the fleet in 2001 and 2002. From 2003 onward, vehicles that emit no NOx (so-called Zero-Emission Vehicles) must account for at least 10 percent of a manufacturer's fleet, while LEV and ULEV vehicles will account for the remainder (EIA 1998b). Many of the larger auto manufacturers have, or will have within the next 5 years, at least one ZEV model in production. For example, GM offers an electric vehicle for lease in a few markets in the southwest U.S., and Honda plans to introduce a ("zero emissions") fuel cell powered vehicle in the U.S. by 2003.

The actual NO_x emissions (3.6 million tons) from passenger vehicles are several times higher than the 0.4 g/mi regulatory standard, considering actual vehicle miles traveled. Older cars on the road met earlier, less stringent, standards. Therefore, were there no increase in vehicle-miles traveled, vehicle replacement would gradually lower actual NO_x emissions by highway vehicles.

Use of Natural Resources

Industrial processes and products require natural resource inputs. When discussing electricity's role in emissions of major air pollutants, we 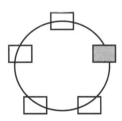 noted that the source of these emissions are fossil fuels, especially coal, combusted by electric power plants. In fact, electric generators account for most domestic coal consumption. Moreover, coal plants account for a significant portion of climate-changing gas emissions. Electric utilities also account for 15 percent of natural gas consumption, 2 percent of petroleum consumption, and 47 percent of domestic water withdrawals (large volumes of water needed for cooling the electric power turbines).

With deregulation of the electric utility industry, coal consumption is expected to increase, a trend that may be offset by implementation of the Kyoto Protocol. Coal already accounts for a much broader share of domestic electricity generation than it does of domestic power plants' available generation capacity. That is to say, coal plants are less likely to be idle than are other plants. Coal accounted for 43.1 percent of operable capacity at U.S. electric utilities as of January 1998. This occurs through underutilization of other sources such as natural gas (EIA 1998a).

With regard to power plants, the Clinton Administration has indicated an intention to track changes in NO_x emissions and to consider a further use of emission credits in a "cap-and-trade" program. The potential environmental impact associated with deregulation of the electric utility industry have intensified debate in this regard. A cap-and-trade program would complement existing EPA and state programs to bring ozone nonattainment areas into compliance – programs likely to be impacted by the outcome of the current debate on the appropriate air quality standards for ozone and particulate matter.

In 1998, the EPA proposed NO_X emission limits for 22 Midwestern states. If implemented, these limits would facilitate continued improvement in urban air quality. In 1999, the agency also proposed lowering the tailpipe emissions standard for cars and light trucks. Nevertheless, establishment of a stricter regulatory standard for ozone concentrations as well as initial reports of air quality for the summer of 1998 are reminders that urban air quality is inadequate for millions of Americans.

Highway vehicle use also has consequences for energy use. Vehicle fuel economy and transportation habits, as well as population and economic growth, affect these trends (see Energy Indicator chapter). In 1996, highway vehicle energy use was 18.75 quadrillion btus – an average annual increase of 1.8 percent from 1970. This also represents a 2.0 percent annual increase from 1990, indicating an acceleration in energy use by autos. Most highway vehicles use oil and gasoline/diesel fuel, while a small portion use natural gas; a negligible portion use other fuels. Overall, transportation accounted for 27.4 percent of U.S. energy consumption in 1997. This is a slight increase from 24.2 percent in 1970. Autos and light trucks accounted for 58.8 percent of transportation energy use in 1996 (EIA 1998b). The key environmental question for the transportation sector is whether the turnover to vehicles with better emissions control technology will outpace the upward trend in vehicle miles traveled.

IV. Water Quality

Water is the basis of life. It circulates constantly from sea to land and back, through precipitation, surface flow, evaporation, and other hydrologic processes. Plants convert water and carbon dioxide into carbohydrates. We need this plant food, and water itself, to survive. We expect unlimited, potable tap water. We enjoy swimming and fishing in clean waters. When *Money* magazine evaluated the best places to live in America in 1996, clean water ranked as the most important criterion for readers.

Unfortunately, millions of Americans drink contaminated tap water. At least 8 percent of the U.S. population was provided drinking water that violated federal standards at least once during 1995. An estimated 900 Americans die and almost 1 million become ill each year from drinking water-related illnesses. The data for recreational water use is also disturbing. More than one-third of the nation's surveyed waters are not clean enough for fishing or swimming. We face this daily in beach closures and fish consumption advisories.

These water quality concerns have financial consequences. Clean water is of paramount importance to the U.S. economy. In May 1996, the EPA estimated that clean water-dependent industries contribute more than $1 trillion to the U.S. economy. The principal economic beneficiaries of clean water include the recreation industry, since beaches, rivers, and lakes are Americans' primary vacation destination; agriculture, since approximately 15 percent of domestic farms use irrigation; commercial fishing and shellfishing; real estate, since proximity to certain water bodies can boost land value; and manufacturing, which uses 13 trillion gallons of water per year (EPA 1996).

This section discusses the potability, swimmability, and fishability of U.S. drinking and surface water as well as the specific pollutants and the regulatory framework.

Potability

Americans use 34 billion gallons of tap water each day. Community water systems served 252.5 million Americans in 1996, equal to 93 percent

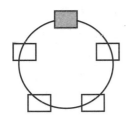

of the resident U.S. population. The remainder of the U.S. population obtains drinking water from private wells or other nonfederally regulated water systems. By EPA definition, a public water system "provides piped water for human consumption to at least 15 service connections or serves an average of at least 25 people for at least 60 days each year." These systems serve schools, hospitals, factories, motels, and other locations. A community water system (CWS) is a public water system "that provides water to the same population year-round." CWSs receive their supply from groundwater and surface water sources (EPA 1997b).

The EPA has developed indicators to measure changes in drinking water quality. One of the Office of Water's core indicators is "Population Served by Community Drinking Water Systems Violating Health-Based Requirements," which is measured once a year. Of the population served by a CWS in 1996, approximately 6.1 percent (15.1 million people) were served by one that violated a health-based drinking water standard at least once that year. This represents an improving trend since 1992, yet only a marginal improvement since 1991 (Figure 6).

The EPA enforces nonhealth-based standards as well, including treatment technique and monitoring/reporting violations. Approximately 18.9 percent (46.6 million people) of the population served by a CWS were served by one that violated some drinking water standard at least once in 1996, whether health-based, reporting-based, or other. This represents a decrease from the 20.9 percent (51.2 million) in 1991 (EPA 1997b). (The EPA acknowledges that the overall rate of noncompliance is understated and that data quality needs improvement.)

Of greatest concern are the approximately 10,000 public water

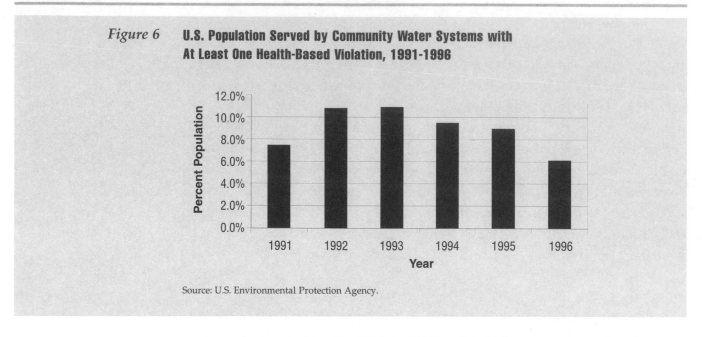

Figure 6   **U.S. Population Served by Community Water Systems with At Least One Health-Based Violation, 1991-1996**

Source: U.S. Environmental Protection Agency.

systems designated by the EPA in 1995 as "significant non-compliers" (SNCs). These water systems have "more serious, frequent, or persistent violations." The SNC criteria vary by contaminant, which are classified into three groups: microbiological/turbidity, chemical/radiological, and surface-water treatment rule. The EPA's policy is to address SNCs in a "timely and appropriate" fashion, which includes EPA action or water system compliance or other resolution within six months (EPA 1996a).

Swimmability/Fishability

The quality of surface waters also impacts Americans' recreational opportunities, the nation's economy, and, for many, their sustenance

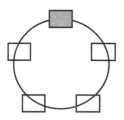

and lifestyle. The United States has 3.5 million miles of rivers, 40.8 million acres of lakes, 34,400 square miles of estuaries, 58,000 miles of ocean shoreline, and 277 million acres of wetlands, as well as 33,000 trillion gallons of ground water. The EPA began measuring "swimmability" and "fishability" of U.S. waters in 1984. Since then, state-level data collected by EPA indicates a gradual deterioration of the nation's waterways.

Nearly 25 years after passage of the Clean Water Act, nearly 40 percent of our surveyed waters remain too polluted for fishing or swimming (EPA 1997c). In 1996, only 61 percent of the nation's surveyed lake-acres, 62 percent of surveyed estuarine square-miles, and 64 percent of surveyed river-miles were clean enough for these activities. The data represents a decline from 1984, when the rate for lake-acres was 78 percent; estuarine square-miles, 82 percent; and river-miles, 73 percent (see Appendix 4). These changes can be viewed in the context of increased population and economic growth as well as improvements in industrial process technology (EPA 1994c, 1995). (There are concerns about the quality of EPA data, therefore

Great Lakes Water Quality

The International Joint Commission, a binational body established by the 1909 Boundary Waters Treaty between the United States and Canada, issues biennial reports on water quality in the Great Lakes. The Commission's 1996 report noted: "[c]onsumption of Great Lakes fish is a major source of human exposure to persistent toxic substances, particularly to polychlorinated biphenyls (PCBs). Some fish, especially the larger salmon and lake trout, pose a particular threat to women of childbearing age and their children." The report called for the virtual elimination of persistent toxic substances from (and for zero discharge of persistent toxic substances into) the Great Lakes ecosystem. Persistent toxic chemicals are toxic chemicals that bioaccumulate or that have a half-life greater than eight weeks in any medium (IJC 1996).

conclusive statements are not possible.)

Passed in 1972, the Clean Water Act aimed to eliminate the discharge of pollutants into the nation's waters by 1985. The act set an interim goal requiring all (surface) waters to be fishable and swimmable by 1983. Needless to say, neither the 1983 nor the 1985 goals were attained. It was not until the fifth National Water Quality Inventory was published in 1984 that the EPA began measuring the overall swimmability and fishability of our waters. Although pre-1984 data is not available, EPA states that surveys of large rivers in 1974 indicated that only 40 percent were safe for fishing and swimming (EPA 1995).

Causes of Contaminated Drinking Water

The EPA notes that drinking water can be contaminated before, during, or after treatment by public water systems. Before treatment, 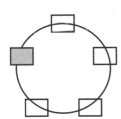 drinking water sources can be contaminated by bacteria from human or animal sources; overflowing storm sewers; agricultural run-off (including pesticides and fertilizers); saltwater; highway runoff; decay products of radon, radium, and uranium; and hazardous products and waste by-products. During treatment, trihalomethanes and other by-products of disinfectants can contaminate drinking water. After treatment, drinking water can be contaminated by materials from corroding, leaking, or permeable pipes or through improper water system connections (EPA 1996a).

As of 1995, the EPA had established regulations for 81 drinking water contaminants, including six microbiological contaminants, four radionuclides, 17 inorganic chemicals, and 54 organic chemicals. Specific contaminants include arsenic, atrazine, copper, cyanide, dioxin, Giardia lamblia, lead, nitrate, radium-226, and total coliform bacteria. Inorganic chemicals include toxic minerals and metals; organic chemicals include fertilizers and pesticides. Microorganisms include bacteria, viruses, and parasites (EPA 1996a).

The Safe Drinking Water Act (SDWA), passed in 1974 and amended in 1986, requires the EPA to regulate 25 contaminants every three years. The EPA failed to meet its statutory obligations, leading to lawsuits by environmental groups. However, changes to the SDWA modified the EPA's obligations.

Consequences of Contaminated Tap Water

Estimates vary widely on the public health burden and risk posed by water pollutants. Certain water-borne diseases (such as cholera and typhoid) have been eliminated. The Centers for Disease Control and Prevention (CDC) estimated 7,400 cases of drinking water-related illness per year in the United States from 1971 to 1985 (EPA 1994). The Environmental Working Group, an advocacy organization, cited a 1987 CDC estimate of 940,000 contaminated drinking water-related illnesses and more than 900 deaths each year, excluding cancer risks from chlorination and radioactive substances in drinking water (Cohen 1995). A 1995 review of recent scientific literature by the Natural Resources Defense Council, a national environmental group, estimated that there are 400,000 to 7 million cases of water-borne disease per year, resulting in an estimated 1,200 deaths. There are lower rates of illnesses for people using water from systems with advanced water treatment filters (Olson 1995). Concern is significant enough that the CDC has advised people with compromised immune systems (such as those with cancer) to consult their physician before drinking tap water. The American Water Works Association, the principal trade association for water utilities, advises all those with the HIV virus to boil tap water before drinking it (EPA/CDC 1995).

International Comparison

The United Nations estimates that 100 percent of people in industrialized countries have access to safe drinking water (UNDP). The World Bank estimates that more than 90 percent of Americans have access to safe drinking water. By comparison, the United Nations estimates that nearly one-third of people (1.2 billion) living in developing countries do not have access to a safe and reliable supply of drinking water (Postel 1997). For example, the World Bank states that 71.3 percent of the population in China have access to safe water (World Bank).

Causes of Surface Water Pollution

The EPA identifies several direct causes of surface water pollution. These include low dissolved oxygen, nutrients, sediment, and siltation; 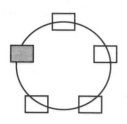 bacteria and pathogens; toxic organic chemicals and metals; pH from mining activities and atmospheric depositions; and habitat modification/hydrologic modification. Bacteria that feed on excess organic material, such as leaves and manure, deprive other aquatic organisms, such as fish, of necessary oxygen. Nitrogen and phosphorus and other compounds over-stimulate growth of aquatic weeds and algae, which clog waters, compete with other species, and deplete oxygen. Small soil particles can physically disrupt aquatic life, affect the aesthetic quality of water, and transport toxic chemicals. Pathogens are found in sewage, manure, and equivalent sources (EPA 1995).

Sources of Water Contaminants

Water pollution sources include natural sources – such as weather and decaying organic matter – and sources related to human activities, such as industrial activity, municipalities, combined sewers, storm sewers/urban runoff, agriculture, silviculture, construction, resource extraction, land disposal, and hydrologic modification. These sources are generally divided

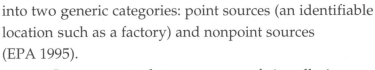

into two generic categories: point sources (an identifiable location such as a factory) and nonpoint sources (EPA 1995).

In contrast to data on sources of air pollution, there is no systematic collection, management, and reporting of specific trendline data on sources of water pollution. Analysis of water pollution is more difficult to report, in comparison to air pollution. Major sources of the main air pollutants are identified, measured, regulated, and reported. While air emissions of nitrogen oxides can be aggregated, one cannot easily aggregate pH values for water sources because the safe values differ markedly by water body type and location. On the other hand, poor air quality can generally be compared from one locale to another. To aggregate water pollutants may have limited meaning, because impacts are specific to individual water bodies.

Role of Nonpoint Sources

Nonpoint sources of pollution are a complicating factor in water quality analysis, as it is difficult to quantify. Sedimentation and siltation

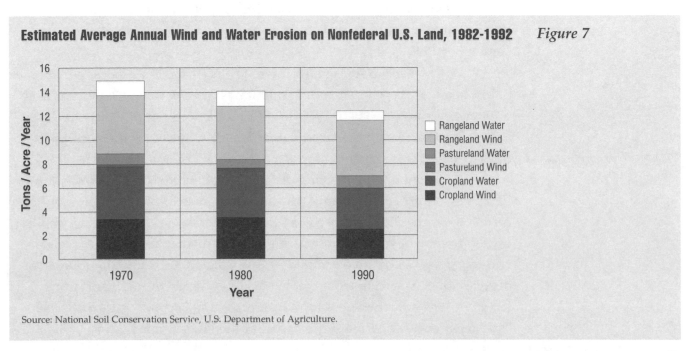

Estimated Average Annual Wind and Water Erosion on Nonfederal U.S. Land, 1982-1992   *Figure 7*

Source: National Soil Conservation Service, U.S. Department of Agriculture.

related to agriculture are an example. Specific data is not tracked by the EPA, but soil loss data is available from the Department of Agriculture. This can serve as a proxy for agricultural runoff. Not included is runoff from residential and industrial development, which will increase as encroachment on natural sites continues.

Intensive agricultural practices affect the availability of topsoil. Erosion contributes to pollution of water and air. Estimated erosion (both wind and water) from cropland, pastureland, and rangeland was 12.7 tons per acre per year in 1992, down from 14.9 tons per acre per year in 1982 (Figure 7). Erosion of cropland and rangeland accounts for most of this loss (Department of Agriculture).

Role of Point Sources

Under the Clean Water Act, industrial and water treatment facilities are required to have a federally issued permit – a National Pollutant Discharge Elimination System permit – to discharge pollutants into national waters. There are more than 57,000 of these permits and compliance is tracked by the EPA. According the U.S. General Accounting Office (GAO), approximately one-sixth of the 7,053 "major" regulated facilities "significantly" violated their permitted discharge limits in 1994. This excludes scheduling and reporting violations. The pollutants that most frequently violated daily maximum limits (in "significant noncompliance") were chlorine, total suspended solids, and biochemical oxygen-demanding pollutants. However, the GAO noted the actual level of violations might be twice as high. The GAO also noted that the EPA's oversight of permits is limited, and that enforcement of significant violations was uneven (GAO 1996). According to the GAO, the EPA is considering regulatory changes and increased emphasis on controlling pollution within watersheds. In addition, the new, more stringent EPA criterion for "significant noncompliance" was updated in September 1995 and was expected to go into effect in September 1996.

With regard to sewage treatment facilities, the EPA states that releases of biochemical oxygen-demanding pollutants have declined 36 percent from 6,700 metric tons per day in 1970 to 4,300 metric tons per day in 1992, despite a 28 percent increase in sewage treated. The EPA attributes the decrease to upgraded sewage treatment, now available to 73 million Americans.

In addition to monitoring permit compliance of point sources, the EPA also requires many manufacturing companies to report the amount of certain toxic chemicals released to surface waters and transferred to publicly owned treatment works and released to other media. In 1994, these releases and transfers, which are permitted by law, totaled 320.8 million pounds, a decrease of 68.6 percent from the one trillion pounds released and transferred in 1987 – the first year for which reporting began (Figure 8). These toxic releases to water are significant, but the law's limited scope does not

Toxic Chemical Releases to U.S. Waters, 1987-1995

Figure 8

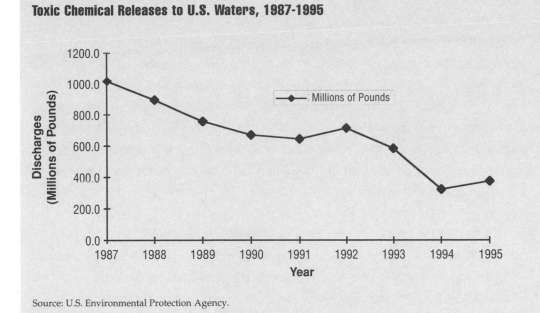

Source: U.S. Environmental Protection Agency.

Groundwater Quality

Underground aquifers account for two-thirds of fresh water supplies worldwide. About half of the U.S. population relies, at least in part, on (under)ground water as a source of drinking water. The percentage is greater in rural areas. States report that groundwater has been contaminated by petroleum compounds, nitrates, metals, VOCs, pesticides and other contaminants from leaking underground storage tanks, agricultural activities, Superfund sites, septic tanks and other sources (EPA 1997c). Where inflow and outflow rates are low, polluted aquifers can take a long time (up to 10,000 years) to "clean" themselves. However, shallow unconfined aquifers account for much water use and are more prone to pollution (Postel 1997).

Aquifer depletion is a key determinant of groundwater quality. Unfortunately, accurate, comprehensive data on U.S. aquifers is not yet available. The U.S. Geological Survey has identified 28 major regional aquifer systems. Water budgets for at least seven regional aquifer systems indicate that development causes an annual decrease in storage – a net depletion of the aquifers. Water budgets are analyses of the natural and anthropogenic in- and outflows of groundwater. Development refers to withdrawal of water and to land use patterns that prevent natural recharge. This suggests a potentially unsustainable use of water in regions containing a large proportion of U.S. population. For example, California's Central Valley, a world supplier of fruits and vegetables, is depleting ground-water aquifers at unsustainable rates. The California Central Valley Aquifer System has a net decrease in storage of 0.7 billion gallons of water per day (USGS 1994). A drought, from 1987 through 1991, reduced water available from streams, increasing dependence on reservoirs and aquifers, exacerbating depletion of these sources.

Aside from effects on the public (e.g. lifestyle, economic impact on farmers), there were adverse environmental impacts (e.g. habitat of freshwater biota, and increased pollution related to fossil fuel replacement of some hydropower). Land subsidence in California's Central Valley has reached 30 feet, and exceeds one foot over thousands of square miles. Because of this, the Central Valley has lost 25 billion cubic meters in storage capacity – an amount equivalent to 40 percent of California's man-made surface storage capacity. Water expert Sandra Postel estimates the replacement cost at $6 billion (Postel 1997).

capture key water pollution concerns. Nonpoint sources, in general, do not report toxic releases to the EPA (EPA 1997d).

Revision in 1996 to the Safe Drinking Water Act were intended to boost potability more efficiently. With regard to swimmability/fishability concerns, the EPA and the DOA are encouraging states to develop water-shed-based plans that address nonpoint pollution. After criticism from the GAO and environmental groups such as the Natural Resources Defense Council, the EPA is considering revising its compliance program for Clean Water Act (point-source) violations. The EPA also has other programs to improve water quality. Efforts to address water use concerns are less clear.

V. Role of Population and Economic Activity

While analysis of the sources of air and water pollution provide insight into the impact of waste on environmental quality, they do not address scale. Environmental impacts are a function of human population, industrial production methods, and the path our society takes to achieve economic growth.

For example, increases in population and economic activity have a significant impact on levels of air pollution. Emissions of nitrogen oxides increased 8.1 percent from 21.6 million tons in 1970 to 23.4 million tons in 1996. Nitrogen oxides are the only major air pollutant for which domestic emissions have increased on an absolute basis. This increase occurred despite technological improvements in products such as automobiles and processes such as power plants that are associated with emissions of this pollutant. However, during this 1970-1996 period, the U.S. population increased 30 percent from 204 million to 265 million. Thus, emissions of nitrogen oxides per capita decreased 16.9 percent from 1970 to 1996. Similarly, economic growth, as measured by chained 1992 dollars of GDP, increased 103.3 percent from $3.4 trillion in 1970 to $6.9 trillion in 1996. Thus, emissions of nitrogen oxides per unit of GDP decreased 46.8 percent during this period. These data reinforce the role of population and economic growth on pollution. While adjusted trends improve analysis of the data, it is the absolute level of waste that affects environmental quality (EPA 1997).

Population and economic activity also affect use of natural resources. Consumption of materials – agricultural, mineral, and other resources – reached an all-time peak of 2.85 billion metric tons in 1995. This is a 34 percent increase from 2.1 billion metric tons consumed in 1970, and 18 times greater than consumption in 1900. However, after adjusting for economic or population growth, there is not a significant increase in use of materials such as gravel, metals, cotton, and wood. In 1995, domestic materials use was 0.930 pounds per dollar of GDP, a 32.7 percent decrease from 1.38 pounds per dollar of GDP in 1970. Daily, per-capita consumption of materials in the United States was 65.3 pounds in 1995, an increase from 1970 of 3.9 percent. Thus, while there was year-to-year variability, materials consumption per capita was not significantly different in 1970 and 1995. In fact, per-capita materials consumption dropped to a decade-low during the economic recession of 1980-81, and climbed to a 20-year high in 1995. Within this time period is a partial economic shift from manufacturing to services (USGS 1997).

Regardless of any improvements on a population- or GDP-adjusted basis, environmental impacts are determined on an absolute basis. If the goal is to reduce total environmental impact, efforts to control pollution must counteract the impacts of a growing population. The Census Bureau expects the U.S. population to increase 15 percent to 318 million over the next 20 years. Pollution, on a per-capita, or per-GDP, basis, must decline by at least that much to maintain current pollution levels.

VI. Conclusion

A 1997 report in *Nature*, by a group of ecologists, economists and geographers, estimated nature's value at $33 trillion. Some critics argued that no economic price could capture the value of the planet's resources, given that no viable alternatives exist. Regardless of the price tag, the state of our environment remains a key quality of life concern for most Americans. Substantive environmental gains were made during the 1970s, and generally maintained during the 1980s and 1990s. Data on key indicators – population breathing unhealthful levels of air pollution, and potability/swimmability/ fishability of U.S. waters – is only available for the 1980s and 1990s. However, the pollution trends that underlie these data indicate that the improvements made in the 1970s – such as the reductions in emissions of VOCs, sulfur dioxide, and lead – have not been maintained in the past two decades. In fact, significant challenges remain to ensure environmental health. Unhealthful levels of ozone affect more than one-quarter of the U.S. population, and about one-third of our waters are too polluted for recreational use. Increased recycling is not offsetting increased generation of waste. This is exacerbating landfill capacity concerns in certain locales. The threats to nonhumans are more significant: a large portion of native animal and plant species are at risk.

Conquering these challenges will require vigorous attention and continued improvement. The only major air pollutant for which emissions have increased on an absolute basis is nitrogen oxides, which contributes to formation of ozone. Electric utilities need to match the success of reducing sulfur dioxide emissions in the reduction of nitrogen oxides. Deregulation threatens to exacerbate the challenges faced in this regard by utilities and their regulators. In 1998, the EPA proposed nitrogen oxides limits in 22 Midwestern states. The agency is also considering an emissions credit trading program. Transportation policies must recognize environmental implications. The pace of technological introduction in the automotive sector, or the expansion of mass transit usage, must start keeping pace with the continued increase in vehicle-miles traveled. Until this point, technology has lost this battle: vehicle-related NO_X emissions have increased despite stricter tailpipe emissions standards and the widespread use of catalytic converters. The challenge is to move toward a net reduction of NO_X, as U.S. passenger vehicle-miles accelerate.

The significant improvements in air quality have not been matched in water quality. Clearly, the United States has fallen short of the Clean Water Act's goal to eliminate the discharge of pollutants into the nation's waters by 1985, and the interim goal that all (surface) waters are fishable and swimmable by 1983. In early 1998, President Clinton proposed an array of new water quality programs under the Clean Water Initiative. The fate of this initiative may have significant consequences for the nation's waterways. Industry/agriculture and government must continue to create win-win programs for themselves and consumers.

Environmental quality is difficult to measure. By definitions the datastreams contained herein are only indicators of concepts such as clean air and water. Additions and improvements are possible. However, more and better data are needed from federal agencies. Recognizing this, several agencies are developing national indicators, and the EPA, as noted above, has established its own set of environmental indicators. These need to be maintained and expanded over time.

Specifically, the EPA should improve its measurements of swimmability and fishability of U.S. waters, in order to legitimize trend analysis. The USGS needs to complete the water budgets for the major regional aquifer systems to provide accurate, comprehensive data on U.S. groundwater supplies. The EPA needs to complete work with states to standardize its municipal solid waste data collection methodology. Analysis is needed of construction and demolition debris as well as mining and agricultural waste. General land use patterns also need to be measured and tracked. Finally, federal agencies should benchmark U.S. performance against global performance and trends.

U.S. Population Living in Counties Not Meeting Federal Air Quality Standards, 1985-1997

Year	Population Total U.S.	Population (Number) in Nonattainment Areas All Pollutants	Ozone	Population (Percent) in Nonattainment Areas All Pollutants	Ozone
1985	237,924,000	N.A.	76,400,000	N.A.	32.1
1986	240,133,000	98,000,000	75,000,000	40.8	31.2
1987	242,289,000	101,800,000	88,600,000	42.0	36.6
1988	244,499,000	121,000,000	111,900,000	49.5	45.8
1989	246,819,000	84,000,000	66,700,000	34.0	27.0
1990	249,398,000	74,000,000	62,900,000	29.7	25.2
1991	252,106,000	86,000,000	69,700,000	34.1	27.6
1992	255,011,000	51,400,000	42,600,000	20.2	16.7
1993	257,795,000	59,100,000	51,300,000	22.9	19.9
1994	260,372,000	62,000,000	50,200,000	23.8	19.3
1995	262,890,000	79,800,000	70,800,000	30.4	26.9
1996	265,284,000	46,600,000	39,300,000	17.6	14.8
1997	267,744,000	52,600,000	47,900,000	19.6	17.9
Rev-1997	267,744,000	107,000,000	101,600,000	40.0	37.9

Source: U.S. Environmental Protection Agency.

Appendix 2   **Classifications of Ozone Nonattainment Areas**

Extreme (2010)

Los Angeles South Coast Air Basin, CA

Severe (2007)

Chicago-Gary-Lake County, IL-IN

Houston-Galveston-Brazoria, TX

Milwaukee-Racine, WI

New York-N. New Jersey-Long Island, NY-NJ-CT

Southeast Desert Modified AQMA, CA

Severe (2005)

Baltimore, MD

Philadelphia-Wilmington-Trenton, PA-NJ-DE-MD

Sacramento Metro, CA

Ventura Co., CA

Serious (1999)

Atlanta, GA

Baton Rouge, LA

Boston-Lawrence-Worcester (E. MA), MA-NH

El Paso, TX

Greater Connecticut

Phoenix, AZ

Portsmouth-Dover-Rochester, NH

Providence (All RI), RI

San Diego, CA

San Joaquin Valley, CA

Santa Barbara-Santa Maria-Lompoc, CA

Springfield (Western MA), MA

Washington, DC-MD-VA

Source: U.S. Environmental Protection Agency.

National Air Pollutant Emissions: 1940-1997, thousands of tons

Appendix 3

Year	CO	NOx	VOCs	SO2	Particulates w/o Dust	Particulates Fug. Dust	Lead
1900	NA	2,611	8,503	9,988	NA	NA	NA
1910	NA	4,102	9,117	17,275	NA	NA	NA
1920	NA	5,159	10,004	21,144	NA	NA	NA
1930	NA	8,018	19,451	21,106	NA	NA	NA
1940	93,615	7,374	17,161	19,954	15,956	NA	NA
1950	102,609	10,093	20,936	22,384	17,133	NA	NA
1960	109,745	14,140	24,459	22,245	15,558	NA	NA
1970	128,761	21,639	30,817	31,161	13,190	NA	220,869
1975	115,968	23,151	25,895	28,011	7,803	NA	159,659
1980	116,702	24,875	26,167	25,905	7,287	NA	74,153
1985	115,644	23,488	24,227	23,230	4,695	40,889	22,890
1986	110,437	23,329	23,480	22,544	4,553	46,582	14,763
1987	108,879	22,806	23,193	22,308	4,492	38,041	7,681
1988	117,169	24,526	24,167	22,767	5,424	55,851	7,053
1989	104,447	24,057	22,383	22,907	4,590	48,650	5,468
1990	96,535	23,792	20,985	23,136	4,639	25,308	4,975
1991	98,461	23,772	21,100	22,496	4,299	25,258	4,168
1992	95,123	24,137	20,695	22,420	4,198	25,308	3,808
1993	95,291	24,482	20,895	21,879	4,086	23,937	3,911
1994	99,677	24,892	21,546	21,262	4,353	26,572	4,043
1995	89,721	23,935	20,586	18,552	4,068	22,820	3,943
1996	88,822	23,393	19,086	19,113	4,068	27,233	3,869
1997	87,100	22,900	19,200	20,300	3,000	NA	5,000

Note: All data in thousands of tons, except lead, which is in tons.

Source: U.S. Environmental Protection Agency.

Appendix 4 **Swimmability/Fishability (%) of U.S. Waters**

Source	1984	1986	1988	1990	1992	1994	1996
River Miles	73	74	70	70	62	64	64
Lake Acres	78	73	74	60	56	63	61
Estuarine Square Miles	82	75	72	67	68	63	62

Source: U.S. Environmental Protection Agency.

REFERENCES

American Lung Association. 1993. *Breath in Danger II*. Washington, DC.

Cohen, Brian, Christopher Campbell, and Richard Wiles. 1995. *In the Drink*. Washington, DC: Environmental Working Group.

Ingram, Colin. 1991. *The Drinking Water Book: A Complete Guide to Safe Drinking Water*. Berkeley, CA: Ten Speed Press.

International Joint Commission. 1996. *Eighth Biennial Report on Great Lakes Water Quality*. Washington, DC: The Governments of the United States of America and Canada.

Olson, Erik D. 1995. *You Are What You Drink…: Cryptosporidium and Other Contaminants Found in the Water Served to Millions of Americans*. Washington, DC: Natural Resources Defense Council.

Postel, Sandra. 1997. *Dividing the Waters: Food Security, Ecosystem Health, and the New Politics of Scarcity*. Washington, DC: Worldwatch Institute.

United Nations Development Programme. 1997. *Human Development Report 1997*. New York, NY: Oxford University Press.

U.S. Department of Commerce. 1998. *Statistical Abstract of the United States 1997: The National Data Book, 117th Edition*. Washington, DC.

U.S. Energy Information Administration. 1998. *Electric Power Monthly* (January).

U.S. Energy Information Administration. 1998a. *Electric Power Annual 1998: Volume I* . Washington, DC.

U.S. Energy Information Administration. 1998b. *Transportation Energy Databook, Edition 18,* Stacy C. Davis, Center for Transportation Analysis, Energy Division, Oak Ridge National Laboratory. Oak Ridge, TN.

U.S. Environmental Protection Agency. 1999. *Emissions Scorecard 1998*, Acid Rain Program, Office of Air and Radiation. Washington, DC.

U.S. Environmental Protection Agency. 1998. *National Air Quality and Emissions Trends Report, 1997,* Office of Air Quality Planning and Standards. Washington, DC.

U.S. Environmental Protection Agency. 1998a. *FY 1997 Compliance Report,* The National Public Water System Supervision Program, Office of Enforcement and Compliance Assurance. Washington, DC.

U.S. Environmental Protection Agency. 1997. *National Air Pollutant Emission Trends, 1900-1996,* Office of Air Quality Planning and Standards. Washington, DC.

U.S. Environmental Protection Agency. 1997a. *USA Air Quality Nonattainment Areas,* http://www.epa.gov/airs/nonattn.html. Washington, DC.

U.S. Environmental Protection Agency. 1997b. *FY 1996 Compliance Report,* The National Public Water System Supervision Program, Office of Enforcement and Compliance Assurance. Washington, DC.

U.S. Environmental Protection Agency. 1997c. *National Water Quality Inventory: 1996 Report to Congress,* Office of Water. Washington, DC.

U.S. Environmental Protection Agency. 1997d. *1995 Toxics Release Inventory: Public Data Release.* Washington, DC.

U.S. Environmental Protection Agency. 1996. *Liquid Assets*, Office of Water Oceans and Wetlands. Washington, DC.

U.S. Environmental Protection Agency. 1996a. *FY 1995 National Compliance Report*, The National Public Water System Supervision Program, Office of Enforcement and Compliance Assurance. Washington, DC.

U.S. Environmental Protection Agency. 1996b. *Characterization of Municipal Solid Waste in the United States: 1995 Update, Executive Summary*. Washington, DC.

U.S. Environmental Protection Agency. 1995. *National Water Quality Inventory: 1994 Report to Congress*, Office of Water. Washington, DC.

U.S. Environmental Protection Agency. 1994. *Is Your Drinking Water Safe?*, Office of Water. Washington, DC.

U.S. Environmental Protection Agency. 1994a. *National Water Quality Inventory: 1992 Report to Congress*, Office of Water. Washington, DC.

U.S. Environmental Protection Agency and Centers for Disease Control and Prevention. 1995. "Guidance for People With Severely Weakened Immune Systems." Washington, DC.

U.S. Fish and Wildlife Service. 1996. *Endangered Species General Statistics*, Division of Endangered Species. Washington, DC.

U.S. General Accounting Office. 1996. *Water Pollution: Many Violations Have Not Received Appropriate Enforcement Attention*. Washington, DC (March).

U.S. General Accounting Office. 1996a. *Water Pollution: Differences Among the States in Issuing Permits Limiting the Discharge of Pollutants*. Washington, DC (January).

U.S. Geological Survey. 1997. *U.S. Consumption of Raw Materials from USA Sources*, Materials Group. Washington, DC.

U.S. Geological Survey. 1994. *Regional Aquifer-System Analysis Program of the U.S. Geological Survey, 1978-1992*, Circular 1099, U.S. Department of the Interior. Washington, DC.

World Bank. 1994. *The Environmental Data Book*. Washington, DC.

World Conservation Monitoring Centre. 1992. *Global Biodiversity: Status of the Earth's Living Resources*.

Chapter 9

Health Indicator

by Constance Battle, M.D. and Mary Jenifer

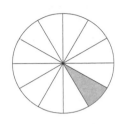

I. Introduction

The United States has gradually, even reluctantly, come to acknowledge that it provides more health care services at higher costs, with approximately two times the physicians per capita than any other country in the
world. The cost of health care rose steadily to 13.6 percent of the Gross
Domestic Product (GDP) where it remained from 1993 through 1996. In 1996
over one billion dollars were spent on health care, amounting to $3,759 per
person on average. Yet some studies indicate only modest improvements in
certain health statistics and none in others. Looking at 1997 data from the
Organization for Economic Cooperation and Development (OECD),
Anderson and Poullier concluded that U.S. health spending per capita grew
more rapidly in the 1990s than did spending in any other OECD country.
Health statistics, however, rated the United States in the bottom half of
reporting countries.

In order to realize substantial improvements in the quality of the
nation's health, we will need to redefine what we mean by the term *health*.
Health must be understood as the product of social environments, incentives, and choices that individuals make on their own behalf and as members
of the communities in which they live. An expanded concept of health
includes acute intervention and remediation along with an expanded recognition of disease prevention and education. The focus has been on a
tenaciously held belief that somehow technology or access to medical professionals is lacking. The solutions rest not with hospitals or service delivery
systems as they are currently configured but with behavior patterns.
Improving diet and nutrition, increasing physical exercise, reducing tobacco
smoking, lowering alcohol and other drug consumption, and reducing crime
and violence are the most salient factors. Public health statistics such as teen
pregnancy rates, premature births, and firearms-related homicides demonstrate that the root causes lie in the problematic and often dysfunctional
social and economic environments, as well as lack of access to health care or
intervention. The health care debate in the United States has often ignored
the root causes of these factors and other social indicators such as high crime
rates, percentage of persons in car accidents, declining educational performance, and persistently high numbers of homeless families. These indicators
have been neglected or ignored as relevant to the core "health" needs of
significant sectors of the U.S. population.

Once health is defined in a broader context, the integral relationship of wellness and the key components of living and working environments must be explored and addressed. The Healthcare Forum Leadership Center's Healthier Communities Partnership has developed an educational program and materials that direct attention to a new way of looking at health and wellness (Healthcare Communities Action Kit 1993). The Healthcare Forum holds that major factors determining the health of the individual, the community, and the nation include: quality education, adequate housing, availability of meaningful employment, access to job skills training, access to efficient public transportation, availability of recreational opportunities, healthy and clean physical environments, along with access to health education and preventive services. Government policies must prioritize an awareness that social and environmental factors are the real determinants of health. Health disparities will continue to exact heavy individual and social tolls not only for the disadvantaged but for the nation as a whole. How the United States resolves these challenges will determine the ability of future generations to enjoy a high quality of life and to compete in a global economy. The challenge to achieve health for American citizens and communities rests upon an approach that sets priorities and makes plans by developing cross-sector responsibility for change.

Few would argue the importance of health to the quality of life, but current measures of economic progress do not value health. GDP, which measures the total value of goods and services bought and sold, values illness more than health. Heart transplants, hospital stays, prescription drugs, and emergency room visits equal money spent and hence add to the GDP. These expenditures are viewed as progress even if they contribute to unhealthy lifestyles, addictions, and violent crimes. New measures for prosperity and progress that give value to health must be developed.

Health: Definition and Measurement

The Calvert-Henderson Health Indicator focuses on two basic questions: "Does one get a chance at life?" and "How long will that life last?" (see Figure 1). To answer these questions, the statistics on infant mortality and life expectancy are discussed. The next sections define the two indicators, describe their strengths and weaknesses, and consider recent data trends. Alternative measures of health are discussed in the final section. Measuring health is a difficult task. It involves a particularly diverse set of measurements. Health involves the physical, psychological, and social aspects of a society and its people. It is difficult to find good indicators because cultures and individuals define health in different ways. Quality of life is affected by people's expectations, their ability to handle limitations, and even their tolerance for pain. Some people accept pain or illness, such as chronic back pain, as an inevitable part of their lives and can adapt to these limitations. Others may find it impossible to deal with similar circumstances.

Calvert-Henderson Health Model

QUIZ:

1. Do You Get a Chance at Life?

2. How Long Will That Life Last?

The subjectivity and complexity of personal health and well-being makes it difficult to define and quantify this statistically elusive condition.

Finding adequate measures of health can be even more difficult in the United States and other areas where the priorities have focused on medical or sick care. Recent debates have focused on cost and availability of health care. Americans have been involved in recent debates about managed care, primary care versus specialty care, length of hospital stays, who pays for care, and new drugs to treat disease. Less frequently discussed are issues about the overall health of people, the socioeconomic variables involved, and what measures can be taken to ensure and improve health.

In the selection of measures to describe health, it is important to choose statistics that are easy to understand, collect, and use for comparison between regions. The most readily available data are the vital statistics, data that record significant events and dates in human life such as births, deaths, and marriage. These data are collected in most nations throughout the world and used by national, state, and local governments and other organizations to analyze and compare characteristics of health. These data allow for trend analysis over time, provide benchmarks for improving health, are relatively easy to collect, and are commonly reported. Data on infant mortality, life expectance, and causes of death from various diseases are regularly collected. The U.S. National Center for Health Statistics is a primary source of information and annually revises its publication, *Health United States.* The World Health Organization collects international data and reports it annually in the United Nations' *Demographic Yearbook.* National data is reported regularly, but the information is broken down by region or characteristics and international data lag several years behind. International health comparisons are widely accepted, since much of the data is standardized. We recognize that health care systems differ radically from country to country. This chapter will focus solely on health outcomes and not delivery systems.

Vital statistics will be used in the Calvert-Henderson Health Indicator because they are available, relatively simple to interpret, and widely accepted despite controversy. Larsen (1991) suggests in his book *The Measurement of Health: Concepts and Indicators* that the further we deviate from vital statistics, the more difficult and costly it is to gather information. Our objective is to unbundle aggregate statistics and present information on health in a clear and direct manner accessible to people interested in both their own health and the health of the nation.

Vital statistics will be used...because they are available, relatively simple to interpret, and widely accepted....

II. Infant Mortality Indicator

The infant mortality rate is used widely throughout the world as a general measure of health in the population. The reason for the importance of accurately measuring death in infancy is that it is the most prevalent form of death worldwide. The World Health Organization estimates that of the 140 million babies born each year, almost four million die within hours or days, and two-thirds of all infant deaths occur during the first 27 days of life. Infant mortality is defined as the ratio of the number of live-born children who die within the first 365 days of life to 1,000 live births reported in a year.

The infant mortality rate and related measures are considered to be the best overall measure of health care in many countries. According to Larson, infant mortality is very sensitive to the factors of accessibility and quality health care in the population. It measures the health of an area's most vulnerable population. "Studies have shown that infant mortality is related to lower socioeconomic status and lower levels of education. Thus, in a sense, infant mortality measures both health and socioeconomic development" (Larson 1991). Infant mortality rates inform us about maternal health, due to the obvious relationship between the mother's health and the survival of a newborn.

Infant Mortality in the United States

In 1995 the infant mortality rate in the United States was 7.6 deaths of infants under one year of age per 1,000 live births. Rates for all races have decreased, but the data shows that there is continuing difference in the mortality between black and white infants. The rate for black infants in 1995 (14.6) is just under two and a half times that of white infants (6.3). Between 1983 and 1995 mortality for white infants declined almost 32 percent, but mortality for black infants declined only 24 percent. Over the same time period the rates for both races decreased, but the gap in mortality rates between the two races increased. In 1995 the infant mortality rate for black infants was 2.3 times that for white infants compared with 2.1 times in 1983. Less dramatic but still significant differences in mortality rates can be seen in other races.

It is interesting to note that the lowest mortality rates occurred among babies born to women in other minority groups whose origins were nonwhite. All Asian or Pacific Islander groups had lower rates than the national average (7.6) in 1995 or white mothers (6.3). Babies born to mothers of Chinese origin had the lowest rate of all women in the United States (3.8). Babies born to mothers of Japanese (5.3), Filipino (5.6), and "other Asian or Pacific Islander" (5.5) origins also had rates lower than those born to white mothers.

This same trend can be seen in mothers of Hispanic origin. The overall rate for babies born to mothers of Hispanic origin (6.3) was the same as that for babies born to white mothers, but many of the individual groups that make up the Hispanic category had lower rates. Babies born to Puerto Rican mothers had a higher rate (8.9) and to mothers of "other or unknown Hispanic" origin had a rate (7.4) lower than babies of all mothers but higher than those of white mothers. Babies born to mothers of Mexican American (6.0), Cuban (5.3), and Central and South American (5.5) origin all

Table 1   **Infant Mortality Rates According to Detailed Race and Ethnicity of Mother**

Race and Ethnicity	1983	1985	1988	1989	1990	1991	1995
All Mothers	10.9	10.4	9.6	9.5	8.9	8.6	7.6
White	9.3	8.9	8.0	7.8	7.3	7.1	6.3
Black	19.2	18.6	17.8	17.8	16.9	16.6	14.6
American Indian or Alaskan Native	15.2	13.1	12.7	13.4	13.1	11.3	13.1
Asian or Pacific Islander	8.3	7.8	6.8	7.4	6.6	5.8	5.3
Chinese	9.5	5.8	5.5	6.4	4.3	4.6	3.8
Japanese	*	*6.0	*7.0	*6.0	*5.5	*4.2	*5.3
Filipino	8.4	7.7	6.9	8.0	6.0	5.1	5.6
Other Asian or Pacific Islander	8.1	8.5	7.0	7.3	7.4	6.3	5.5
Hispanic Origin	9.5	8.8	8.3	8.1	7.5	7.1	6.3
Mexican American	9.1	8.5	7.9	7.7	7.2	6.9	6.0
Puerto Rican	12.9	11.1	11.6	11.7	9.9	9.7	8.9
Cuban	*7.5	8.5	7.2	6.2	7.2	5.2	5.3
Central and South American	8.5	8.0	7.2	7.4	6.8	5.9	5.5
Other and unknown Hispanic	10.6	9.5	9.1	8.4	8.0	8.2	7.4
White, non-Hispanic	9.2	8.7	8.0	7.8	7.2	7.0	6.3
Black, non-Hispanic	19.1	18.3	18.1	18.0	16.9	16.6	14.7

*Infant mortality rates for groups with fewer than 1,000 births are considered unreliable. Rates with fewer than 7,500 births are considered highly unreliable and are not shown.

Source: Health United States, 1998.

had lower infant mortality than babies of white mothers (6.3). Babies of women who described their origin as "White, non-Hispanic" also had the same rate as white mothers. Babies born of mothers identified as American Indian or Native Alaskan had the second highest infant mortality rate among all races (9.0) closely followed by babies born to mothers identified as Puerto Rican (8.0).

The infant mortality rates within the U.S. vary by region. All rates are reported for two-year periods. For the period 1991-1993, the District of Columbia, with a rate of 19.4 per 1,000, had the highest number of infant deaths in the nation. This is more than twice the national rate. The next closest rate is for Mississippi (11.6). New Hampshire (5.9) and Massachusetts (6.4) reported the lowest rate for the same period. By regions, New England had a lower rate (6.7) than other areas. The Pacific region has the next lowest rate (7.1), followed by the Mountain (7.7), West North Central (8.3) and West South Central (8.3). All other regions were higher than the national average

Infant Mortality Rates By Geographic Region and State:
Average Annual for Specified Time Periods

Table 2

Geographic Division and State	1981-83	1986-88	1991-93
United States	11.5	10.1	8.6
New England	10.1	8.3	6.7
Maine	9.5	8.3	6.4
New Hampshire	9.8	8.4	5.9
Vermont	8.6	8.4	6.6
Massachusetts	9.6	7.9	6.4
Rhode Island	11.2	8.6	7.6
Connecticut	11.1	8.9	7.4
Middle Atlantic	11.8	10.3	8.8
New York	12.0	10.7	8.9
New Jersey	11.3	9.7	8.4
Pennsylvania	11.6	10.2	8.9
East North Central	12.1	10.6	9.6
Ohio	11.7	9.9	9.3
Indiana	11.5	10.8	9.2
Illinois	13.3	11.7	10.2
Michigan	12.4	11.0	10.0
Wisconsin	9.8	8.8	7.8
West North Central	10.5	9.3	8.3
Minnesota	9.9	8.6	7.4
Iowa	9.7	8.7	7.7
Missouri	11.7	10.3	9.1
North Dakota	10.2	9.2	8.0
South Dakota	10.8	11.1	9.4
Nebraska	9.9	9.2	8.0
Kansas	10.7	8.8	8.8
South Atlantic	13.2	11.6	9.9
Delaware	12.5	11.7	9.8
Maryland	12.1	11.5	9.6
District of Columbia	21.8	21.2	19.4
Virginia	12.4	10.5	9.4
West Virginia	11.8	9.7	8.7
North Carolina	13.3	12.0	10.4
South Carolina	15.7	12.7	10.6
Georgia	13.3	12.6	10.7
Florida	12.8	10.7	8.8

Continued

Table 2 *continued*				
East South Central	13.1	11.6	10.0
Kentucky	11.9	10.1	8.5
Tennessee	12.5	11.1	9.6
Alabama	13.3	12.5	10.7
Mississippi	15.3	12.8	11.6
West South Central	11.6	9.7	8.4
Arkansas	10.9	10.4	10.2
Louisiana	13.4	11.6	10.3
Oklahoma	11.7	9.7	9.1
Texas	11.2	9.2	7.7
Mountain	10.0	9.3	7.7
Montana	9.9	9.4	7.3
Idaho	10.0	10.2	8.2
Wyoming	10.1	9.7	8.3
Colorado	9.7	9.3	7.9
New Mexico	10.4	9.2	8.0
Arizona	10.2	9.5	8.2
Utah	9.9	8.5	6.0
Nevada	10.7	9.0	7.5
Pacific	10.0	9.0	7.1
Washington	10.2	9.5	6.9
Oregon	10.4	9.5	7.2
California	9.9	8.8	7.1
Alaska	12.0	10.9	8.6
Hawaii	9.3	8.5	7.0

Source: Health United States 1995.

with the highest rates reported in the East South Central (10.0) and South Atlantic (9.9) regions.

Another interesting way to look at infant mortality is by the educational attainment of the mother. Data from 1995 show that the infant mortality decreases as the educational attainment of the mother increases. Looking at babies born to all mothers, the infant mortality rate is 8.9 for babies whose mothers attained less than twelve years of education, 7.8 for babies of mothers with a high school diploma, and 5.4 for babies of mothers who attended at least one year of education beyond high school. It is important to note that though infant mortality rates for blacks decrease as the education level of the mothers increase, the rates are still significantly higher than average for all mothers. The infant mortality rate for babies of black mothers who completed thirteen or more years of education (11.9) is lower than that for black mothers completing less than twelve years (17.0). The rate for black mothers with thirteen or more years of education (11.9) is still

Infant Mortality Rates for Mothers 20 Years of Age and Over According to Education Attainment, Race, and Ethnicity of Mother

Table 3

Demographic Characteristics of Mother	1983	1985	1988	1989	1990	1991	1995
Less Than 12 Years of Education							
All Mothers	15.0	14.3	13.6	12.9	10.8	10.5	8.9
White	12.5	12.2	11.2	10.8	9.0	8.8	7.6
Black	23.4	21.5	21.0	20.1	19.5	19.6	17.0
American Indian or Alaskan Native	*16.4	*16.7	*14.8	14.5	*14.3	*12.9	*
Asian or Pacific Islander	*9.7	*8.0	*8.6	*8.8	6.6	6.3	5.7
Hispanic Origin	10.9	10.4	10.2	8.8	7.3	6.9	6.0
12 Years of Education							
All Mothers	10.2	9.9	9.6	9.5	8.8	8.6	7.8
White	8.7	8.5	7.9	7.9	7.1	6.9	6.4
Black	17.8	17.6	17.0	16.8	16.0	16.2	14.7
American Indian or Alaskan Native	*15.5	*10.9	11.2	12.7	13.4	11.0	7.9
Asian or Pacific Islander	10.0	8.0	7.5	-	7.5	6.6	5.5
Hispanic Origin	8.4	9.1	8.7	7.1	7.0	6.5	5.9
13 or More Years of Education							
All Mothers	8.1	7.7	7.0	6.9	6.4	6.1	5.4
White	7.2	6.6	5.9	5.9	5.4	5.2	4.7
Black	15.3	15.8	14.5	14.2	13.7	13.1	11.9
American Indian or Alaskan Native	*	*	*	*9.1	*6.9	*8.7	*5.9
Asian or Pacific Islander	6.6	6.2	5.6	5.8	5.1	4.5	4.4
Hispanic Origin	9.0	6.4	7.0	6.4	5.7	5.5	5.0

*Infant mortality rates for groups with fewer than 1,000 births are considered unreliable. Rates with fewer than 7,500 births are considered highly unreliable and are not shown.

Source: Health United States 1998.

greater than for all mothers who completed less than twelve years of education (8.9).

International Comparisons

Looking at international comparisons of 1994 data, Japan (4.25) had the lowest infant mortality rate among all countries that reported. The United States reported a rate of 8.02 which is almost 89 percent higher than in Japan and more than 21 percent higher than in Canada (6.30). The United States ranked 25 out of the 38 countries reported by the World Health Organization. Between 1989 and 1994, infant mortality rates decreased in all countries where the data were reported, except in Bulgaria and the Russian Federation, where rates increased by 2.6 percent and 0.6 percent respectively.

Table 4 **Infant Mortality Rates and Average Annual Percent Change: Selected Countries**

Country	1989	1994	Average Annual Percent Change	Country	1989	1994	Average Annual Percent Change
Japan	4.59	4.25	-1.5	Spain	7.78	6.69	-3.0
Singapore	6.61	4.34	-8.1	New Zealand	10.32	7.24	-8.5
Hong Kong	7.43	4.43	-9.8	Israel	10.6	7.80	-6.2
Sweden	5.77	4.45	-5.1	Greece	9.78	7.93	-4.1
Finland	6.03	4.72	-4.8	Czech Republic	9.97	7.95	-4.4
Switzerland	7.34	5.12	-7.0	United States	9.81	8.02	-3.9
Norway	7.72	5.23	-7.5	Portugal	12.18	8.06	-7.9
Denmark	7.95	5.45	-7.3	Belgium	8.53	8.20	-1.3
Germany	-	5.60	-	Cuba	11.08	9.40	-4.0
Netherlands	6.78	5.64	-3.6	Slovakia	13.46	11.19	-3.6
Ireland	7.55	5.93	-4.7	Puerto Rico	14.27	11.47	-4.3
Australia	8.46	6.05	-6.5	Hungary	15.74	11.55	-6.0
Northern Ireland	6.90	6.05	-2.6	Chile	17.06	11.99	-6.8
England and Wales	8.45	6.20	-6.0	Kuwait	17.33	12.68	-4.4
Scotland	8.73	6.20	-6.6	Costa Rica	13.90	13.71	-0.3
Austria	8.31	6.25	-5.5	Poland	15.96	15.13	-1.1
Canada	7.13	6.30	-3.0	Bulgaria	14.37	16.31	2.6
France	7.54	6.47	-3.8	Russian Federation	18.06	18.58	0.6
Italy	8.77	6.63	-5.4	Romania	26.90	23.89	-2.3

Source: World Health Organization 1998.

The most dramatic decreases were in Hong Kong (-9.8 percent) and Singapore (-8.1 percent), which had the second and third lowest rates reported.

III. Life Expectancy

Life expectancy is the number of years of life that can be expected for a particular age group at a given time. For the purposes of this indicator, life expectancy at birth will be used. It is the average number of years of life remaining to a person at birth and is based on a given set of age-specific death rates, generally the mortality conditions existing in the period mentioned. Life expectancy data are easy to collect and reliable. It is also a relatively easy concept for people to understand. It answers the question, "How long will life last given current mortality rates?" The statistic can be misleading because it focuses on how long a person lives but says nothing about the quality of that life. Life expectancy may continue to rise, but there can be corresponding rises in disability and morbidity.

Life Expectancy in the United States

In 1996 life expectancy at birth for women was 79.1 years, 6 years longer than for men at 73.1 years. Life expectancy has increased since 1950, when men could expect to live 65.6 years and women 71.1 years. The overall increase for women, however, has been greater than for men with women's life expectancy increasing by 8 years and men's by 7.5 years. In fact, the life expectancy for women in the United States has been continuously higher than that for men since 1900, when U.S. death registration began. The Department of Health and Human Services reports that between 1992 and 1996 overall life expectancy at birth declined slightly to 75.5 years reflecting the impact of two influenza outbreaks in 1993.

Life Expectancy at Birth in the United States   *Table 5*

Year	Both Sexes	Male	Female
1980	73.7	70.0	77.4
1985	74.7	71.1	78.2
1990	75.4	71.8	78.8
1991	75.5	72.0	78.9
1992	75.8	72.3	79.1
1993	75.5	72.2	78.8
1994	75.7	72.4	79.0
1995	75.8	72.5	78.9
1996	76.1	73.1	79.1

Source: Health United States 1998

In 1996 life expectancy at birth for blacks was 70.2 years, 6.6 years less than the rate for whites (76.8). Between 1980 and 1996 life expectancy increased overall for all groups, except for the slight 1993 decline mentioned earlier. The rate for white women has almost remained steady at 79.6 in 1994 and 1995 and an increase to 79.7 in 1996. The 1996 life expectancy increased for all other groups. It should be noted that 1995 is the first year the rate for black males has been above that of 1985 (65.0). The rate for black males began to drop between 1984 and 1989. This rate began increasing again in 1990 and equaling the 1984 rate in 1992, but not surpassing it until 1996. The difference in the life expectancy between races continues to grow. The difference in rates between white males and black males narrowed from 6.9 years in 1980 to 6.8 years in 1985, but in 1993 the difference increased to a high of 8.5 years, a greater gap than in 1980. The continuing increase in life

Table 6   **Life Expectancy at Birth According to Race and Sex: United States**

Year	White		Black	
	Male	Female	Male	Female
1980	70.7	78.1	63.8	72.5
1985	71.8	78.7	65.0	73.4
1990	72.7	79.4	64.5	73.6
1991	72.9	79.6	64.6	73.8
1992	73.2	79.8	65.0	73.9
1993	73.1	79.5	64.6	73.7
1994	73.3	79.6	64.9	73.9
1995	73.4	79.6	65.2	73.9
1996	73.9	79.7	66.1	74.2

1995 and preliminary 1996 from Monthly Vital Statistics Report, 1997.

Source: Health United States 1998.

expectancy of black males decreased the gap in 1996 to about 7.8 years, which is still greater than the 1980 gap. A smaller, but similar difference can be seen in data for women.

International Comparisons

Worldwide life expectancy is increasing. In industrialized countries, women outlive men an average of six years. In most reporting countries, average life expectancy is now over 70 years. The majority of developing countries still have a life expectancy below 50 years. There is, however, a group of developing countries – including Argentina, Cuba, Singapore, and Sri Lanka – already enjoying a life expectancy of 70 years or more (WHO Report 1993). In 1994 Japan had the highest life expectancy for men (76.6) and for women (83.3). Of 33 reporting countries, the United States had the twenty-second highest rate for men (72.4) and seventeenth for women (79.0). Canadian men had the seventh highest life expectancy (74.8) for men. Canadian women had the sixth highest (81.0).

Life Expectancy at Birth According to Sex: Selected Countries

Table 7

Country	Male 1987	Male 1994	Female 1987	Female 1994
Australia	73.2	75.1	79.8	80.9
Austria	71.6	73.3	78.2	79.8
Bulgaria	68.3	67.1	74.6	74.7
Canada	73.3	74.8	80.2	81.0
Chile	70.0	71.4	75.7	76.3
Cuba	73.0	-	76.5	-
Czech Republic	67.9	69.5	75.2	76.6
Denmark	71.9	72.7	78.0	77.9
England and Wales	72.6	73.8	78.3	79.7
Finland	70.7	72.8	78.9	80.2
France	72.6	73.8	81.1	82.1
Germany	-	73.0	-	79.6
Greece	74.1	75.2	78.9	80.2
Hungary	65.7	64.9	73.9	74.3
Ireland	71.6	72.6	77.3	78.2
Israel	73.4	75.1	77.0	78.9
Italy	72.7	74.0	79.2	80.7
Japan	75.9	76.6	82.1	83.3
Netherlands	73.6	74.6	80.3	80.4
New Zealand	71.0	73.3	77.3	78.9
Northern Ireland	71.1	72.5	77.2	79.7
Norway	72.8	74.2	79.8	80.3
Poland	66.8	67.4	75.2	76.0
Portugal	70.6	71.5	77.5	78.6
Puerto Rico	70.7	69.6	78.9	78.9
Romania	67.1	66.0	72.7	73.3
Russian Federation	65.0	57.7	74.6	73.1
Scotland	70.5	71.4	76.6	77.7
Singapore	71.3	73.5	76.5	79.0
Slovakia	68.3	68.3	76.5	76.5
Spain	73.1	73.7	79.7	81.1
Sweden	74.2	76.1	80.4	81.4
Switzerland	74.0	75.1	81.0	81.9
United States	71.4	72.4	78.3	79.0

Source: Health United States 1998.

IV. Discussion

The Calvert-Henderson Health Indicator reveals several things about the quality of life for Americans and may help us make decisions about the future health of our communities. All of the health data reported show trends and differences that may lead to discussion and debate. For example, the indicator reveals the continuing differences between rates in race and ethnicity in various regions of the country and the world. The fact that educational attainment seems to lower infant mortality rates should influence decisions about spending cuts in education and school programs in local and national budgets. Even after the high rate in the District of Columbia is removed, infant mortality rates vary by state and region by as much as 4.8 infant deaths per 1,000 live births. Looking at life expectancies in different counties in the United States, Dr. Christopher Murray remarked at a scientific meeting organized by the Federal Centers for Disease Control and Prevention that the vast differences in life expectancies within the United States is the sort found between poverty ridden and wealthy countries. Women in some counties died around the age of 83, while men in an area in South Dakota, that contains two reservations, have a life expectancy of only 61 (Murray and Lopez 1994). This information raises serious concerns and leads to discussion about the impact of inequalities in economic levels, education systems, and health care delivery on the quality of life.

Comparisons of infant mortality and life expectancy on an international level may help people make decisions about future changes in health care policy. For example, in 1994 Japan had the highest life expectancy for both males and females and the lowest infant mortality reported. Health expenditures per capita in the same year in Japan were $1,454. The United States spent more than twice as much at $3,497 per capita. International comparisons may also lead to increased discussion of differences in diet, exercise habits, and lifestyle.

Speaking on the connection between economy and health, Dr. Amartya Sen, the 1998 winner of the Nobel Prize in economics, noted in a recent address that a robust economy does not necessarily translate into better health. "He pointed out that African Americans in the United States may be poor in relation to whites, but are 'tremendously rich' when their incomes are compared with Third World places such as China and India. Yet longevity is higher in these impoverished locales than in Black America." Dr. Sen suggests that we need "an integrated view" of health (McManus 1999).

All of this health data has been presented to the public throughout the years. Most people realize that there are differences in infant mortality rates and life expectancy along racial lines. This information has been presented in disjointed ways and seldom has been presented in the context of the quality of life of American citizens. This organized presentation, in conjunction with indicators on education, environment, income, and other areas, will prove an effective tool for guiding discussion and improving decision-making. Hopefully it will help create a true integrated view of health.

Future Measures of Health

It is difficult to limit the determination of a nation's health to one or two indicators. Infant mortality and life expectancy provide a simple proxy for more complex issues surrounding health. Neither says anything about what makes people ill or what kills them. As interest grows in measuring the quality of life and improving methods for collecting data, other indicators should be considered.

Using other measures we can begin to answer additional questions about the health of a nation's people. An important question is "What's killing people?" Mortality rates tell us the age at which people die, but this provides a limited description of our health. A decrease in the mortality rate does not, by itself, indicate improved health, because mortality rates can decrease while persons suffer from increased illness and disability. In addition, mortality rates are criticized for inaccuracy in reporting and measurement. For example, only one cause of death may be recorded on a death certificate, though there may be several causes. In addition, insurance companies may influence the reporting of the cause of death, and the cause of death is not as thoroughly investigated among the elderly as among the young (Turns and Newber 1983).

The question "What's making people sick?" can be answered using morbidity rates, which measure the occurrence of disease in a population. Morbidity is often considered a better measure of health than mortality because it reflects the presence or absence of serious disease. Morbidity can indicate more about health than the death of an individual but can be unreliable since the statistics are not as widely available or uniform as measures of mortality. Problems in reporting can occur wherever a stigma is attached to illness or where a group within a population does not have the same values as those collecting data. For example, some health problems affecting women – those related to abortion, adolescent pregnancy, female genital mutilation, and domestic violence – are controversial and difficult to document. Even in industrial countries, illness or injury to women and children are underreported according to the World Bank (1994).

Another important question that might be considered is "Are people living healthfully?" To answer this we can examine deaths that could have been prevented by lifestyle changes. We can look at disease caused by environmental impacts or occupational safety and health issues. A population's dependence on alcohol, cigarettes, and other narcotics can also act as an indicator of health. Measurements of the number of people who are overweight and people who have elevated blood pressure, cholesterol, or blood sugar are also important health indicators. This information is currently collected in the United States, but data collection needs to be improved before this information can be used for comparison among other nations or even regions within the country.

The question "Can people get health care?" should also be considered. This answer could include the presence of prenatal and antenatal care, the number of providers per population, the availability of primary care, and the availability of affordable care. Access and availability of health insurance should also be monitored.

Another indicator that deserves attention is birth weight. Low birth weight is one of the most serious public health problems in the world today. It is estimated that more than 20 million low-birth-weight children are born worldwide every year. More than 90 percent of these children are born in developing countries. These low-birth-weight babies, who are born weighing less than 2,500 grams, account for a high proportion of infant mortality. Looking at 1995 data, the National Center for Health Statistics reported that 63 percent of all infant deaths were among low-birth-weight babies. In her article "Healthy Families Make Healthy Babies," Moreno (1993) points out that when low-birth-weight babies survive, these infants suffer higher rates of childhood illnesses and, often, severe disabling conditions, such as mental retardation, behavioral disorders, cerebral palsy, and impairment of vision and hearing. She concludes that birth weight is linked to socioeconomic, lifestyle, or behavioral factors on the part of the mother and family. Contributing factors include insufficient antenatal care, inadequate maternal nutrition, pregnancy at extreme ages, insufficient birth spacing, smoking, excessive physical activity during pregnancy, and psychosocial and occupational stress. Many expect that measuring birth weight is a better indicator of health than infant mortality. As data collection improves, this measure should be a good indicator of health because it looks at a larger number of infants whose quality of life was compromised from the start. It reflects not only infants who die, but also those who survive with a variety of health problems.

Finally, measures of disability should also be considered as indicators of health. According to the United Nations, approximately one out of every ten persons is affected by disability (1992). In developing nations, the incidence may be twice as high. Disability is reported regularly in the United States through surveys conducted by the National Center for Health Statistics. The measures include days of restricted activity, bed days, and work-and school-loss days. Data collection is expensive and even in the United States is limited to a national profile, excluding information on states. International data are even more limited. The impact of disability should not, however, be ignored.

It is very difficult to provide an accurate and comprehensive measure of health. This does not mean that an attempt should not be made to do so. Quality of life is dramatically affected by health and it is important that health be included when measuring the prosperity and progress of a nation.

Indicators give people the information they need to develop healthier communities. Life expectancy and infant mortality are offered here as starting points, but efforts to improve information on health need to continue locally and internationally.

Vital Statistics *Appendix 1*

Vital statistics are not ideal. There is criticism about data collection and questions about which statistics are really the best measure of health. The quality of data also varies by region, internationally or within the U.S. Sophisticated data are not available in developing countries because many countries lack complete and accurate vital registration systems. In all countries, even where vital registration systems exist, the data can be underreported due to a variety of social, religious, emotional, and practical factors, such as the stigma of abortion and AIDS, or the desire to avoid an official inquiry (World Bank 1994). Reporting in areas distant from local governments or health care delivery systems can also be infrequent and inaccurate.

Statistics on mortality and morbidity were also considered as indicators but were not chosen because of the necessity to list mortality or morbidity as a result of a wide variety of diseases that lead to sickness and health. This group of numbers would not have as much meaning as a single indicator. A low incidence of cancer, for example, can be a very good thing in an industrialized country. In a developing nation, a low incidence of cancer often means that persons do not live to an age where chronic diseases become a problem. Many developing nations are only beginning to see an increase in chronic disease because they are just beginning to control the number of deaths caused by infectious diseases. Finally, the use of a crude death rate, reporting the number of total deaths in a population, would eliminate the need to list all of the causes of death, but that number alone would also be difficult to interpret because of the multiple variables (natural disasters, war) that impact the rate.

Indexes, or combinations of single indicators such as mortality and morbidity, were considered but not chosen because the meaning of the indexes are complex and often based on multiple assumptions. Moreover, indexes are difficult to interpret and could lead to improper conclusions.

REFERENCES

Anderson, Gerard F. and Jean-Pierre Poullier. "Health Spending, Access, and Outcomes: Trends in Industrialized Countries." *Health Affairs,* Vol. 18, No. 3, pp. 178-192.

Bunker, John P., Howard S. Frazier, and Frederick Mosteller. 1994. "Improving Health: Measuring Effects of Medical Care." *The Milbank Quarterly,* Vol. 72, No. 2, pp. 225-258.

Cobb, Clifford, Ted Halstead, and Jonathan Rowe. 1995. "If the GDP is Up, Why is America Down?" *The Atlantic Monthly,* pp. 59-78 (October).

Healthier Communities Action Kit: A Guide for Leaders Embracing Change – Module 1: Getting Started. 1993. San Francisco: Healthier Communities Partnership.

Larson, James S. 1991. *The Measurement of Health: Concepts and Indicators.* New York: Greenwood Press.

McManus, Rich. 1999. "Sen's 'Relational Reach' Links Health, Economy." *The NIH Record,* Vol. LI, No. 14, 1 and 6.

McDowell, Ian and Claire Newell. 1987. *Measuring Health: A Guide to Rating Scores and Questionnaires.* New York: Oxford University Press.

Miller, C. Arden. "Infant Mortality in the U.S." *Scientific American,* Vol. 253, No. 1, pp. 31-37.

Moreno, Elsa Margarita. 1993. "Healthy Families Make Healthy Babies." *World Health,* pp. 23-25 (May/June).

Murray, CJL and AD Lopez, eds. 1994. *Global Comparative Assessments in the Health Sector: Disease Burden, Expenditures and Intervention Packages.* Geneva: World Health Organization.

Mushkin, Selma and David Dunlop, eds. 1979. *Health: Is It Worth It? Measures of Health Benefits.* New York: Pergamon Press.

National Center for Health Statistics. 1998. *1998 Fact Sheets: New Study Identifies Infants at Greatest Risk.* Hyattsville, MD: Public Health Service (February 26).

National Center for Health Statistics. 1996. *Health United States, 1995.* Hyattsville, MD: Public Health Service.

Robine, Jean-Marie, Colin D. Mathers, and Denis Bucquet. 1993. "Distinguishing Health Expectancies and Health-Adjusted Life Expectancies from Quality-Adjusted Life Years." *American Journal of Public Health,* Vol. 83, No. 6, pp. 797-798.

Satcher, David. 1995. "The Lessons and Challenges of Emerging and Re-emerging Infectious Diseases." Presented at The George Washington University School of Medicine and Health Sciences Convocation, Washington, D.C. (September 12).

"Surprises in a Study of Life Expectancies." 1997. *The New York Times,* p. 24 (December 4). "Taking the World's Pulse: The WHO Report." 1993. *World Health,* pp. 4-5 (May/June).

Testa, Marcia A. and Donald C. Simonson. 1996. "Assessment of Quality-of-Life Outcomes." *The New England Journal of Medicine,* Vol. 334, No. 13, pp. 835-840.

Turns, Daniel and Larry Newbu. 1983. "The Measurement of Health Status." *Assessing Health and Human Services Needs.* Roger Bell, ed. New York: Human Sciences Press.

United Nations. 1992. *World Programme of Action Concerning Disabled Persons.* New York: United Nations.

Vita, Anthony J., Richard B. Terry, Helen B. Hubert, and James F. Fries. 1998. "Aging, Health Risks, and Cumulative Disability." *New England Journal of Medicine,* Vol. 338, No. 15, pp. 1035-1041.

Voelker, Rebecca. 1994. "Born in the USA: Infant Health Paradox." *The Journal of the American Medical Association,* Vol. 272, No. 23, pp. 1803-1804.

World Bank. 1994. *A New Agenda for Women's Health and Nutrition.* Washington, D.C.

Chapter 10

Human Rights Indicator

by Alya Kayal, Esq.

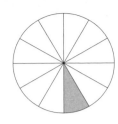

I. Introduction

The objective of the Calvert-Henderson Human Rights Indicator is to provide an overview of the constitutional and other legal state of our human rights. This Indicator provides a holistic framework, presented by the Calvert-Henderson Human Rights model, from which we can begin to evaluate the protection of our human rights. In future editions, we will examine the ramifications of human rights protections, as well as analyze the degree to which our rights are protected in the United States.

The United States has some of the most advanced and best legal protections in the world, including a large community of human rights and social justice activists. Despite this, many Americans continue to face human rights violations. An increasing number of people, particularly African-Americans, are being incarcerated; the mistreatment of female and immigrant prisoners is reported by the press; the death penalty continues to be on the rise despite worldwide appeals; racism and discrimination are prevalent; and young women continue to work in garment sweatshops. The most basic of human rights, security of person, is still not effectively protected for millions of women and children, who face domestic violence and abuse in their own homes. In addition, our political system continues to be influenced by wealthy contributors and corporate political action committees who gain an advantage over those who have fewer resources. These growing social justice concerns emphasize the need to understand human rights in the United States. The Calvert-Henderson Human Rights Indicator seeks to educate and remind Americans of the rights to which each of us is entitled.

Toward this end, we present the Human Rights model as a tool for viewing our rights in the United States. The model comprises of four areas: (1) fundamental or "security of person" rights, (2) private sphere human rights, (3) public sphere human rights, mainly the U.S. Bill of Rights and Amendments to the Constitution, and (4) U.S. government impact on noncitizens. The explicit conjunction of these areas is crucial to the understanding of human rights in America. The foundation underlying the Human Rights model is the U.S. Bill of Rights and Amendments to the Constitution from which our rights are derived.

The Calvert-Henderson Human Rights Indicator is valuable to the human rights literature in several ways. First, it is a unified presentation of multiple categories of human rights as they relate to our constitutional protections. Typically, human rights in the United States tend to focus on one or more traditional human rights issues (such as freedom of expression, right of assembly, etc.), and is often viewed as discrete issues by many nonprofit organizations (e.g., women's rights organizations focus on women's human rights; justice groups focus on death penalty etc.). The Indicator provides a broader and more inclusive framework portraying the evolving nature of human rights by including many areas of human rights, such as private sphere issues. It also recognizes the connection to security of person issues, such as human rights to food, nutrition, medical care, and clothing. In general, the model provides a framework from which we can evaluate multiple categories of human rights systematically. Second, the Calvert-Henderson Human Rights Indicator is useful because, unlike current human rights literature that focuses on U.S. compliance with international treaties, this Indicator expressly links the evaluation of international human rights to those legal rights guaranteed by our own country by the U.S. Constitution, the Bill of Rights, and other amendments.

The Human Rights model is a tool for viewing our rights in the United States.

The Calvert-Henderson Human Rights Indicator will be presented in two parts. Section II defines human rights in the unique context of the American experience. Section III provides an explanation of the Calvert-Henderson Human Rights model as a tool for viewing human rights in this country and provides readers with selected data to illustrate the level of human rights enjoyed in the United States and conversely, where human rights are being violated today.

II. Definitions of Human Rights and Its Relation to the United States

Defining human rights is controversial, particularly because it is deeply rooted in moral philosophy, notions of justice, and respect for human beings. Whether human rights are to be viewed as divine, moral, or legal entitlements is still debated. Although discussions of human rights are found in ancient literature, the philosophical basis for modern human rights is that people have certain inalienable human rights. Human rights professor Jack Donnelly explains the rationale behind why human beings are considered to have certain rights: "The term human rights indicates both their nature and their source. They are the rights that one has simply because one is human" (Donnelly 1998, p.18).

International human rights scholar Louis Henkin proposes a working definition for human rights that is more descriptive of the types of rights one is entitled to:

> Every human being has, or is entitled to have, "rights" – legitimate, valid, justified claims – upon his or her society; claims to various "goods" and benefits…. They are benefits deemed essential for individual well-being, dignity and fulfillment, and that reflect a

Calvert-Henderson Human Rights Model

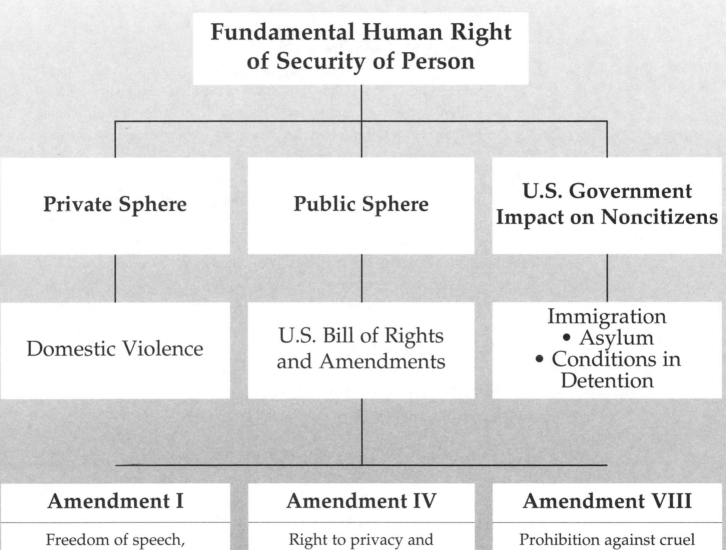

Fundamental Human Right
of Security of Person

Private Sphere	Public Sphere	U.S. Government Impact on Noncitizens
Domestic Violence	U.S. Bill of Rights and Amendments	Immigration • Asylum • Conditions in Detention

Amendment I

Freedom of speech, religion & assembly

Amendment IV

Right to privacy and protection against unreasonable search and seizure

Amendment VIII

Prohibition against cruel and unusual punishment

Amendment XIII

Prohibition against slavery and involuntary servitude

Amendment XIV

Right to due process and equal protection

Amendments XII, XV, XIX, XXIV and XXVI

Rights to political participation

Note: the model was co-created with Adrienne Fitch-Frankel, Research Associate at Calvert Group when this indicator was developed.

common sense of justice, fairness, and decency. . .Human rights are universal: they belong to every human being in every human society (Henkin 1990, p.2-3).

The protection of our human rights is viewed as the responsibility of our government:

[A]ll human rights are universal, indivisible and interdependent and interrelated....[w]hile the significance of national and regional partic-ularities and various historical, cultural, and religious backgrounds must be borne in mind, it is the duty of the States, regardless of their political, economic, and cultural systems, to promote and protect all human rights and fundamental freedoms" (Vienna Declaration and Programme of Action 1993).

Human rights comprise five general categories: civil, political, economic, social, and cultural rights. The definitions of these categories are described in the Universal Declaration of Human Rights ([UDHR] 1948) and the International Bill of Rights (1966). These rights were expanded further by various international conventions, such as the Convention on the Rights of the Child (1989) and the Convention on the Elimination of All Forms of Discrimination Against Women ([CEDAW] 1979; see Appendix 1). The UDHR and the International Bill of Rights are described below.

Universal Declaration of Human Rights

The modern practice of human rights is defined by the UDHR; human rights advocates and practitioners refer to this document as the primary definition of human rights. Fifty years ago, the United States and other countries came together to define "human rights" by drafting and signing the UDHR. The United States, represented by Eleanor Roosevelt, was a key participant in negotiating the text of this declaration. The frame-work of the UDHR, based largely on the U.S. Bill of Rights, includes 30 articles guaranteeing the rights of all people through a broad spectrum of economic, social, cultural, political, and civil rights, which governments agree to observe. Since the UDHR is not a binding document, the United Nations interpreted the provisions of the UDHR by drafting binding treaties: the International Covenant on Civil and Political Rights (ICCPR); the International Covenant on Economic, Social, and Cultural Rights (ICESCR); and the Optional Protocol to the Civil and Political Rights Covenant.

The five broad types of human rights (grouped under the two inter-national conventions, the ICCPR and ICESCR) are defined below:
- *Civil and Political Rights* – These include the right to self-determina-tion; right to life, liberty, and security of person; right to freedom of thought and freedom of association; and the right to be free from

slavery and torture and from cruel, inhuman, or degrading punishment. Civil and political rights are immediately applicable to all
countries that ratify the ICCPR treaty, so that governments must
protect these rights at once. The United States has ratified the
ICCPR.

- *Economic, Social, and Cultural Rights* – These include the right to
  freely dispose natural wealth; right to social security; right to join
  trade unions; right to education; and right to participate in cultural
  life. Unlike political and civil rights, these economic, social, and
  cultural rights are to be accomplished only progressively by
  ratifying governments "as resources permit." The United States
  has not ratified the ICESCR.

Human rights codified in the UDHR commit the government to
several different types of action. In some cases, a government pledges to
restrain itself from violating human rights. In other cases, a government
promises to restrain private individuals or organizations from violating
human rights. Governments also promise to seek to guarantee access to basic
human needs and improve the quality of life. These international conventions on human rights are designed to apply to the national context. Since
governments cannot be expected to monitor their own abuses of power and
failures to guarantee human rights, all countries pledge to preserve human
rights for their own citizens by declaring their commitments to human rights
in public international documents with the world as witness. As a signatory
of the UDHR, and a party to the binding ICCPR, the United States has
endorsed this broad-based definition of human rights and has vowed to
protect human rights for its own citizens, as much as it promises to be a
witness and monitor for other nations.

The American Experience: Civil Rights to Human Rights

Social movements struggling to expand human rights have been a
hallmark of American political history, from the fight for independence in the
18th century, to the abolition movements in the 19th century and movements
for worker and women's rights in the 20th century. The civil rights
movement elevated its cause to such prominence that civil rights is practi-
cally synonymous with human rights in common parlance today. The
concept and use of the term "human rights" are experiencing a renaissance in
recognition as an issue relevant to the American context. Several states (e.g.,
Minnesota, Washington, Vermont, and Tennessee) as well as several cities
(e.g., San Francisco, Denver, and New York) have human rights commissions
and/or laws. Recognition of human rights as an issue is evident at the federal
level as well. In a report to the United Nations, the State Department states
that it is "meant to offer to the international community a sweeping picture of
human rights observance in the United States" (U.S. DOS 1994, p.1).

The concept of human rights is very much part of the American historical experience. The U.S. Bill of Rights and other amendments to the U.S. Constitution are closely linked to those rights enumerated in the UDHR and the international covenants. Given the unique role of the United States as a leader in the development of international human rights principles, our government drew heavily on its own constitutional and legal experience when drafting the UDHR. However, the UDHR and the international covenants modernize human rights by going beyond those individual rights guaranteed in the Bill of Rights. For example, the UDHR includes the rights to asylum in other countries from persecution, to marriage and family, rest and leisure, social security, and participation in cultural life. Our Constitution does not expressly articulate such rights. Nevertheless, both the UDHR and U.S. Bill of Rights and other amendments include human rights guarantees that fall into one of the categories of human rights: civil, political, economic, social, and cultural.

In summary, the definition, nature, and scope of human rights are fluid and evolve over time due to political, social, cultural, and ideological changes. Some of these rights may be interpreted differently by different people at different times, and their universality may be contentious. There continue to be ongoing debates over whether human rights are individual or collective rights; whether economic, social, and cultural rights should take precedence over civil and political rights; and whether present definitions of human rights have a Western bias that places emphasis on individual rather than community rights. Nevertheless, there is some consensus that certain human rights are universal and timeless, setting a "common standard of achievement for all peoples and all nations" (UDHR 1948).

III. The Calvert-Henderson Human Rights Model

The Calvert-Henderson Human Rights model provides a framework from which we can evaluate multiple categories of human rights systematically. The model has four key components. The author has placed security of person at the top of the model because of its paramount importance. Next, given that constitutional rights have shaped modern definitions of international human rights and because our human rights are directly derived from them, the author has placed selected U.S. Bill of Rights and Amendments as a focus of the Human Rights model, under the public sphere. Moving away from traditional ways of looking at human rights, the author has included human rights in the home/private sphere in the model. Finally, since the United States is a land of immigrants, the author includes the human rights of noncitizens as an important part of the model. These four key concepts provide a comprehensive overview of human rights in the United States. The following is a discussion of the four components of the Calvert-Henderson Human Rights model.

Security of Person Rights

The security of person rights have been placed at the top of the Calvert-Henderson Human Rights model. Although there is some discussion about whether rights to food and shelter are human rights, these rights to basic human needs are seen by many as the most fundamental of all human rights and are included in international human rights conventions. People are considered to have a right of access to that which is necessary for survival. Without protection of survival and security of the person, other important human rights can be meaningless or immaterial. The founding fathers of this country also held sacred the "pursuit of life," listed in Article 3 of the UDHR as the right to life, liberty, and security of person. Although the UDHR enumerates human rights to food, clothing, housing, medical care, social services, education, and participation in cultural life, the U.S. Constitution and Bill of Rights do not expressly enumerate these rights. The Calvert-Henderson Quality of Life project includes indicators that describe in detail some of our fundamental security of person rights. For example, the Health Indicator looks at infant mortality and life expectancy and the Shelter Indicator looks at affordability and access to housing. In addition, the Human Rights Indicator points to private sphere rights or security of person rights in the home.

Private Sphere Human Rights

Because the status of women and children are important indicators for measuring the quality of life, the Calvert-Henderson Human Rights Indicator includes human rights in the private sphere. Human rights theory has traditionally been relegated to the protection of rights of people (predominantly protection of men) from abuse of power by the state. As a result, human rights split off from that of women's or children's rights. Governments are not the only violators of human rights; institutions or individuals in our society can violate human rights as well. An unequal distribution of power and monopolies or the use of force can affect the family, the most basic unit of society. Therefore, the human rights of women and children need protection in the domain where they are most vulnerable to abuse of power, the home. In a 1997 public opinion survey, approximately 22 percent of women stated that they had been physically abused by their spouse or companion (Sourcebook for Criminal Justice Statistics Online 1998). In 1996, approximately 25 percent of women reported that they were raped or physically assaulted in their lifetime by an intimate partner (U.S. Department of Justice, National Institute of Justice, U.S. Department of Health and Human Services, and Centers for Disease Control and Prevention, 1998). See discussion on private sphere human rights by Riane Eisler entitled "Toward a Holistic Model of Human Rights" below.

The human rights of women and children need protection in the domain where they are most vulnerable to abuse of power, the home.

The Private Sphere - Toward a Holistic Model of Human Rights
by Riane Eisler, Ph.D.

The movement of human rights only goes back 300 years, to the 17th century beginnings of the Enlightenment. At that time, the focus of political discourse gradually began to shift from words such as fealty, loyalty, and obedience to words such as freedom, equality, and progress. This shift in discourse – and with it, the emergence of the idea that there are human rights – did not happen in a vacuum. It came along with the destabilization of many entrenched beliefs and institutions through exponentially rapid technological change. As the Industrial Revolution began to go into high gear, more and more once taken-for-granted ways of working and living began to unravel. This brought great dislocation and stress. But it also brought a growing consciousness that entrenched traditions of domination – be it the rule of kings over their "subjects" or the rule of men over the women and children in the "castles" of their homes – were not immutable.

In short, the emergence of the concept of human rights heralds the onset of modern democracy, and with it a better general quality of life. Indeed, despite periodic regressions, the thrust of the modern human rights movement has been toward the expansion of the scope of human rights to encompass more people, as well as more areas of our lives.

Nonetheless, in the United States, which generally receives high rankings in international human rights indexes, progress has been uneven. All along, there have been large gaps between enumerated rights and real-life application. The human rights of large segments of the U.S. population, including women and children, are in both legal theory and actual practice still often selectively protected.

The Public and Private Spheres

During the first two centuries of the modern struggle for human rights, the primary emphasis was on the protection of political rights in the so-called public sphere. This was the emphasis of both the American and later French revolutions, as well as important documents such as the U.S. Constitution and Bill of Rights. But politics (or participation in government and the making of laws and public policies) was during that time viewed as an exclusive male preserve. Hence, during its first formative centuries, the modern movement of human rights was literally what it is still often called: the movement to protect the "rights of man."

Philosophers, such as John Locke of the 17th century and Jean Jacques Rousseau in the 18th century, who proposed the then novel idea that men have "inalienable rights" never spoke of the same rights for women and children. For them, rather than being individuals innately possessed of "natural rights," women and children were merely members of men's households, "naturally" to be controlled by them. However, there were women, such as Mary Wollstonecraft and Abigail Adams in the 18th century and Elizabeth Cady Stanton and Sojourner Truth in the 19th century, who argued that women too have human rights. There were also a number of men (e.g., the British philosopher John Stuart Mill and the African-American abolitionist leader Frederick Douglass) who made this point. But by and large, such views were effectively banished to the intellectual ghetto of feminism.

Thus, the splitting off of "women's rights" and later also "children's rights" from "human rights" (which in theory and practice focused primarily on the rights of adult, free, propertied, white males) was established. And this split was perpetuated by the continuing distinction in human rights theory and practice between the "public" (or men's) world and the "private" world, to which women and children were still generally confined to by custom, and sometimes by law. The purview of human rights theory was originally limited only to adult members of the male half of the population. In the United States until after the Civil War, it was limited to free men, which effectively meant only white men, since most African-American men, women, and children were slaves.

Political and Economic Rights

This gendered and racial double standard for human rights applied both to political and economic rights. Regarding political participation, it was not until the Nineteenth Amendment in 1920 (over a century after the U.S. Constitution was adopted) that the female half of the American population finally won the right to vote. Women's economic rights were also severely abridged. Until the mid-19th century, many American states had laws that deprived women of any control over property – even property a wife brought to her marriage or monies she earned by working outside her home. Until these laws were changed a wife's body and her work were viewed as her husband's legal property.

The right to enter high paying professions was also generally denied to women. It was not until the second half of the 19th century that the first wave of modern feminism began to make significant strides in its struggle for female access to institutions of higher learning. Only after the second half of the 20th century did American civil rights and women's liberation movements begin to be successful in the struggle for laws prohibiting race and gender-based employment discrimination.

Theory and Reality

The Equal Rights Amendment (which women's groups began to introduce during the late 19th century to protect women from discriminatory government policies and action) is not yet part of the U.S. Constitution. Hence, although in theory all Americans have equal protection under the Constitution, it was not until the second half of the 20th century that the U.S. Supreme Court declared women persons under the Equal Protection Clause of the 14th Amendment.

Similarly, even though most human rights scholars would agree that the most fundamental right is the right to security of person – most basically, the right to protection from violence – in accordance with the double standard for human rights and women's/children's rights, this violence is still generally treated as merely "domestic violence." Even though the U.S. Surgeon General's office found that violence in their homes is America's number one health threat to women, the police will often consider it merely a "domestic squabble" rather than a serious crime had it been a stranger. Therefore, unconscious biases against traditionally disempowered groups, such as women and minorities, and their traditional lack of political and economic influence, are a factor impeding the equal protection of human rights.

The Future of Human Rights

Clearly the situation in the United States is far better than in many other nations where torture of political prisoners, public stoning of women for suspected sexual independence, enormous government restrictions of freedom of speech and assembly, and other blatant human rights violations are still the norm. However, our most basic of human relations are between women and men and between them and their daughters and sons. It is here that we learn to value every human being or to treat difference as the basis for discrimination, cruelty, and violence. As long as discrimination, cruelty, and violence in people's intimate and family relations are condoned rather than condemned, these acts will continue from generation to generation and will spread to outside the family.

The arbitrary distinction in human rights theory and practice between what happens in the private and public spheres is thus not just a theoretical nicety, but something that has very real, often tragic, consequences. Our first lessons about human relations (and also about human rights) are learned not in the public, but in the private sphere. This is where people learn to respect the rights of others to freedom from violence, cruelty, oppression, and discrimination. Thus, whether intimate relations orient persons to what my research identifies as either a "partnership" or "dominator" model profoundly affects the quality of life for all. Also important in the movement toward an integrated partnership model for human rights are the many United Nations declarations and conventions that during the past decade have begun to integrate the private and public spheres, as well as economic and social rights.

In summary, the scope of human rights theory and action has greatly expanded during the last three centuries. And today, in bits and pieces, we are beginning to see movement toward a reformulation of human rights theory and action in ways that integrate not only the private and public spheres and the rights of women, men, and children but also political, social, and economic rights and responsibilities. It is impossible to predict if and when these bits and pieces will coalesce into the fully integrated approach to human rights appropriate for a social organization based primarily on partnership, rather than domination. What we can predict is that if and when this occurs there will be vast improvement in the quality of life worldwide.

Public Sphere

In light of the fact that universally accepted definitions of human rights enumerated in the UDHR are not legally binding in U.S. courts, and because the U.S. Bill of Rights and other amendments to the Constitution contain nearly every human right enumerated in the UDHR, we have selected the U.S. Bill of Rights and the other amendments to the Constitution as the foundation for the Calvert-Henderson Human Rights Indicator. The U.S. Bill of Rights and other amendments most powerfully represent human rights for Americans and are the "highest law of the land." The Bill of Rights is legally binding, enforceable, and designed to protect people in the United States.

Since the Constitution was ratified in 1789, there have been 27 amendments. The first 10 amendments are known collectively as the Bill of Rights. According to the U.S. government, these amendments provide for the basic protection of those individual rights that are fundamental to the democratic system of government; they remain at the heart of the U.S. legal system today. Amendments to the Constitution subsequent to the original Bill of Rights cover a wide range of subjects.

The following constitutional amendments have been selected for the Calvert-Henderson Human Rights Indicator because of their focus on individual rights as strong indicators of human rights. Other amendments were not selected because they focus on governance issues (e.g., elections of senators, conditions of terms of Presidents, judicial power, etc.); taxes; right to bear arms; prohibition of alcohol (later repealed); and due process issues in judicial trials. Although there are some human rights issues associated with the amendments left out of the model, the author chose to select those amendments firmly associated with human rights.

> **Amendment I [1791]**
> "Congress shall make no law respecting an establishment of religion, or prohibiting the free exercise thereof; or abridging the freedom of speech, or of the press; or of the right of the people peaceably to assemble, and to petition the Government for a redress of grievances."

The First Amendment protects the freedom of speech, religion, and association. Freedom of speech is protected against government interference, and also actions by private individuals who are closely associated with government officials. Freedom of speech includes symbolic speech, such as flag burning, as well as certain rights to seek and receive information. Given that early European-Americans fled religious persecution, freedom of religion is also among the most fundamental human rights of Americans. The rights of association, which are supplemented by labor legislation, are implicit in the rights of assembly, speech, and expression (NAACP v. Claiborne Hardware Co., 458 U.S. 898, 1982).

Human rights groups state that the United States violates the First Amendment by curtailing the flow of information both into and out of the country. According to a 1993 report by Human Rights Watch and the American Civil Liberties Union, visas to foreign visitors are still denied for ideological reasons; restrictions on international travel interfere with the rights of Americans to seek and share information; and restrictions on press coverage of military operations include limits on press access, harassment of journalists, and censorship of war-related news (Human Rights Watch/ACLU 1993, p.149). There are, however, permissible limitations to the right to freedom of speech.[1] For example, federal employees may not advocate the overthrow of our constitutional form of government or be a member of an organization they know to advocate this idea (5 United States Code § 7311).

Hate crimes are another example of restrictions on the freedom of speech. While America prides itself on its diversity, hate crimes caused by prejudice are on the rise. Under the "Hate Crimes Statistics Act of 1990," the Federal Bureau of Investigation (FBI) collects statistics on bias-motivated crimes based on race, color, religion, or national origin. More than 40 states have hate crimes laws, with 21 states and the District of Columbia covering sexual orientation, 22 covering gender, and 21 covering disability. Nine states have no hate crimes laws. In April 1999, President Clinton asked Congress to expand federal hate crime laws to include offenses based on sexual orientation. The new bill would make federal prosecution of hate crimes easier.

Despite laws against hate crimes, a recent rise in hate crimes has shocked the nation. In the past year, an African-American man was dragged to his death behind a pick-up truck by a white supremacist in Texas; a gay college student was killed in Wyoming; and another gay man was burned to death in Alabama. Reported hate crimes have more than doubled from 4,755 in 1991 to 9,861 in 1997 (Appendix 2). This represents an increase of about 108 percent within six years. During those years, intimidation accounted for approximately 30 to 40 percent of annual offenses, destruction of property for about 20 to 30 percent, and simple assault for about 15 to 20 percent.[?] Ninety-eight persons have been murdered in 1991-1997 in hate-motivated incidents. Over sixty percent of the hate crimes in the 1990s have been race-based, while approximately 15 percent have been religion-based. Hate crimes based on sexual orientation have risen sharply from approximately 11 percent in 1994 to almost 14 percent in 1997 - an increase of over 25 percent in just three years (Appendix 3).

Amendment IV [1791]

"The right of the people to be secure in their persons, houses, papers, and effects, against unreasonable searches and seizures, shall not be violated, and no Warrants shall issue, but upon probable cause, supported by Oath or affirmation, and particularly describing the place to be searched, and the persons or things to be seized."

The primary protection against the government's unwarranted deprivation of a person's liberty is in the Fourth Amendment. The U.S. Supreme Court has defined "search" under this amendment to be a government infringement of a person's privacy (Rakas v. Illinois, 439 U.S. 128, 1978). This amendment requires that an arrest must be reasonable and there must be probable cause. It also protects the reasonable expectation of privacy (Katz v. United States, 389 U.S. 347, 1967). Under this analysis, people have no subjective or reasonable privacy interest in property that they have abandoned (Hester v. United States, 265 U.S. 57, 1924) or in items that they have exposed to the public (Coolidge v. New Hampshire, 403 U.S. 443, 1971). In addition, if an individual has no reasonable expectation that his conduct/possessions will be private, there is no requirement that government agents secure a warrant and is therefore not subject to Fourth Amendment protection. Concerns about family planning (e.g., contraception and abortion issues); privacy at home (e.g., warrantless searches); correspondence (except for mail entering the U.S. from abroad); and electronic surveillance or wire tapping are also privacy issues falling under the protection of the Fourth Amendment.

> **Amendment VIII [1791]**
> "Excessive bail shall not be required, nor excessive fines imposed,
> nor cruel and unusual punishments inflicted."

The Eighth Amendment prohibits cruel and unusual punishment. These punishments include uncivilized and inhuman punishments, punishments that fail to comport with human dignity, and punishments that include physical suffering (Furman v. Georgia, 408 U.S. 238, 1972). This amendment applies to punishments provided for by statute or imposed by a court after a criminal conviction (e.g., death penalty); as well as prison conditions and prisoner mistreatment, such as solitary confinement, prison work that involves physical labor beyond the strength of the inmate, and inmates who are victims of excessive force by prison guards or government officials.

Death Penalty

The death penalty is an important indicator for the Calvert-Henderson Human Rights Indicator because it is a violation of the fundamental right to life. The death penalty has come under criticism for several reasons, including arguments that it is a government-authorized killing; its application is racist and arbitrary against the poor, minorities, and those unable to secure competent attorneys; execution and the wait on death row are torturous and cruel; it does not deter crime; and it does not exclude mentally disabled or juvenile offenders. In addition, there is a great risk of executing innocent persons, especially given that between 1973 and 1996, at least 59 wrongfully convicted death row inmates have been released, some of whom were within days of execution (Death Penalty Information Center 1996, p. 9). In 1996 alone, at least four prisoners were removed from death row and all charges on capital offense were dropped (Sourcebook of Criminal Justice Statistics 1998, p. 534).

In 1972, there was a ban on the death penalty in the United States as the U.S. Supreme Court found, in the case of Furman v. Georgia, that the death penalty was unconstitutional because it was "cruel and unusual" and the laws were being administered in an "arbitrary and capricious" manner. However, four years later, the Supreme Court lifted that ban after finding that a Georgia statute provided the protection necessary to permit the death penalty to be applied with "guided discretion" (Gregg v. Georgia, 428 U.S. 153, 1976). This finding opened the door to more death penalty statutes and currently, such statutes exist in 38 states and under federal and military law (Death Penalty Information Center 1996). Also, the United States has executed at least eight juvenile offenders since 1990, more than any other country (Amnesty International USA, 1998, p.113).

While the United Nations continues to urge signatories to end the

There is a great risk of executing innocent persons, especially given that between 1973 and 1996, at least 59 wrongfully convicted death row inmates have been released, some of whom were within days of execution.

death penalty, executions are on the rise in the United States. The American death row population is at an all-time high. As of 1997, approximately 3,335 people were on death row; of whom 56 percent were white and 42 percent were nonwhite (Appendix 4). Between 1978 and 1998, 357 prisoners were executed by the U.S. civil authorities (Appendix 5). In total, between 1930-1996, 4,217 persons have been executed. It appears that 1999 will set the record for the modern death penalty, with 100 executions nationwide, a third of which will take place in Texas (*Newsday*, 1999). There were 25 people executed in 1987, and this number almost doubled to 45 persons in 1996, of whom 68 percent of those executed were white and 31 percent were black.

One of the greatest concerns with the death penalty is the discriminatory racial impact. Expert and statistical evidence indicate injustices in the death penalty (Death Penalty Information Center 1996). African Americans continue to be sentenced to death and executed in far greater numbers than their proportion in the U.S. population. For example, African Americans constituted only 12 percent of the U.S. population in 1996, but represented 42 percent of the population on death row and 31 percent of those executed that year. In addition, racial disparities based on race of the victim is a critical factor. In 1990, the U.S. General Accounting Office (GAO) found that in 82 percent of the studies, "race of victim was found to influence the likelihood of being charged with capital murder or receiving the death penalty, i.e. those who murdered whites were found to be more likely to be sentenced to death than those who murdered blacks." (GAO 1990, p. 5). One study in Kentucky, using the federal GAO methodology in reviewing 572 murder trials from 1976-1991, concluded that defendants were more likely to be executed if their victims were white (Keil and Vito 1995). Similarly, a study of more than 2,000 murder cases in Georgia found that defendants of white victims were 4.3 times more likely to receive a death sentence than defendants with black victims, and that race of the victim determined the sentence imposed in up to one-third of the death sentences (Baldus, Woodworth, and Pulaski 1990). Other factors, such as socio-economic status and residence also influenced sentencing (Baldus, Woodworth, and Pulaski 1990).

Prisoner Mistreatment

Concerns surrounding the treatment of prisoners also fall under the Eighth Amendment. Currently, the United States has among the highest known incarceration rate in the world – with over 1 million people in prison in 1996 – half of whom were African American (Appendix 6). The proliferation of "three strikes and you're out" laws,[3] the proposals to end or severely limit parole, the push to build prisons, and mandatory minimum sentences for nonviolent crimes mean that prison populations will continue to grow. As the prison population rises, so does violence in prisons. According to Amnesty International, guards fail to stop inmates assaulting each other, or in many cases, beat or sexually abuse inmates, including pregnant women or the mentally ill (Amnesty International USA 1998). Solitary confinement and inadequate physical and mental healthcare are also serious concerns. In addition, women inmates also face serious mistreatment in prisons that fail to adjust to gender-specific needs of this population. For example, in September 1998, Human Rights Watch found that in Michigan, where approximately 2,000 women are incarcerated in state prisons, male corrections employees allegedly raped female prisoners, abused them, and compelled female prisoners to have sex (Human Rights Watch 1998). Although Michigan was used as an example, the report states that these issues are representative of those facing corrections departments throughout the United States.

Disproportionate Sentencing

In common law, punishment must fit the crime. However, there are a number of examples of disproportionately severe sentences in the United States. For example, a 1997 report by Human Rights Watch, titled "Cruel and Unusual: Disproportionate Sentences for New York Drug Offenders," criticizes the human rights impact of harsh criminal drug sentences in New York for low-level or marginal offenders. In New York, a person convicted of a single sale of two ounces of cocaine faces the same mandatory prison term as a murderer, which is 15 years to life. Although long prison sentences may be proportionate for traffickers who run large violent drug distribution enterprises, in New York, the vast majority of drug offenders sentenced to prison were involved in nonviolent minor drug deals (Human Rights Watch 1997).

Section 1983 Lawsuits

There is considerable evidence of increasing mistreatment of prisoners. Section 1983 of Title 42 of the U.S. code allows prisoners to file civil lawsuits in U.S. District Court challenging the conditions of confinement in prisons and jails. These lawsuits claim that state correctional officials have deprived persons of their constitutional rights such as adequate medical treatment, protection against excessive force by corrections officers or violence by other inmates, due process in disciplinary hearings, access to law libraries, or freedom of religious expression. In 1991, there were over 25,000 Section 1983 lawsuits filed in federal courts (Sourcebook of Criminal Justice Statistics).

Amendment XIII [1865]

"Section 1: Neither slavery nor involuntary servitude, except as a punishment for crime whereof the party shall have been duly convicted, shall exist within the United States, or any place subject to their jurisdiction."

Abolition of slavery dates from the Emancipation Proclamation of 1863 and the Thirteenth Amendment. This amendment also prohibits "involuntary servitude," which means when an individual is forced to labor for another individual through the use or threatened use of physical or legal coercion (United States v. Kozminski. 487 U.S. 931, 1988). In the United States, there is no constitutional or statutory prohibition against "hard labor," although it may be prohibited under the Eighth Amendment if prison work is beyond the strength of the inmate, endangers their lives, or causes undue pain (Ray v. Mabry, 556 F, 2d 881, 8th Cir. 1977).

Nevertheless, forced labor and involuntary servitude still exist in the United States. Migrant farm workers are forced to perform agricultural work under oppressive conditions in labor camps. According to the U.S. government, these workers are often recruited through force or deceit to work in agriculture, were not informed that they would be charged for food and shelter, and often cannot leave work until they pay off their debts (U.S. Department of State 1994). In addition, vulnerable groups such as undocumented immigrants, mentally ill persons, and children have been held under involuntary servitude on certain occasions in the United States. For example, sweatshops still exist in the United States. In August 1995, a government raid of a sweatshop just outside Los Angeles, found more than 70 Thai workers held against their will, some as long as seven years, and forced to sew garments for well-known companies (Jameson 1999). There have been many more government raids of oppressive working conditions, including a recent discovery of sweatshops in Saipan, a U.S. territory in the Northern Marianas.

Prison Labor

Prison labor is an important indicator of human rights because it is an aspect of coerced or forced labor. There is a proliferation of prison labor in the United States as inmates take jobs ranging from telemarketing to manufacturing license plates, blue jeans, shoes, eyeglasses, lingerie, etc. For example, the Prison Blues company makes jeans at a medium-security prison in Oregon (*Boston Globe* 1998). In 1979, a federal program, Prison Industry Enhancement (PIE) allowed prison enterprises. The number of inmate workers has more than doubled to 2,600 in 35 states over the past six years, with California having one of the most extensive programs (Haynes 1998). Some of these operations are operated by private businesses that lease prison sites for substantially less than the cost of operating their own plants. While these businesses pay the area's prevailing wage, they do not offer medical coverage. Meanwhile, working inmates must pay income tax as well as contribute to room and board, victim-assistance, and family support programs. In addition, currently 19,000 of the 106,000 federal inmates work in industry programs similar to PIE, and make more than 150 products that are sold only to other government agencies (Hallinan 1998). While private prison labor programs keep inmates busy and benefit the state and the companies, they receive much criticism, particularly from labor organizations. While supporting opportunities for prisoners to learn useful trades, organized labor and some human rights groups have condemned the use of convict labor in private sector jobs as a source of cheap and "captive" labor. Critics claim that inmates lack workplace protections and grievance systems, and prison labor sets up incentives for incarceration (Tyson 1999).

Amendment XIV [1868]

"Section 1: All persons born or naturalized in the United States, and subject to the jurisdiction thereof, are citizens of the United States and of the State wherein they reside. No State shall make or enforce any law which shall abridge the privileges or immunities of citizens of the United States; nor shall any State deprive any person of life, liberty, or property, without due process of law; nor deny to any person within its jurisdiction the equal protection of the laws."

The Fourteenth Amendment has been interpreted to apply the protections of the Bill of Rights to the states. It includes provisions of government services and benefits, such as education, employment and housing; legal representation for indigent persons; race discrimination; excessive force on pretrial detainees; redlining; and voting. This amendment also guarantees men and women equality before the law. The U.S. courts interpret the Fourteenth Amendment as imposing different levels of protections. For example, discrimination based on race, religion, and national origin receive the strictest scrutiny and must be justified as necessary to a "compelling government interest" (Korematsu v. United States, 323 U.S. 214, 1944; Brown v. Board of Education, 347 U.S. 483, 1954). Discrimination based on gender, alienage, and birth status (illegitimacy) receive a mid-level or heightened scrutiny, while discrimination based on economic status and property receive a mere rationality test.

Race disparities in prison are one reflection of inequality. African Americans are held in prisons or jails at a higher rate than white people. In 1996, black men were held at a rate of 6,607 per 100,000 adult residents, whereas white men were held at a rate of 944 per 100,000 residents (Appendix 7). Similarly, African American women were held at a rate of 474 per 100,000 residents while white women were held at a rate of 73. These numbers are high particularly because African Americans constitute only 12 percent of the population. There are several reasons for the high rate of African Americans in prisons, including disproportionately high sentences.

Equality in sentencing is a major social justice issue in the United States. For example, African Americans receive higher average sentence lengths than white Americans (Appendix 8). In 1996, for example, African Americans served an average of 91.9 months in prison compared with 48.9 months for whites. The average sentence length for African Americans has consistently increased since 1988 from 63.2 months to 91.9 months in 1996, while the average sentence length for white Americans decreased from 54.2 months in 1988 to 48.9 months in 1996.

Amendment XII [1804]
"But in choosing the President, the votes shall be taken by states, the representation from each State having one vote."

Amendment XV [1870]
"Section 1. The right of citizens of the United States to vote shall not be denied or abridged by the United States or by any State on account of race, color, or previous condition of servitude."

Amendment XIX [19201
"[1] The right of citizens of the United States to vote shall not be denied or abridged by the United State or by any State on account of sex."

Amendment XXIV [1964]
"Section 1. The right of citizens of the United States to vote in any primary or other election for President or Vice President, for electors for President or Vice President, or for Senator or Representative in Congress, shall not be denied or abridged by the United States or any State by reason of failure to pay any poll tax or other tax."

Amendment XXVI [1971]
"Section 1. The right of citizens of the United States, who are eighteen years of age or older, to vote shall not be denied or abridged by the United States or by any State on account of age."

The right to vote is the principle mechanism for participating in the U.S. political system, and hence political participation is one of the strongest indicators of human rights in a democracy. The U.S. Supreme Court's interpretation of the Fourteenth Amendment has resulted in an expansion of voting rights for certain groups over the past century, such as women, African Americans, and non-English speakers. The Voting Rights Act of 1965 was created to eliminate racial discrimination in voting. An amendment to the Act in 1975 extended protections to a large number of "language minorities" (e.g., Native Americans, Asian Americans, Hispanics, etc.). Despite these protections there have been a number of serious setbacks in voting rights in America by white voters who have challenged the creation of a majority black congressional district (See Shaw v. Reno, 61 U.S.L.W. 4818, U.S. June 28, 1993).

Despite our right to vote, only 54.2 percent of Americans voted during the 1996 Presidential election, which has dropped from 59.2 percent in 1976. (Appendix 9). Among women the voting rate was 55.5 percent compared to 52.8 percent among men. Among African Americans, the voting rate was 50.6 percent compared to 56 percent among the white population. The number of American citizens actually voting is pitifully low for one of the largest democracies in the world.

Women and Minorities in Congress

An essential factor in political participation is the demographic composition of public officers. One measurement of an open political process is whether the gender and racial composition of the country is reflected in state and federal legislatures. Although the number of women in Congress has increased slowly, in the 1997-1999 period women held 65 of the 435 seats in the U.S. House of Representatives (15 percent) (Appendix 10). In that same period, women held only 9 out of 100 seats in the U.S. Senate (9 percent) (Appendix 11). In addition, there has never been a woman Speaker of the House or majority or minority leader of the Senate, even though women make up approximately 50 percent of the eligible U.S. voting population (Statistical Abstract, 1998). In comparison, political participation of women in many western countries is fairly high. For example, the United Nations reports that in Sweden and Norway, women comprise 40 percent and 36 percent of the parliament respectively (United Nations Development Report 1998).

Similarly, minority representation in Congress remains low. In the 1997-1999 period, African Americans held only 39 seats in the House (9 percent) and only 1 in the Senate (one percent). That year, there were only 17 Hispanic representatives (4 percent) and no senators. No minority group members serve in the top congressional leadership as Speaker of the House or Senate majority or minority leader, although they do chair certain committees. African Americans and Hispanics make up approximately 12 percent and 10 percent of the eligible voting population respectively.

Political Action Committees (PACs)

Money in politics is an important indicator of human rights because it can undermine the political participation of citizens by not affording equal access to the political process. A factor that impacts the political participation process of the citizenry is the growing political influence of the wealthy, particularly corporate influence through Political Action Committees (PACs) (Appendix 12). Corporate PACs consistently outnumber those connected with labor and other groups. In 1996, there were 1,642 corporate PACs out of

Money in politics is an important indicator of human rights because it can undermine the political participation of citizens by not affording equal access to the political process.

a total of 4,079 (40 percent) compared to only 332 labor PACs (8 percent). PACs spent approximately $430 million in 1995/1996, out of which $130.6 million was spent by corporate PACs alone (30 percent) (Appendix 13).

The concerns surrounding both PACs and calls for campaign finance reform are the vast amounts of money driving the political process in America, with millions of dollars pouring into political campaigns. In a landmark ruling in 1976, the U.S. Supreme Court associated restrictions on money in campaign finance with limiting freedom of speech (Buckley v. Valeo, 424 U.S. 1). Therefore, the Court found that it is constitutional to limit how much individuals and PACs can *contribute* to political candidates ($1,000 limit), but not how much candidates can *spend* in political campaigns. The argument is that limiting spending restricts political speech, but contributions could be capped to prevent a perception of corruption. Nevertheless, unlimited expenditures by political candidates can result in an unfair advantage to those who are already wealthy over those who are not, as well as resulting in significant time spent raising money. At the time of this writing, the U.S. Supreme Court is currently re-visiting this decision.

U.S. Government Impact on Noncitizens

In addition to the private and public sphere human rights discussed above, a comprehensive analysis of human rights must also include the U.S. government's treatment of noncitizens. In the United States, the U.S. Bill of Rights and amendments guarantee certain rights to immigrants and refugees who are within the jurisdiction of the United States, regardless of citizenship. The 1967 U.N. Protocol Relating to the Status of Refugees sets the standard and states that no country shall return a refugee to a country "where his life or freedom would be threatened on account of race, religion, nationality, membership in a particular social group or political opinion" (known as the *non-refoulement* principle). The 1980 Refugee Act brings our country into compliance with its obligations under the Refugee Protocol.

The United States views itself as a land of immigrants, a land with people from diverse cultural, religious, and social backgrounds. Approximately 660,477 immigrants were admitted into the United States in 1998, out of which 54,709 (8 percent) were refugees and political asylees (Appendix 14). The United States is approving fewer applications for asylum. Approved applications for asylum has been falling since 1980 from 55.2 percent approval rate to 20 percent in 1995 (Appendix 15).

In 1996, Congress passed the Illegal Immigration Reform and Immigrant Responsibility Act, which allegedly makes for a more efficient asylum system and prevents abuses by speeding up the asylum process and enhancing enforcement. However, there is much controversy about the "expedited removal" procedure, which is a screening process at U.S. ports of entry to quickly identify and remove individuals who are not entitled to enter the United States. The concern is that this procedure violates non-refoulement principles by potentially jeopardizing valid claims of asylum as candidates are rushed through without proper procedural protections. This process may risk returning refugees to a country where their life can be threatened. In addition, once immigrants are in the United States, they can still face human rights violations. For example, there is legislation on federal and state levels that cut off both legal and undocumented immigrants from public welfare benefits (Stoll 1997). Indigent immigrants also have no right to appointed counsel in deportation proceedings. Therefore, even though the Immigration and Naturalization Service (INS) detainees may be eligible for relief from deportation, they may not be able to obtain the relief. In 1997, over 114,000 aliens were deported from the United States, up from 22,000 in 1987 (Appendix 16).

Immigrant Abuse

There continues to be documented human rights violations against immigrants and refugees in the United States. Border Patrol Agents of the INS have been accused of verbally and physically abusing immigrants (Bailey 1996). One area of abuse is at the U.S./Mexico border. According to a study by the Urban Institute, there are approximately 2.7 million undocumented Mexicans residing in the United States (Rothenberg & Gzesh 1998). Mexicans are the largest group of undocumented immigrants and the INS enforcement efforts are directed disproportionately against them. Although Mexicans have been traveling to the United States for work since the 1800s, current U.S. immigration legislation strengthens the Border Patrol and increases penalties for those entering the country illegally. Although cases of shootings of immigrants at the border have declined, beatings, rough treatment, and sexual and verbal abuse still continue. "Because of flawed complaint, review and disciplinary procedures and poor management, abusive agents are rarely disciplined or prosecuted criminally for their behavior."

Immigrants in INS Detention

The numbers of both legal and undocumented immigrants populating jails and prisons in every state of the United States is growing rapidly. According to Corrections Compendium April 1995, most of them were from Mexico, Cuba, and the Dominican Republic. Government records are not accurate enough to provide reliable statistics on how many are legal, illegal, where they are from etc. However one survey of incarcerated foreign nationals found that, in states where the Department of Corrections record the citizenship, there were approximately 71,294 foreign nationals in U.S. prisons. That means that there were more foreign nationals in U.S. prisons than the total prison populations of Massachusetts, Mississippi, New Mexico, Oregon, Utah, Virginia, Rhode Island, and the District of Columbia combined (Corrections Compendium 1995).[4] The report states that it is surprising so little is known about foreign national inmates, who have unique problems such as language barriers and communication problems. At the time of this writing, the INS announced that it would review thousands of cases of immigrants with criminal histories who have been jailed pending deportation (Pan 1999).

In addition to the number of foreigners in U.S. prisons, there are concerns about detaining asylum seekers in jail. The INS holds more than 60 percent of its 15,000 detainees in local jails throughout the country (Human Rights Watch 1998). By locking them up, many indefinitely, individuals are being punished for seeking asylum, a basic human right. These asylum seekers in jails are subjected to punitive treatment and may be mixed with criminal inmates. Abusive conditions include denial of appropriate medical care, frequent and unexplained transfers to other jails, language problems, excessive or inappropriate discipline, commingling with accused or criminal inmates, isolation from family and friends, and restricted correspondence and visitation policies. Instead of receiving special protection for allegedly fleeing persecution, asylum seekers may face abuse after arriving in this country. In addition, children seeking asylum are also detained by the INS in jail-like conditions for long periods of time (Human Rights Watch 1998). Similarly, a report of women held in a Pennsylvania INS facility found that they were incarcerated indefinitely for months, or even years, when they had committed no crime but to seek protection in the United States (Women's Commission for Refugee Women and Children 1995).

IV. Conclusion

Human rights are a key quality of life concern for all those in the United States. We are all responsible for the protection or violation of human rights, whether it be in the private sphere of the home, in the public arena, or towards noncitizens. This is the essence of democracy. Although our country was founded on human rights principles, has contributed greatly to the development of international human rights laws, has played a special role in the spread of human rights ideas around the world, and has developed among the best federal and state legal safeguards to protect a wide range of human rights, it appears that human rights violations still exist here. Our country's historical leadership on human rights is being challenged by those who want our government to reduce the suffering of people within its jurisdiction.

The Calvert-Henderson Human Rights Indicator correlates with the other indicators in this volume and, through the Human Rights model, provides a framework from which we can view multiple human rights issues in a holistic manner. We realize that the protection or abuse of human rights in the United States cannot be reduced to case law or quantitative data alone. Human rights protections under the law may not be enforced, may not be recorded, credible, or technically accurate given the illegalities.

We are all responsible for the protection or violation of human rights, whether it be in the private sphere of the home, in the public arena, or towards noncitizens.

Therefore, the Calvert-Henderson Human Rights Indicator is theoretically driven, not data driven. However, we recognize that human rights data may be critical to evaluating the level of human rights experienced in a country and have, therefore, selected data to illustrate the existence of human rights protection according to the U.S. government and reputable private sector sources. In subsequent editions, the Calvert-Henderson Human Rights Indicator will analyze the ramifications and circumstances surrounding the reasons for human rights violations in the United States.

ENDNOTES

[1] There are essentially two broad restrictions on the freedom of speech. One restriction is that which does not regulate content, but promotes substantial government interest by the least intrusive means (e.g., a law regulating the distribution of handbills to reduce litter). Another category of restriction is the type of speech. Speech posing "clear and present danger" to public order if that speech is intended to incite or produce imminent lawless action; "fighting words" can be proscribed if the words inflict injury or incite a breach of the peace; obscenity or patently offensive representations of sexual conduct without redeeming value; and some forms of commercial speech so as not to mislead or coerce consumers. See Civil and Political Rights in the United States, U.S. Department of State, July 1994, p. 158.

[2] It should be noted that because of poor cooperation from many law enforcement agencies combined with victim under-reporting, the actual number of cases most likely far exceed those actually reported. For example, in 1994, agencies participating in the hate crime reporting program covered only 58 percent of the population compared with 97 percent for the overall crime reporting system. See "FBI Reports Decline in Hate Crimes in 1994," Klanwatch Intelligence Report, (Montgomery, Alabama), October 1995.

[3] "Three strikes and you're out" laws mandate that any person convicted of three felonies must be sentenced to life without parole. Some states only consider violent felonies, while other states include any felony convictions.

[4] The Corrections Survey states that the estimate of 71,294 incarcerated foreign nationals is a very rough – and probably egregiously low – figure, since there is no accurate means of determining which inmates are indeed U.S. citizens and which are not. The birth country of inmates does not always reflect citizenship.

The United States is a member of the United Nations, the International Labour Organization, and the Organization of American States. The United States generally becomes a party to a treaty by ratification, which commences by the President signing the treaty and submitting it to the U.S. Senate for advice and consent. If two-thirds of the Senate consent, the treaty is returned to the President, who then completes the process by signing the instrumentation of ratification. Generally when the United States ratifies a treaty, it may make a "reservation" stating that unless implementing legislation is passed by Congress, the treaty cannot be implemented in this country. Implementing legislation can take several years.

The United States has ratified the following international human rights treaties:

- International Covenant on Civil and Political Rights (1966). Entered into force for the U.S. on 9/8/92.

- International Convention on the Elimination of All Forms of Racial Discrimination (1965). Entered into force for the U.S. on 11/20/94.

- Convention Against Torture and Other Cruel, Inhuman, and Degrading Punishment (1984). Entered into force for the U.S. on 11/20/94.

- Convention to Suppress the Slave Trade and Slavery (1926) and its Amended Protocol (1953). Entered into force for the U.S. on 3/21/29 and then on 3/7/56.

- Supplementary Convention on the Abolition of Slavery, the Slave Trade and Institutions and Practices Similar to Slavery (1956). Entered into force for the U.S. on 12/6/67.

- Protocol Relating to the Status of Refugees (1967). Entered into force for the U.S. on 11/1/68.

- Inter-American Convention on the Granting of Political Rights to Women (1953). Entered into force for the U.S. on 5/24/76.

Continued

Appendix 1
continued

- Convention on the Political Rights of Women (1953). Entered into force for the U.S. on 7/7/76.

- Convention on the Prevention and Punishment of the Crime of Genocide (1948). Entered into force for the U.S. on 2/23/89.

- Four Geneva Conventions for the Protection of Victims of Armed Conflict (1949). Entered into force for the U.S. on 2/2/56.

- Convention Concerning the Abolition of Forced Labor/ILO Convention No. 105 (1957). Entered into force for the U.S. on 9/25/92.

The United States is being urged by human rights advocates to ratify a number of treaties, including the Convention on the Elimination of All Forms of Discrimination Against Women (1979), the International Covenant on Economic, Social, and Cultural Rights (1966), and the Convention on the Rights of the Child (1989).

Bias-Motivated/Hate Crimes Known to Police by Offense, 1991-1997

Appendix 2

Offenses	1991	%	1992	%	1993	%	1994	%
Murder	12	0.3	17	0.2	16	0.2	13	0.2
Forcible rape	7	0.1	8	0.1	15	0.2	5	0.1
Robbery	119	2.5	172	1.9	161	1.8	126	1.7
Aggravated assault	773	16.3	1,431	16.0	1,452	16.1	1,012	14.0
Burglary	56	1.2	69	0.8	88	1.0	61	0.8
Larceny-theft	22	0.5	36	0.4	61	0.7	47	0.6
Motor vehicle theft	0	0.0	5	-0.1	9	0.1	3	0.1
Arson	55	1.2	47	0.5	53	0.6	63	0.9
Simple assault	796	16.7	1,765	19.8	1,754	19.5	1,324	18.2
Intimidation	1,614	33.9	3,328	37.3	3,056	34.0	2,843	39.1
Destruction/damage/ vandalism of property	1,301	27.4	2,040	22.9	2,294	33	1,758	24.2
Other	-	-	-	-	28	0.3	7	0.1
TOTAL	4,755	100	8,918	100	8,987	100	7,262	100

Offenses	1995	%	1996	%	1997	%
Murder	20	0.2	12	0.1	8	0.08
Forcible rape	12	0.1	10	0.09	9	0.09
Robbery	194	1.9	155	1.4	144	1.5
Aggravated assault	1,268	12.8	1,444	13.4	1,237	12.5
Burglary	96	1.0	140	1.3	111	1.1
Larceny-theft	53	0.5	75	0.7	95	1.0
Motor vehicle theft	5	0.05	7	0.06	7	0.07
Arson	62	0.6	75	0.7	60	0.6
Simple assault	1,796	18.1	1,762	16.4	1,800	18.3
Intimidation	4,048	41.0	4,130	38.5	3,814	38.7
Destruction/damage/ vandalism of property	2,315	23.4	2,874	26.8	2,549	25.8
Other	26	0.2	5	0.04	12	0.1
TOTAL	9,895	100	10,706	100	9,861	100

Source: U.S. Department of Justice, Federal Bureau of Investigation

Appendix 3 **Bias-Motivations in Hate Crimes by Race, Ethnicity, Religion, and Sexual Orientation 1994-1997**

	1994	%	1995	%	1996	%	1997	%
Race	**4,431**	**61.0**	**6,170**	**62.4**	**6,767**	**63.2**	**5,898**	**59.8**
Anti-white	1,269	17.5	1,511	15.3	1,384	12.9	1,267	12.8
Anti-black	2,693	37.0	3,805	38.5	4,469	41.7	3,838	38.9
Anti-American Indian/ Alaskan Native	24	0.3	59	0.6	69	0.6	44	0.4
Anti-Asian/Pacific Islander	269	3.7	484	4.9	527	4.9	437	4.4
Anti-multi-racial group	176	2.4	311	3.1	318	3.0	312	3.2
Ethnicity	**790**	**10.9**	**1,022**	**10.3**	**1,163**	**10.9**	**1,083**	**11.0**
Anti-Hispanic	446	6.1	680	6.9	710	6.6	636	6.4
Anti-Other Ethnicity/ National Origin	344	4.7	342	3.4	453	4.2	447	4.5
Religion	**1,244**	**17.1**	**1,414**	**14.3**	**1,500**	**14.0**	**1,483**	**15.0**
Anti-Jewish	1,088	15.0	1,145	11.6	1,182	11.0	1,159	11.8
Anti-Catholic	19	0.3	35	0.4	37	0.3	32	0.3
Anti-Protestant	31	0.4	47	0.5	80	0.7	59	0.6
Anti-Islamic	17	0.2	39	0.4	33	0.3	31	0.3
Anti-other religions	72	1.0	122	1.2	139	1.3	173	1.8
Anti-multireligious group	14	0.2	25	0.3	27	0.3	26	0.3
Anti-atheism/agnosticism	3	0.05	1	0.01	2	0.01	3	0.03
Sexual orientation	**793**	**10.9**	**1,266**	**12.8**	**1,256**	**11.7**	**1,375**	**13.9**
Anti-male homosexual	567	7.8	915	9.2	927	8.6	912	9.2
Anti-female homosexual	121	1.7	189	1.9	185	1.7	229	2.3
Anti-homosexual	79	0.1	125	1.3	94	0.9	210	2.1
Anti-heterosexual	16	0.2	19	0.2	38	0.4	14	0.1
Anti-bisexual	10	0.1	18	0.2	12	0.1	10	0.1
Multiple Bias	**4**	**0.05**	**23**	**0.2**	**20**	**0.2**	**10**	**0.1**
Disability	**N/A**		**N/A**		**N/A**		**12**	**0.1**
TOTAL	**7,262**	**100**	**9,895**	**100**	**10,706**	**100**	**9,861**	**100**

Source: U.S. Department of Justice, Federal Bureau of Investigation.

**Prisoners Under Sentence of Death (Death Row) by Race
1978-1997**

Appendix 4

Year	Total	White	Non-White
1978	445	261	184
1979	567	344	223
1980	688	418	270
1981	838	488	350
1984	1,420	806	614
1985	1,575	896	679
1986	1,800	1,013	787
1987	1,967	1,128	839
1988	2,117	1,235	882
1989	2,243	1,308	935
1990	2,346	1,368	978
1991	2,466	1,450	1,016
1992	2,575	1,508	1,067
1993	2,727	1,575	1,152
1994	2,905	1,653	1,252
1995	3,064	1,732	1,332
1996	3,242	1,833	1,358
1997	3,335	1,876	1,406

Source: U.S. Bureau of Justice Statistics.

**Prisoner Executions by Civil Authority
1978-1996**

Appendix 5

(Total=357)

Year	Total	White	Black
1978	0	0	0
1979	2	2	0
1980	0	0	0
1981	1	1	0
1982	2	1	1
1983	5	4	1
1984	21	13	8
1985	18	11	7
1986	18	11	7
1987	25	13	12
1988	11	6	5
1989	16	8	8
1990	23	16	7
1991	14	7	7
1992	31	19	11
1993	38	23	14
1994	31	20	11
1995	56	33	23
1996	45	31	14

Note: There were no executions from 1968-1976. Totals exclude executions by military authorities.

Source: U.S. Law Enforcement Assistance Administration and U.S. Bureau of Justice Statistics.

Appendix 6 **Prisoners Under Jurisdiction of State and Federal Correctional Authorities by Race**

Year	Total	White	Black	American Indian/ Alaska Native	Asian/ Pacific Islander	Not known
1978	306,602	157,208	143,376	2,584	699	2,735
1979	314,006	161,642	145,383	2,928	749	3,304
1980	328,695	169,274	150,249	3,011	842	5,319
1981	368,772	190,503	168,129	3,307	1,170	5,663
1982	414,362	214,741	189,610	3,758	1,504	4,749
1983	437,238	225,902	200,216	4,086	1,577	5,457
1984	462,442	239,428	209,673	4,474	2,180	6,687
1986	544,133	274,701	246,833	5,291	1,850	16,458
1987	581,020	291,606	262,958	5,461	1,997	18,998
1988	627,600	308,712	289,462	5,350	2,177	21,899
1989	712,563	343,550	334,952	5,994	2,480	25,587
1990	774,375	369,485	367,122	6,251	2,806	28,711
1991	824,133	385,347	395,245	7,407	3,423	32,711
1993	946,946	431,780	456,570	8,300	5,408	44,888
1994	1,054,774	464,167	501,672	9,283	6,005	73,647
1995	1,126,287	455,021	544,005	10,176	6,483	110,602
1996	1,180,524	478,308	565,549	11,393	7,582	117,692

Source: U.S. Department of Justice, Bureau of Justice Statistics.

Appendix 7 **Rate of Adults Held in Prisons or Jails (per 100,000 adult residents)**

Year	White Male	White Female	Black Male	Black Female
1985	528	27	3,544	183
1986	570	29	3,850	189
1987	594	35	3,943	216
1988	629	41	4,441	257
1989	685	47	5,066	321
1990	711	48	5,161	329
1991	732	51	5,503	346
1992	766	53	5,793	356
1993	797	55	6,032	393
1994	842	61	6,443	426
1995	907	65	6,618	456
1996	944	73	6,607	474

Source: U.S. Department of Justice Statistics.

Average Length of Sentence Imposed on Offenders Sentenced to Incarceration in U.S. District Courts (months)

Appendix 8

Year	White	Black	Other
1988	54.2	63.2	46.8
1989	51.9	65.4	49.9
1990	53.9	77.4	53.8
1992	56.8	84.1	60.8
1994	50.4	83.6	49.9
1996	48.9	91.9	55.9

Note: Offenses include violent offenses, property offenses, drug offenses, and public order offenses.

Source: U.S. Department of Justice, Bureau of Justice Statistics.

Percentage of Population Who Voted During Presidential Election Years

Appendix 9

Year	Total	Male	Female	White	Black
1976	59.2	59.6	58.8	60.9	48.7
1980	59.2	59.1	59.4	60.9	50.5
1984	59.9	59.0	60.8	61.4	55.8
1988	57.4	56.4	58.3	59.1	51.5
1992	61.3	60.2	62.3	63.6	54.0
1996	54.2	52.8	55.5	56.0	50.6

Source: U.S. Bureau of the Census.

Appendix 10 **Number of Congressional Representatives by Sex and Race 1949-1999**

Years	Total Number of Representatives	Female	Black	Asian/Pacific Islander	Hispanic
1949-1951	435	9	2	0	1
1951-1953	435	10	2	0	1
1953-1955	435	12	2	0	1
1955-1957	435	17	3	0	1
1957-1959	435	15	4	1	1
1959-1961	436	17	4	2	1
1961-1963	437	18	4	2	2
1963-1965	435	12	5	1	3
1965-1967	435	11	6	2	3
1967-1969	435	11	5	2	3
1969-1971	435	11	10	2	4
1971-1973	435	15	13	2	5
1973-1975	435	16	16	3	5
1975-1977	435	19	17	4	5
1977-1979	435	20	17	3	5
1979-1981	435	17	17	4	6
1981-1983	435	23	19	5	7
1983-1985	435	24	21	5	10
1985-1987	435	25	21	5	11
1987-1989	435	25	23	6	11
1989-1991	435	31	24	6	10
1991-1993	435	33	27	5	11
1993-1995	435	55	39	6	17
1995-1997	435	59	39	6	17
1997-1999	435	65	39	5	17

Source: Congressional Research Service.

Number of Senators by Sex and Race
1949-1999

Appendix 11

Years	Total Number of Senators	Female	Black	Asian/Pacific Islander	Hispanic
1949-1951	96	1	0	0	1
1951-1953	96	1	0	0	1
1953-1955	96	3	0	0	1
1955-1957	96	1	0	0	1
1957-1959	96	1	0	0	1
1959-1961	98	2	0	1	1
1961-1963	100	2	0	1	1
1963-1965	100	2	0	2	1
1965-1967	100	2	0	2	1
1967-1969	100	1	1	2	1
1969-1971	100	1	1	2	1
1971-1973	100	2	1	2	1
1973-1975	100	0	1	2	1
1975-1977	100	0	1	2	1
1977-1979	100	2	1	3	0
1979-1981	100	1	0	3	0
1981-1983	100	2	0	3	0
1983-1985	100	2	0	2	0
1985-1987	100	2	0	2	0
1987-1989	100	2	0	2	0
1989-1991	100	2	0	6	0
1991-1993	100	3	0	5	0
1993-1995	100	7	1	6	0
1995-1997	100	9	1	6	0
1997-1999	100	9	1	5	0

Source: Congressional Research Service.

Appendix 12 — Number of Political Action Committees by Committee Type

Committee Type	1978	1980	1985	1989	1991	1992	1993	1994	1995	1996
Total	1,653	2,551	3,992	4,178	4,094	4,195	4,210	3,954	4,016	4,079
Corporate	785	1,206	1,710	1,796	1,738	1,735	1,789	1,660	1,674	1,642
Labor	217	297	388	349	338	347	337	333	334	332
Trade/Membership/ Health	453	576	695	777	742	770	761	792	815	838
Non-connected	162	374	1,003	1,060	1,083	1,145	1,121	980	1.020	1,103
Cooperative	12	42	59	59	57	56	56	53	44	41
Corporation without stock	24	56	142	136	136	142	146	136	129	123

Source: U.S. Federal Election Commission.

Appendix 13 — Disbursements by Political Action Committees (millions of dollars)

Type	1979-1980	1981-1982	1983-1984	1985-1986	1987-1988	1989-1990	1991-1992	1993-1994	1995-1996
Total	131.2	190.2	266.8	340.0	364.2	357.6	394.8	388.1	430.0
Corporate	31.4	43.3	59.2	79.3	89.8	101.1	112.4	116.8	130.6
Labor	25.1	34.8	47.5	57.9	74.1	84.6	94.6	88.8	99.8
Trade/Membership/ Health	32.0	41.9	54.0	73.3	83.7	88.1	97.5	94.1	105.4
Non-connected	38.6	64.3	97.4	118.4	104.9	71.4	76.2	75.1	81.3
Cooperative	2.7	3.8	4.5	4.7	4.5	4.8	4.9	4.5	4.2
Corporation without stock	1.3	2.1	4.2	6.4	7.2	7.7	9.2	9.2	8.7

Source: U.S. Federal Election Commission.

Number of Immigrants Admitted to USA in 1989-1998

Appendix 14

Year	Total	Refugees and Asylees
1989	1,090,924	84,288
1990	1,536,483	97,364
1991	1,827,167	139,079
1992	973,977	117,037
1993	904,292	127,343
1994	804,416	121,434
1995	720,461	114,664
1996	915,900	128,565
1997	798,378	112,158
1998	660,477	54,709

Source: U.S. Immigration and Naturalization Service.

Asylum Cases Filed with Immigration and Naturalization Service

Appendix 15

Year	Cases Received	Approved	Percentage Approved	Denied
1980	26,512	1,104	55.2	896
1981	61,568	1,175	26.0	3,346
1982	33,296	3,909	35.0	7,255
1983	26,091	7,215	30.0	16,812
1984	24,295	8,278	20.4	32,344
1985	16,622	4,585	24.4	14,172
1986	18,889	3,359	29.9	7,882
1987	26,107	4,062	54.0	3,454
1988	60,736	5,531	39.2	8,582
1989	101,679	6,942	18.0	31,547
1990	73,637	4,173	14.7	24,156
1991	56,310	2,108	33.6	4,167
1992	103,964	3,919	37.6	6,506
1993	144,166	5,012	21.8	17,979
1994	146,468	8,131	22.0	28,892
1995	154,464	12,454	20.0	14,091
1996	128,190	13,532	-	2,504

Source: U.S. Immigration and Naturalization Service.

Appendix 16   Aliens Deported from the United States

Year	Total
1980	17,341
1981	16,720
1982	14,518
1983	18,232
1984	17,607
1985	21,358
1986	22,302
1987	22,224
1988	23,119
1989	30,425
1990	26,203
1991	33,189
1992	43,649
1993	42,452
1994	45,524
1995	50,672
1996	69,317
1997	114,060

Source: U.S. Immigration and Naturalization Service.

REFERENCES

Amnesty International USA. 1998. *United States of America: Rights for All; Killing with Prejudice: Race and the Death Penalty.* New York (October).

Bailey, Jennifer. 1996. "Abuse and Impunity Along the US/Mexican Border." Human Rights Watch/Americas and Jesuit Refugee Service/USA. *The Mustard Seed.* Washington, D.C. (Fall).

Baldus, David, George Woodworth, and Charles Pulaski. 1990. *Equal Justice and the Death Penalty: A Legal and Empirical Analysis.* Boston: Northeastern University Press.

Corrections Compendium. 1995. "Prison Population Projections." (March).

Death Penalty Information Center. 1996. "Twenty Years of Capital Punishment: A Re-Evaluation." Washington, D.C. (June).

Death Penalty Information Center. 1996. "Facts About Death Penalty." Washington, D.C.

Donnelly, Jack. 1998. *International Human Rights, Second Edition.* Boulder, CO: Westview Press.

Eisler, Riane. 1996. "The History and Future of Human Rights in the United States." California: Center for Partnership Studies.

Hallinan, Joseph T. 1998. "Hard Labor at $7 an Hour: But Is It Right to Turn Inmates Into Employees?" *Boston Globe,* August 23, p. E1.

Haynes, V. Dion. 1998. "Factories Behind Prison Walls: A New Drill for Model Inmates." *Chicago Tribune,* December 29, p. 4.

Henkin, Louis. 1990. *The Age of Rights.* New York: Columbia University Press.

Human Rights Watch and American Civil Liberties Union. 1993. *Human Rights Violations in the United States. New York* (December).

Human Rights Watch. 1997. "Cruel and Unusual: Disproportionate Sentences for New York Drug Offenders." Washington, D.C. (March).

Human Rights Watch. 1998. "Nowhere to Hide: Retaliation Against Women in Michigan State Prisons." Washington, D.C. (September).

Human Rights Watch. 1998. "Locked Away: Immigration Detainees in Jails in the United States." Washington, D.C. (September).

Human Rights Watch. 1998. "United States: Detained and Deprived of Rights: Children in the Custody of the U.S. INS." Washington D.C. (December).

International Covenant on Civil and Political Rights. 1966.

International Covenant on Economic, Social, and Cultural Rights. 1966.

Jameson, Marnell. 1999. "Sweatshop Fire Led to Changes in Workplace." *Los Angeles Times,* September 28, p.4.

Keil, Thomas J. and Vito, Gennaro F. 1995. "Race and the Death Penalty in Kentucky Murder Trials: 1976-1991." *American Journal of Criminal Justice.* University of Louisville. Vol. 20, No. 1.

Keil, Thomas J. and Vito, Gennaro F. "Race and the Death Penalty in Kentucky Murder Trials: 1976-1991: A Study of Racial Bias as a Factor in Capital Sentencing," paper presented at the "Variations in Capital Punishment" panel, Academy of Criminal Justice Science, Chicago, Illinois.

Klanwatch Intelligence Report. 1995. "FBI Reports Decline in Hate Crime in 1994." Montgomery, Alabama (October).

Pan, Philip P. 1999. "INS Shifting Policy on Immigrant Detention." *Washington Post,* August 9, p. A1.

Rothenberg, Daniel, and Gzesh, Susan. 1998. "Open Fields, Closed Doors: A Retrospective of

Mexican Migration to the United States." *The Mustard Seed.* Jesuit Refugee Service/USA. No. 48, Washington D.C. (Summer).

Saul, Stephanie. 1999. "A Record for the Death Penalty?" *Newsday,* August 16, p. A18.

Stoll, David. 1997. "The Immigration Debate." *Borderlines.* Silver City, New Mexico: Interhemispheric Resource Center (April).

Tyson, James. 1999. "The Rise of a Cellblock Workforce." *Christian Science Monitor,* July 12, p.13.

Universal Declaration of Human Rights. 1948.

U.S. Department of State. July 1994. *Civil and Political Rights in the United States: Initial Report of the United States to the UN Human Rights Committee under the International Covenant on Civil and Political Rights.* Washington, D.C.: United States Department of State.

United States Department of Justice, National Institute of Justice, the U.S. Department of Health and Human Services, and the Centers for Disease Control and Prevention. 1998. "Prevalence, Incidence, and Consequences of Violence Against Women: Findings from the National Violence Against Women Survey." NCJ-172837. Washington D.C., p. 7.

United Nations Development Report. 1998. New York: Oxford University Press.

United States General Accounting Office Report to Senate and House Committees on the Judiciary. 1990. "Death Penalty Sentencing: Research Indicates Pattern of Racial Disparities." Vol. 5-6.

Vienna Declaration and Programme of Action. 1993.

Women's Commission for Refugee Women and Children. 1995. "An Uncertain Future, A Cruel Present: Women in INS Detention." New York (September).

Chapter 11

Income Indicator

by Lawrence Mishel, Ph.D.

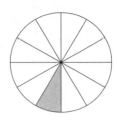

I. Introduction

Any quality of life assessment will include indicators of economic well-being. For this purpose, however, measures of aggregate economic growth (Gross Domestic Product) and of the "macroeconomy" (inflation, unemployment, and productivity) are limited. For one, they exclude important nonmonetary components of well-being such as leisure. Second, aggregate measures do not take account of living arrangements; since most people live in households or families that share income it is the growth of income in these units that matter to their well-being. Third, growing income inequality over the last 25 years has meant that the incomes of typical working families have not fared as well as the "average" family. This is because averages reflect income growth at the very top as well as at the very bottom of the income scale. As an illustration of the degree to which "averages" conceal important information, consider the situation of a person with one foot in a bucket of boiling water and the other foot in a bucket of ice water – this person is "on average" comfortable. That is, one must look underneath the "average" or aggregate to understand how the standard of living for the vast majority is faring.

The Calvert-Henderson Income Indicator focuses on trends in the standard of living as reflected in monetary measures of family income. In particular, the trends in the level and distribution of family income are examined and explained (Section III), with a particular focus on what has been the key determinant of family income trends, the changes in the level and distribution of hourly wages (Section IV). An explanation of stagnant and unequal wage growth is presented in Section V. Other aspects of living standard trends are reviewed elsewhere in this volume. The Calvert-Henderson Income model, the framework for the analysis in this indicator, is reviewed in Section II.

II. The Income Model

The Calvert-Henderson Income model describes the relationship of the various determinants of economic well-being, at least as reflected in monetary income. The unit of analysis is a living unit, either a *family* (a group of two or more legally related persons) or the more inclusive notion of a *household* (a family, a single person living alone, or a group of unrelated individuals residing together). The Income Indicator focuses on families but the findings reported would characterize households as well.

It is useful to separately identify *income* and *wealth* as contributors to economic well-being. *Income* is the money received from wages or salaries, pensions, government cash assistance (e.g., welfare, Social Security), interest, dividends, and other sources. For nearly all families, their ability to purchase what they need is based almost entirely on their annual income. Families, however, can also draw upon their *wealth,* or net worth. Based on savings, gifts, investments, and inheritances, families can accumulate houses, bank accounts, stocks, businesses, and other assets. Of course, families also accumulate debts, including mortgages, credit card loans, and other "liabilities." A family's wealth, therefore, needs to be considered in terms of its net worth, the difference between its assets and its liabilities.

Wealth is important for two reasons: One is that it generates income (capital gains from stock, interest income, etc.) and services (the benefits one receives from having a house to live in or a car to drive). Second, and perhaps more important, a family's wealth allows it to contend with financial emergencies, such as illness or unemployment, and provide for future needs, such as retirement income or college expenses for children. This indicator limits its scope to income trends. It should be noted, however, that wealth is even more unevenly distributed than income, that wealth-holding has become more unequal since the early 1980s, that a large portion of families (40 percent or so) have little or no wealth, and that the wealth of the typical (median) family has not grown since the early 1980s (Mishel and Bernstein 1997; Wolff 1996).

For most families, the amount of income they receive is almost entirely determined by their employment income, the amount of wage or salary income received in the labor market. As the Income model indicates, wage and salary income (labor market income) is determined both by how much paid work a family performs and by the hourly pay received for that work, including both wages (and salaries) and benefits (such as health insurance and pensions). The amount a family works, of course, depends on how many members work, how many hours each employed person works (based on hours per week and weeks of employment) and whether family members experience spells of unemployment or underemployment (such as working part-time when wanting a full-time job). The pay workers receive not only depends on their skills and education but also whether they face gender or race discrimination, have a union, work in a high-paid industry, or work at the minimum wage level.

Income other than labor market income is important for certain segments of the population. Some low-income families rely on government cash transfer programs (welfare) or noncash assistance (food stamps). These are considered "means-tested" programs, meaning that only people with a certain low-income level are eligible. In contrast, there are non-means-tested government transfers such as Social Security, which is provided to senior citizens based on prior earnings but is received by both high- and low-earning

Calvert-Henderson Income Model

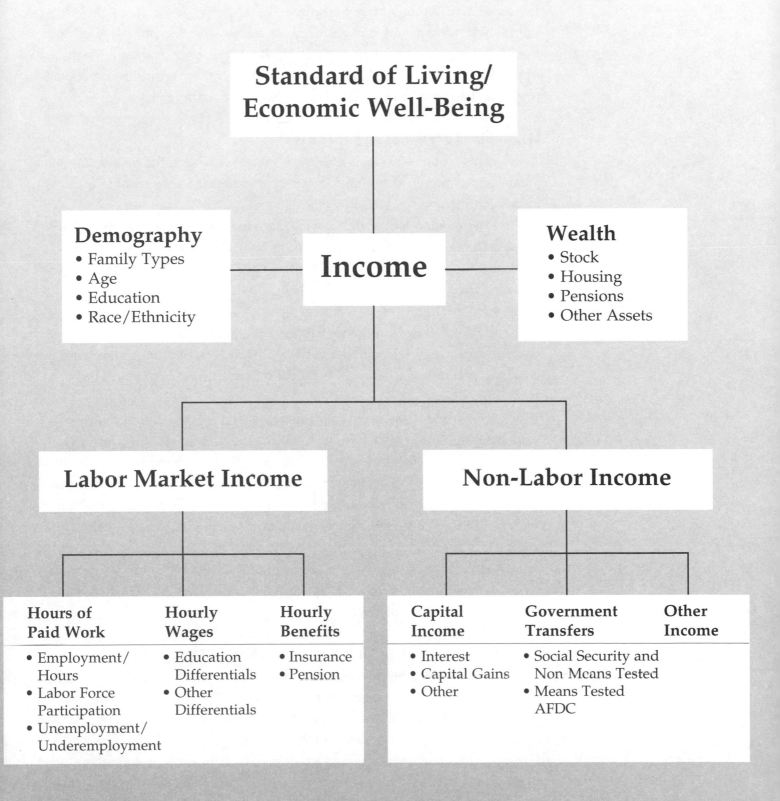

**Standard of Living/
Economic Well-Being**

Demography
- Family Types
- Age
- Education
- Race/Ethnicity

Income

Wealth
- Stock
- Housing
- Pensions
- Other Assets

Labor Market Income

Non-Labor Income

Hours of Paid Work	Hourly Wages	Hourly Benefits	Capital Income	Government Transfers	Other Income
• Employment/ Hours • Labor Force Participation • Unemployment/ Underemployment	• Education Differentials • Other Differentials	• Insurance • Pension	• Interest • Capital Gains • Other	• Social Security and Non Mcans Tested • Means Tested AFDC	

workers. Last, some families, particularly those with the highest income, receive income generated by the assets they hold – "capital income," such as capital gains, interest, and dividends.

There are noneconomic, or demographic, factors that also affect the level and distribution of family income. For instance, a shift to a younger population or more single-parent families tends to lead to more low-income families and more income inequality. Higher levels of education have the opposite effect by raising income levels, although there would be no impact on the distribution of income unless disparities in education grow.

III. Trends in Family Income

This section examines how the economy, through the production of jobs, wages, and returns on investment, has generated slow growth and increasing inequality in family incomes.

The median family (those with more income than half of all families but less than the other half – a "middling family") has fared poorly in the 1990s: for the first time in the post-war period, family income fell four years in a row, declining each year from 1989 to 1993. The initial decline was attributable to the recession that began in 1990, but the median continued to fall as the recovery got under way in 1992. Median family income finally responded to overall growth between 1993 and 1996, but the median family was still $990 less well off in 1996 than it was at the peak of the last business cycle, in 1989.

This trend is disturbing for several reasons. First, although it is not surprising that incomes fell as unemployment rose between 1990 and 1992, the amount of the decline is greater than would be expected from a rise in the unemployment rate from 5.5 percent to 7.4 percent. Second, it is unique in the post-war period to have median family income fall during a recovery year, as it did in 1992-1993 as unemployment fell, average incomes rose, and gross domestic product expanded. The $990 fall in median family income from 1989 to 1996 represents a 2.3 percent decline. However, after two more years of growth from 1996 to 1998, family incomes grew 6.4 percent to surpass the income level of 1989.

The 1989-1996 period has also seen an expansion in the growth of income inequality, a trend that began in earnest in the late 1970s. While incomes fell (or rose more slowly) for all family types and for families throughout the income distribution, the pattern of decline did not slow the growth of inequality. Those at the lower end of the income scale lost ground at an even more rapid pace than in the previous decade, while the richest 5 percent of families continued to experience income growth, though at a slower rate.

Why have income trends continued to be so negative in the 1990s? Along with overall slow growth, the primary reason is the continuing wage deterioration among middle- and low-wage earners, now joined by white-collar and even some groups of college-educated workers. Another key factor in understanding recent income trends is the contribution of working wives.

In the 1980s, many families compensated for falling hourly compensation, which was particularly steep for male workers, by working more hours (either through more family members working or through longer hours by those employed). This strategy – working longer for less – is most notable among families with children, in part because these families tend to have more potential workers. In fact, in the absence of increased hours and earnings by working wives in married-couple families with children in the 1980s, the incomes of the bottom 60 percent of families would have fallen.

In the 1990s, however, there was a slowdown in the growth (for some, even a decline) of hours and earnings among working wives in families with children, particularly among low- and middle-income women. Unlike the prior decade, wives' contributions were no longer able to offset the lower earnings of husbands, whose wages continued to fall, for all but the top 5 percent. By 1994, all but the top 5 percent would have experienced flat or declining incomes in the absence of wives' work. And even with wives' contributions, middle-class incomes fell.

Another major factor fueling growing inequality in the 1980s and 1990s was the acceleration of capital-income growth due to high real interest rates, high profitability, and the stock market boom, all of which primarily benefited the richest families. For example, the capital income of families in the top one percent doubled between 1979 and 1989. In contrast, hourly wages and fringe benefits, which provide support for most families, grew more slowly than inflation. Inequality among wage earners also rose as real wages rose among high-income groups but fell among the broad middle class and lower-income groups.

The large increases in the capital incomes of the rich result in large part from the increase in the rate of profit, or the return to capital holdings. Profit rates continue to soar in the 1990s, but these gains have not led to increased investment in capital stock, nor have they been accompanied by increases in efficiency, as measured by productivity growth until 1999. Their main effect has been to increase the incomes of the richest families at the expense of the broad working class.

The following sections provide greater detail on the character of and explanation for the slow and unequal growth of family incomes.

Family Income Growth

Income growth over the last two business cycles – 1979-1989 and 1989-1996 (the latest data are for 1996) – was slow and the gains were unequally distributed. Appendix 1 shows changes in family income, adjusted for changes in consumer prices, in various cyclical peak (or low-unemployment) years since World War II. The data examine income changes from business-cycle peak to business-cycle peak in order to eliminate the distortion caused by the fact that incomes fall significantly in a recession and then recover in the subsequent upswing.

Family income increased substantially in the two decades immediately following World War II (1947-1967). During that time, median family income increased by more than $14,000, for an annual rate of growth of 2.8 percent. Family incomes continued to grow into the early 1970s, but since 1973 have risen slowly. In 1989, the median family's income was about $1,000 greater than it was in 1979, translating into growth of just 0.4 percent per year from 1979 to 1989, or only two-thirds of the sluggish 0.6 percent annual growth of the 1973-1979 period and only one-seventh the rate of the post-war years prior to 1973.

The recession that began in 1990 and ended in 1991 (or in 1992 in terms of high unemployment) significantly reduced incomes through 1993 (see Appendix 2). Despite income growth from 1993-1996, the median family income in 1996 was 2.3 percent, or $990, below its 1989 level. The 1989-1996 income decline appeared to reflect more than the unemployment accompanying a normal business-cycle downturn. First, it was large, considering the less-than-average recessionary increase in unemployment, up 2.1 percent (from 5.3 percent to 7.4 percent). Second, the income decline reflected several ongoing and new structural shifts in income growth, such as the falloff in wages among white-collar and college-educated workers that preceded the recession, continuing reductions in blue-collar wages, and a slowdown in labor-force growth.

The fact that the median income had yet to return by 1996 to its pre-recessionary peak is historically unique. Typically, job growth, falling unemployment, and increasing productivity – all of which occurred in the recovery that began in 1991 – would have helped to return the median family income to its previous level.

The stagnation of family income over the last few decades has occurred among families of every race, every age group, and every type (single-parent, married couples). For instance, the median income among white families grew by 0.5 percent annually over the 1979-1989 period (falling in the 1989-1996 period), far more slowly than the 2.8 percent annual growth over the 1947-1967 period (see Appendix 3). Black family income grew faster than that of white families in the 1990s but lagged by comparison to the 1970s and 1980s. Hispanic family income grew the least over this period.

Married-couple families with the female partner in the paid labor force saw better income growth since 1973 (Appendix 4) than other married-couple families or single-parent families (male-headed or female-headed). Nevertheless, each type of family experienced far slower income growth after 1973 than in the pre-1973 period. In particular, the growth in income from 1989 to 1996 was negative or very modest (the 0.3 percent annual growth for couples with the female partner in the labor force) for every type of family. This suggests that changes in the composition of the family have not driven the trend towards faltering incomes.

Growing Inequality of Family Income

The vast majority of American families have experienced either modest income growth or an actual erosion in their living standards over the 1989-1996 period, while the small minority of upper-income families had substantial income growth. The result has been an increase in inequality such that the gap between the incomes of the well-off and those of everyone else is larger now than at any point in the post-war period. The rich have gotten richer, low-income and even poor families are more numerous and are poorer than they have been in decades, and the middle has been "squeezed."

Appendix 5 presents information on the share of all family income received by families at different points in the income distribution. Families have been divided into fifths, or "quintiles," of the population, and the highest income group has been further divided into the top 5 percent and the next 15 percent. The 20 percent of families with the lowest incomes are considered the "lowest fifth," the next 20 percent of families are the "second fifth," and so forth. The appendix also shows the trend in the "Gini ratio," a standard measure of inequality wherein higher numbers reveal greater inequality. Because the Census Bureau raised the "top-codes" (i.e., the highest income levels it would record) in 1994, income shares beyond that year are less comparable to those of prior years. Estimates suggest that, in the 1989-1995 period, perhaps half of the increase in inequality at the top of the income scale is due to this change.

The upper 20 percent received 46.8 percent of all income in 1996. The top 5 percent received more of total income, 20.3 percent, than the families in the bottom 40 percent, who received just 14.2 percent. In fact, the 1996 share of total income in each of the three lowest-income fifths (i.e., the bottom 60 percent of families) was smaller than in 1947. Income in the United States is distributed far more unequally than in other industrialized countries (Gottschalk and Smeeding 1997).

The 1980s was a period of sharply increasing income inequality, reversing the trend toward less inequality over the post-war period into the 1970s. Between 1979 and 1989, the bottom 80 percent lost income share and only the top 20 percent gained. Moreover, the 1989 income share of the upper fifth, 44.6 percent, was far greater than the share it received during the entire post-war period and even higher than the 43 percent received in 1947. Even among the rich, the growth in income was skewed to the top: between 1979 and 1989, the highest 5 percent saw their income share rise 2.1 percentage points (from 15.3 percent to 17.9 percent), accounting for the bulk of the 2.9 percentage-point total rise in the income share of the upper fifth.

The increase in inequality continued unabated over the 1989-1996 period. For example, the share received by the top 5 percent grew from 17.9

percent in 1989 to 20.3 percent in 1996 (recall that perhaps half of this increase is due to lifting the top-code, a statistical artifact).

The increase in the income gap between upper- and lower-income groups is illustrated in Appendix 6, which shows the ratio of the average incomes of families in the top 5 percent to the average incomes of those in the bottom 20 percent from 1947 to 1996. The gap between the top and the bottom incomes fell from 1947 to 1979 but grew to a historic high of 19.1 percent by 1996, reversing three decades of lessening inequality.

Another way of viewing this recent surge in income inequality is to compare the "income cutoff" (the income of the best-off family in each group) of families by income group, as in Appendix 7. By focusing on this measure, we are able to discuss income gains and losses for complete groupings of families (e.g., the bottom 40 percent). Over the early post-war period, from 1947 to 1973, there was even income growth across the income spectrum. From 1947 to 1967, for instance, the growth in the top value in each fifth ranged from the 2.5 percent annual pace obtained by the top 5 percent to the 2.9 percent annual pace obtained by those in the second fifth. Because incomes grew slightly faster for lower- and middle-income families from 1947 through 1967, there was a general decline in income inequality, as shown by the falling Gini ratio in the previous appendix.

The pattern of income growth since 1973 has been far more uneven and far slower than in the earlier period. From 1973 to 1979 the fastest income growth was the 1.3 percent annual growth among the top 5 percent of families, which, though modest, was nearly twice the 0.6 percent to 0.5 percent annual income growth among the first and second fifths. Income cut-offs continued to grow slowly in the 1979-1989 period, but the pattern of growth was even more unequal. The families with the lowest incomes actually lost ground from 1979 to 1989 (incomes fell 0.3 percent annually), while the top 5 percent accelerated to a 1.5 percent annual rate. In the most recent period, 1989-1996, growth was flat on average, but inequality continued to grow. The bottom 40 percent of families lost 0.5 percent and 0.4 percent per year, while the top 5 percent gained 0.3 percent.

Appendix 8 reveals the unequal annual growth of average incomes over the full post-war period. The top panel, covering the years 1947-1973, shows strong and even growth. The bottom panel reveals the highly unequal nature of growth in the 1973-1996 period.

Sources of Income

The fortunes of individual families depend heavily on the sources of their incomes: wage and salary income, capital income, or government assistance. To understand changes in the structure of family income one needs to track the trends in these various types of income.

Appendix 9 presents data that show the sources of income for families in each income group in 1989. The top fifth received a larger share of its income (13.8 percent) from financial assets (capital) compared to the other 80 percent of the population. For instance, the top 1 percent received 41.0 percent of its income from financial assets. The other income groups in the upper 10 percent received from 12 percent to 19 percent of their income from capital. In contrast, the bottom 80 percent of families relied on capital income for less than 8 percent of their income in 1989.

Those without access to capital income depend either on wages (the broad middle) or on government transfers (the bottom) as their primary source of income. As a result, the cutback in government cash assistance primarily affects the income prospects of the lowest 40 percent of the population, but particularly the bottom fifth. For instance, roughly 40 percent of the income of families in the bottom fifth is drawn from government cash assistance programs (e.g., Unemployment Insurance, Social Security, Supplemental Security Income). The income prospects of families in the 20th to 99th percentile, on the other hand, depend primarily on the level and distribution of wages and salaries.

Thus, to understand changes in income at the bottom of the income scale one must examine changes in both wage and salary income and in government transfers. At the other end, incomes at the very top are set by both labor income and capital income. For the vast middle, however, incomes are set by what happens to labor income.

The Role of Demographic Factors

Some analysts have attributed the growth of income inequality to various demographic factors, such as more single-parent households. In fact, it is changes in the structure of the economy rather than demography that have driven income inequality. This can be seen in Appendix 10, which presents an analysis of the impact of changes in a number of demographic factors on the growth of median household income in the 1970s and 1980s. The factors considered are the age (are they younger?) and race (more minorities?) of households, the types of households (more single persons or single-parent households?), and the level of education. Two conclusions stand out. First is that demographic change *lowered* median income in the 1970s (by $1,486) but raised it in the 1980s ($658). Therefore, demographic shifts are in no way responsible for the income problems of the 1980s and probably not a factor in the 1990s. Second, even the most adverse demographic shift – to more single-parent or female-headed households – was less adverse in the 1980s than in the 1970s, -$1,417 versus -$2,548. It follows that the continued shift towards female-headed households cannot explain why income problems that were not present in the 1970s emerged in the 1980s. As the Income Model shows, if demographic factors were not driving these trends then structural changes, often policy driven, in wage and salary income and other types of income (interest, capital gains, government transfers) are the primary factors driving the process.

Appendix 11 presents direct evidence that changes in family composition have not been the important factor in the growth of recent income inequality. As the first column indicates, the growth of income inequality (as measured by the Gini ratio) was much greater over the 1979-1993 period than in the 1969-1979 period while inequality fell over the 1959-1969 period. Was this faster growth of inequality after 1979 driven by a shift in family composition to more single-parent (or female-headed) families? The second column in Appendix 11 shows the effect of family composition changes on the growth of inequality in each period. As with the analysis above, family composition changes have been a force for growing inequality, but a rather steady force over the entire period from 1969 to 1993. Thus, the faster growth of inequality after 1979 reflects a greater impact of other causes (economic factors) rather than demographic shifts. In fact, the big story is that "economic factors" were leading to *lesser* inequality in the 1960s but were a force for *greater* inequality after 1979. It is for this reason that the next part of this chapter focuses on the growth of wage inequality.

Working Harder for Less

Family-earnings growth has not only been slow and unequal, it has also come increasingly from greater work effort – from a rise in the number of earners per family and in the average weeks and weekly hours worked per earner.

The primary source of the increased work effort was women, including many with children. Since there has also been a fall in real wages for men and for some groups of women the result has been increases in annual earnings primarily through more work rather than through higher hourly wages.

This trend is troublesome for several reasons. Depending on increased work effort as the primary source of income growth is self-limiting, because it can only go on until all adult (or even teen) family members are full-time, full-year workers. Second, there are significant costs and problems associated with this type of growth, one of the most significant being the lack of adequate, affordable child care.

The problem is not that more women or mothers are working but that they are doing so because it is the only way to maintain family incomes in the face of lower real wages. Increased work elicited through falling real wages is a sign of poor performance of the economy. In addition, families are clearly worse off and family life suffers if, to obtain higher incomes, they must work more hours rather than rely on regular pay increases.

Married-couple families (76.3 percent of all families in 1996, Appendix 4) are most able to increase income through greater work effort because they have two potential adult workers. Single-parent families and individuals, however, can only increase work effort by having the adult work more weekly hours and/or more weeks in a year. It is for this reason that we focus first on the greater work hours of married couples with children.

The increase in family work effort is documented in Appendix 12, which shows the annual hours worked by families according to their income fifth. There was a steady increase in family hours worked in the 1980s (0.5 percent annually) and a drop in the 1990s (-0.1 percent annually), with the largest increases among married couples with children (0.7 percent annually over 1979-1989 and 0.4 percent annually over 1989-1996).

Which types of families have been increasing their work effort the most? Work hours increased among families in all income fifths, but the fastest growth has been among middle-income married-couple families in the second and middle-income fifths. For instance, a middle-income married-couple family with children worked 3,232 hours in 1979, the equivalent of having 1.55 full-time workers (at 2,080 annual hours). By 1996, these middle-income families were working 3,762 hours, the equivalent of 1.81 full-time workers, 530 more hours per year than in 1979.

Note that this growth in family work hours over the last two decades is greater than the growth of family income. For instance, middle-income families (with children) increased their hours by 11.7 percent from 1979 to 1989 but saw only a 4.2 percent growth in income (see Mishel and Bernstein 1997, Table 1.25). Similarly, hours have increased faster than income in the 1990s, as middle incomes grew slowly while hours grew 0.9 percent per year. It is on this basis that families are considered to be working more for less. This dynamic can be considered to be a troubling "quality" of growth, i.e., that growth is being driven by more work rather than higher hourly pay.

The Role of Taxation

The standard of living of middle- and low-income families can be affected by the amount of taxes they pay either because tax rates increase (with presumably no increase in government services) or because the distribution of the tax burden is shifted onto them. Thus, it is a key issue in the analysis of income growth and income inequality to ascertain how much of the changes affecting middle- and low-income families is due to changes in pre-tax incomes or changes in taxes that put a "wedge" between pre-tax and after-tax income.

A supposed increase in taxation is one basis for the claim that "big government" is the problem behind faltering living standards. In fact, federal tax rates on middle-income families are no higher now than in 1977, as seen in Appendix 13. This graph shows the trend in "effective federal tax rates," based on a Congressional Budget Office analysis of the percent of their income that a family pays in all federal taxes, including income, payroll, excise, and corporate income taxes. Appendix 13 also shows that taxes for the top one percent were cut considerably from 1977 to 1989 but that their tax rate was increased over the 1989-96 period. Tax rates on the lowest fifth of families were reduced over the 1989-96 period, the result of the increased generosity of the Earned Income Tax Credit (EITC).

Appendix 13 also shows that the federal tax system as a whole is "progressive," meaning that tax rates are higher on families with higher incomes. This progressivity is almost entirely due to the fact that the federal income tax is steeply progressive, as seen in Appendix 14. In 1996, the top one percent of families paid 24.4 percent of their income in federal income taxes while the middle fifths paid 6.1 percent of their income in federal income taxes. The bottom fifth actually received (from the EITC) more than they paid in federal taxes.

One can believe that the federal tax, and specifically the income tax, system should be more or less progressive. However, it is a basic fact that there is progressivity to the basic system. One can also believe that federal taxes are too high or too low. However, it is a basic fact that the reason for the slow growth in family income is what has happened to pre-tax incomes, since middle- and low-income families did not pay a greater share of their income to the federal government in 1996 than in 1977 (there was a slight increase to state and local taxes). Likewise, the shifts in the income distribution are almost entirely due to a growing inequality of pre-tax incomes rather than a change in the distribution of taxes (see Mishel and Bernstein 1997, Table 2.5). This finding further motivates the identification of changes in the distribution of wages as the key determinant of growing wage inequality (see Parts IV and V below).

Poverty

One last topic in the area of income distribution deserves special attention, the trends in poverty over the last two decades. According to the Census Bureau, any family of four (two adults, two children) that had an income less than $16,036 in 1996 is considered "poor." There are a variety of other ways to measure poverty, some of which would show higher or lower poverty rates than that shown by the Census Bureau (see National Research Council 1995 and Mishel and Bernstein 1997, Chapter 6, for a discussion). All measures of poverty, however, show the same trend over time and therefore our use of Census Bureau data does not drive our findings.

Appendix 15 presents the trends in the poverty rate over the 1959-1996 period. Poverty declined steadily over the 1959-1996 period overall and among both white and black families. This was the period when "a rising tide lifted all the boats," meaning economic growth led to lower poverty.

Since the late seventies there has been no further progress in reducing poverty. Among whites, poverty has grown over the last two decades, rising from 9.0 percent in 1979 to 11.2 percent in 1996. There was an even larger growth in poverty among Hispanics, growing from 21.8 percent to 29.4 percent. Among blacks, however, poverty fell over the 1979-1996 period.

It is noteworthy that poverty has failed to decline over the last two decades despite growth in the economy. A higher tide no longer lifts the rowboats as well as the yachts. This cannot be explained by changes in culture or the growth of female-headed households or out-of-wedlock births. These demographic factors have been present and growing for many decades. The factors that have changed are the way the economy distributes its rewards, an increased inequality of market-based incomes such as wages, and the failure of government transfer programs to offset poverty-inducing economic trends (Mishel and Bernstein).

Wealth

Average wealth per household has grown about 2.1 percent per year in the 1990s, but the growth has not been evenly distributed. The distribution of wealth is even more concentrated at the top than is the distribution of income, with the top one percent of households controlling 38.5 percent of all wealth, compared to 14.4 percent of all household income in 1995. As with the income distribution, the wealth distribution has become more uneven since 1983. The share of all wealth held by the upper 1 percent grew from 33.8 percent in 1983 to 39.1 percent in 1997 (Mishel, Bernstein, and Schmitt 1998).

The real value of financial assets, which are held in highly concentrated form by a relatively small share of the population, increased 3.8 percent per year between 1989 and 1997, largely reflecting the prolonged increase in the value of the stock market. Over the same period, the value of nonfinancial assets, which include real estate and are generally more widely held, *fell* at a 1.9 percent annual rate. As a result, the inflation-adjusted value of the wealth held by the middle fifth of the population declined about $1,600 between 1989 and 1997 and was no higher than in 1983. Over roughly the same period, the share of households with zero or negative wealth (families with negative wealth owe more than they own in assets) increased from 15.5 percent to 18.5 percent of all households. Almost one-third (31.3 percent) of black households had zero or negative wealth in 1995.

The stock market boom of the 1980s and 1990s has not enriched working families for the simple reason that most working families do not own much stock. While the share of households owning stock has risen in the 1990s, by 1995 almost 60 percent of households still owned no stock in any form, including mutual funds. Moreover, many of those new to the stock market have only small investments there. Fewer than one-third of all households, for example, had stock holdings greater than $5,000. In the same year, almost 90 percent of the value of all stock was in the hands of the best-off 10 percent of households. Not surprisingly, then, wealth projections through 1997 suggest that 85.8 percent of the benefits of the increase in the stock market between 1989 and 1997 went to the richest 10 percent of households.

IV. Wage Trends

Wage trends have been the primary determinant of the slow growth in income and the greater income inequality experienced in recent years. This should not be surprising, since wages and salaries make up roughly three-fourths of total family income; the proportion is even higher among the broad middle class. This section examines what has happened to the wage structure and why wages continue to deteriorate for most workers throughout most of the 1990s (the data presented goes to 1995).

The widespread deterioration of wages that began in the 1980s has continued over the current business cycle from 1989 to 1995. The deterioration of wages over the 1989-1995 period has been broad, encompassing the bottom 80 percent of men and the bottom 60 percent of women. The decline in the median wage of women workers in the 1990s represents a reversal from the 1980s, when the median woman's wage grew modestly at 0.5 percent per year.

Many high-wage workers, particularly men, have failed to see real wage improvements in recent years. Male white-collar wages, including those for managers and technical workers, have declined, and the wages of male college graduates have stagnated and remain lower than their level in the mid-1980s or early 1970s. The wages of new college graduates have declined sharply among both men (-9.5 percent) and women (-7.7 percent) over the 1989-1995 period, indicating that each year's graduating class is accepting more poorly paying jobs.

The deterioration of wages among noncollege-educated workers, who make up 75 percent of the workforce, has continued in the 1990s at a somewhat faster pace than in the 1980s. Moreover, the wages earned by new high school graduates continued to decline in the 1989-1995 period, as it did in the 1979-1989 period. For instance, the entry-level wages of high school graduates in 1995 were 27.3 percent and 18.9 percent less for young men and women respectively than in 1979.

What is driving this widespread erosion of wages? Not poor productivity performance: productivity has been growing more than 1 percent per year since 1979, and positive productivity cannot explain falling real wages. Growth in benefits, particularly health benefits, is not responsible, since the trend in compensation (wages and benefits) has paralleled that of wages (see Mishel and Bernstein 1997, Chapter 3) in recent years.

There is no "smoking gun," or single factor, that can explain all or even most of the shift in the wage structure. However, a number of factors, in total, seem to account for most of the shifts. Significant institutional shifts, such as a severe drop in the value of the minimum wage and deunionization, explain one-third of the growing wage inequality among prime-age workers, and the expansion of low-wage service-sector employment has perhaps contributed one-fifth. Similarly, the increasing globalization of the economy – immigration, offshore outsourcing, capital mobility and trade – has created more wage inequality, explaining, in my judgment, from 15 percent to 25 percent of the total. Together, the combined effects of industry shifts and globalization (which overlap and are not cumulative) can conserv-atively account for another 25-35 percent of the growth of wage inequality.

The notion that the growth of wage inequality reflects primarily a technology-driven increase in demand for "educated" or "skilled" workers is flawed. There is evidence that the overall impact of technology on the wage and employment structure was no greater in the 1980s or 1990s than in the 1970s. Moreover, skill demand and technology have little relationship to the growth of within-group wage inequality (i.e., inequality among workers with similar levels of experience and education), which was responsible for a significant part of the overall growth of wage inequality in the 1980s. Technology has been and continues to be an important force, but there was no "technology shock" in the 1980s or 1990s, and no ensuing demand for "skill" that could not be satisfied by the continuing expansion of the educa-tional attainment of the workforce.

The late 1990s saw a "bidding up" of the wages of "more-skilled" and "more-educated" workers. Yet the wages of many college graduates and white-collar workers, especially men, had fallen each year since the mid-1980s and were stagnant over the 1989-1995 period. Moreover, it is mislead-ing to label as "less educated" or "less skilled" a group constituting three-fourths of the workforce (and whose educational status ranges from high school dropouts to holders of associate-college degrees).

More Hours and Stagnant Wages

To understand changes in wage trends it is important to distinguish between trends in annual, weekly, and hourly wages. Trends in annual wages, for instance, are driven by changes in both hourly wages and the amount of time spent working (weeks worked per year and hours worked per week). Likewise, weekly wage trends reflect changes in hourly pay and weekly hours.

Appendix 16 illustrates the importance of distinguishing between annual, weekly, and hourly wage trends. The annual wage and salary of the average worker in inflation-adjusted terms grew 0.4 percent annually between 1989 and 1994. However, much of this growth was due to longer working hours. For instance, the average worker worked 1,740 hours in 1994, 26 more – the equivalent of half an hour more each week – than the 1,714 hours worked in 1989. Correspondingly, that 0.4 percent yearly growth in annual wages was driven by a 0.3 percent yearly growth in annual hours and a minimal 0.1 percent yearly growth in real hourly wages. Any wage analysis that focuses on annual wages would miss the fact that most of the growth from 1989 to 1994 was due to more work rather than higher hourly wages.

The 1979-1989 period was also characterized by growing hours of work (up 94, from 1,620 to 1,714), while the real hourly wage was stagnant – growing 24 cents over 10 years, or 0.2 percent annually. The 0.6 percent year-ly growth in hours worked was driven by the increase in the average work year to 44.5 weeks from 42.7 weeks, a 0.4 percent annual growth, and a slight increase in the hours of the average workweek, to 38.5 hours. In the 1973-1979 period, when hourly wages were essentially flat (falling 0.1 percent annually) and annual hours grew slowly (0.2 percent), the annual wage grew only 0.1 percent. In contrast, real hourly wages rose 2.9 percent annually between 1967 and 1973, while annual hours declined 0.4 percent. Thus, the post-1973 trend of greater work effort coupled with modestly rising or falling wages replaced a trend of strong real annual wage growth based on higher real hourly wages and reduced work time.

Productivity growth (measured as the growth of output per hour worked) over the last two decades has been less than that of the pre-1973 economy (Appendix 16), but these lower numbers are not sufficient to explain the modest growth in real wages. After all, hourly productivity actually *increased* by 1.1 percent or 1.0 percent over the last three business cycles, 1973-1979, 1979-1989, 1989-1994.

Since 1979, few groups in the labor force have been able to enjoy even the modest growth in the "average wage" because of the large and continuing growth of wage inequality: high-wage workers received real-wage gains while the remainder of the wage structure fell.

Wages by Occupation

Appendix 17 presents post-1973 average wage trends by occupation for men and women; it uses a data source that has wage, but no benefit, information. The decline in hourly wages from 1989 to 1995 among men was evident in nearly every aggregate occupation category (although some specific, detailed occupations have seen wage increases), although greater among blue-collar (-7.1 percent) than white-collar (-1.4 percent) men. For blue-collar men, who made up 41.5 percent of male employment in 1995, these recent wage setbacks follow the deep real wage declines of the 1979-1989 period. Men in the higher-paid white-collar occupations, on the other hand, enjoyed real wage growth in the 1980s, so their recent experiences represent a turnaround. White-collar men in 1995 earned slightly less, $18.05, than their counterparts did in 1973, $18.21.

Nearly three-fourths (74 percent) of women workers were white-collar workers in 1995, and their wage growth of 3.3 percent in the recent period from 1989 to 1995 was slow relative to the 9.2 percent growth in the prior decade, even after taking the different lengths of these time periods into account. The wages of women in blue-collar, service, and lower wage white-collar occupations (administrative, clerical, or sales) did not do well in either the 1980s or 1990s.

Wage Trends by Wage Level

For any given trend in average wages, there will be different outcomes for particular groups of workers if wage inequality rises, as it has in recent years. Appendix 18 provides data on wage trends for workers at different points (or levels) in the wage distribution, thus allowing us to characterize wage growth for low-, middle-, and high-wage earners. The data, presented for the cyclical peak years 1973, 1979, and 1989 and for the most recent year for which we have data, 1995, show that the deterioration in real wages since 1979 was both broad and uneven. The breadth of recent wage problems is clear from the fact that real wages fell for the bottom 60 percent of wage earners over the 1979-1989 period, while wages fell among the bottom 80 percent over the 1989-1995 period. That is, only workers in the upper 20 percent of the wage scale obtained real wage growth.

The decline in wages was greater the lower the wage. Over the 1979-1995 period, wages fell just 0.4 percent at the 80th percentile but were down 11.1 percent and 17.0 percent at the 20th and 10th percentiles respectively. The wage of the median worker, who earned more than half of the workforce but also less than half of the workforce, fell 2.4 percent from 1979 to 1989 and another 4.6 percent from 1989 to 1995.

This overall picture, however, masks somewhat different outcomes for men and women. Among men, wages have fallen more and at nearly all parts of the wage distribution (Appendix 19). In the middle, the median male hourly wage fell 9.1 percent between 1979 and 1989 and another 6.3 percent between 1989 and 1995, for a total fall of 14.9 percent. Even high-wage men (those at the 80th percentile) experienced a decline in wages of 2.0 percent over the 1979-1989 period, followed by a 3.6 percent drop after 1989. Wages among low-wage men fell the most – about 18 percent – from 1979 to 1995. These data thus show significant wage deterioration for nearly all men, with the bottom 60 percent suffering between a 12 percent and 18 percent wage reduction from 1979 to 1995. Since 1979, the median male hourly wage has fallen $2.04, or about one percent per year. Even the high-wage men at the 90th percentile who earned nearly $25 per hour have done well only in relative terms, since their wage was a marginal one percent higher in 1995 than in 1979.

The structure of male wage deterioration shifted in the 1980s and 1990s. In the 1980s, wages fell most the lower the wage, while in the 1990s there was an almost uniform wage decline among the bottom 60 percent. Thus, the wage spread between middle- and low-wage men did not grow in the 1990s, although the gap between high-wage men and middle- and low-wage men continued to grow.

The only significant wage growth between 1979 and 1995 appears to have been among higher-wage women (Appendix 20). For instance, wages grew 18.0 percent and 21.5 percent at the 80th and 90th percentiles between 1979 and 1995, but they declined among the lowest-wage women at the 20th percentile and below and grew modestly at the median, 4.0 percent over 16 years.

The surprising trend is the modest but pervasive decline in wages from the 20th to the 60th percentile among women in the 1989-1995 period. Even high-wage women received only modest real wage gains after 1989. Thus, while women's wages were the bright spot of the 1980s, the wage trends for women have been far less favorable in the 1990s. One positive trend, however, is that wages for the lowest-wage women (the 10th percentile) stopped falling in the recent period, perhaps because of the rise in the minimum wage in the 1990s.

The Male-Female Wage Gap

From 1979 to 1995, the median hourly wage fell $2.04 for men and rose $0.35 for women (Appendices 19 and 20). These changes led to a growth in the hourly wage ratio between men and women by 13.9 percentage points, from 62.8 percent in 1979 to 76.7 percent in 1995, representing a sizable reduction in gender wage inequality. Even after this progress, however, women still roughly earned about one-fourth less than men in 1995.

Two aspects of this improvement in gender equity are disheartening. First, this narrowing of the male/female wage gap has primarily occurred because male wages fell (accounting for 82 percent of the narrower gap). Second, since 1989, the wages for both the median-wage male and median-wage female have been *falling*. Therefore, any progress in lessening gender inequality resulted from women's wages falling more slowly than men's wages.

The Expansion of Low-Wage Jobs

Another useful way of characterizing changes in the wage structure is to examine the trend in the proportion of workers earning low or "poverty-level" wages. The poverty-level wage is the hourly wage that a full-time, year-round worker must earn to sustain a family of four at the poverty threshold, which was $7.28 in 1995 (in 1994 dollars).

Appendix 21 shows a significant expansion of workers earning less than poverty-level wages over the 1980s and 1990s. In 1979, 23.7 percent of the workforce earned low wages, rising to 29.7 percent by 1995. This growth was fueled by the increase of low earners among men, whose share nearly doubled from 12.8 percent in 1973 to 23.3 percent in 1995. On the other hand, the prevalence of low earnings among women fell over this time period, although it has remained far higher than among men. As Appendix 22 shows, this growth of low earners occurred among each race/ethnic group.

Rising Education Wage Differentials

Another important dimension of the wages structure that has changed is the wage gaps between different educational groups. The growth in "education wage differentials" is partly responsible for greater wage inequality in the 1980s and 1990s and helps explain the relatively faster wage growth among high-wage workers.

Appendices 23, 24, and 25 present the wage trends and employment shares (percentage of the workforce) for all men and women workers at various education levels over the 1973-1995 period. It is common to point out that the wages of "more-educated" workers have grown faster than the wages of "less-educated" workers since 1979, with the real wages of "less-educated" workers falling sharply. This pattern of wage growth is sometimes described in terms of a rising differential, or "premium," between the wages of the college-educated and high school-educated workforces.

The usual terminology of the "less educated" and "more educated" is misleading. Given that workers with some college education (from one to three years) also experienced falling real wages (down 9.9 percent from 1979 to 1995), it is apparent that the "less-educated" group with falling wages makes up more than three-fourths of the workforce. The last column of Appendix 23 shows the average noncollege wage falling 11.9 percent over the 1979-1995 period. Moreover, the "college-educated" group consists of two groups: one is those with just four years of college, who enjoyed a minimal 4.3 percent wage gain over the 1979-1995 period, and the other is the more-educated ("advanced degree") but smaller (6.9 percent of the workforce in 1989) group that enjoyed 12.1 percent wage growth.

This increased differential between college-educated and other workers is frequently ascribed to a relative increase in employer demand for workers with greater skills and education. Yet an increased relative demand for educated workers is only a partial explanation, especially if ascribed to a benign process of technology or other factors leading to a higher value for education thus bidding up the wages of more-educated workers. Note, for instance, that the primary reason for an increased wage gap between college-educated and other workers is the precipitous decline of wages among the noncollege-educated workforce and not any strong growth of the college wage. Moreover, as discussed below, there are many important factors (that may not reflect changes in demand for skill), such as the shift to low-wage industries, deunionization, a falling minimum wage, and import competition, that can also lead to a wage gap between more- and less-educated workers.

Among men (Appendix 24), the wages of noncollege-educated workers have been falling steadily since 1979: wages fell 10.1 percent over the 1979-1989 period and another 7.2 percent between 1989 and 1995. The decline in wages was sizable even among men with "some college" – 13.4 percent from 1979 to 1995. The wage of the average high school-educated male fell somewhat more, 16.7 percent from 1979 to 1995, while the wages of those without a high school degree fell 27.0 percent. In contrast, the wages of male college graduates did not rise at all over the 1989-1995 period and rose just 0.6 percent from 1979 to 1989. As shown in the last column, the estimated college-high school wage premium grew from 27.3 percent in 1979 to 41.8 percent in 1989 and to 44.4 percent in 1995.

A somewhat different pattern has prevailed among women

(Appendix 25). In the 1979-1989 period wages fell modestly (2.8 percent) among high school-educated women but significantly among those without a high school degree (10.7 percent). Women with some college, unlike their male counterparts, saw wage gains in the 1980s (6.3 percent), but not as much as college-educated women (12.9 percent). This pattern of wage growth, however, still resulted in an equivalent growth of the college-high school wage differential from 30.8 percent in 1979 to 46.0 percent in 1989. Thus, inequality grew as quickly among women as among men but the relative losers – non-college-educated women – saw stagnant, not declining, wages.

Young Workers Have Been Hurt Most

Since 1973, the wages of younger workers have been falling faster than the wages of older workers. As a result, there have been significant changes in the wage differentials between younger and older workers. Since the wages of both younger and noncollege-educated workers have fallen most rapidly, it follows that the wages of workers who are both young and noncollege educated have fallen dramatically. These adverse wage trends were strongest among men. Appendix 26 presents trends in "entry-level" wages for high school graduates as reflected in the wages of workers with one to five years of experience. The entry-level hourly wage of a young, male high school graduate in 1995 was 27 percent less than that for the equivalent worker in 1979. Young women high school graduates earned 19 percent less in 1995 than in 1979.

Entry-level wages among male college graduates (Appendix 27) were stagnant over the 1973-1989 period and fell 9.5 percent from 1989 to 1995. Thus, new male college graduates earned $1.54 less per hour in 1995 than their counterparts did in 1973. This sharp decline in entry-level wages of college graduates also took place among women, where the wage fell 7.7 percent over the 1989-1995 period. The fact that entry-level wages for college graduates remain higher than for high school graduates means that it still makes economic sense for individuals to complete college. Nevertheless, men who obtain a college degree will have a lower wage than that obtained by an earlier generation of male college graduates.

V. Explaining Wage Trends

The wage problem confronting workers over the last few decades can be characterized as slow growth and growing inequality, the combination of which has led to broad-based real wage deterioration.

There are two factors that explain the slow overall growth in hourly wages (or hourly wages and benefits). The primary reason for the slow growth in average wages is the slow growth in productivity since 1973. When the pie grows more slowly (i.e., output per hour, or productivity, increases the pie more slowly), it follows that an individual's piece of pie will grow more slowly. However, another factor has emerged in the 1990s –

the shift of income from compensation to capital income (profits and interest), as discussed in an earlier section. This redistribution has been an additional factor that slowed compensation growth in the 1990s.

That slow growth in productivity is not enough to explain wage problems as illustrated in Appendix 28. Although slower than in earlier periods, the more than one percent annual productivity growth since 1973 should have generated a growth in hourly compensation for the typical worker. In fact, as Appendix 28 shows, total productivity grew roughly 25 percent between 1973 and 1995 but the hourly compensation of the median worker fell over that period and the hourly compensation of the median male worker fell roughly one percent annually from 1979 to 1995. This gap between rising average hourly compensation and the stagnant or falling wages is due to a growth in wage inequality.

There are two clusters of factors that can explain the growth of wage inequality: (1) the erosion of labor market institutions and (2) the impact of globalization and the shift to service industries. These factors are examined in the following two sections.

Labor Market Institutions

The weakening of labor market institutions can most easily be documented by examining the erosion of union representation and a lowering of the minimum wage. As Appendix 29 shows, the percentage of workers represented by unions fell rapidly in the 1980s, after having been stable in the 1970s.

This falling rate of unionization has lowered wages for noncollege educated workers, not only because some workers no longer receive the higher union wage but also because there is less pressure on nonunion employers to raise wages. There are also reasons to believe that there has been a weakening of union bargaining power, a qualitative shift beyond the quantitative decline. This erosion of bargaining power is partially related to a harsher economic context for unions because of trade pressures, the shift to services, and ongoing technological change. However, analysts have also pointed to other factors, such as employer militancy and changes in the application and administration of labor law, which have helped to weaken unions.

The real value of the minimum wage has fallen considerably since its high point in the late 1960s (Appendix 30). The decline was particularly steep and steady between 1979 and 1989, when inflation whittled down the real minimum wage (in 1995 dollars) from $5.97 to $4.12, a fall of 31.1 percent. Despite the legislated increases in the minimum wage in 1990 and 1991, its value of $4.25 in 1995 was $1.72, or 28.8 percent, less than in 1979. In fact, the minimum wage's purchasing power in 1995 ($4.25) was 23.7 percent less than that of the minimum wage 28 years earlier, in 1967.

Congress voted to increase the minimum wage to $5.15 in 1997. This is a modest increase that will not restore the value of the minimum wage to anywhere near its value of 20 to 30 years ago. Even with the increase, the minimum wage will be 26.7 percent below its 1979 level in the year 2000.

The analysis in Appendix 31 examines the impact of changes in labor-market institutions on wage inequality by quantifying the effect of specific factors on the wage gap between high- and middle-wage workers and between middle- and low-wage workers. The analysis also covers several subperiods (1973-1979, 1979-1988, 1988-1992), so one can observe how a factor's impact can shift over time.

Over the 1973-1979 period there was growth in the minimum wage and stability of union representation. The result of the strong minimum wage was a sizable lowering of the middle/low wage gap among women (4.6 percentage points) and a slight lowering of the wage gap at the bottom among men (0.3 percentage points). Changes in unionism in this period were equalizing among men but disequalizing among women.

The results for the 1979-1988 period make clear that deunionization was an important factor in the growth of male wage inequality at the top, contributing 4.0 of the 11.9-percentage-point growth in the high/middle wage gap. The reduction of the minimum wage over the 1979-1988 period, on the other hand, generated 15.0 of the 24.3-percentage-point growth in the middle/low wage gap among women and a large part (5.0) of the 7.6-percentage-point growth in the male middle-/low-wage gap. Thus, a lower minimum wage was a major factor in lowering the wages of low-wage men and women relative to the middle. Deunionization, in contrast, primarily allowed high-wage men to fare better than middle-wage men.

In the 1988-1992 period, a modest rise in the minimum wage tightened the wage structure at the bottom, and continued deunionization helped to widen the male wage structure at the top.

Looking at the 1979-1992 period as a whole, deunionization was a major factor driving wage inequality at the top of the wage structure, responsible for 5 of the 14.4 percentage point rise of the high-/middle-wage gap (contributing 35 percent of the total growth). The erosion of the minimum wage, on the other hand, was the major factor generating women's wage inequality (contributing 66 percent of the growth), which primarily occurred at the bottom, and the wage gap at the bottom for men (contributing 69 percent of the growth). Together, the shifts in labor-market institutions – deunionization and a lower minimum wage – over the 1979-1992 period can explain 36 percent and 44 percent of the growth of overall wage inequality respectively (the top/bottom wage gap) among men and women.

Globalization and the Shift to Services

There was a large employment shift to low-wage sectors in the 1980s and 1990s. This shift is a consequence of trade deficits and deindustrialization as well as stagnant or falling productivity growth in service-sector industries. This "industry-shift" effect is not the consequence of some natural evolution from an agriculture to a manufacturing to a service economy.

For one, a significant part of the shrinkage of manufacturing is trade related. More important, industry shifts would not provide a downward pressure on wages if service-sector wages were more closely aligned with manufacturing wages, as is the case in other countries. Moreover, since health coverage, vacations, and pensions are related to the specific job or sector in which a worker is employed, the sectoral distribution of employment matters more in the United States than in other countries. An alternative institutional arrangement found in other advanced countries sets health, pensions, vacation, and other benefits through legislation in a universal manner regardless of sector or firm. Therefore, the downward pressure of industry shifts can be said to be the consequence of institutional structures.

The extent of the shift to low-wage industries is evident in an analysis of changes in the shares of the workforce in various sectors (Appendix 32). Several high-wage sectors, such as construction, transportation, wholesale, communications, and government, increased employment in the 1980s or 1990s but ended up providing a smaller or similar share of overall employment over time. A lower share of employment in these high-wage sectors puts downward pressure on wages. Overall, the share of the workforce in low-paying services and in retail trade was 10.3 percentage points higher in 1995 than in 1979. The parallel trend was the 10.3-percentage-point drop in the share of the workforce in high-paying industries, such as manufacturing, construction, mining, government, transportation, communications, and utilities. In the 1990s, the only private-sector industry to significantly expand its employment share was services.

The process of "globalization" in the 1980s and 1990s has also been an important factor both in slowing the growth rate of average wages and in reducing the wage levels of workers with less than a college degree. The increase in international trade and investment flows affects wages through several channels. First, increases in imports of finished manufactured goods, especially from countries where workers earn only a fraction of what U.S. workers earn, reduces manufacturing employment in the United States. While increases in exports create employment opportunities for some domestic workers, imports mean job losses for many others. Large, chronic trade deficits over the last 15 years suggest that the jobs lost to import competition have outnumbered the jobs gained from increasing exports. Given that export industries tend to be less labor intensive than import-competing industries, even growth in "balanced trade" (where exports and imports both increase by the same dollar amount) would lead to a decline in manufacturing jobs.

Second, imports of intermediate manufactured goods (used as inputs in the production of final goods) also help to lower domestic manufacturing employment, especially for production workers and others with less than a college education. The expansion of export "platforms" in low-wage countries has induced many U.S. manufacturing firms to "outsource" part of their production processes to low-wage countries. Since firms generally find it most profitable to outsource the most labor-intensive processes, the increase in outsourcing has hit noncollege-educated production workers hardest.

Third, low wages and greater world capacity for producing manufactured goods can lower the prices of many international goods. Since workers' pay is tied to the value of the goods they produce, lower prices internationally can lead to a reduction in the earnings of U.S. workers, even if imports themselves do not increase.

Fourth, in many cases the mere threat of direct foreign competition or of the relocation of part or all of a production facility can lead workers to grant wage concessions to their employers.

Fifth, the very large increases in international investment flows (in percentage terms the increases are much larger than for international trade) have meant shifted investment in the domestic manufacturing base and significant growth in the foreign manufacturing capacity capable of competing directly with U.S.-based manufacturers.

Finally, the effects of globalization go beyond those workers exposed directly to foreign competition. As trade drives workers out of manufacturing and into lower-paying service jobs, the new supply of workers to the service sector (from displaced workers plus young workers not able to find manufacturing jobs) lowers the wages of those already employed in service jobs.

The analysis of the impact of globalization on wage inequality is a relatively new, and controversial, topic in economics. Some analysts dismiss this factor as "small" or "trivial." However, if trade creates no costs and does not disproportionately hurt lower-wage workers then trade must not be creating any benefits (the logic of trade making us better off requires workers and resources to be shifted from "less productive to more productive" uses). On the other hand, even though our economy is now more integrated into a world economy it is still primarily driven by domestic factors.

A reasonable estimate of the impact of globalization would be that it has generated 15 percent to 25 percent of the growth of wage inequality (see Schmitt and Mishel 1996 and Cline 1997). The shift to low-paying industries can also be considered to be responsible for about 20 percent of the growth of wage inequality. Since these factors are related (i.e., trade leading to a shrinkage of manufacturing employment), the combined effect of industry shifts and globalization can account for about one-third of the growth of wage inequality (including the effect of immigration, which is not discussed here).

The Shift of Income From Labor to Capital

Another reason for the slow growth in average wages and compensation in the 1990s and another reason that real wages deteriorated for the broad majority is that a "profit squeeze" on wages has taken place. In the mid-1990s economic return (profits and interest) to assets (the structures and equipment owned by corporate businesses) has been very high by historical standards. This has led to an increase in the share of income generated by corporate businesses that is paid as capital income (i.e., profits and interest).

The higher profitability in the 1990s was partly the result of greater investment productivity. It was also the ability of business to "control labor costs," meaning the ability to keep wage and compensation growth low, that led to the higher profitability.

The growth of the returns to capital, or "profitability," is shown in Appendix 33. In 1996, profitability was 70 percent greater than in 1989 and significantly greater than in any year since 1959 (when the government began collecting the data). Appendix 34 shows the trend in the share of corporate income paid to capital (i.e., as profits and interest), which in 1996 was the highest in 30 years. For instance, capital's income share rose from 17.6 percent in 1989 to 21.1 percent in 1996, two years of comparably low unemployment.

Economics provides little guidance as to the appropriate division of income between business income and employee compensation, but an historical perspective might help (Mishel 1997; for contrary view, Poterba 1997). The income return to capital in 1996 was about 25 percent higher than in the 1960s, the best decade on record for both productivity and profitability in the post-war period. Had business received the rate of return realized in the 1960s, then hourly compensation could have been about 5 percent higher or roughly $1,950 more per worker in 1996. This is not a trivial amount of money and represents more than double the actual growth of average hourly compensation over the 1989-1996 period.

Technology's Impact

Technological change can affect the wage structure by displacing some types of workers and by increasing demand for others. Given the seemingly rapid diffusion of microelectronic technologies in recent years, many analysts have considered technological change as a major factor in the recent increase in wage inequality. Unfortunately, because it is difficult to measure the extent of technological change and its overall character (whether it is generally de-skilling or up-skilling and by how much), it is difficult to identify the role of technological change on recent wage trends. More than a few analysts, in fact, have simply assumed that whatever portion of wage inequality is unexplained can be considered to be the consequence of technological change. This type of analysis, however, only puts a name to our ignorance.

It is easy to understand why people might consider technology to be a major factor explaining recent wage and employment trends. We are often told that the pace of change in the workplace is accelerating, and there is widespread visibility of automation and robotics; computers and microelectronics provide a visible dimension evident in workplaces, such as offices, not usually affected by technology. The economic intuition goes beyond this; research has shown that the most recent wage inequality and the employment shift to more-educated workers has occurred within industries and has not been caused primarily by shifts across industries (i.e., more service jobs, fewer manufacturing jobs). Research has also shown that technological change has traditionally been associated with an increased demand for more-educated or "skilled" workers. This pattern of change suggests an increase in "skill-biased technological change" driving large changes within industries.

There are many reasons to be skeptical of a technology-led increase in demand for "skill" as an explanation for growing wage inequality. First, note that there has been little growth in multifactor productivity (a commonly used proxy for technological change) for decades, nor has there been any greater growth in labor productivity in recent years. However, the technology explanation assumes that there was a large technology-led transformation of the workplace that substantially decreased the need for "unskilled" workers and thereby led to a large shift in wage differentials. It is implausible that there has been a technology shock that has transformed workplaces but has not boosted productivity growth.

Second, the experience since the mid- to late 1980s does not accord with a technology explanation, whose imagery is of a computer-driven technology that bids up the wages of "more-skilled" and "more-educated" workers, leaving behind a small group of workers with inadequate skills. The facts are hard to reconcile with the notion that technological change grew as fast or faster in the 1990s than in earlier periods. If technology were adverse for "unskilled" or "less-educated" workers, then we would expect a continued expansion of the wage differential between middle-wage and low-wage workers. Yet, the middle/low wage gap has been stable or declining among both men and women since 1986 or 1987. Instead, we are seeing the top earners pulling away from nearly all other earners. Therefore, there seems to be factors driving a wedge between the top 10 percent and everyone else, rather than a single factor aiding the vast majority but leaving a small group of unskilled workers behind. Further confirmation of the breadth of those left behind is that wages have been stable or in decline for the bottom 80 percent of men and the bottom 70 percent of women over the 1989-1995 period, with wages falling for the entire noncollege-educated workforce (roughly 75 percent of the workforce). Of course, even high-wage, white-collar, or college-graduate men have failed to see real wage growth in 10 years.

The flattening of the growth of education differentials in the late 1980s and 1990s among men also does not easily fit a technology story. Since the wages of college-graduate men are not being "bid up" relative to others at the same pace as in the early and mid-1980s, one can only conclude that there has been a deceleration of the relative demand for education (given that the supply of college workers did not accelerate). This would not be the case if technology were being introduced into workplaces at the same or a faster pace in the late 1980s or in the 1990s. Moreover, the late 1980s to mid-1990s period has been one of continued growth of wage inequality as the top pulls away from the middle and bottom; since this growing gap is not being driven by wider education differentials (the primary mechanism by which technology leads to greater wage inequality), it is hard to believe that technology is playing a major role.

Third, there is no evidence that the growth of wage inequality over the entire 1973-1995 period has been primarily driven by changes in the economic return to education or experience, the most easily measured dimension of skill. Rather, wage inequality has been largely driven by the growth of within-group wage inequality – the growing gap among workers with similar education and experience. The growth of within-group inequality may be related to technological change if it is interpreted as a reflection of growing economic returns to worker skills that are not easily measured (motivation, aptitudes for math, etc.). However, there are no signs that the growth of within-group wage inequality has been fastest in those industries where the use of technology grew the most. It is also unclear why the economic returns for measurable skills (e.g., education) and unmeasured skills (e.g., motivation) should not grow in tandem. In fact, between-group and within-group inequality has not moved together in the various subperiods since 1973.

Finally, the notion that technology has been "bidding up" the wages of the "skilled" relative to the "unskilled" is debatable given the facts presented earlier. Or, it holds true in a "relative" but not an "absolute" sense. The wages of skilled men, defined as white-collar, college-educated, or 90th-percentile workers, have been flat or declining since the mid-1980s. We also know that white-collar men have increasingly become displaced and beset by employment problems. High-wage women have continued to see their wages grow, but it does not seem likely that technology is primarily affecting skilled women but not skilled men.

Last, the discussion of technology's role in growing wage inequality assumes that we have entered a new era of technological change, signified by the computer revolution. In this scenario, either the rate of introduction of new technologies or the types of technologies being introduced is creating a new situation in today's workplace, along with an enhanced demand for cognitive skills. Some analysts have explicitly talked in terms of a "technology shock." This widely expressed view assumes an *acceleration* of technology's impact on relative demand, suggesting that one test of the technology hypothesis is whether technology had a greater impact on skill demand in the 1980s or 1990s than in the 1970s or earlier periods. A series of studies have shown that there has not been an acceleration of technology's employment impact in the 1980s and 1990s relative to the 1970s (Autor, Katz, and Krueger 1997 and Mishel and Bernstein 1997).

VI. Conclusion

There have been dramatic changes in the wage structure over the last 16 years. The real hourly wages of most workers have fallen, and the group experiencing the greatest wage decline has been noncollege-educated workers, especially new entrants to the labor force. Given that three-fourths of the workforce has not earned a four-year college degree, the continuing deterioration of the wages of high school graduates (whose wages fell somewhat less than those of high school dropouts but somewhat more than those of workers with "some college") means that the vast majority of men and many women are working at far lower wages than their counterparts did a generation earlier. More recently (i.e., since the mid-1980s), wages have been falling or stagnant among college graduates and white-collar workers, especially men.

The wage trends of the 1989-1995 period mirror those of the 1980s in that wage inequality at the top of the wage scale has continued to grow and median male wages have continued their one percent annual decline. The difference between the 1980s and 1990s is that there is a broader decline of wages among women, including a decline at the median, and there has been no growth in inequality at the bottom – wages at the median and the 10th percentile are falling in tandem.

Incomes: An Update

Since this indicator was prepared there has been some new data released and, more importantly, some impressive improvements in income across the income spectrum. Specifically, the median family's income grew 6.4 percent from 1996 to 1998 and has finally surpassed the income level of 1989, the endpoint of the last recovery. This income growth also benefited those at the bottom, where incomes grew by 5.9 percent over the 1996-98 period. Incomes at the upper end (the best-off 5 percent) grew somewhat faster, 9.2 percent, over the same period. Income inequality has remained roughly stable over the last few years while the poverty rate has now fallen back to its 1989 level.

How do these income developments alter our judgement about the economy's performance in raising living standards? These welcomed income developments should reaffirm our belief in the beneficial effect of having persistently low unemployment and provide confidence that it is possible to have broadly shared income growth. At the same time, we should be mindful that several strong years of growth at the end of a recovery have not produced "the best economy in thirty years" or "unimagined prosperity." After all, even with the recent strong growth, the income gains over this business cycle – 0.4 percent annual growth from 1989 to 1998 – just matches the gains of the 1980s, is below that of the 1970s, and is far below that of the 1950s and 1960s. That inequality has neither fallen nor risen is not good news since in most recoveries inequality falls as wage and hiring gains disproportionately benefit the bottom half.

By the yardstick of productivity – the growth in output per hour that reflects the expansion of the "economic pie" – incomes have not fared well: productivity has grown nearly 20 percent but the wages of the typical worker in 1998 were still on par with wage levels of 1989.

Yet, there may be reason to believe that the economy can deliver more, and to more people, than earlier assessments would have suggested. If productivity growth at the higher levels of 1996-98 is sustained into the future – a big if – then we will see higher growth in incomes that, with appropriate policies and institutions, could lower poverty and provide a lasting prosperity for all.

Median Family Income,* 1947-96 (1996 Dollars)

Appendix 1

Year	Median Family Income*
1947	$19,651
1967	34,285
1973	40,059
1979	41,530
1989	43,290
1996	42,300
Total Increases	
1947-67	$14,638
1967-73	5,770
1973-79	1,471
1979-89	1,760
1989-96	-990

* Income includes all wage and salary, self-employment, pension, interest, rent, government cash assistance, and other money income.

Source: Author's analysis of U.S. Bureau of the Census (1996) and unpublished Census data.

Annual Growth of Median Family Income, 1947-96 (1996 Dollars)

Period	Median Family Income Growth		Adjusted for Family Size
	Percent	Dollars	Percent
1947-67	2.8%	$732	n.a.
1967-73	2.6	962	2.8%
1973-79	0.6	245	0.5
1979-89	0.4	176	0.5
1989-96	-0.3	-141	-0.3

Source: Author's analysis of U.S. Bureau of the Census (1996) and unpublished Census data.

Appendix 2   **Median Family Income, 1947-96**

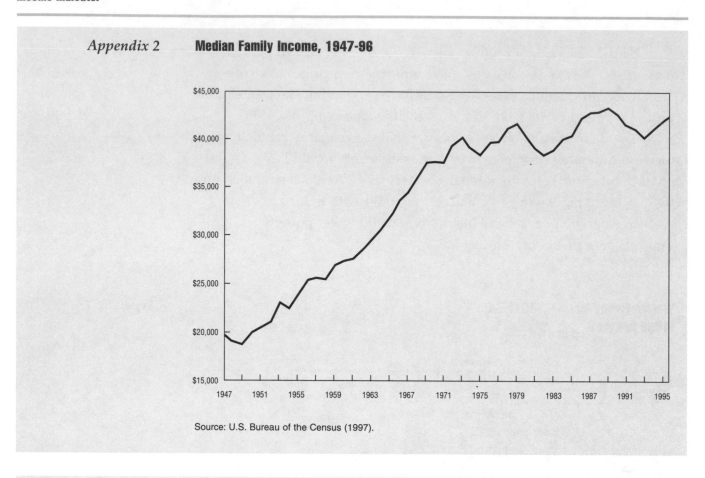

Source: U.S. Bureau of the Census (1997).

Appendix 3   **Median Family Income by Race/Ethnic Group, 1947-96
(1996 Dollars)**

Year	White	Black*	Hispanic**	Ratio to White Family Income of: Black	Ratio to White Family Income of: Hispanic
1947	$20,468	$10,464	n.a.	51.1%	n.a.
1967	35,590	21,071	n.a.	59.2	n.a.
1973	41,868	24,163	$28,970	57.7	69.2%
1979	43,336	24,540	30,042	56.6	69.3
1989	45,520	25,571	29,667	56.2	65.2
1996	44,756	26,522	26,179	59.3	58.5
Annual Growth Rate					
1947-67	2.8%	3.6%	n.a.		
1967-73	2.7	2.3	n.a.		
1973-79	0.6	0.3	0.6%		
1979-89	0.5	0.4	-0.1		
1989-96	-0.2	0.5	-1.8		

*   Prior to 1967, data for blacks include all nonwhites.

**   Persons of Hispanic origin may be of any race.

Source: Author's analysis of U.S. Bureau of the Census (1996) and unpublished Census data.

**Median Family Income by Family Type, 1947-96
(1996 Dollars)**

Appendix 4

| Year | Married Couples | | | Single | | All Families |
	Total	Wife in Paid Labor Force	Wife Not in Paid Labor Force	Male-Headed	Female-Headed	
1947	$20,157	n.a.	n.a.	$19,035	$14,082	$19,651
1967	36,485	43,033	32,897	29,452	18,560	34,289
1973	43,307	50,650	37,955	35,708	19,270	40,059
1979	45,435	52,712	37,542	35,637	20,948	41,530
1989	48,774	57,276	36,374	35,235	20,804	43,290
1996	49,707	58,381	33,748	31,600	19,911	42,300
Annual Growth Rate						
1947-67	3.0%	n.a.	n.a.	2.2%	1.4%	2.8%
1967-73	2.9	2.8%	2.4%	3.3	0.6	2.6
1973-79	0.8	0.7	-0.2	-0.0	1.4	0.6
1979-89	0.7	0.8	-0.3	-0.1	-0.1	0.4
1989-96	0.3	0.3	-1.1	-1.5	-0.6	-0.3
Share of Families						
1951*	86.7%	19.8%	66.9%	3.0%	9.9%	99.7%
1967	86.4	31.6	54.8	2.4	10.6	99.4
1973	85.0	35.4	49.7	2.6	12.4	100.0
1979	82.5	40.6	41.9	2.9	14.6	100.0
1989	79.2	45.7	33.5	4.4	16.5	100.0
1996	76.3	47.3	29.0	5.5	18.2	100.0

* Earliest year available.

Source: Author's analysis of U.S. Bureau of the Census (1996) and unpublished Census data.

Appendix 5 **Shares of Family Income Going to Various Income Groups and to Top 5%, 1947-96**

Year	Lowest Fifth	Second Fifth	Middle Fifth	Fourth Fifth	Top Fifth	Breakdown of Top Fifth		Gini Ratios
						Bottom 15%	Top 5%	
1947	5.0%	11.9%	17.0%	23.1%	43.0%	25.5%	17.5%	0.376
1967	5.4	12.2	17.5	23.5	41.4	25.0	16.4	0.358
1973	5.5	11.9	17.5	24.0	41.1	25.6	15.5	0.356
1979	5.4	11.6	17.5	24.1	41.4	26.1	15.3	0.365
1989	4.6	10.6	16.5	23.7	44.6	26.7	17.9	0.401
1996*	4.2	10.0	15.8	23.1	46.8	26.5	20.3	0.425
Point Change								
1947-67	0.4	0.3	0.5	0.4	-1.6	-0.5	-1.1	-0.018
1967-73	0.1	-0.3	0.0	0.5	-0.3	0.6	-0.9	-0.002
1973-79	-0.1	-0.3	0.0	0.1	0.3	0.5	-0.2	0.009
1979-89	-0.8	-1.0	-1.0	-0.4	3.2	0.6	2.6	0.036
1989-96	-0.4	-0.6	-0.7	-0.6	2.2	-0.2	2.4	0.024

* These shares allow the top-code to increase and thus reveal greater inequality.

Source: Author's analysis of unpublished Census data.

Ratio of Family Income of Top 5% to Lowest 20%, 1947-96

Appendix 6

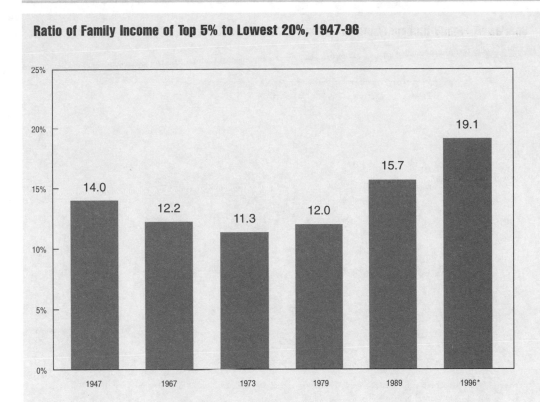

* Part of the increase in inequality in 1996 is attributable to changes in data collection methodology.

Source: Author's analysis of U.S. Census Bureau data (1997).

Real Family Income Growth by Income Group, 1947-96, Upper Limit of Each Group (1996 Dollars)

Appendix 7

Year	Lowest Fifth	Second Fifth	Middle Fifth	Fourth Fifth	Top 5%	Average
1947	$10,270	$16,572	$22,472	$31,886	$52,335	$22,990
1967	17,760	29,154	39,095	53,597	86,118	38,041
1973	20,214	33,355	46,538	64,000	99,774	45,282
1979	20,908	34,380	48,707	67,068	107,595	47,316
1989	20,249	35,429	51,625	75,350	125,220	52,518
1996	19,680	34,315	51,086	75,316	128,000	53,676
Annual Growth Rate						
1947-67	2.8%	2.9%	2.8%	2.6%	2.5%	2.5%
1967-73	2.2	2.3	2.9	3.0	2.5	2.9
1973-79	0.6	0.5	0.8	0.8	1.3	0.7
1979-89	-0.3	0.3	0.6	1.2	1.5	1.0
1989-96	-0.4	-0.5	-0.1	-0.0	0.3	0.3

Source: Author's analysis of unpublished Census data.

Appendix 8   **Annual Growth in Family Income by Income Group**

1947-73

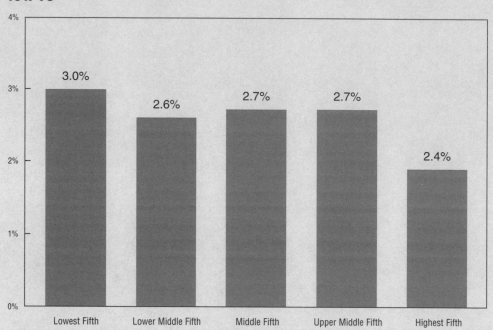

1973-96

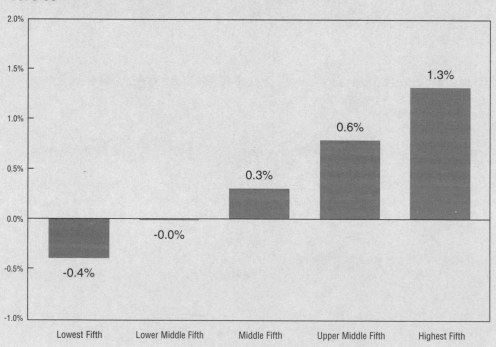

Source: U.S. Bureau of the Census (1997).

Source of Family Income for Each Family Income Group, 1989

Income Group	Labor	Capital*	Government Transfer	Other	Total
All	75.3	12.9	6.7	5.1	100.0
Bottom Four-Fifths					
First	46.3	4.6	39.9	9.1	100.0
Second	69.6	7.7	14.3	8.4	100.0
Middle	79.1	8.0	6.7	6.2	100.0
Fourth	83.4	8.0	3.9	4.7	100.0
Top Fifth	80.0	13.8	2.0	4.2	100.0
81-90%	83.6	9.6	2.4	4.3	100.0
91-95%	81.8	12.3	1.9	4.0	100.0
96-99%	74.3	19.4	1.6	4.6	100.0
Top 1%	57.6	41.0	0.4	1.1	100.0

* Includes rent, dividend, interest income, and realized capital gains.

Source: Author's analysis of Family Income Data Series.

Detailed Effects of Demographic Changes on Median Household Income, 1970s and 1980s

Median Household Income, 1989 (1995 dollars): $35,527

Variable	1970s	1980s
Age	-$678	$354
Race	-135	-103
Household Type	-2,548	-1,417
Education	1,875	1,824
All Demographic	-1,486	658

Source: U.S. Bureau of the Census (1997).

Growth in Income Inequality as Measured by the Gini Ratio, 1959-93

	Annual Growth In Gini Ratio (X100)	Annual Growth Due to: Family Composition Changes*	Annual Growth Due to: Other Causes	Percent of Change Due to: Family Composition Changes	Percent of Change Due to: Other Causes
1959-69	-0.460	0.050	-0.510	-10.9%	110.9%
1969-79	0.120	0.110	0.010	91.7	8.3
1979-93	0.386	0.100	0.286	25.9	74.1

* Change in annual growth rate due to shift from married-couple to male- or female-headed households.

Source: Author's analysis of Karoly and Burtless (1995) and Burtless (1995).

Appendix 12 — Changes in Family Hours Worked by Family Type, 1979-96

	Bottom	Second	Middle	Fourth	Top	Average
All Families						
1979	999	2,107	2,913	3,436	4,156	2722
1989	1,096	2,243	3,049	3,619	4,255	2852
1996	1,069	2,194	3,093	3,791	4,217	2873
Annual Percent Change						
1979-89	0.9	0.6	0.5	0.5	0.2	0.5
1989-96	-0.4	-0.3	0.2	0.7	-0.1	-0.1
Married Couples with Children						
1979	2,186	2,943	3,232	3,700	4,288	3270
1989	2,395	3,268	3,609	3,918	4,294	3497
1996	2,296	3,344	3,762	4,051	4,292	3549
Annual Percent Change						
1979-89	0.9	1.1	1.1	0.6	0.0	0.7
1989-96	-0.4	0.6	0.9	0.8	0.0	0.4
Unrelated Individuals						
1979	649	1,387	1,822	2,034	2,170	1612
1989	759	1,603	1,944	2,091	2,246	1729
1996	671	1,572	1,889	2,104	2,265	1700
Annual Percent Change						
1979-89	1.6	1.5	0.7	0.3	0.3	0.7
1989-96	-1.5	-0.1	-0.0	0.1	0.1	-0.1

Source: Author's analysis.

Federal Tax Burden, 1977-96(p)

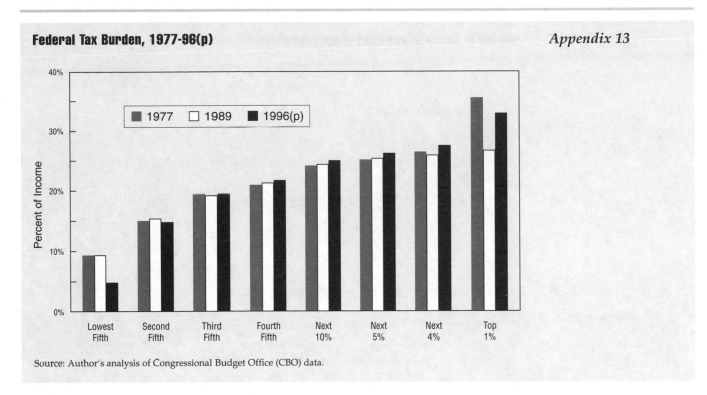

Source: Author's analysis of Congressional Budget Office (CBO) data.

Personal Income Tax Burden, 1977-96(p)

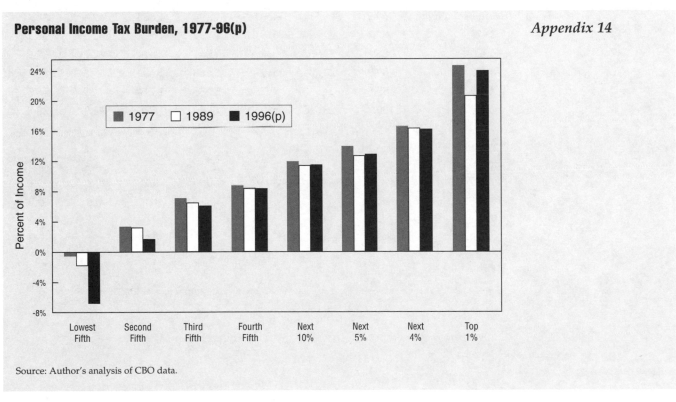

Source: Author's analysis of CBO data.

Appendix 15   Persons in Poverty, by Race/Ethnicity, 1959-96

Year	Total	White	Black	Hispanic
1959	22.4%	18.1%	55.1%	n.a.
1967	14.2	11.0	39.3	n.a.
1973	11.1	8.4	31.4	21.9
1979	11.7	9.0	31.0	21.8
1989	13.1	10.2	30.8	26.3
1996	13.7	11.2	28.4	29.4

Source: U.S. Bureau of the Census, Historical Data Series.

Appendix 16   Trends in Average Wages and Average Hours, 1967-94 (1995 Dollars)

Year	Productivity per Hour (1992=100)	Wage Levels			Hours Worked		
		Annual Wages	Weekly Wages	Hourly Wages	Annual Hours	Weeks per Year	Hours per Week
1967	69.2	$19,511	$459.59	$11.96	1,633	42.4	38.4
1973	80.7	22,694	536.01	14.22	1,598	42.3	37.7
1979	86.4	22,862	534.92	14.11	1,620	42.7	37.9
1983	89.9	22,334	519.45	13.88	1,609	43.0	37.4
1989	95.8	24,600	552.42	14.35	1,714	44.5	38.5
1994	100.7	25,070	558.96	14.40	1,740	44.9	38.8
*Annual Growth Rate**							
1967-73	2.6%	2.5%	2.6%	2.9%	-0.4%	-0.0%	-0.3%
1973-79	1.1	0.1	-0.0	-0.1	0.2	0.2	0.1
1983-89	1.1	1.6	1.0	0.6	1.1	0.6	0.5
1979-89	1.0	0.7	0.3	0.2	0.6	0.4	0.2
1989-94	1.0	0.4	0.2	0.1	0.3	0.1	0.2

* Log growth rates.

Source: Author's analysis of Current Population Survey (CPS) data and Murphy and Welch (1989).

Changes in Hourly Wages by Occupation, 1973-95
(1995 Dollars)

Occupation*	Percent of Employment 1995	Hourly Wage				Percent Change		
		1973	1979	1989	1995	1973-79	1979-89	1989-95
Males								
White Collar	45.4%	$18.21	$18.21	$18.31	$18.05	-0.0%	0.6%	-1.4%
Managers	13.1	20.17	20.28	21.71	21.36	0.5	7.1	-1.6
Professional	12.6	20.21	19.74	20.79	20.92	-2.3	5.3	0.6
Technical	3.3	17.18	16.94	17.41	16.97	-1.4	2.8	-2.5
Sales	10.0	15.82	16.03	15.00	14.44	1.3	-6.5	-3.7
Admin., Clerk	6.5	13.85	13.93	12.79	11.97	0.6	-8.2	-6.5
Service	10.5%	$11.41	$10.47	$9.54	$9.23	-8.2%	-8.9%	-3.2%
Protective	3.2	14.72	13.30	13.35	13.15	-9.7	0.4	-1.5
Other	7.3	9.78	9.17	7.89	7.49	-6.2	-13.9	-5.1
Blue Collar	41.5%	$13.73	$13.79	$12.51	$11.62	0.5%	-9.2%	-7.1%
Craft	18.7	15.70	15.40	14.18	13.33	-1.9	-7.9	-6.0
Operatives	8.6	12.30	12.74	11.65	10.65	3.5	-8.5	-8.6
Trans. Op.	7.5	12.92	13.20	11.74	11.03	2.2	-11.1	-6.0
Laborers	6.7	11.28	11.18	9.53	8.78	-0.9	-14.7	-7.9
Females								
White Collar	74.0%	$11.06	$10.89	$11.89	$12.28	-1.5%	9.2%	3.3%
Managers	12.9	12.73	12.49	14.47	14.80	-1.9	15.8	2.3
Professional	17.7	14.77	13.80	15.64	16.35	-6.6	13.3	4.6
Technical	4.0	11.65	12.18	13.04	12.87	4.6	7.1	-1.3
Sales	12.1	7.61	8.80	8.77	8.88	15.6	-0.3	1.2
Admin., Clerk	27.3	9.92	9.68	10.07	9.86	-2.4	4.0	-2.1
Service	15.6%	$7.21	$7.44	$6.96	$6.94	3.2%	-6.4%	-0.3%
Protective	0.7	n.a.	n.a	n.a	n.a	n.a	n.a	n.a.
Other	14.9	7.16	7.39	6.81	6.76	3.2	-7.8	-0.8
Blue Collar	10.4%	$8.39	$8.91	$8.57	$8.36	6.3%	-3.9%	-2.4%
Craft	2.1	9.63	10.08	10.22	9.97	4.7	1.4	-2.4
Operatives	5.7	8.22	8.68	8.05	7.88	5.6	-7.2	-2.2
Trans. Op.	0.9	n.a	n.a	n a	n.a	n.a	n.a.	n.a.
Laborers	1.7	n.a	n.a	n.a	n.a	n.a	n.a	n.a.

* Data for private household and farming, forestry, and fishing occupations not shown and not included in wage calculations.

Source: Author's analysis of CPS data.

Appendix 18   **Wages for All Workers by Wage Percentile, 1973-95
(1995 Dollars)**

Year	Wage by Percentile						
	10	20	40	50	60	80	90
Real Hourly Wage							
1973	$5.76	$6.96	$9.61	$11.02	$12.64	$16.79	$21.10
1979	6.10	6.96	9.62	10.88	12.60	17.37	21.33
1989	5.12	6.37	9.13	10.61	12.39	17.64	22.28
1995	5.06	6.19	8.70	10.13	11.98	17.30	22.35
Dollar Change							
1973-79	$0.34	$0.00	$0.00	$-0.14	$-0.04	$0.58	$0.23
1979-89	-0.98	-0.59	-0.48	-0.27	-0.21	0.27	0.95
1989-95	-0.06	-0.19	-0.43	-0.48	-0.41	-0.34	0.07
1979-95	-1.04	-0.77	-0.92	-0.75	-0.62	-0.08	1.02
Percent Change							
1973-79	5.8%	0.1%	0.0%	-1.3%	-0.3%	3.5%	1.1%
1979-89	-16.1	-8.5	-5.0	-2.4	-1.7	1.5	4.5
1989-95	-1.1	-2.9	-4.7	-4.6	-3.3	-1.9	0.3
1979-95	-17.0	-11.1	-9.5	-6.9	-4.9	-0.4	4.8

Source: Author's analysis based on CPS data.

Appendix 19   **Wages for Male Workers by Wage Percentile, 1973-95
(1995 Dollars)**

Year	Wage by Percentile						
	10	20	40	50	60	80	90
Real Hourly Wage							
1973	$6.80	$8.73	$11.79	$13.37	$15.15	$19.19	$24.45
1979	6.71	8.53	11.93	13.66	15.51	20.20	24.62
1989	5.86	7.34	10.67	12.41	14.61	19.80	24.80
1995	5.49	6.93	9.91	11.62	13.58	19.08	24.88
Dollar Change							
1973-79	$-0.09	$-0.20	$0.14	$0.29	$0.35	$1.01	$0.18
1979-89	-0.85	-1.19	-1.26	-1.25	-0.90	-0.40	0.17
1989-95	-0.37	-0.41	-0.76	-0.79	-1.03	-0.72	0.08
1979-95	-1.22	-1.59	-2.02	-2.04	-1.92	-1.12	0.25
Percent Change							
1973-79	-1.3%	-2.3%	1.2%	2.2%	2.3%	5.2%	0.7%
1979-89	-12.7	-13.9	-10.6	-9.1	-5.8	-2.0	0.7
1989-95	-6.4	-5.5	-7.1	-6.3	-7.0	-3.6	0.3
1979-95	-18.2	-18.7	-16.9	-14.9	-12.4	-5.5	1.0

Source: Author's analysis based on CPS data.

**Wages for Female Workers by Wage Percentile, 1973-95
(1995 Dollars)**

Appendix 20

Year	Wage by Percentile						
	10	20	40	50	60	80	90
Real Hourly Wage							
1973	$4.80	$5.96	$7.49	$8.44	$9.50	$12.34	$15.26
1979	5.82	6.31	7.64	8.58	9.75	12.64	15.78
1989	4.76	5.87	7.80	9.07	10.36	14.63	18.36
1995	4.84	5.77	7.76	8.92	10.28	14.92	19.17
Dollar Change							
1973-79	$1.02	$0.35	$0.15	$0.14	$0.25	$0.30	$0.52
1979-89	-1.06	-0.44	0.16	0.49	0.61	1.98	2.58
1989-95	0.08	-0.10	-0.04	-0.15	-0.09	0.29	0.81
1979-95	-0.98	-0.53	0.12	0.34	0.52	2.28	3.39
Percent Change							
1973-79	21.3%	5.9%	2.0%	1.6%	2.7%	2.5%	3.4%
1979-89	-18.2	-7.0	2.1	5.7	6.2	15.7	16.3
1989-95	1.6	-1.6	-0.5	-1.7	-0.8	2.0	4.4
1979-95	-16.8	-8.5	1.6	4.0	5.3	18.0	21.5

Source: Author's analysis based on CPS data.

Percent of Workers Earning Poverty-Level Wages, 1973-96

Appendix 21

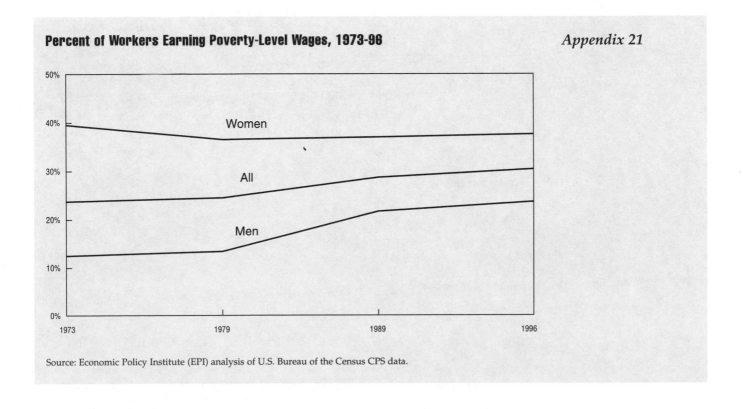

Source: Economic Policy Institute (EPI) analysis of U.S. Bureau of the Census CPS data.

Appendix 22 **Percent of Workers Earning Poverty-Level Wages, by Race/Ethnicity, 1973-96**

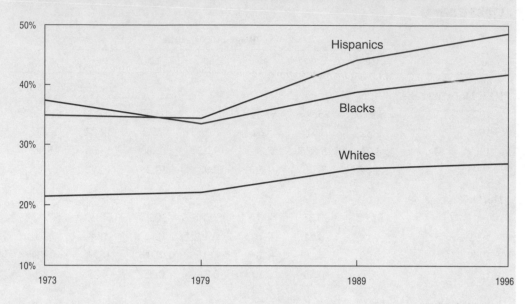

Source: EPI analysis of U.S. Bureau of the Census CPS data.

Appendix 23 **Change in Real Hourly Wage by Education, 1973-95 (1995 Dollars)**

Year	Less Than High School	High School	Some College	College	Advanced Degree	Memo: Non-College Educated**
Hourly Wage						
1973	$10.65	$12.17	$13.45	$17.66	$21.52	$11.89
1979	10.59	11.86	12.92	16.55	20.34	11.80
1989	8.91	10.79	12.53	16.98	22.07	10.96
1995	8.16	10.46	11.64	17.26	22.81	10.39
Percent Change						
1973-79	-0.6%	-2.6%	-3.9%	-6.3%	-5.5%	-0.8%
1979-89	-15.9	-9.0	-3.1	2.6	8.5	-7.1
1989-95	-8.4	-3.0	-7.1	1.6	3.3	-5.2
1979-95	-23.0	-11.8	-9.9	4.3	12.1	-11.9
Share of Employment*						
1973	28.5%	41.7%	15.1%	8.8%	3.6%	85.4%
1979	20.1	42.1	19.2	11.0%	5.0	81.3
1989	13.7	40.5	22.3	14.0%	6.9	76.5

* Since the shares of those with one year of schooling beyond college are not shown, the presented shares do not sum to 100. There are no reliable data for 1995 using same definitions.

** Those with less than four years of college.

Source: Author's analysis based on CPS data..

Change in Real Hourly Wage for Men by Education, 1973-95 (1995 Dollars)

Appendix 24

Year	Less Than High School	High School	Some College	College	Advanced Degree	Memo: Non-College Educated**	College-H.S.Wage Differential***
1973	$12.45	$14.65	$15.43	$20.32	$22.62	$14.00	32.5%
1979	12.22	14.25	15.14	19.43	22.15	13.89	27.3
1989	10.09	12.51	14.27	19.54	24.43	12.49	41.8
1995	8.92	11.87	13.11	19.55	25.28	11.59	44.4
Percent Change							
1973-79	-1.9%	-2.7%	-1.9%	-4.4%	-2.1%	-0.7%	
1979-89	-17.4	-12.2	-5.7	0.6	10.3	-10.1	
1989-95	-11.6	-5.1	-8.1	0.0	3.5	-7.2	
1979-95	-27.0	-16.7	-13.4	0.6	14.1	-16.5	
*Share of Employment**							
1973	30.6%	38.1%	15.6%	8.9%	4.5%	84.3%	
1979	22.3	38.6	18.8	11.5	6.1	79.7	
1989	15.9	38.7	21.0	14.2	7.8	75.5	

* Since the shares of those with one year of schooling beyond college are not shown, the presented shares do not sum to 100. There are no reliable data for 1995 using same definitions.

** Those with less than four years of college.

*** Estimated with controls for education, experience as a quartic, four regions, marital status, and race.

Source: Author's analysis based on CPS data.

Appendix 25   **Change in Real Hourly Wage for Women by Education, 1973-95 (1995 Dollars)**

Year	Less Than High School	High School	Some College	College	Advanced Degree	Memo: Non-College Educated**	College-H.S.Wage Differential***
1973	$7.51	$9.26	$10.31	$13.70	$18.42	$8.92	43.0%
1979	7.84	9.28	10.16	12.42	16.19	9.19	30.8
1989	7.00	9.02	10.79	14.02	18.51	9.27	46.0
1995	6.99	8.95	10.20	14.84	19.54	9.05	51.8
Percent Change							
1973-79	4.5%	0.2%	-1.5%	-9.4%	-12.1%	3.0%	
1979-89	-10.7	-2.8	6.3	12.9	14.3	0.9	
1989-95	-0.3	-0.8	-5.5	5.9	5.5	-2.4	
1979-95	-10.9	-3.6	0.4	19.5	20.7	-1.5	
Share of Employment*							
1973	25.6%	47.7%	14.4%	8.7%	2.3%	87.1%	
1979	17.2	46.7	19.6	10.4	3.5	83.6	
1989	11.2	42.6	23.9	13.8	5.8	77.8	

* Since the shares of those with one year of schooling beyond college are not shown, the presented shares do not sum to 100. There are no reliable data for 1995 using same definitions.

** Those with less than four years of college.

*** Estimated with controls for education, experience as a quartic, four regions, marital status, and race.

Source: Author's analysis based on CPS data.

Entry-Level Wages of High School Graduates, 1973-96

Appendix 26

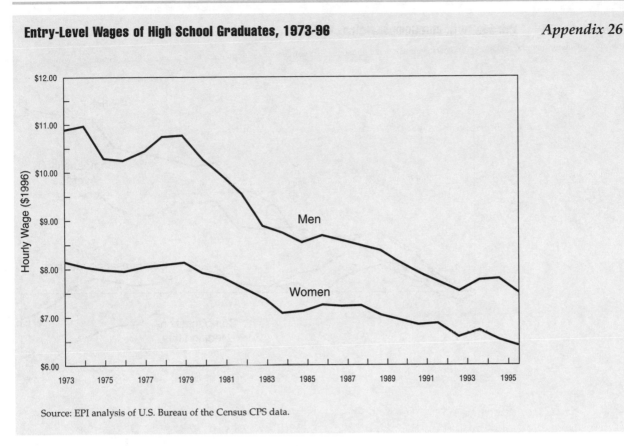

Source: EPI analysis of U.S. Bureau of the Census CPS data.

Entry-Level Wages of College Graduates, 1973-96

Appendix 27

Source: EPI analysis of U.S. Bureau of the Census CPS data.

Appendix 28   **Productivity and Compensation, 1973-96**

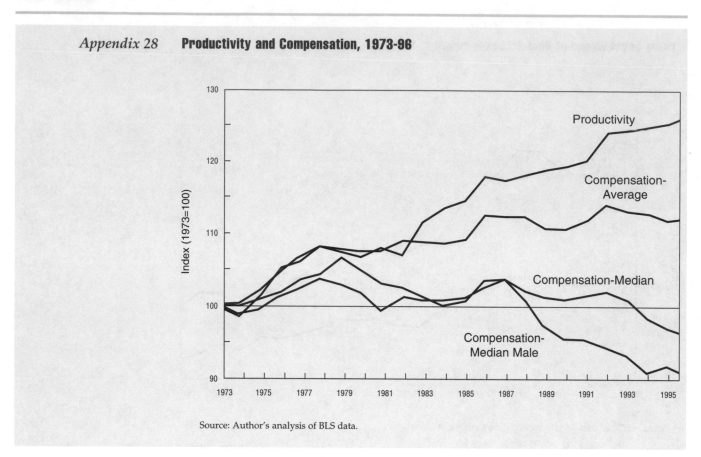

Source: Author's analysis of BLS data.

Appendix 29   **Union Membership, 1973-96**

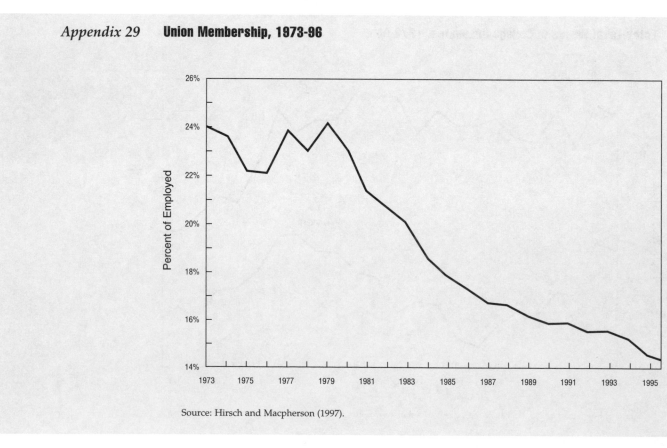

Source: Hirsch and Macpherson (1997).

Value of the Minimum Wage, 1947-96

Appendix 30

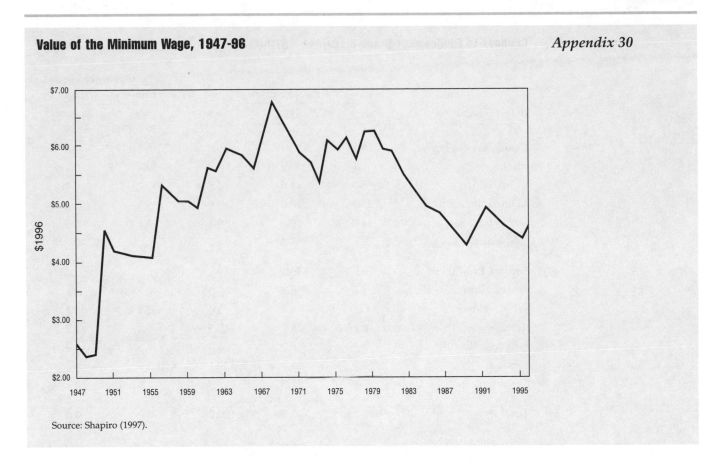

Source: Shapiro (1997).

The Impact of Labor-Market Institutions on Wage Differentials, 1973-92

Appendix 31

Period	Men			Women		
	90/10	90/50	50/10	90/10	90/50	50/10
1973-79						
Total Change	-0.4	-1.8	1.5	-1.7	-1.6	-0.1
Minimum Wage	-0.2	0.1	-0.3	-4.4	0.3	-4.6
Unions	-0.9	-1.0	0.2	0.7	0.1	-0.5
1979-88						
Total Change	19.5	11.9	7.6	32.8	8.5	24.3
Minimum Wage	4.9	0.0	5.0	14.8	-0.2	15.0
Unions	2.1	4.0	-1.9	0.4	1.4	-1.0
1988-92						
Total Change	2.0	2.5	-0.5	1.9	3.7	-1.9
Minimum Wage	-0.1	0.0	-0.1	-0.4	-0.1	-0.3
Unions	0.9	1.0	-0.1	0.2	0.2	0.0
Contribution to Growing Wage Inequality **1979-92**						
Total	100%	100%	100%	100%	100%	100%
Minimum Wage	22	0	69	42	-2	66
Unions	14	35	-28	2	13	-5

Source: Fortin and Lemieux (1996).

Appendix 32	**Changes in Employment Share by Sector, 1979-95**				
	Share of Employment			Change in Employment Share	
Industry Sector	1979	1989	1995	1979-89	1989-95
Goods Producing	29.5%	23.4%	20.8%	-6.1	-2.6
Mining	1.1	0.6	0.5	-0.4	-0.1
Construction	5.0	4.8	4.5	-0.2	-0.3
Manufacturing	23.4	18.0	15.8	-5.5	-2.2
Durable Goods	14.2	10.6	9.1	-3.6	-1.5
Nondurable Goods	9.2	7.4	6.7	-1.8	-0.7
Service Producing	70.5%	76.6%	79.2%	6.1	2.6
Trans., Comm., Util.	5.7	5.2	5.3	-0.5	0.1
Wholesale	5.8	5.7	5.4	-0.1	-0.3
Retail	16.7	18.0	17.9	1.4	-0.2
Fin., Ins., Real Est.	5.5	6.2	6.0	0.6	-0.2
Services	19.1	24.9	28.1	5.9	3.2
Government	17.8	16.5	16.5	-1.3	0.1
Total	100.0%	100.0%	100.0%	0.0	0.0

Source: Author's analysis.

Corporate Profit Rates, 1959-96   *Appendix 33*

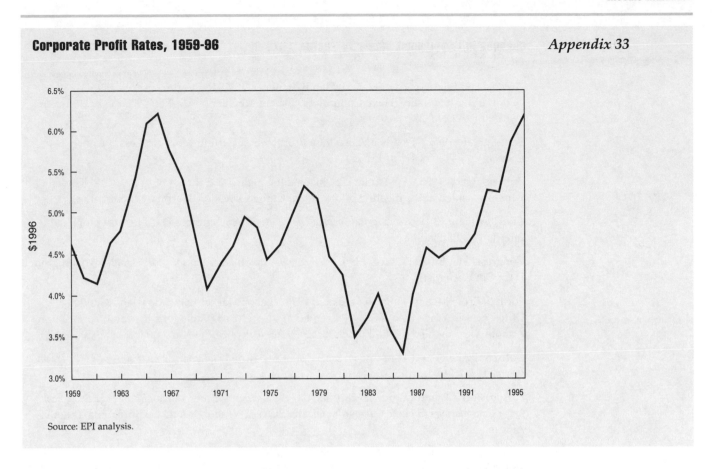

Source: EPI analysis.

Factor Income Shares in the Corporate Sector, 1959-96   *Appendix 34*

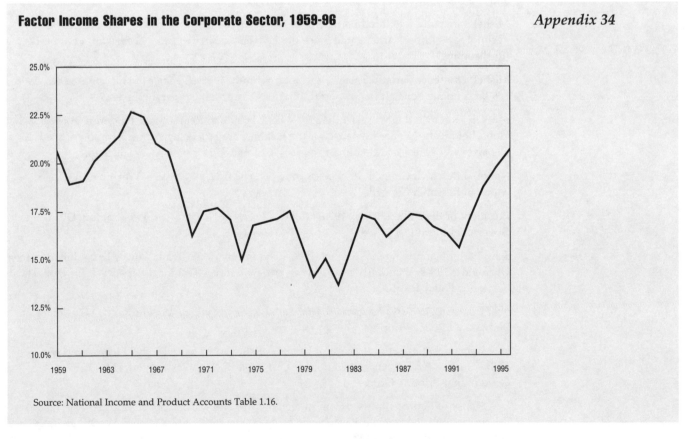

Source: National Income and Product Accounts Table 1.16.

REFERENCES

Autor, David, Lawrence Katz, and Alan B. Krueger. 1997. Revised from July 1996. "Computing Inequality: Have Computers Changed the Labor Market?" *Princeton University Working Paper* No. 377.

Baker, Dean. 1996. "Trends in Corporate Profitability: Getting More for Less?" *National Tax Journal*, Vol. 44, No. 4, pp. 451-75.

Burtless, Gary. 1995. "Widening U.S. Income Inequality and the Growth in World Trade." Paper presented at the meeting of the Tokyo Club in Dresden, Germany (September).

Cline, William R. 1997. *Trade and Income Distribution.* Washington, D.C.: Institute for International Economics.

Congressional Budget Office. 1995. *The Economic and Budget Outlook: An Update.* Washington, D.C.: CBO (August).

Fortin, Nicole M. and Thomas Lemieux. 1996. "Labor Market Institutions and Gender Differences in Wage Inequality." Presented at the Industrial Relations Research Association Annual Meeting held in San Francisco, CA (January).

Gottschalk, Peter and Timothy M. Smeeding. 1996. *Cross National Comparisons of Earnings and Income Inequality.* Unpublished.

Hirsch, Barry T. and David A. Macpherson. 1995. *Union Membership and Earnings Data Book 1994: Compilations from the Current Population Survey.* Washington, D.C.: Bureau of National Affairs.

Karoly, Lynn A. and Gary Burtless. 1995. "Demographic Change, Rising Earnings Inequality, and the Distribution of Personal Well-Being, 1959-89." *Demography*, Vol. 32, No. 3, pp. 379-405.

Mishel, Lawrence and Jared Bernstein. 1997. "Technology and the Wage Structure: Has Technology's Impact Accelerated Since the 1970s?" *Research in Labor Economics*, Volume 17 (forthcoming).

Mishel, Lawrence, Jared Bernstein, and John Schmitt. 1998. *The State of Working America, 1998-1999.* Economic Policy Institute Series. Ithaca, NY: Cornell University Press.

Murphy, Kevin and Finis Welch. 1989. "Recent Trends in Real Wages: Evidence from Household Data." Paper prepared for the Health Care Financing Administration of the U.S. Department of Health and Human Services. Chicago, IL: University of Chicago.

National Research Council. 1995. *Measuring Poverty: A New Approach.* Washington, D.C.: National Research Council.

President of the United States. 1996. *Economic Report of the President.* Washington, DC: U.S. Government Printing Office.

Schmitt, John and Lawrence Mishel. 1996. "Did International Trade Lower Less-Skilled Wages During the 1980s? Standard Trade Theory and Evidence." Technical Paper. Washington, D.C.: Economic Policy Institute.

Shapiro, Isaac. 1997. *No Escape: The Minimum Wage and Poverty.* Washington, D.C.: Center on Budget and Policy Priorities.

U.S. Department of Labor, Bureau of Labor Statistics. 1995. *International Comparisons of Manufacturing Productivity and Unit Labor Cost Trends, 1994.* Washington, D.C.: U.S. Government Printing Office.

U.S. House of Representatives, Committee on Ways and Means, Subcommittee on Human Resources. 1991. *Background Material on Family Income and Benefit Changes.* Washington, DC: U.S. Government Printing Office.

Wolff, Edward N. 1996. "Trends in Household Wealth During 1989-1992." Paper submitted to the Department of Labor. New York: New York University.

Chapter 12

Infrastructure Indicator

by William J. Mallett, Ph.D.

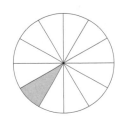

I. Introduction

On a Saturday in 1996 in Manhattan's garment district, a 94-year-old water main, part of a 6,000-mile network under New York City, ruptured, releasing millions of gallons of water onto city streets and into subway lines. In addition to snarling traffic around Times Square and shutting all west side subway lines, the flood of water, knee-deep in some places, damaged merchandise in several stores, interrupted water and power service in several buildings, and damaged asphalt on surrounding streets. Fortunately no one was hurt. The mayor was reported as saying that he was glad the break had not occurred on a weekday (Alvarez 1996).

Infrastructure consists of the long-lived structures and equipment systems that provide basic services to households and firms. This includes systems of transportation that provide passenger and freight mobility; systems of communication by telephone, television, and computer; public utilities providing water, electricity, and gas; and systems of education and health. Good infrastructure, in developed countries no less than developing ones, enables agriculture and manufacturing, helps prevent the spread of disease, and underpins almost every aspect of daily life.

Occasionally, dramatic infrastructure failures – like the water-main break in New York City and the 1993 collapse of the Mianus River Bridge in Connecticut that resulted in three deaths – provide a shocking reminder of its importance. Yet, infrastructure problems are experienced daily by large sections of the population. According to a 1995 report by the General Accounting Office (GAO), one-third of the nation's public schools attended by 14 million children need extensive repairs (GAO 1995). Every day people suffer the frustration of highway congestion, which in 1996 was estimated to have cost $74 billion in 70 of the nation's largest urban areas (Texas Transportation Institute 1998). Congestion is also a growing problem with the relatively new infrastructure of the internet, slowing data traffic on the so-called information superhighway (Sprout 1996).

The size and quality of a nation's infrastructure is a function of investment and consumption. Each year the United States, like every country, consumes part of its collective income and leaves a portion to be invested. Investment can include spending on public or private capital; income-producing assets abroad; human capital through education, health, and science and technology; and the maintenance and conservation of natural resources and the environment (Munnell 1993). All of these investments have the potential for expanding a country's capital stock, defined as assets with the potential to produce future output and income.

Recently researchers at the World Bank argued that a country's capital stock – including natural capital, produced capital, human capital, and social capital – is a much better indicator of a country's development and future prospects than current output and income traditionally measured in national accounts (Serageldin 1996). Current income and output can be generated in unsustainable ways, including borrowing from abroad, over-exploiting natural resources, and using but not maintaining capital goods such as infrastructure. Government accounting procedures have begun to recognize these ideas with the development of a "green" Gross Domestic Product (Carson 1994) and the reconceptualization of government spending based on assets used for more than one year as investment – not consumption – in the National Income and Product Accounts (Parker, Dobbs and Pitzer 1995). However, the debate continues over whether, once this asset budgeting is fully implemented, there should also be deductions for wear and tear over the nation's entire stock of such capital assets. Such depreciation (also used in corporate asset accounts) of national capital stocks gives a picture of a much larger "deficit" in our infrastructure investment. Environmental statisticians have called for similar depreciation of natural resource stocks (World Bank 1997).

The Calvert-Henderson Infrastruture Indicator examines the nation's commitment to its stock of infrastructure capital. Is the country investing for the future by building up its stock or is it producing current income by drawing down these assets? And, more specifically, are there specific elements of the nation's infrastructure that are improving through investment while others are deteriorating?

To answer these questions the indicator of the nation's infrastructure capital stock is calculated from 1947 to 1994. Typically, measures of the nation's infrastructure are limited to public capital, even though significant elements, including telecommunications, transportation, education, health, and public utilities are privately owned. The Calvert-Henderson Infrastructure Indicator, therefore, includes both public and private systems of infrastructure. This approach is particularly important as fiscal problems in government at all levels have encouraged private development of infrastructure, privatization, and public-private partnerships. The movement toward deregulating infrastructural industries, such as telecommunications and electric utilities, provide another rationale for beginning the measurement of private infrastructure capital. On the public side the indicator includes nonmilitary built assets for all levels of government such as highways and streets, water and sewer systems, utilities, transit systems and airports, educational and hospital buildings, conservation and development structures (levees, seawalls, canals, etc.), and equipment.

The Infrastruture Indicator reveals that there has been a substantial

The Calvert-Henderson Infrastructure Indicator includes both public and private systems of infrastructure.

Calvert-Henderson Infrastructure Model

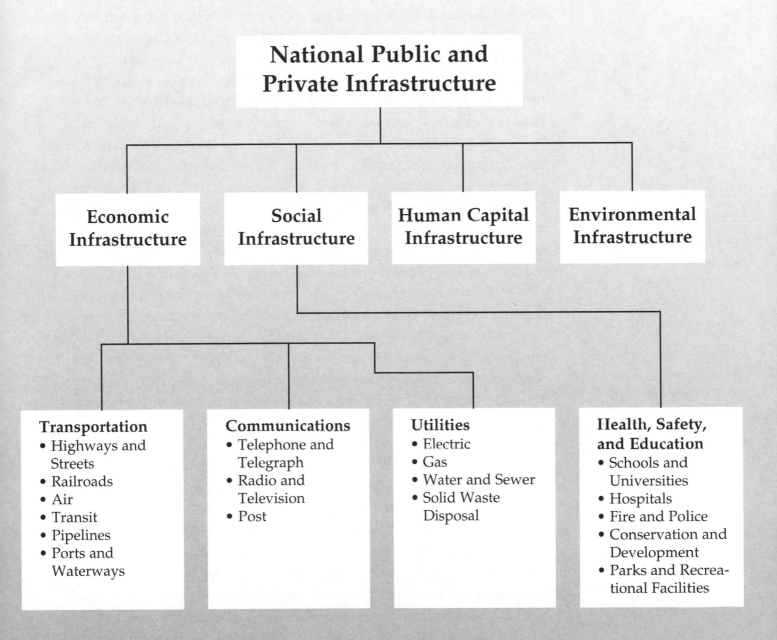

National Public and Private Infrastructure

Economic Infrastructure

Social Infrastructure

Human Capital Infrastructure

Environmental Infrastructure

Transportation
- Highways and Streets
- Railroads
- Air
- Transit
- Pipelines
- Ports and Waterways

Communications
- Telephone and Telegraph
- Radio and Television
- Post

Utilities
- Electric
- Gas
- Water and Sewer
- Solid Waste Disposal

Health, Safety, and Education
- Schools and Universities
- Hospitals
- Fire and Police
- Conservation and Development
- Parks and Recreational Facilities

slowdown in infrastructural development since the early 1970s in both the public and private sectors, pointing to one cause of current problems with deterioration and congestion. The early 1980s were particularly poor years for both private and public infrastructural investment. On the public side the slow growth in the capital stock is attributable to declines in highways and streets and educational facilities, while other parts of the infrastructure, such as other transportation assets and water and sewer assets, have grown but relatively slowly. On the private side there have been noticeable declines in most sectors of transportation from the late 1970s, except for air transportation. By contrast there has been significant investment in electricity and telephone systems, and, to a lesser extent, in sanitation and health infrastructure.

Presentation of the Infrastructure Indicator begins with a definition of infrastructure and then moves on to consider the importance of infrastructure, its benefits, and other views on the state of the nation's infrastructure. Data used to estimate the indicator are outlined in section IV along with some limitations of the indicator. Section V discusses the research findings by detailing infrastructure trends in relation to the size of the population and the overall economy. Implications are discussed in the final section.

II. Defining Infrastructure

Infrastructure can be defined in many different ways. Narrow definitions are limited to economic infrastructure – large capital intensive assets needed for the delivery of key services such as water, electricity, and transportation. Many economic studies also limit their analysis to those elements of the economic infrastructure capital stock owned by the public sector. Broader definitions of infrastructure add social infrastructure, the built assets underlying the delivery of education, health, and recreation such as schools, hospitals, and parks. The broadest definitions of infrastructure, however, also include human capital and environmental assets that allow for the provision of basic services (National Research Council 1987, Forsyth 1995). In this view, water supply, for instance, involves water resources (natural assets), water-supply facilities (economic assets), and the human skills (human capital assets) needed to build and manage water supply (Lemer 1992). The development of the necessary human skills, of course, also relies on a population's education that, in part, is dependent on an infrastructure of schools and colleges (social assets).

The Calvert-Henderson Infrastructure Indicator is predicated on the broader definition of infrastructure because of the very important interrelationships between the four key infrastructure elements: economic, social, human capital, and environmental. The model of our infrastructure indicator, which includes these four elements, appears on the previous page.

As the model suggests, places that have heavily polluted water will have poor water-system infrastructure no matter how sophisticated (and costly) the water purification structures and equipment. Another example of the interrelationships between these elements is the very real problem faced by many cities today with polluted land. Contaminated by years of industrial production there are now thousands of acres that are difficult to redevelop no matter how well developed the surrounding system of roads, sewers, and telecommunications. Indeed, in some places, New York's Love Canal being the most famous example, whole built infrastructures have been abandoned because of polluted land. Human skills and social institutions (e.g., government and legal systems) are other important components of infrastructure because without them economic and social infrastructure cannot be constructed and, if constructed, cannot be properly operated or maintained. Politically weak governments, for instance, often cut infrastructure spending before reducing spending on other more immediate concerns like income supplements and wages for military and other government personnel.

Despite the importance and interrelationships between the four key elements of infrastructure, the Calvert-Henderson Infrastructure Indicator is limited to economic and social infrastructure, the built components of a country's infrastructure capital stock. Human capital is addressed elsewhere in this volume in the Education and Health Indicators, while national assets and environmental wealth are more fully captured by the Calvert-Henderson Environment Indicator and the World Bank's Wealth Index. Military structures and equipment are also excluded from our infrastructure indicator because defense spending, while connected to the quality of life is not logically included as a part of social infrastructure, and is treated as part of the Calvert-Henderson National Security Indicator.

Economic Infrastructure

Economic infrastructure is at the center of most definitions of infrastructure. Economic assets have several key characteristics (Kay 1993). They are networks that deliver services to households and firms, services that are an indispensable input into many activities. For instance, not only is clean water indispensable to sustain life and to prevent the spread of disease, but it is also an input in the production of commodities such as chemicals and food. Other services such as telecommunications and transportation are also used as inputs in the production process of most if not all commodities. As a result, infrastructure investment has a large impact on the productivity of labor and capital in the entire economy. Infrastructure failure, therefore, typically results in large losses in many sectors disproportionate to the expense of the breakdown itself (Musgrave 1990).

Another key characteristic of infrastructure systems is that they are often natural monopolies in which competitive provision would be inefficient, exhibiting what has been termed "publicness," although infrastructure is not necessarily limited to public capital (Biehl 1991, Peterson 1990, Gramlich 1993).[1] Infrastructure, therefore, is often provided by the public sector or by a closely regulated private sector activity, which sometimes includes the public protection of a market. Many facilities have been built and operated by private enterprise, in partnerships of public and private organizations, or acquired by private firms from public entities through privatization. Railroads, for instance, were built privately, but with public financial support. Of course, private development of infrastructure is not a 19th century idea. The first private toll roads built this century were opened a few years ago in northern Virginia and Orange County, California. Telecommunications infrastructure and most public utilities today are held privately. Large elements of the nation's infrastructure such as wastewater treatment plants have recently been transferred to the private sector.

High capital costs relative to running costs are another feature of economic infrastructure. The sunk costs are often very high and usually must be borne in large quantities before a service can be offered. A road is a good example as construction costs are the greatest expense, and once built roads cannot be used for other purposes and must be connected to an expensive network of other roads to be of use.

In sum, economic infrastructure includes three main systems:
- Transportation, including highways, streets, roads, and bridges; mass transit; airports and airplanes; ports, waterways, and vessels; railroads and rail equipment; and gas and petroleum pipelines.
- Utilities, including water supply and sewerage; solid waste treatment and disposal; and electric power generation and transmission.
- Telecommunications and postal communications.

Social Infrastructure

Another important component of infrastructure is social infrastructure – sometimes called social overhead capital – including the built components of education, health, safety, and recreation systems. Such systems are not so obviously a crucial input into the production process, nor are the capital costs disproportionately large in comparison to running costs. But as Lemer notes, social infrastructure "facilities – not as individual buildings, but tied together by the functional and administrative systems they house – provide important services to the public at large, in much the same fashion as highways and water supply facilities" (1992:363). Moreover, social assets underpin the development of human capital; failure in these systems can have widespread impacts.

In the District of Columbia, for instance, the deterioration of public school buildings delayed school openings following the summer recess for three out of four years between 1994 and 1997, impacting the education of thousands of children. In the long run, of course, poorly educated children make poor workers as well as poor citizens, threatening economic productivity and political stability as discussed by Swensen in the Education Indicator. In the short run, the delayed school openings caused economic disruption as thousands of parents had to make alternative arrangements for day care or take unscheduled leave from their jobs. Systems of recreation are another type of social infrastructure that are frequently taken for granted. It is instructive to review the construction of parks in industrial cities during the 19th century; assets actively sought by businesses as well as liberal reformers improved the lives of the working class and tamed social unrest (see Lubove 1969 for a discussion of parks development in Pittsburgh).

III. The Benefits of Infrastructure

Infrastructure is fundamental to several aspects of the quality of life, including health, safety, recreation, and aesthetics. Despite the reemergence of water quality concerns around the nation (EPA 1997), the problems associated with individuals having to dispose of their own wastes, collecting and purifying their own water, and gathering their own fuel, are for most people in the United States not even a distant memory. Philadelphia was the first large city in the United States to construct a municipal water supply, between 1779 and 1801, following a yellow fever epidemic (Tarr 1984). But infrastructure can be important to health in more surprising ways. Researchers have found that the psychological health of the elderly can be dramatically affected by their mobility, partly a function of infrastructure systems such as public transit. Those that cannot travel to visit family and friends, to worship, and to shop often suffer from feelings of uselessness, anxiety, and depression (Carp 1988). Transportation can also enhance people's leisure hours by providing them access to a wide range of recreational opportunities.

Economic Growth

Infrastructure also underpins a country's economic productivity and competitiveness. Over the past decade economists have debated the contribution of infrastructure investment, at least public economic infrastructure investment, to economic productivity (Gramlich 1993, Hulten and Schwab 1995). Research by Auschaer (1990) suggests that the economic rate of return from public investment in core public infrastructure – highways, water, and sewerage – is very large. Although much of this work has been discredited, more credible research by Nadiri and Mamuneaus (1996) on transportation infrastructure reached the same conclusion. They found that the social rate of return on highways was 35 percent a year in the 1950s and 1960s, compared with the social rate of return for private investment of 14 percent a year.[2] The social rate of return declined throughout the 1970s to about 10 percent a year by the 1980s, much lower but still equal to the return on private investment in that time period. Federal highways were found to have a much higher rate of return than local projects.

Research in developing countries demonstrates that a high rate of return on infrastructure investment is not automatic. On the contrary, investment must be made in line with a country's level and pattern of development to satisfy existing and latent demand. Of course, determining future

needs is fraught with uncertainty. But most agree that developing a sophisticated telecommunications infrastructure in an agricultural society that has a
poor transportation system would likely provide few benefits. Infrastructure
projects that relieve bottlenecks, unsurprisingly, are much more likely to
produce very high rates of return and promote economic growth. Hence, it is
often said that, although infrastructure does not guarantee growth, it is a
necessary precondition (World Bank 1994).

Current Research

Opinion is divided on whether the United States is experiencing an
infrastructure problem (Gramlich 1993). The doomsaying that began in the
early 1980s with the publication of *America in Ruins* (Choate and Walter
1981) – detailing problems with roads, bridges, water-supply facilities – and
other studies based on needs assessments has largely been discredited by
experience over the past 15 years and more careful analysis (Peterson 1991).
Problems with underdeveloped infrastructure and infrastructure deterioration remain, such as water quality, traffic congestion, and school building
deterioration. But there have been encouraging signs of improvement in
some areas. The number of structurally deficient and functionally obsolete
bridges, for instance, decreased by about 40,000 between 1988 and 1992
(Dunker and Rabbat 1995). The condition of highway pavement also
improved from the early 1980s through the early 1990s (U.S. Department of
Transportation 1996 and 1997).

Nonetheless, Thurow (1995) argues that the country is underinvest-
ing in infrastructure, particularly in relation to its main competitors, Japan
and Western Europe. Munnell (1993) also finds that the United States invests
less than many countries in Western Europe. The World Economic Forum
(1996), which rates national competitiveness, argues, on the other hand, that
America's infrastructure is one of its greatest strengths. At least part of the
confusion stems from what is measured. Public investment, what both
Thurow and Munnell refer to, does appear to be lower in the United States
than in Western Europe, but that is to be expected with the relatively larger
public sector in Europe. Including private infrastructure investment, as we
do in the Calvert-Henderson Infrastructure Indicator, quite possibly alters
this view of insufficient infrastructural development.

IV. Measuring Infrastructure: Methodology and Data

Infrastructure is most usually measured as a capital stock, the monetary market value of infrastructure (Aschauer 1990, Munnell 1993, Winston
and Bosworth 1993). In a cross-regional comparison, Biehl (1991) uses infrastructure capacity to construct an infrastructure index. Such an approach,
among other things, causes enormous problems with standardization across
different types of infrastructure investments over time. Hence, the capital
stock approach is used here.

Capital stock is estimated across all sectors by the U.S. Department of Commerce's Bureau of Economic Analysis (BEA). The BEA data are currently being revised for integration into the National Income and Product Accounts (NIPA), for better conceptualization of government capital spending and to better estimate depreciation. Before 1996, all goods and services purchased by government, whether they be school meals for children or a new highway, are considered to be consumed in the same period in which they are purchased. The revision will depreciate public investments over time (as is done in the private sector) to allow for a better estimation of investment and savings in the national accounts.

Capital stock is measured by BEA using the perpetual inventory method. This method estimates net capital stock in a given period by totaling previous investment and deducting for depreciation due to wear and tear, obsolescence, accidental damage, and aging. Depreciation in the current series is based on a straight line formula in which it is assumed that the value of an asset declines an equal dollar amount over its service life. Adjustments are made for major natural disasters like hurricanes and earthquakes. The new depreciation methodology assumes more accurately that an asset loses a constant percentage amount over its service life, hence a greater dollar value early in its life (Parker, Dobbs, and Pitzer 1995).

Ideally, each functional element of the national infrastructure (i.e., transportation, water, sewer, telecommunications, etc.) would be measured across the public and private sectors, allowing one to draw conclusions about each system. However, current data make this difficult if not impossible to achieve. Even within the categories of public and private data there are problems determining trends in functional systems because some types of infrastructure are included in catch-all categories, for instance, "utilities, transit systems, and airports" on the public side. As a result, the infrastructure indicator is calculated for total national infrastructure, but disaggregated into public and private elements and further by type of infrastructure within these categories, as is shown by the data in Appendix 1.

The public sector part of the Infrastructure Indicator includes all public sector structures by functional system. All public sector equipment is grouped together. Military structures and equipment are excluded. Highways, streets, sewer, water, utilities, and transportation facilities form the core of public infrastructure systems and thus are grouped together in Appendix 1. The table also collapses the federal and state/local government distinction and combines several of the categories into more understandable groups.

The private sector infrastructure part of the indicator includes both structures and equipment by functional system. Functional systems are estimated by industry based on Standard Industrial Classification codes, not by type of structure or equipment. Using data by industry results in including structures and equipment owned by a certain industry that may not be obviously part of the infrastructure of that industry. For example, a company car owned by a railroad company will show up as part of the railroad infrastructure.

In addition to data problems that hinder the full and accurate specificity of the indicator, the national capital stock approach leaves several important questions on the quality of the nation's infrastructure unanswered. The indicator does not tell us anything about spatial differences of infrastructure quality and condition within the United States. Infrastructure in some areas may be extensive and well-maintained while in other areas it may be underdeveloped and/or poorly maintained. Nor does the indicator allow us to say anything about the quality of infrastructure investments and its contribution to people's quality of life. For instance, urban sprawl requires substantial infrastructural investments that many argue are wasteful.

V. Post-War Infrastructure Trends

Between 1947 and 1994, the infrastructure capital stock of the United States more than tripled in real terms to stand at $3.4 trillion (in 1987 dollars). However, calculating infrastructure in relation to the size of the population and the overall economy shows that there has been a significant slowing of infrastructure investment since the early 1970s. On a per capita basis infrastructure capital stock grew by 87 percent between 1947 and 1994 (from $7,000 to $13,100), but nearly two thirds of the gain was made before 1970. In 1982 and 1983 net investment (spending minus depreciation) was so small in relation to population growth that there was a decline in the per capita infrastructure capital stock. Similarly infrastructure capital stock as a percentage of GDP shows that the nation's commitment to infrastructure investment has waned significantly since the early 1970s. Despite a number of swings in the measure, it stood at 80 percent in 1975, the same as it was in 1947. Since then there has been almost a steady decline to 64 percent in 1994. The steepest decline in infrastructure investment as a percentage of GDP was in the early 1980s.

Between 1947 and 1994, the value of public infrastructure grew more than the value of private infrastructure, both absolutely and relatively. On a per capita basis, the stock of public infrastructure doubled from $4,100 in 1947 to $8,200 in 1994 while private infrastructure grew 67 percent from $2,900 in 1947 to $4,800 in 1994. Net public infrastructure investment far outstripped net private investment in the period up to 1970 (Appendix 2). As a result, the per capita stock of public infrastructure grew by 72 percent compared with only 33 percent of growth on the private side in this period. But, net private infrastructure investment picked up in the 1960s to match public investment in the early 1970s and was even greater for a time in the mid- to late-1970s, although this was to some extent a result of the dearth of public investment. In the late 1980s and early 1990s, public investment recovered somewhat, though at levels far below those in the 1960s, while private investment continued to lag.

Despite the lack of public investment in the 1970s and 1980s, government is still the dominant provider of the country's infrastructure. In 1994, public infrastructure capital stock accounted for 63 percent of the total national infrastructure, a little lower than its high of 65 percent in 1968, but well above the low in the post war period of 57 percent in 1950. State and local governments are the most important owners of infrastructure, notwithstanding the fact that state and local government infrastructure is often financed by federal grants (Appendix 3). State and local governments owned 87 percent of public infrastructure in 1994. The capital stock of the federal government per capita has remained virtually constant in the post-war period.

The rapid growth of the public infrastructure stock from the end of World War II to the early 1970s was largely due to spending on highways and educational buildings, the two largest elements of public infrastructure (Appendices 4 and 5). The value of both of these types of assets declined in the mid-1970s and did not begin to recover until the early 1990s. In part the slowing of highways and streets reflects the end of the building of the interstate highway system. The decline in the value of educational buildings to some extent mirrors the growth and decline in the numbers of school-age children. Nevertheless, lack of investment in school buildings has become a significant problem in many areas of the country (GAO 1995).

Other elements of the core public infrastructure (utilities, transit systems, airports, water, and sewer systems) have grown steadily but slowly since 1947. The value of sewer systems has grown the most, followed by utilities, transit systems, airports, and water supply systems (Appendix 4). Data problems make it difficult to separate the value of publicly owned transit systems from airports and utilities, but it is likely that there was a spurt of growth in the value of public-owned transit systems in the 1970s in a wave of public takeovers from troubled private operators in the late 1960s (Department of Transportation [DOT] 1997). Airport development and redevelopment has also been particularly important over the past 25 years, with the growth in air transportation (DOT 1996).

The public stock of conservation and development structures – primarily for water-resources protection and control such as levees, seawalls, and canals – has grown modestly over the past 47 years but started to decline in 1982. This may have significant implications for places prone to river or coastal flooding. Other public buildings (general office and industrial buildings, police and fire stations, courthouses, auditoriums, garages, and passenger terminals) have grown in value by 75 percent in per capita terms since 1947, although most of that growth has occurred since the late 1960s (Appendix 5).

Unlike growth in the public sector, the private infrastructure capital stock grew as much from 1971 to 1994 as it did from 1947 to 1970. Overall growth of the private infrastructure from 1947 to 1994 is mostly due to growth in electric and gas utilities and telecommunications (Appendices 6 and 7). On the other hand, many sectors of private transportation infrastructure, particularly railroads, have declined (Appendix 8).

The value of private utilities infrastructure has grown across the board, although both the growth and its share of infrastructure is dominated by electric capital stock. Electric infrastructure grew from $555 per person in 1947 to $1,800 per person in 1994, but since the late 1980s the value of electric infrastructure on a per person basis has declined. Gas infrastructure per person has approximately doubled over the period to stand at $395 a person. Private sanitation infrastructure has been valued at about $50 per person since 1947, but nearly quadrupled between 1985 to 1994 as a result of privatization and increased spending on pollution abatement facilities and equipment. For instance, spending on solid waste pollution abatement, including recycling facilities, has increased from $10 billion in 1972 to $30 billion in 1993 (Rutledge and Vogan 1995).

Telecommunications infrastructure grew rapidly between 1947 and 1994, especially radio and television since 1978. The value of telephone and telegraph grew steadily from 1947 to the early 1980s, but has since stagnated. The slowdown in the growth of the value of telephone and telegraph infrastructure coincides with the breakup of the AT&T monopoly in 1984. Radio and television infrastructure by contrast grew slowly until the late 1970s, and since 1978 has more than tripled in per capita terms.

The value of stock in the private transportation per capita has declined or remained unchanged over the past 47 years in all sectors, except air transportation. The decline has been most precipitous in the railroads, falling from $1,400 per capita in 1947 to about $400 per capita in 1994. This has resulted mainly as a result of competition from highway transportation for both passengers and freight. The shrinkage of railroad track has recently caused congestion problems due to the robust growth in freight rail shipments (Welty 1996). There has also been decline in local and interurban passenger transit and water transportation. The capital stock of trucking and warehousing has rapidly declined since 1979 after very rapid growth from about 1970 to 1979. Investment in air transportation infrastructure has been the exception in private transportation, growing more than seven fold in per capita terms since 1947. Nevertheless, growth since 1970 has been very modest (Appendix 9).

Finally, on the private side there has been a great percentage growth in social infrastructure, including health and educational services, going from $22 per person in 1947 to $325 in 1994. Their proportion of the country's total infrastructure stock remains very small, however.

VI. Conclusions

Infrastructure is vital to the health, welfare, and economic productivity of the United States. Current trends in the capital stock of infrastructure

Infrastructure is vital to the health, welfare, and economic productivity of the United States.

suggest that investment in infrastructure, in both the public and private sectors, has not been pursued vigorously since the mid-1970s. Although it cannot be concluded that the slowing of infrastructure development has caused productivity problems in the recent past, it does raise questions of the nation's commitment to the future. Moreover, the evidence provided in the Infrastructure Indicator points to problem areas that may support other more specific infrastructure studies. Clearly, the condition of infrastructure varies by the type of system. Stagnation and decline are evident in the value of the nation's transportation infrastructure, with the most startling decline in railroads. Educational infrastructure has also suffered since the late 1970s. On the whole utilities and communications infrastructures appear to be in relatively good shape, although infrastructure trends in both of these systems need watching in the future as deregulation proceeds in these industries.

Building infrastructure is, however, not always the answer to infrastructure problems. Another important task is the management of existing infrastructural resources for efficient use. In transportation, for instance, several states are experimenting with roadway pricing to encourage travelers to shift the timing of trips or to forego trips altogether to reduce congestion. It is hoped such schemes will reduce the need for additional road building and lessen transportation's negative effects, which include, among other things, air and noise pollution. More fundamentally, several states and localities are trying to shape land use patterns in order to maximize the benefits of infrastructure spending. Maryland, for instance, has recently announced an initiative called Smart Growth that will attempt to guide residential and commercial development to areas that have existing infrastructural capacity.

Lagging infrastructure investment since the early 1970s, nonetheless, does suggest that the country has been consuming more and investing less of the national product than in the past. Sufficient investment in the nation's infrastructure, however, is as much a political problem as it is an economic one. Infrastructure projects, particularly big ones, have become much more difficult politically with the rising distrust of government, a proliferation of interest groups, and the spread of NIMBY (Not In My BackYard) objections. While questioning the benefits and costs of infrastructure projects – including the social distribution of costs and benefits – is important, these factors have hurt the ability of governments to raise capital for investment, lengthened the time it takes to build infrastructure, and increased the costs of infrastructure development for both public and private organizations. Hence, in the future the ability to quickly build consensus on infrastructure projects and find efficient ways to deal with the negative impacts of infrastructure projects will be at least as important as balancing investment in infrastructure with consumption on current needs.

ENDNOTES

[1] Recent experience in very mature economies like the United States suggests that natural monopolies are very rare. Indeed, competition has developed in industries like telecommunications and electrical utilities. Less mature economies, however, may still need a long period of regulated monopoly to develop a sophisticated infrastructure.

[2] The social rate of return is defined as the sum of economic gains due to highway investment for all the nation's industries, less the depreciation cost of the highways.

Infrastructure Capital Stock, 1947-1994 (millions of 1987$)

Appendix 1

	1947	1950	1960	1970	1980	1990	1994	Percent Change, 1947-1994
Total National Infrastructure	1,006,863	1,076,923	1,502,796	2,232,125	2,800,232	3,202,972	3,399,860	238
Population (millions)	144	152	181	205	228	250	260	81
GDP (millions 1987 dollars)	1,252,800	1,418,500	1,970,800	2,873,900	3,776,300	4,897,300	5,344,000	327
Infrastructure per capita	6,992	7,085	8,303	10,888	12,282	12,812	13,076	87
Infrastructure per GDP	80	76	76	78	74	65	64	(21)
Total Public Infrastructure	588,661	616,129	918,105	1,440,030	1,728,367	1,978,472	2,142,560	264
Core Infrastructure	314,608	335,499	490,379	772,364	935,293	1,069,562	1,154,682	267
Highways and Streets	211,233	223,961	340,716	535,191	606,118	651,036	692,926	228
Sewer Systems	35,889	39,414	59,435	88,311	134,624	169,195	184,470	414
Water Supply Systems	32,693	34,679	45,091	67,738	79,529	100,324	113,733	248
Utilities, Transit Systems, and Airports	34,793	37,445	45,137	81,124	115,022	149,007	163,553	370
Buildings	170,454	176,413	276,149	438,150	530,347	577,100	624,821	267
Educational	66,274	73,915	142,192	259,213	292,005	279,909	297,189	348
Hospital	18,626	23,208	31,722	41,057	51,355	54,340	56,719	205
Other[a]	85,554	79,290	102,235	137,880	186,987	242,851	270,913	217
Conservation and Development	56,923	64,654	85,040	123,092	146,654	155,424	156,209	174
Equipment	46,676	39,563	66,537	106,424	116,073	176,386	206,848	343
Total Private Infrastructure[b]	418,202	460,794	584,691	792,095	1,071,865	1,224,500	1,257,300	201
Transportation	268,035	270,253	251,110	263,697	302,003	255,600	240,000	(10)
Railroad	201,008	199,402	168,149	134,214	120,480	98,200	93,600	(53)
Local and Interurban Passenger Transit	15,286	14,212	8,568	5,856	4,667	5,900	4,200	(73)
Water Transportation	15,873	15,080	18,119	21,445	32,989	20,400	17,800	12
Pipeline, excluding Natural Gas	11,382	12,349	13,397	15,117	24,024	17,900	17,200	51
Air Transportation	3,918	4,121	11,232	35,995	44,309	50,100	53,500	1,265
Trucking and Warehousing	14,871	18,727	23,106	32,633	57,535	44,800	36,100	143
Telecommunications	32,505	43,846	82,372	159,569	256,459	306,100	318,000	878
Telephone and Telegraph	30,475	41,322	77,315	148,463	236,282	256,900	257,600	745
Radio and Television	2,029	2,524	5,057	11,107	20,177	49,200	60,400	2,877
Utilities	114,464	142,303	238,546	340,299	472,090	587,100	614,700	437
Electric	79,940	99,950	170,000	249,039	367,406	456,700	460,800	476
Gas	27,361	35,307	61,217	82,493	92,343	93,200	102,700	275
Sanitary	7,163	7,046	7,329	8,767	12,341	37,300	51,200	615
Education and Health	3,198	4,392	12,663	28,530	41,313	75,700	84,600	2,545
Health Services	2,803	3,823	11,506	26,937	39,525	72,300	80,400	2,768
Educational Services	395	569	1,157	1,593	1,788	3,400	4,200	963

[a]Includes general office and industrial buildings, police and fire stations, courthouses, auditoriums, garages, and passenger terminals
[b]All categories include structures and equipment

Source: U.S. Department of the Commerce, Bureau of Economic Analysis 1993.

Appendix 2 **Annual Change in Per Capita Public and Private Infrastructure Capital Stocks, 1947-1994 (constant 1987$)**

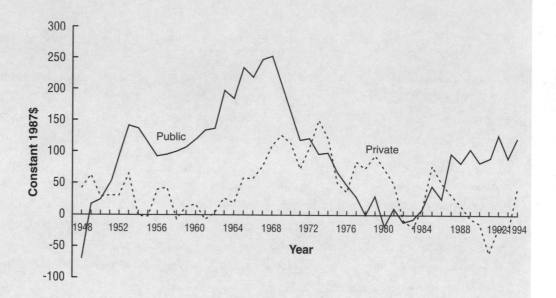

Source: U.S. Department of Commerce, Bureau of Economic Analysis 1993 and unpublished updates.

**Infrastructure Capital Stock by Level of Government, 1947-1994
(constant 1987$)**

Appendix 3

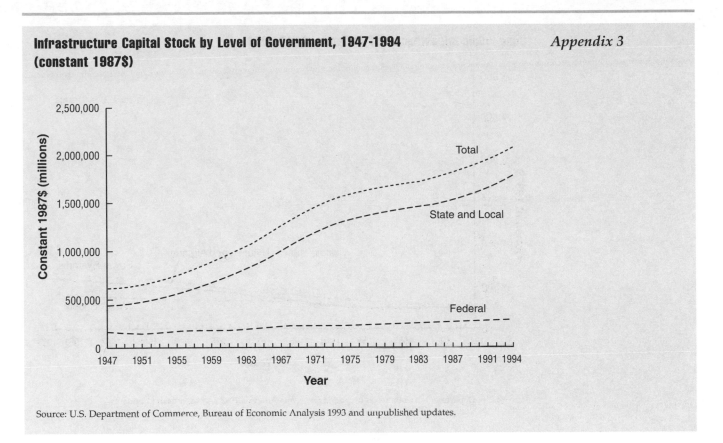

Source: U.S. Department of Commerce, Bureau of Economic Analysis 1993 and unpublished updates.

Appendix 4   **Core Public Infrastructure Per Capita, 1947-1994**

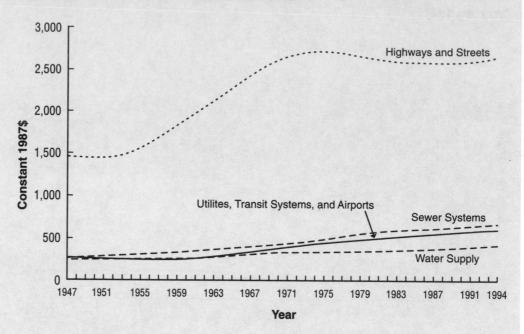

Source: U.S. Department of Commerce, Bureau of Economic Analysis 1993 and unpublished updates.

Elements of the Public Infrastructure Capital Stock Per Capita, 1947-1994 (constant 1987$)

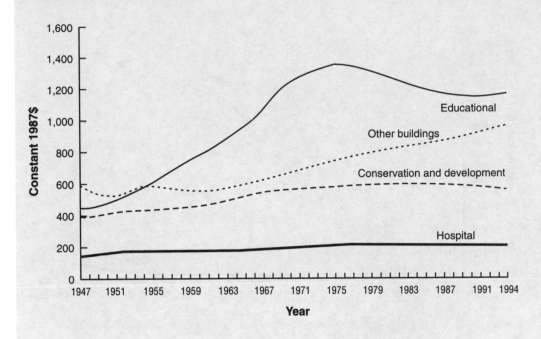

Source: U.S. Department of Commerce, Bureau of Economic Analysis 1993 and unpublished updates.

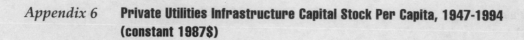

Appendix 6 **Private Utilities Infrastructure Capital Stock Per Capita, 1947-1994 (constant 1987$)**

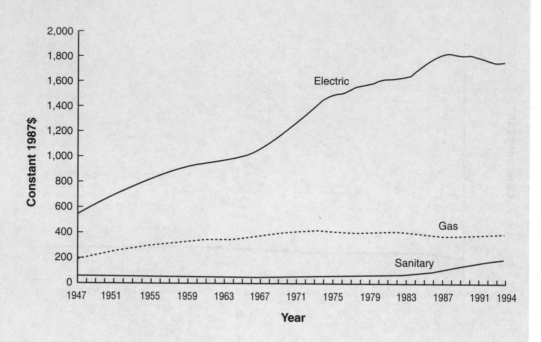

Source: U.S. Department of Commerce, Bureau of Economic Analysis 1993 and unpublished updates.

Private Telecommunication Infrastructure Capital Stock Per Capita, 1947-1994 (constant 1987$)

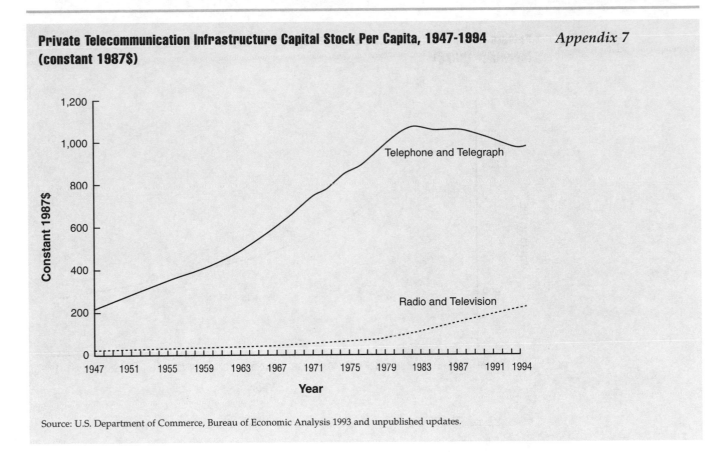

Source: U.S. Department of Commerce, Bureau of Economic Analysis 1993 and unpublished updates.

Appendix 8   **Private Railroad Infrastructure Capital Stock Per Capita, 1947-1994 (constant 1987$)**

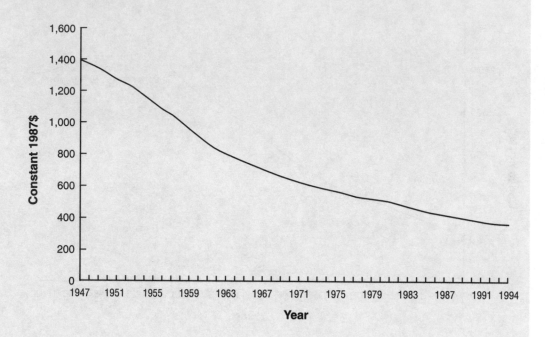

Source: U.S. Department of Commerce, Bureau of Economic Analysis 1993 and unpublished updates.

Elements of the Private Infrastructure Capital Stock Per Capita, 1947-1994 (constant 1987$)

Appendix 9

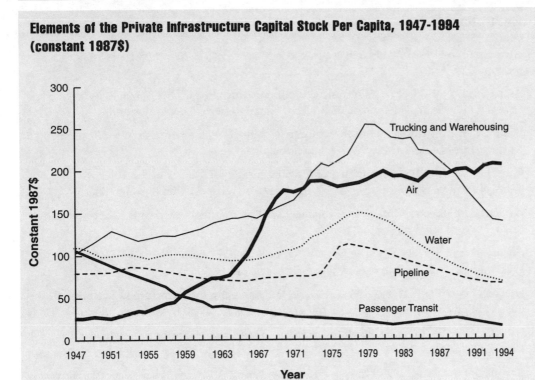

Source: U.S. Department of Commerce, Bureau of Economic Analysis 1993 and unpublished updates.

REFERENCES

Alvarez, Lizette. 1996. "A Broken Main Floods Midtown." *The New York Times,* May 5, Section A, p.1.

Aschauer, D.A. 1990. "Why is Infrastructure Important?" in Alicia H. Munnell (ed), *Is There a Shortfall in Public Capital Investment?* Boston: Federal Reserve Bank of Boston.

Biehl, D. 1991. "The Role of Infrastructure in Regional Development," in R.W. Vickerman (ed), *Infrastructure and Regional Development.* London: Pion Press.

Carp, Frances M. 1988. "Significance of Mobility for the Well-Being of the Elderly." *Transportation in an Aging Society.* Washington, D.C.: Transportation Research Board.

Carson, Carol S. 1994. "Integrated Economic and Environmental Accounts." *Survey of Current Business,* April, pp. 33-49.

Choate, P. and S. Walter. 1981. *America in Ruins: Beyond the Public Works Pork Barrel.* Washington, D.C.: Council of State Planning Agencies.

Dunker, Kenneth F. and Basile G. Rabbat. 1995. "Assessing Infrastructure Deficiencies: The Case of Highway Bridges." *Journal of Infrastructure Systems,* Vol. 1, No. 2, pp. 100-119.

Forsyth, A. 1995. "Privatization: Infrastructure on the Urban Edge." *Journal of Urban Affairs,* Vol. 17, No. 3, pp. 241-262.

Gramlich, Edward M. 1993. "Infrastructure Investment: A Review Essay." *Journal of Economic Literature,* Vol. XXXII, pp. 1176-1196.

Harden, Blaine. 1997. "Highway Project Shovels Cash to Shore Up Bostonian Support." *Washington Post,* September 17, Section A, p.1.

Hulten, Charles R. and Robert. M. Schwab. 1995. "Infrastructure Spending: Where Do We Go From Here?" *National Tax Journal,* pp. 261-273.

Kay, J. 1993. "Efficiency and Private Capital in the Provision of Infrastructure." *Infrastructure Policies for the 1990s.* Paris: Organization for Economic Cooperation and Development.

Lemer, A.C. 1992. "We Cannot Afford Not to Have a National Infrastructure Policy." *Journal of the American Planning Association,* Vol. 58, No. 3, pp. 362-367.

Lubove, Roy. 1969. *Twentieth Century Pittsburgh: Government, Business, and Environmental Change.* New York: John Wiley and Sons.

Munnell, A.H. 1993. "An Assessment of Trends in, and Economic Impacts of, Infrastructure Investment." *Infrastructure Policies for the 1990s,* Paris: Organization for Economic Cooperation and Development.

Musgrave, R.A. 1990. "Discussion," in Alicia H. Munnell (ed), *Is There a Shortfall in Public Capital Investment?* Boston: Federal Reserve Bank of Boston.

Nadiri, M.I. and T.P. Mamuneas. 1996. "Contribution of Highway Capital to Industry and National Productivity Growth." Prepared for the U.S. Department of Transportation, Federal Highway Administration, Office of Policy Development (September).

National Research Council. 1987. *Infrastructure for the 21st Century.* Washington DC: National Academy Press.

Parker, R. P., D.T. Dobbs, and J.S. Pitzer. 1995. "Preview of the Comprehensive Revision of the National Income and Product Accounts: Recognition of Government Investment and Incorporation of a New Methodology for Calculating Depreciation." *Survey of Current Business,* September, 33-41.

Peterson, G. E. 1990. "Is Public Infrastructure Undersupplied?" in Alicia H. Munnell (ed), *Is There a Shortfall in Public Capital Investment?* Boston: Federal Reserve Bank of Boston.

Peterson, G. E. 1991. "Historical Perspectives on Infrastructure Investment: How Did We Get Where We Are?" American Enterprise Institute, Discussion Paper, February.

Roborgh, L.J., R.R. Stough, and A.J. Toonen (ed.s). 1988. *Public Infrastructure Redefined.* Bloomington, Ind.: School of Public and Environmental Affairs.

Rutledge, G.L. and C.R. Vogan. 1995. "Pollution Abatement and Control Expenditures, 1993." *Survey of Current Business,* May, pp. 36-45.

Serageldin, Ismail. 1996. "Sustainability and the Wealth of Nations: First Steps in an Ongoing Journey." World Bank: Environmentally Sustainable Development Studies and Monographs Series No. 5.

Sprout, Alison L. 1996. "Waiting to Download." *Fortune,* August 5, pp. 64-70.

Tarr, J.A. 1984. "The Evolution of the Urban Infrastructure in the Nineteenth and Twentieth Centuries," in Royce Hanson (ed), *Perspectives in Urban Infrastructure.* Washington, D.C.: National Academy Press.

Texas Transportation Institute. 1998. *Urban Roadway Congestion: Annual Report, 1998.* College Station, Texas: Texas Transportation Institute.

Thurow, Lester C. 1995. *The Future of Capitalism.* New York: William Morrow and Company, Inc.

U.S. Department of Commerce, Bureau of Economic Analysis. 1993. *Fixed Reproducible Tangible Wealth in the United States, 1925-1989.* Washington, D.C.: U.S. Government Printing Office.

U.S. Environmental Protection Agency (EPA). 1997. *Drinking Water Infrastructure Needs Survey: First Report to Congress.* Washington, D.C.: Government Printing Office.

U.S. General Accounting Office. 1995. *School Facilities: Condition of America's Schools.* (GAO/HEHS-95-61). Washington, D.C.: U.S. Government Printing Office.

U.S. Department of Transportation. 1995. *1995 Status of the Nation's Surface Transportation System: Condition and Performance.* Washington, D.C.: Government Printing Office.

U.S. Department of Transportation, Bureau of Transportation Statistics. 1996. *Transportation Statistics Annual Report, 1996.* Washington, D.C.: U.S. Government Printing Office.

U.S. Department of Transportation, Bureau of Transportation Statistics. 1997. *Transportation Statistics Annual Report, 1997.* Washington, D.C.: U.S. Government Printing Office.

Welty, Guy. 1996. "Greater Volume, Limited Capacity: How a Shrinking Industry Is Coping with Growth." *Railway Age,* September.

Winston, C. and B. Bosworth. 1993. "Public Infrastructure, "in Henry J. Aaron and Charles L. Shultze (eds), *Setting Domestic Priorities: What Can Governments Do?* Washington, D.C.: Brookings Institution.

World Bank. 1994. *World Development Report 1994: Infrastructure for Development.* Oxford: Oxford University Press.

World Bank. 1997. *Expanding the Measure of Wealth: Indicators of Environmentally Sustainable Development.* Washington, D.C.: World Bank.

World Economic Forum. 1996. *Global Competitiveness Report 1996.* Geneva, Switzerland.

Chapter 13

National Security Indicator

by Colonel Daniel M. Smith, Ret.

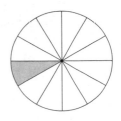

I. Introduction

Supreme Court Justice Potter Stewart once observed that although he could not define pornography, he knew it when he saw it. The same observation could be made about U.S. national security. It is a state of mind, something we feel or sense. It is a way of being affected by and having an effect on the world, rather than an absolute state of existence that can be precisely defined in everyday life. Nonetheless, some people have strong views about the state of national security, with one person believing (for what seem valid reasons) that the nation is secure from its enemies while another (for equally valid reasons) sees great dangers looming.

Our political and military leaders annually attempt to articulate their interpretation of the state of the nation's ability to protect its vital interests and the American way of life against unwanted intrusions and influences. Thus in its broadest sense, national security is a negative concept that individuals and groups, from the family to the nation-state and increasingly to the world community, apply to the specific conditions of their environment. In this century there have been three great statements of what constitutes national security and its essential complements, individual and international security. The first was Woodrow Wilson's Fourteen Points (1918). These addressed the conditions without which international security in a post-World War I Europe of paranoid, vengeful, victorious nation-states would be impossible. Wilson's failure at the Versailles peace conference presaged both his failure to gain Senate approval of the League of Nations and Europe's rapid return to a new world war.[1]

The second great statement was Franklin Roosevelt's Four Freedoms (1941). These embodied the conditions of individual security that Roosevelt believed were fundamental for the political health and security of nations: freedom of speech and expression, freedom of worship, freedom from want, and freedom from fear of physical violence.[2] Of particular interest is that only freedom from fear of physical violence even remotely addresses war and conflict.

The third statement of national security, the Charter of the United Nations (1945), is more inclusive than Wilson's Fourteen Points and Roosevelt's Four Freedoms, for it brings the three fundamental aspects of security – individual, national, and international – into a single statement and single vision for the world. The preamble to the charter affirms that the objectives of the United Nations are "to save succeeding generations from the scourge of war;... to reaffirm faith in fundamental human rights, in the dignity and worth of the human person, in the equal rights of men and women and of nations large and small; to establish conditions under which justice and respect for the obligations arising from treaties and other sources of international law can be maintained; and to promote social progress and better standards of life in larger freedom."

The explicit conjunction of individual, national, and international spheres is crucial for understanding the American approach to national security. Security of the individual within the state (free to seek economic opportunity and personal well-being and to be free from crime and intimidation), and the state within the international community (national identity, economic and environmental well-being) are equally the most fundamental obligations of democratic government.

II. National Security: What Is It, Who Determines It

Keeping in mind the fundamental elements of individual and nation state security, the Calvert-Henderson National Security Indicator examines the process and pressures that impinge on the formation and execution of national security policies as illustrated in the National Security Model.

National security determinations are of necessity iterative. Over time, the list of national interests changes as national and world conditions change. For example, in the early days of the nation the government worried less about invasion by European nations than about confrontations with Native Americans as settlements expanded westward across the continent. As international commerce expanded, freedom of the seas became more important. In the last few decades, we have come to realize that the quality of the environment carries implications for overall national security as well.

Just as national security is multifaceted, so too are the structures of government that define, fund, and implement policies and programs that contribute to security in the United States. The President sets the country's international relations agenda by defining vital and lesser but still important national objectives, the threats that might thwart attaining these objectives, and the diplomatic-military-economic initiatives that will negate or mitigate these threats. Through the annual budget proposal, the President provides to the Congress priorities and a blueprint of how the national security apparatus will operate and cooperate. The Departments of State and Defense have the primary responsibility in international relations, followed by the Departments of Commerce, Justice, Treasury, and the Central Intelligence Agency. Insofar as the President sets the overall objectives for international relations, he also has the initial advantage in rallying domestic public opinion behind his programs.

Congress, in turn, disposes of the President's proposals by its power over the purse. Committees in both chambers are involved in setting budget targets (ceilings) while authorization and appropriations subcommittees and

Calvert-Henderson National Security Model

Public Opinion

President's National Security Strategy
(Prevent/Deter/Defeat)

Congressional Budget Process

Diplomatic Strategy
and Activities
(Prevent/Deter)

Military Strategy
and Programs
(Deter/Defeat)

Consultations
and
Nonmilitary
Interventions

U.N. & Other
Alliances
& Treaties

Forces
Plans
Operations

Defense
Industry and
Technology

If effective

NATIONAL MILITARY SECURITY

Threat

committees minutely examine proposed programs. Eventually both chambers vote the dollars that will actually be spent. Any disagreements between the final bills produced by each chamber must be resolved before the legislation goes to the President for signature or veto. But regardless of how national interests may change over time, regardless of the interplay between the executive and legislative branches, national security has one fundamental and vital premise: the survival of the nation-state as an independent sovereign entity with its territorial integrity intact. Diplomatic and military activity to achieve this condition occurs simultaneously and, in the best of circumstances, in tandem with each other. Diplomatic instruments include treaties and agreements, multinational organizations, and regular diplomatic representations. Military instruments include forces and weapons, plans and operations, and the industrial base that supports the military's effort to provide comprehensive defenses for the nation.

The processes that determine the instruments to be used are not unidirectional. Rather they are influenced by the government's perceptions of what has been achieved and what still needs to be accomplished with regard to national security. Similarly, the perception of threats and public opinion about foreign affairs help shape the forms that national security assumes. For instance, the spectacular successes in space of the former Soviet Union in the late 1950s gave rise first to the U.S. perception of a missile gap and then an all-out commitment, widely supported by the nation, to develop the technology to reach the moon. Because of the interchangeability of civilian and military space functions and technology, the Pentagon was a significant player in missile technology developments. In the aftermath of the Soviet Union's collapse and with a number of international agreements about nuclear weapons, public interest in the missile issue waned, although it remains visible in Congress because of the recent tests by North Korea, Iran, India, and Pakistan of intermediate range ballistic missiles.

The key point behind the Calvert-Henderson National Security Indicator is not to quantify the nation's resources to be expended for national security. The critical element is determining the correct division of resources between the military and nonmilitary spheres that can best guarantee the nation's total national security. The irreducible criterion is the willingness to spend what is needed where it is needed but to resist spending one cent more than is required in either category. Overspending in one sphere entails opportunity costs in the other, for both human and monetary resources are finite. For example, failing to apply this standard to defense spending risks starting down the road of destroying the value of the very things we seek to defend – life, liberty, and the opportunity to develop individual capabilities to their fullest.

III. National Security and the Nation's Quality of Life

"This world in arms is not spending money alone. It is spending the sweat of its laborers, the genius of its scientists, the hopes of its children" (Eisenhower 1953). This was President Dwight D. Eisenhower's assessment of the impact of the nuclear and conventional arms races that began in the aftermath of World War II.

As a professional soldier who had risen to the highest rank and commanded millions of men and women in war, Eisenhower understood the necessity of a strong military in a world of competing and ideologically hostile nation-states. Yet his first-hand experience of modern warfare's all-consuming annihilation, made possible by human ingenuity and science, also convinced him that the human race risked all its achievements and possibly its very existence by its pursuit of the weapons of war.

The essential question posed by President Eisenhower remains relevant today: How much of our resources – labor, education, science, finance, psychology – is the nation willing to commit to the various components of national security so that our quality of life and that of our children is protected and preserved from external threats but not unduly diminished or circumscribed by the perceived necessity of national survival?

There really is no easy answer to this question. Just as the quality of our lives changes over time as a reflection of our wages, housing, health, environment, public safety, and so on, so too does the perception of how much national defense is enough. As the national and individual sense of safety from physical harm grows, each is able to reallocate resources to desirable goals beyond the need for security. For the nation-state in particular, the process is iterative until the goals and resources one nation desires for its quality of life compete with the goals and resources desired by other nations. At this point, decisions have to be made either to cooperate, to share, to search for alternative resources, or to seize resources by force on the Athenian premise that the state that does not rule others is soon ruled itself (Thucydides 1954, Durant and Durant 1966).[3]

In a democracy, citizens ultimately make the decisions about what course to follow in achieving and maintaining their quality of life. Their decisions are translated at the ballot box in terms of who is elected to govern. Government, as the people's representative to other governments, further translates these decisions into foreign policy, traditionally diplomatic and military but increasingly financial (trade and currency), informational, and environmental. In this manner, national security ultimately cannot be separated from the values and goals that a people hold. It is therefore important that citizens ensure that their goals and values are not put at unnecessary risk either from an overreaching or negligent government.

The essential question remains: How much of our resources is the nation willing to commit to the various components of national security?

IV. National Security in U.S. Policy

Threats and the perceptions of the public about the adequacy of military forces to counter these threats are the external forces driving the national security process as noted in the Calvert-Henderson National Security Model. There is in U.S. government circles an official definition of national security. According to the Joint Chiefs of Staff, national security is a state of affairs achieved by a combination of favorable advantages in foreign relations (diplomacy) and military affairs through which a government can successfully resist overt or covert political, military, and economic encroachments of other nation-states (U.S. Department of Defense 1994). This condition can be reached by identifying external and internal threats (those that could weaken the ability of the state to withstand external pressures) and devising strategies that effectively counter both existing and anticipated threats to the survival of the nation-state.

Achieving national security is not really the main difficulty nations face. Normally, war or the threat of war is sufficient to convince a populace that they are in danger. The difficulty lies in sustaining this state of mind among citizens who, experiencing long periods of relative peace or having no credible threat near their borders, tire of indefinitely supporting elaborate military establishments. A healthy skepticism, key to functioning democracies, too easily can turn to cynicism when the military and political elite cannot sway public opinion about the existence of credible near- or long-term threats to the nation.

The history and geography of the United States makes achieving national security doubly difficult. Until the 1940s, with vast oceans on two sides of the continent and quiescent nations on our borders, the United States did not fear a substantive, direct enemy attack. The 45-year Cold War, with its threat of nuclear missiles a mere 30 flight minutes away and a huge Soviet Army seemingly poised on the edge of the inter-German border, changed that perception. Our response was to maintain, for the first time in our history, a large and expensive standing military in peacetime. The military rather than the diplomat took center stage. "Where are the [aircraft] carriers" and "send in the Marines" became the first response and the primary concern of presidents in dealing with international affairs during the Cold War.

In 1999, eight years after the dissolution of the threat of massive conventional war in Europe, the United States is slowly but surely returning to its pre-1940s tradition. This is evident by progress – albeit sometimes halting – in reducing nuclear arsenals and the renewed emphasis on using the National Guard and Reserve Forces to augment active duty units. Examples are the use of reserve components to help staff the Multinational Force of Observers that monitors activities in the Sinai Desert between Egypt and Israel; flying air missions in support of U.S. policies in the Persian Gulf, Bosnia, and Kosovo; the creation of special chemical and biological emergency assessment response teams; and the serious proposal to replace an active duty company with a National Guard company in Army infantry and armor battalions. But this reversion still faces significant opposition, as evident in the manner elected officials and the Pentagon continue to formulate the fundamental issues pertaining to national security: strategy, forces, military equipment, threats, and public opinion.

For example, the May 7, 1998, issue of *Roll Call,* a newspaper that covers the activities of Congress, contained a special section on national defense. The overall theme was the decline of U.S. military forces. The authors, from both the administration and Congress and from both political parties, cited what they saw as decreased readiness; an inability to shape events, forcing a reactive military posture; increased personnel stress because of repeated unaccompanied and dangerous overseas assignments; and the lack of a national missile defense. None of the articles addressed the positive contributions of the reserve components to national defense.

V. National Security Strategy and Structure

National security strategy is the umbrella term encompassing all elements of national strength that are brought to bear to secure our national interests. It is the perception of unwarranted opposition to the national interests of self-preservation, independence, national integrity, military security, economic well-being, and international order or stability that drives the development of strategies to prevent others from unilaterally depriving us of achieving these ends. After all, if nations could completely harmonize their efforts so that everyone proportionately shared these interests, we would have security.

President Clinton first encapsulated the post-Cold War U.S. national security strategy as "engagement and enlargement," a dual approach to international relations whose objective is to draw increasing numbers of nation-states into a web of economic relationships among democratic countries. Ironically, in this first attempt to translate his theory into practice, the President chose a patently negative troika of activities: prevent/deter/defeat. Perhaps realizing the defensive tone of this formulation, the second iteration became "shaping the international environment, responding to the full spectrum of crises, and preparing now for an uncertain future" (the White House 1997, Cohen 1998).

By prevention, President Clinton means that the United States must be able to foresee and forestall the emergence of serious opposition, particularly military opposition, to U.S. goals. Should foresight fail, we must then have the diplomatic and military means to deter a hostile power from directly or indirectly attacking the United States. This would include attempts to subvert friendly regimes as well as attacks on U.S. allies with whom we have concluded mutual defense treaties. Lastly, should deterrence also fail, U.S. military forces must be able to defeat an enemy quickly and decisively, ensuring that the United States emerges from battle without unacceptable losses or damage to the homeland.

Many executive branch departments have a part to play in implementing this national security strategy, most prominent of which is the Department of Defense. Thus it is no surprise that the Pentagon's definition of national security strategy is the usual starting point for consideration of this subject.

The Pentagon defines national security strategy as "the art and science of developing and using the political, economic, and psychological powers of a nation, together with the armed forces, during peace and war, to secure national objectives" (U.S. Department of Defense 1994). In past times national objectives were always unilateral, a focus that inevitably led to wars and other conflicts. Today, they are often cast in the rhetoric of environmental, free-market, and democratic inclusiveness. Nonetheless, the underlying rationale remains that of narrow national power and the pursuit of national objectives.

Using the President's national security strategy as its starting point, the Pentagon formulates the national military strategy, which it defines as "the art and science of distributing and applying military power to attain national objectives in peace and war." Since World War II the United States has divided the world geographically into military theaters or areas of military responsibility. Five war-fighting commanders-in-chief are responsible for employing military force within defined geographical areas if so ordered by the President.

VI. Congressional Budget Process

The executive branch does not have the defense arena to itself. While the President and the Defense Department articulate the national security and military security strategies, they remain little more than ideas and goals until Congress, in the second step of the national security process, validates them through appropriating money to run the activities of government.

This is a long process. The President submits the budget to Congress in late January or early February of each year. By mid-April Congress is responsible for passing a budget resolution setting guidelines for all government expenditures for the coming fiscal year. Various committees hold hearings on the President's budget proposal. Some committees authorize expenditures while others actually appropriate funds, adding, deleting, or leaving the President's requests unchanged. Each House then votes on the 13 funding bills for the entire government. If any of the Senate and House bills differ, a joint conference is held to develop a compromise. Both chambers vote on the compromise bill, which then goes to the President for signature into law or veto. If the latter, the bill goes back to Congress for further consideration or for votes to override the presidential veto. Quite often, Congress fails to complete its work before October 1, the start of each new fiscal year. It must then either pass continuing resolutions to temporarily fund the government or – as in 1996 – the government closes.

National defense and foreign policy funding follow this same process. How quickly they move through the process depends in part on the intensity of partisan politics that comes into play. For example, a frequent cliché of the early Cold War era was that "partisanship stopped at the water's edge," meaning that in foreign affairs Congress and the administration of the day would stand virtually shoulder to shoulder when the question was the content and direction of U.S. international relations (Vandenberg 1952). However, such singularity of purpose was less prevalent among policymakers than many remember, particularly when Congress was controlled by one party and the White House by the other (e.g., during the Nixon and the latter years of the Reagan presidencies).

In recent years, this putative unified public posture is under new strains as the demands for balanced budgets and tax relief clash with demands to maintain and even increase military spending and operations. In the mid-1990s, congressional hawks failed to obtain real spending increases for defense even though they did add dollars to the annual defense budget submitted by the White House, specifically $7 billion in Fiscal Year (FY)1996, $11.2 billion in FY1997, and a mere $3.7 billion in 1998. But for FY1999, although still constrained by the 1997 balanced budget agreement with the Clinton White House, Congress has already added over $19 billion in supplemental defense spending – that is, spending that does not have to be offset by cuts in other programs – and it will probably consider a third supplemental funding bill before the end of the fiscal year. Furthermore, the Pentagon has received a small windfall from lower than anticipated inflation. Unlike other executive branch departments, the Pentagon has been allowed to keep the funds not needed to cover inflation related costs.

As important as these factors have been in the debates about military spending, a new and very powerful factor was added in late 1998. The continued air patrols over northern and southern Iraq, missile tests by North Korea and other countries, and the relatively large numbers of military men and women leaving active duty led to a public call by the Joint Chiefs of Staff for an additional $27.5 billion to fully restore America's military might. In response, the administration increased its military spending request for FY2000 by $12.6 billion over what it had planned to seek from Congress just one year earlier. In the same budget, the President also projected that the Pentagon would receive $112 billion more for the next six years than was planned in his FY1999 budget. Congress, long critical of military spending cuts that actually began in the second Reagan Administration, seems prepared to give the Pentagon more than what it is seeking. Such additions may escape close scrutiny by many because national wealth is expanding so rapidly that the $300 billion for military programs projected for FY2001 will constitute only 2.8 percent of projected gross domestic product (GDP) in that year

(Executive Office of the President 1999, U.S. Department of Defense FY2000).

Still, voices of fiscal conservatives are being raised, reflecting the inability of proponents of a large, standing peacetime military force to completely convince American taxpayers that there is a serious military-based threat to American national security. Public interest polls conducted by organizations such as the University of Maryland's Program on International Policy Attitudes (1997) reveal that policymakers consistently misread public attitudes on military spending. Given a choice between increasing or cutting defense spending, 60 percent of the general public chose to cut whereas 50 percent of those in Congress wanted higher defense spending.

This split between the general public and the political, military, and defense industry elites is also reflected in the sometimes dire warnings about public apathy toward today's "serious threats" to U.S. national interests. Parallels are drawn between the 1920s and 1930s and the current post-Cold War period. An example is a commentary in the June 22, 1998, issue of *Army Times* by General Gordon Sullivan, who retired as Chief of Staff of the Army in 1995. He wrote: "We must not regress to the conditions of the 1920s and '30s, between the two world wars…. Today…there is only downhill drift toward unreadiness, fragility of quality-of-life programs and perilous fracturing of the technological superiority of our forces. American political leadership and American citizens must be brought into this debate before the millennium. The QDR [Quadrennial Defense Review] to be initiated in 2000 must be preceded by a national awareness and debate on national defense."

This debate is very important, but the comparisons with 50 or 60 years ago seem strained. In the era between the two World Wars, the national security state of mind was more "fortress America" than internationalist (as exemplified by the Senate's rejection of U.S. membership in the League of Nations). Today, President Clinton's drive for engagement and enlargement manifestly keeps the United States involved in world affairs. Yet the "serious threats" to national security are frequently seen by the public as unresponsive to the historical 20th century military solutions of large armies conducting multi-faceted military campaigns.

Financing the National Security Process

One way some in Congress judge the adequacy of national security is the percent of GDP that military spending consumes. Defense expenditures as a percentage of GDP have fluctuated between 3 and 7 percent over the past 20 years. In the post-World War II era, not until FY1978 did the defense budget exceed $100 billion (current year dollars) in outlays, representing 4.7 percent of total GDP. Defense outlays rose through the 1980s, peaking at $319.7 billion in 1991. By comparison, the nonmilitary foreign affairs budget category of "International Programs" did not peak until 1993 when it reached a mere $21.6 billion, up from $8.5 billion in 1978 (Congressional Budget Office, 1998).

Between 1991 and 1997 defense outlays decreased to a low of $266 billion before rising to just over $268 billion in 1998, the last complete fiscal year as this book goes to press. Even with this upturn, the 1998 figure represents just 3.2 percent of GDP (valued at $8.4 trillion). The fact that GDP increased by more than $2.5 trillion between 1991 and 1998 (a 31 percent increase) while defense-related outlays fell only $33 billion (11 percent) from its high point in this period suggests that basing the adequacy of defense spending on GDP may not be a sound approach.

A second measure of the adequacy of national security spending is actual dollar outlays. The FY2000 budget request projects defense outlays rising from $280.8 billion in FY2000 to $333 billion in FY2005 (U.S. Department of Defense FY2000). But these amounts in themselves tell us nothing about the degree of security the nation enjoys. Money can pay for troops and weapons, but security depends on the ability of political and military leaders to forge an effective and efficient military establishment. It is easy to throw money at a problem; it may be quite hard to make proposed improvements work.

Thus, judging the adequacy of national defense on money spent or as a percent of GDP is both seductive and inappropriate. These methods essentially look inward at the process of government rather than outward at the nature of the threats to national security. Using threat projections as the basis for military spending supports the important premise that a nation should spend what is necessary for security but not any more than is necessary. Under this approach, disagreements would center on the key issue: defining the threat.

Implementing the President's national security strategy, as modified by congressional actions, falls primarily to the Departments of State and Defense. Each has unique functions in this regard but shares others. The Department of State relies on treaties and consultations with allies, on the United Nations and other multinational fora, and on nonmilitary intervention, such as economic sanctions, to prevent or deter challenges to national security. The Department of Defense, on the other hand, develops military strategies, forces, and plans (supported by the output of the defense industry) to help deter or, if necessary, defeat these same challenges. The degree to which the Departments of State and Defense (and other agencies with lesser roles in international affairs) are effective determines the state or condition of our national military security.

National Security and the Balance-of-Power Model

Although we are at the dawn of the 21st century, the Pentagon continues to formulate the question of national security in terms of organizations and weaponry that have been employed in this century to implement the traditional roles and missions of the armed forces, which can be summarized as:

- safeguarding U.S. territorial integrity against attack or invasion,
- rescuing American citizens caught in civil strife in foreign countries,
- assisting allies and friends who are attacked or threatened by aggression, and
- participating in internationally approved or sanctioned civil-military operations and military operations other than war.

As long as the rules of international relations rested on the balance-of-power system that emerged in Europe after 1648, nations could judge their national security by their ability to conduct successful military operations that exemplified the roles and missions listed above. But with the collapse of the Soviet Union and the Warsaw Pact in 1990-1991, the balance-of-power system also collapsed, leaving the United States without a military peer or near-peer competitor. Policymakers and opinion molders initially celebrated this turn of events and many inside and outside the government predicted that the nation would reap a large peace dividend. But as measured by military appropriations in the 1990s, the anticipated dividend never materialized. Why?

In a perverse way, a traditional peacetime balance-of-power system can actually help regulate the growth of military expenditures. The system is fundamentally a zero-sum game: when one side gains an ally, the other suffers a loss of influence. When one side develops a new military capability, the other develops a countermeasure. Military spending admittedly increases, but given the initial relative balance that creates this system, the increases tend to be measured responses. This pattern persisted throughout much of the bipolar Cold War system in which the dominance of two superpowers ensured stability and guaranteed a degree of predictability in international affairs.

But with the economic collapse of the Soviet Union in the 1980s, the entire balance-of-power structure and its competitive restraints also collapsed. From the perspective of U.S. policymakers, the post-Cold War unipolar world that emerged was less predictable, less stable, and more threatening because clear choices and plans could not be made. Furthermore, for the United States to so suddenly be essentially unchecked in the exercise of its sovereign power in pursuit of national security proved to be more debilitating than liberating.

With the old, clearly identifiable threats gone, the Pentagon sought to identify new, sufficiently precise military threats on which to focus the public's national security mindset and justify continued funding for its traditional roles and missions (Layne 1998). Just how difficult this task became after the end of the "evil empire' was illustrated as early as 1991 by then Chairman of the Joint Chiefs of Staff Colin Powell when he told Congress he was "running out of demons."

Allocating Resources: State Department vs. Defense Department

If predictability characterized the Cold War, the watchword for the 1990s is instability. The sources of instability are legion: the remaining rogue state demons, organized terrorism, international crime, insufficient control over and accountability of nuclear (fissile) materials and technology (as evident from the 1998 nuclear tests by India and Pakistan), the spread of biological and chemical warfare means and missile delivery systems, civil wars, famine, and refugee floods. Faced with this array of problems, Congress has continued to appropriate well over a quarter of a trillion dollars annually – the equivalent of 90 percent of the annual peacetime Cold War budgets – for military programs and equipment. At the same time, Congress has become even more parsimonious with the International Affairs budget, which includes State Department operations as well as foreign aid and foreign assistance, the very activities that should be the meaningful first line of defense of U.S. interests by nonmilitary means.

For example, in its FY2000 budget the administration noted that Congress appropriated $18.7 billion in new budget authority for International Affairs (the "150" account) for FY1999 against a request of $20.2 billion. New budget authority for National Defense (the "050" account) for FY1999, including $4.5 billion in supplemental FY1999 funding already released when the new budget went to Congress, is $276.2 billion against an original request of $270.6 billion. Thus in each case – the administration's request as well as what Congress appropriated – the 150 account is less than 10 percent of the 050 account (U.S. Department of State 1999).

The administration's FY2000 request shows a further widening of the gap. In FY2000 the International Affairs request rises to $20.2 billion while National Defense goes to $280.8 billion; by FY2004 the numbers are $19.6 and $321.7 billion, respectively.

One reason for this congressional attitude is the failure to regard the State Department and foreign assistance as elements of national defense. Yet, like Pentagon satellites and military attaches, Foreign Service officers provide intelligence and early warning about potential trouble. They are trained to resolve disputes before conflict erupts and extensive military intervention or humanitarian relief becomes necessary. Globalization means the United States has a continuing interest in the ability of other nations to protect the environment and to fight international crime, narcotics, and terrorism – issues not susceptible to military resolution.

The reluctance to regard diplomatic and international monetary institutions as contributing to national defense has forced the United States on several occasions to abandon important initiatives as new crises arose. Finding funds to help stabilize Haiti meant reducing economic aid to Turkey, a key NATO ally in the Middle East. Aid for the West Bank and Gaza came from funds originally earmarked to demobilize opposing armed forces in Central America as part of a peace settlement on which the United

States had labored for years. The inability to find $2 million to monitor a cease-fire between Kurdish factions gave Saddam Hussein a pretext to move his own forces into northern Iraq, a move that subsequently is costing the United States much more for Operation Northern Watch (Brookings Institution and Council on Foreign Relations 1997).

The ability of the United States to garner multinational support is also being undermined by the failure of Congress to pay arrearages due the United Nations. As of 1998, of some $2 billion owed to the United Nations by some 166 nations, the United States owed $1.3 billion or almost two-thirds of the total for regular dues and peacekeeping assessments. A June 1998, U.S. General Accounting Office (GAO) report notes that this level of arrears has already cost the United States its seat on the U.N. budget committee, stopped negotiations on reducing the United States assessment rate, and may even cost the United States its vote in the General Assembly.

This growing disparity between Pentagon and State Department funding unfortunately sends to other nations the message that the United States will, for the foreseeable future, rely more on its military muscle than its diplomatic leadership. Yet our diplomats, more so than our military, are on the front line of democracy every day. Their success or failure in containing and resolving disputes is a key factor that determines the need for, and thus the size of, America's military forces. Shortchanging our diplomatic efforts guarantees continuing growth in Pentagon budgets.

To help understand why this disparity between State and Defense funding continues to grow eight years after the demise of the Soviet Union, we must look more closely at how the government, especially the Pentagon, identifies both the current threats to national security and the future threats (those beyond 2015) and uses them to formulate and justify its budget. The most relevant vehicles for this examination are Secretary of State Madeleine Albright's June 11, 1998, congressional testimony defending the administration's foreign operations budget request for FY1999 and the Pentagon's recent strategy and force structure review known as The Quadrennial Defense Review (U.S. Department of Defense 1999).

VII. Current Security Environment
Diplomatic Strategy and Activities: Prevent/Deter

On June 11, 1998, Secretary Albright appeared before the Senate Foreign Operations Appropriations Subcommittee seeking support for the State Department's budget request. The first section of her remarks dealt with "Peace and Security." She developed her theme in large part by focusing on the countries that make the 1990s a "more dangerous world." These are the countries that the State Department and the Pentagon believe the United States must be able to dominate militarily. They always include Iran (even given the thaw in the 20-year-old hostility between Iran and the United States), Iraq, Libya, Cuba, and Sudan. North Korea and Syria are often included unless the subject of the reference is the negotiations on replacing nuclear power facilities (North Korea) or the Madrid-Middle East peace process (Syria).

Unofficially, and in some academic and policy organizations, Russia and China are mentioned as long-term, near-peer competitors that the United States must watch carefully for signs of rapid technological advances that might presage a challenge to U.S. interests. A related danger is that these powers, particularly China, will form alliances with some of the rogues in an attempt to embroil the United States in regional disputes, particularly in the Persian Gulf region. China is also in the spotlight because of its alleged assistance to Pakistan's effort to develop both a nuclear weapons capability and the missiles to delivery these weapons.

Secretary Albright also pointed to other trouble spots such as the Caucasus, Cyprus, Israel-Palestine, and the former Yugoslavia, where potential (Bosnia) or actual armed conflict (Kosovo) seems to be the norm. But unlike the rogue states, whose policies are explicitly anti-American and against whom the United States therefore combines military and diplomatic actions, this second set of countries (other than Kosovo in 1999) has displayed antithesis to military intervention in their willingness to participate in consultations, confidence-building measures, economic support, and nation-building. These actions obviously fall more towards the first and second elements of the prevent/deter/defeat triad, as do the other major elements Secretary Albright discussed, such as arms control, antiterrorism, anticrime and antidrug initiatives, sustainable economic growth, human rights and the rule of law, and humanitarian assistance.

Consultations and Nonmilitary Interventions

Consultations and nonmilitary interventions (such as special representatives) are one of two main diplomatic activities routinely employed to offset perceived or possible threats to national security. Although the precise threat the seven rogue countries plus China and Russia might represent to U.S. dominance may not lie in the diplomatic arena and may not always be declared in the military sphere, the fact that these are nation-states (as opposed to subnational or terrorist groups) makes them ostensibly vulnerable to traditional diplomatic action. In terms of prevent/deter/defeat, the United States can seek international support to isolate diplomatically, economically, and culturally those countries that flout international norms. Economic sanctions used judiciously, as against Iraq and Serbia, have been instrumental in obtaining varying levels of compliance with U.N. Security Council Resolutions. Applied indiscriminately, however, as in the case of the Helms-Burton Act affecting Cuba, the effort can backfire even with close allies.

Following the overall national security objective of engaging and enlarging, the United States continues to conclude agreements and treaties with other nations. These, the second main arrow in the diplomats' quiver, serve to bind the world ever more closely together through the mechanism of reciprocal obligations. A case in point is the array of late-Cold War and post-Cold War agreements between the United States and Russia concerning the reduction of nuclear arsenals and the control of remaining nuclear weapons and fissile materials.

An increase in the number of international accords can be seen as an indicator of increased stability in the world and therefore of improved national security (see Appendix 1 for a list of treaties since 1949). This is particularly true if treaties and agreements carry with them a verification mechanism such as on-site inspections of military or military-related facilities. In fact, by incorporating verification mechanisms, pacts such as the Strategic Arms Reduction Treaties (START I and START II) of the early 1990s have introduced a significant reversal in the methods used by traditional nation-states to amass sovereignty and ensure their security. The verification regimes of these treaties included provisions for mandatory compliance within 24 hours of a request to conduct challenge inspections of declared weapon sites. The 1991 Open Skies Treaty, yet to be ratified by key powers such as Russia, Belarus, and Ukraine, is another example of sovereign states mutually foregoing certain aspects of their sovereignty because these modifications enhance rather than decrease the security of all signatories.

But to achieve this state of improved national security requires the participants to see through the apparent paradox that treaties present in terms of prevent/deter/defeat. As the world's unchallenged military power, the United States theoretically has the capability to act unilaterally almost anywhere. Yet by voluntarily limiting our autonomy, we actually increase our national security because we are linking other nations into obligations that they must consistently honor and thus limit their options to act.

This interlocking web, spread widely enough, also contributes to resolving crises before conflict occurs or mitigates the level of violence should fighting begin. Even in the absence of a direct threat of international conflict spilling onto U.S. territory, the effect on our perception of current U.S. national security (increasing, decreasing, unchanged) can be surmised by the number of on-going major armed conflicts (i.e., those involving over 1,000 deaths) and particularly cross-border conflicts (see Appendix 2).

Fewer active conflicts in the world (as has been the general trend since 1989) presumably translate into greater stability and predictability, which, in turn, allows for increased engagement and enlargement of the circle of democratic, free-market nations. Concurrently, in such a stable world, there should be less need for large purchases of arms and, although lagging further behind, a general decline in total military expenditures as military forces are reduced.

Arms Trading and Conflicts

Although a direct correlation is not statistically supportable, the general downward trend in the number of major armed conflicts over the past decade has been matched by a decrease in the monetary value of the international arms trade and in overall worldwide military expenditures (see Appendices 3 and 4).

Initially, the waning of the Cold War superpower rivalry ended support for client governments and factions, but participants in many conflicts were so well armed already that they were not seriously inconvenienced initially by this rapport. The concurrent "lifting of the Cold War lid" also allowed old ethnic, religious, and socio-political animosities to reignite. Thus, while the value of arms deliveries steadily declined by over 50 percent between 1987 and 1995 and world military expenditures dropped 40 percent during the same period, the number of major armed conflicts did not start to decrease from its average of 36 until 1990. There was a subsequent rise in the number of conflicts in 1992, followed by a downward trend in 1994 to a level of 25 in 1997, the most recent year for which data are available (Stockholm International Peace Research Institute Yearbook 1998).

Peace Operations

In terms of a possible national security need to deploy U.S. military forces unilaterally or as part of multinational operations, these indicators portray an increasingly stable if not benign international environment in the mid-1990s.

This conclusion is supported by another completely independent measurement: the number of international peacekeeping, peace-enforcing, and peace-monitoring missions undertaken or sanctioned by the United Nations (Appendices 5 and 6). Prior to 1987, the U.N. Security Council, responding to recommendations by successive Secretary-Generals, had authorized 13 peace operations, of which eight had been completed. The U.N.'s 1987 budget for these operations stood at US$233 million and involved 20,000 personnel drawn from numerous countries that agreed to send people and materials. By the end of 1995, these figures stood at 22 completed operations, 17 ongoing operations, a budget of US$3.6 billion, and 70,000 peacekeepers. By November 1998 the totals reached 33 completed and 16 ongoing missions, annual costs (July 1998-June 1999) were US$859 million, and the number of troops, military observers, peacekeepers, and civilian police had decreased to approximately 14,500. In addition, in late 1998, there were 12 other U.N. special missions or special representatives of the Secretary-General and 19 missions or other field offices operating under the auspices of the Organization for Security and Cooperation in Europe (OSCE). Of these latter, one is in Albania, five are associated with the breakup of the former Yugoslavia, and thirteen with the demise of the Soviet Union (Worldwatch Institute 1998, SIPRI 1998, OSCE 1999).

VIII. Military Strategy and Programs: Deter/Defeat

If diplomacy is oriented toward prevention and deterrence, its counterpart, the military component of national security, focuses on deterring and, when required, defeating an enemy. Deterrence is accomplished in part by the purchase of various types and quantities of weapons, creating and paying for military forces, stationing and deploying these forces, and conducting military exercises with allies to demonstrate capabilities and resolve. Should deterrence falter, all these preparations will then be employed in fighting the nation's wars.

All this costs money. But it is important to remember that dollars spent on Pentagon programs do not translate directly into either international influence or national power. Indeed, one of the late 20th century historical anomalies is that nation-states can wield significant international power through their prowess in creating wealth in lieu of raising and maintaining a huge military establishment. Measured by gross national product, Japan, with the world's second largest economy behind the United States, has the world's 24th largest military. Europe's economic engine, Germany, has the fourth largest economy and the 17th largest military. Japan does not allow its combat forces to go beyond its land or sea borders, a practice followed by Germany until NATO's aerial campaign in Kosovo began in March 1999. Yet both are respected, if not feared, by their neighbors.

What this suggests is that nonmilitary factors, such as the ability to create wealth and to properly identify the probable current and foreseeable threats to the nation's well-being, may be more significant for overall national security than huge military forces-in-being. The challenge is to structure and combine all elements of national security, including diplomatic, intelligence and counterintelligence, economic, trade, and military, to best implement the prevent/deter/defeat strategy.

As an example, for a number of years various presidents have singled out terrorism as one of the major threats to national and international security. Since 1978, the State Department and the Central Intelligence Agency have reported the number of international terrorist incidents and resulting casualties (Appendices 7 and 8). The measurement of incidents, especially when further subdivided regionally to reveal localized patterns of terrorist activity, provides the basis for the State Department to issue warnings to Americans to leave or avoid certain areas until security conditions improve. Fewer incidents, of course, do not necessarily translate into fewer casualties (e.g., the terrorist bombs that blew up the U.S. embassies in Tanzania and Kenya in 1998 killed 227 people and wounded over 5,000). But fewer incidents do reduce the occasions when U.S. or allied forces might have to be used on rescue missions.

What is significant about modern terrorism *per se* is not that it occurs but that it is occurring on a large scale as a substitute for and not in conjunction with traditional warfare. This tends to make traditional military

Nonmilitary factors, such as the ability to create wealth and to properly identify the probable current and foreseeable threats to the nation's well-being, may be more significant for overall national security than huge military forces-in-being.

responses, military forces, many 20th century weapons systems such as high performance fighter planes and tanks, and the money spent for all of the above less useful for national security than in the past.

The reason for this is simple: many terrorists operate in small groups or cells that are difficult to find, penetrate, and target. As such, unless these small groups come together for a more traditional force-on-force attack or operation, high technology weapons are not really useful in controlling or eliminating this threat.

But modern terrorists themselves are changing because of technology. Unable to achieve their aims through political means and equally unable to confront the size and firepower of regular armed forces, they are choosing what are often called "asymmetrical' responses to traditional military power. These responses include bombs, chemical and biological agents, and even nuclear materials as the principal components of the terrorists' arsenals. Because such weapons are difficult to detect, relatively easy to make, and wielded by small, secretive organizations, conventional military forces are largely ineffective against this national security threat.

IX. Forces/Plans/Operations

Three real-world trends of the 1990s further suggest that the old approaches and responses to national security challenges need reexamination: (1) the range of asymmetrical threats to national security, (2) the shift in the day-to-day focus of military planning and operations from major conflicts involving huge numbers of military personnel and equipment to peace operations, and (3) the growing weight of economics in determining international influence.

In spite of three major Pentagon reviews since 1991 – the last being the 1997 Quadrennial Defense Review (QDR) – and the recognition by many analysts that the nature of the threats to national security have changed substantially, Pentagon requests and congressional appropriations continue to emphasize weapons systems whose genesis can be traced back to the era of World War II. High-value capital ships (such as aircraft carriers), high-performance jet aircraft (including stealth aircraft), and armored vehicles have become increasingly vulnerable to the more lethal surface-to-surface, surface-to-air, and antitank weapons being acquired by many nations. Together with the proliferation of submarine, nuclear, and ballistic missile technology, these trends in weaponry suggest that the U.S. military needs to carefully consider whether its current programs can successfully deter and defeat the changing threat or if it needs to place a higher priority on developing smaller, lighter, and more mobile weapons as well as forces that are more effective against and less vulnerable to these threats.

Many critics of Pentagon policies, including a special QDR review panel mandated by Congress, contend that the U.S. military has been slow to make force structure and equipment changes to counter this diffusion of technology and the acquisition of effective and relatively cheap weapons by unfriendly nations (National Defense Panel 1997).

Moreover, as the newer technology is incorporated into the forces, it will have an effect on military planning, training, and operations. In the end, the synergy of these changes, together with the American penchant for innovation, will help reshape the way the United States evaluates and responds to crises.

X. The Role of Defense Industry

The natural human and institutional reluctance to abandon what has been successful in the past is reinforced in military affairs by domestic politics and the domestic economic engine. Large standing military forces require large amounts of sophisticated military hardware. American industries that supply the Pentagon directly employ hundreds of thousands of men and women and indirectly create thousands of other jobs that produce goods and services consumed by well-payed defense workers. Over the course of the Cold War, jobs associated with defense-oriented industries, along with jobs on sprawling military bases, became the economic engines of many cities and towns. Local taxes helped finance services from police to schools to roads. National level politicians from areas where a significant percentage of local employment was in the defense industrial sector worked hard to obtain defense contracts for their constituents. For their part, defense contractors discovered that one avenue to continued economic success lay in spreading contracts throughout as many states and among as many vendors as possible. The practical result of these actions was the creation of what President Dwight D. Eisenhower in the 1950s called the "military-industrial complex."

The public's attitude about the military component of U.S. national security strategy continues to be influenced by political candidates and defense industry spokespersons, who constantly promote the need for ever newer and more expensive weapons to ensure the nation will be adequately defended. In the mid-1950s, based on Soviet subterfuge during a Moscow May Day military parade, the Pentagon raised the specter of a large disparity in the size of the Soviet and U.S. bomber fleets. The result was a crash building program to close the "bomber gap." In the run-up to the 1960 presidential election, candidate John F. Kennedy used early Soviet successes in launching satellites to suggest the existence of a missile gap. The post-Vietnam War Army was characterized as "hollow," meaning that it had too few trained troops to properly staff its units. A mantra of the mid-1990s by some in Congress is the "readiness gap," that is, the U.S. military has so many missions and so little equipment and so few people that the forces would not be able to handle the Pentagon's two-war contingency plan. Today, the public is being told that the United States faces an incipient technology gap that will be precluded only if the United States can seize and dominate what the Pentagon calls the Revolution in Military Affairs (Copper 1994; Metz,

Johnsen, Johnson, Kievit, and Lovelace 1996; Tilford 1997; Williams 1997).

Future National Security Predictors

The real challenge and the truest test of a successful national security policy for the 21st century lies not in being able to fight and win wars or even in deterring wars from beginning. While these two capabilities are indispensable elements of national security, resorting to either indicates that the core challenge of anticipating and resolving the conditions that give rise to armed conflict has failed.

Yet crystal ball-gazing by both the political-military elites and their critics has been spectacularly unsuccessful. In large measure this is because national security, whether measured by force size, equipment, capabilities, and budgets or merely sensed by the public at large, is overwhelmingly dependent on the actions and intentions of the many other participants in the game of nation-state relations. Russia's success or failure in overcoming its economic troubles will affect its evolution as a democratic nation and its attitude toward the United States. China's continuing emergence as a modern Asian power will affect all of Asia and the United States as a Pacific Ocean power. Among the rogue states, the evolution of U.S.-Iranian relations will have a significant influence on the Persian Gulf and the Middle East.

XI. Threats and Public Opinion/Perception

Threats

All of this brings us back to where we started with threat and the public's perception of threat. As already noted, the United States has no current or foreseeable military competitor with the power to threaten our vital interests. Only one nation, Russia, has the capability of delivering a major blow to the United States in the form of nuclear weapons, but President Yeltsin has said that Russian missiles are no longer targeted against the United States. All the major industrial nations in the world are our allies, and this situation seems likely to remain so until (or if) China emerges technologically or if Russia reemerges as an unfriendly nation.

Where conflicts occur, the United States theoretically has the luxury to choose whether, when, and under what conditions we might become engaged diplomatically, militarily, or economically. For example, the United States played an important role in brokering the most recent peace agreement in Northern Ireland. Conversely, the United States was slow to intervene with its allies to stop the killing in Bosnia and sent only a small airfield control unit to help with the delivery of relief supplies to the hundreds of thousands who fled the slaughter of Rwanda's civil war. In Kosovo we and our NATO allies hesitated before beginning direct military action to try to stem the ethnic cleansing and resulting humanitarian crisis that threatened to undermine the stability of Macedonia and Albania.

Public Opinion

Although the United States possesses what is universally acknowledged as the best trained and equipped military in the world, the public consistently evinces great reluctance to use this well-oiled machine. In light of this attitude, echoed by the Pentagon in the same breath that it declares the world to be a dangerous place, it is puzzling why 35 to 45 percent of Americans continue to affirm that the nation is "spending about the right amount" for defense (Kay 1995, University of Maryland 1997, Gallup 1998).

Some observers attribute the public's reluctance to actually use the military option to a fear of high casualties for inconsequential reasons, as occurred in Somalia. Reports indicate that this same reason has been voiced behind the scenes by the uniformed military whenever deployment plans are being seriously discussed, as in preparing for the Haiti invasion and the peacekeeping effort in Bosnia. These views make it increasingly difficult for politicians to use or threaten to use the military option under any circumstances short of war for national survival.

Improving National Security in the Future

Under such circumstances, the burden of extending into the future current favorable trends in international relations, predicting the nature of emerging significant threats to the United States, and trying to prevent the rise of conditions leading to conflicts must fall more and more to the diplomats and special envoys engaged in foreign affairs.

One significant area of diplomatic activity is the effort to continue reducing the level of worldwide military expenditures and the volume of international trade in armaments. But these efforts will be hampered unless the United States, which spends more than one-third of total world military expenditures and sells or gives away more arms than any other nation, takes the lead in developing an approach to national security problems that does not depend as heavily on taking costly military actions unilaterally.

Nation-states are obligated to maintain military forces for self-defense, but the size of such establishments ought to reflect realistic threats to be countered. Lowering U.S. military costs below the current 90 percent of the annual Cold War average could encourage others to reduce their expenditures.

Similarly, as the undisputed heavyweight in the international arms transfer market, the United States should be in the forefront in pressing for a worldwide curtailment of this trade. Arms trade agreements (both between governments and between commercial firms and foreign governments), which are only a rough predictor of the level of actual future arms deliveries, have fallen to half their 1988 total (US$132.0 billion in FY2000 dollars) for four of the last five years (1992-1996). However, with the 1996 total rising to US$62.4 billion (the U.S. share at $40.6 billion in FY2000 dollars), the likelihood for further curtailing conflicts by cutting off weapon supplies is not promising.

A second significant diplomatic effort could be directed toward expanding the web of international treaties and agreements. In addition to existing treaties awaiting ratification, the Senate will be asked to ratify amendments to the Conventional Forces in Europe Treaty negotiated with the Russians in 1995. In May 1998, the Senate ratified the change to the NATO Treaty to allow the admission of Poland, Hungary, and the Czech Republic. On the nuclear front, the administration and many in Congress seem willing to begin negotiating further reductions in nuclear arsenals (START III) even though the Russian Duma has not ratified START II. Such a step would help reassure the Russians that the United States does not seek advantage during their current economic and political restructuring and might hasten the beginning of future talks that would include other declared nuclear weapons states.

XII. Conclusion

In the American system the people are sovereign. Our system has served us well, and for this reason we believe it recommends itself to others. But it serves us because at its heart is the idea of the preeminence of the rule of law as the foundation for human and political rights, a preeminence enshrined in our Constitution.

If the world is to move away from armed conflict as the means for settling international disagreements, it too must accept the rule of law as the foundation of international relations and diplomacy. In the 20th century, under Woodrow Wilson, the United States strode upon the world stage asserting this very point: that the rule of law should apply to all international relations. But during the Cold War, the positive aspects of applying the rule of law in international relations were overwhelmed by the view that international law and international treaties were punitive and negative; they only told us what we could not do. The opposition to increased reliance on international norms and treaties was strengthened by a belief that our main adversary had no intention of observing any restraints on its actions, even those restraints contained in agreements it had signed. The solution for the United States was to follow the Soviet example and refuse to abide by international laws that we thought might limit our activities to the detriment not only of the development of international law but also to our own sovereignty and security.

If we are to escape a militaristic world in which the force of arms is the primary force, we must be willing to return to the beginning of the 20th century to recapture and bring with us into the 21st century Wilson's emphasis on law and apply it to national security considerations. This is not to say we should ignore the need to retain a strong military. We still live in a contentious world in which some will stubbornly continue to defy international standards. What such an emphasis does proclaim is that, for the United States, the use of force will again become a choice that is well down

Our system has served us well because at its heart is the idea of the preeminence of the rule of law as the foundation for human and political rights.

the scale, rather than the first, of the possible national responses in international disputes.

ENDNOTES

[1] The first five of Wilson's Fourteen Points were general precepts: open covenants openly arrived at, freedom of the seas in war and peace, eliminating economic barriers among nations, reducing armaments, and adjusting colonial claims by taking into account the wishes of the indigenous inhabitants and the competing claims of colonial powers. The next eight points dealt with specific post-war European issues, and the last point called for establishing a world body, the ill-fated League of Nations.

[2] As with President Wilson 23 years earlier, Roosevelt first enunciated his Four Freedoms in his annual report to Congress. They were later partially incorporated into the Atlantic Charter of August 14, 1941, which echoed many of the themes of Wilson's Fourteen Points.

[3] The Melian Dialogue recorded by Thucydides provides an insight into the Athenian view of conquest and empire. The Dialogue is followed by the account of the ill-fated attempt by Athens to subjugate the city-state of Syracuse on the isle of Sicily. The Athenian defeat in this venture led to the eventual defeat of Athens itself by her enemies. See the discussion of Thucydides' account in Will and Ariel Durant (1996).

Name and Dates of International Treaties since 1949   *Appendix 1*

Name of Treaty	Signed	Ratified	Entered Into Force
Accidents Measures Agreement	9-30-71		9-30-71
African Nuclear-Weapon-Free Zone Protocols	4-11-96	Pending	Pending
The Antarctic Treaty	12-1-59	8-18-60	6-23-61
Anti-Ballistic Missile Treaty	5-26-72	8-3-72	10-3-72
Anti-Ballistic Missile Protocol	7-3-74	3-19-76	5-24-76
Ballistic Missile Launch Notification Agreement	5-31-88	-	5-31-88
Biological Weapons Convention	4-10-72	1-22-75	3-26-75
Charter of Paris for a New Europe	11-21-90	-	-
Chemical Weapons Convention	1-31-93	4-24-97	4-29-97
Comprehensive Nuclear Test-Ban Treaty	9-24-9	-	-
Confidence and Security	9-19-86	-	9-19-86
Conventional Forces in Europe Treaty	8-19-90	12-12-91	11-9-92
Conventional Forces in Europe Treaty-1A	7-10-92	-	11-9-92
Environmental Modification Convention	5-18-77	12-13-79	10-5-78
Geneva Protocol	6-17-25	4-10-75	2-8-28
Hot Line Agreement	6-20-63	-	6-20-63
Hot Line Expansion Agreement	7-17-84	-	7-17-84
Hot Line Modernization Agreement	9-30-71	-	9-30-71
Incidents at Sea Agreement	5-25-72	-	5-25-72
Inhumane Weapons Treaty	4-8-82	3-29-95	12-2-83
Interim Agreement (SALT I)	5-26-72	9-30-92	10-3-72
Intermediate Range Nuclear Forces	12-8-87	5-27-88	6-1-88
Latin American Nuclear-Free-Zone Treaty Protocols I and II	5-26-77 4-1-68	11-23-88 5-12-77	4-22-68
Limited Test-Ban Treaty	8-5-63	10-7-63	10-10-63
Missile Technology Control Regime Guidelines	4-1-87	N/A	N/A
Non-Proliferation Treaty	7-1-68	11-24-69	3-5-70
North Atlantic Treaty Organization	4-4-49	-	7-21-49
Nuclear Material Convention	3-3-80	9-4-81	2-8-87
Nuclear Risk Reduction Centers	9-15-87	-	9-15-87

Continued

Appendix 1
continued

Name of Treaty	Signed	Ratified	Entered Into Force
Open Skies Treaty	3-24-92	-	Pending
Outer Space Treaty	1-27-67	4-25-67	10-10-67
Peaceful Nuclear Explosions Treaty	5-28-76	12-8-90	12-11-90
Prevention of Nuclear War Agreement	6-22-73	-	6-22-73
Seabed Arms Control Treaty	2-11-71	2-15-72	5-18-72
South Pacific Nuclear Free Zone Treaty Protocols	8-8-86	Pending	12-11-86
Strategic Arms Limitation Talks (SALT II)	6-18-79	-	6-18-79
Strategic Arms Reduction Treaty I	7-31-91	10-1-92	12-5-94
Strategic Arms Reduction Treaty II	1-3-93	1-26-96	Pending
Threshold Test Ban Treaty	7-3-74	12-8-90	12-11-90
U.S. IAEA Safeguards Agreement	11-18-77	7-2-80	12-9-80
U.S. Soviet Bilateral Memorandum of Understanding (stockpiles)	9-23-89	-	9-23-89
U.S. Soviet Bilateral Memorandum of Understanding (destruction)	6-1-90	-	Pending
Vienna Document 1990	11-17-90	-	-

Source: U.S. State Department.

Note: Executive Agreements do not have to be ratified although the President may decide to do so to garner political support. When Executive Agreements are not ratified, they usually enter into force on the date signed.

Appendix 2 **Major Armed Conflicts, 1986-1997**

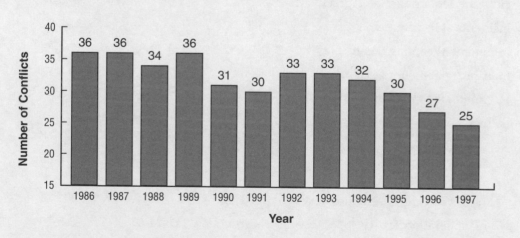

Source: Stockholm International Peace Research Institute Yearbooks, multiple years.

Value of World Arms Transfer Deliveries, 1978-1996 (constant 2000$)

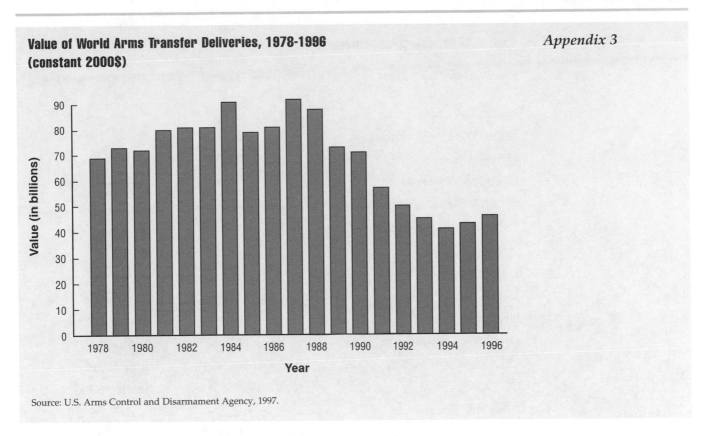

Source: U.S. Arms Control and Disarmament Agency, 1997.

Worldwide Military Expenditures, 1978-1995 (constant 2000$)

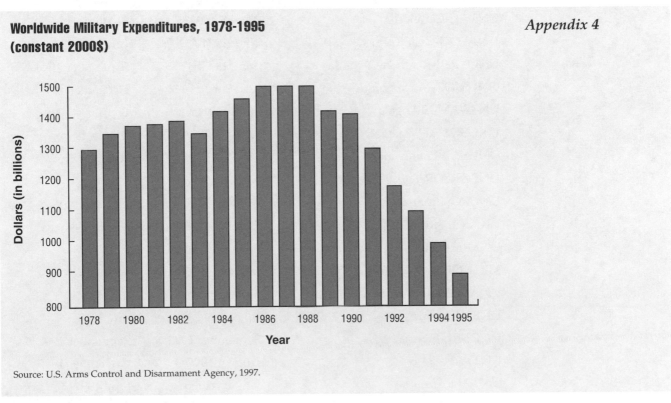

Source: U.S. Arms Control and Disarmament Agency, 1997.

Appendix 5   **Completed Peacekeeping Missions**

Peacekeeping Operations	Date Started	Date Completed
UNOGIL-Lebanon	June 1958	December 1958
UNSF-West New Guinea	October 1962	April 1963
ONUC-Congo	July 1960	June 1964
UNYOM-Yemen	July 1963	September 1964
UNIPOM-India/Pakistan	September 1965	March 1966
DOMREP-Dominican Republic	May 1965	October 1966
UNEF-Middle East	November 1956	June 1967
UNEF II-Middle East	October 1973	July 1979
UNGOMAP-Afghanistan/Pakistan	April 1988	March 1990
UNTAG-Namibia	April 1989	March 1990
UNIIMOG-Iran/Iraq	August 1988	February 1991
UNAVEM I-Angola	January 1989	June 1991
ONUCA-Central America	November 1989	January 1992
UNAMIC-Cambodia	October 1991	March 1992
UNOSOM I-Somalia	April 1992	March 1993
UNTAC-Cambodia	March 1992	September 1993
UNASOG-Chad/Libya	May 1994	June 1994
UNOMUR-Rwanda/Uganda	June 1993	September 1994
ONUMOZ-Mozambique	December 1992	December 1994
UNAVEM II-Angola	June 1991	February 1995
UNOSOM II-Somalia	March 1993	March 1995
ONUSAL-El Salvador	July 1991	April 1995
UNPORFOR-Former Yugoslavia	March 1992	December 1995
UNCRO-Croatia	March 1995	January 1996
UNAMIR-Rwanda	October 1993	March 1996
UNMIH-Haiti	September 1993	June 1996
MINUGUA-Guatemala	January 1997	May 1997
UNAVEM III-Angola	February 1995	June 1997
UNSMIH-Haiti	July 1996	July 1997
UNOMIL-Liberia	September 1993	September 1997
UNTMIH-Haiti	August 1997	November 1997
UNTAES-Croatia	January 1996	June 1997
Croatia-UN Civilian Police Support Group	January 1998	October 1998

Source: United Nations Department of Peacekeeping Operations, 1998.

Peacekeeping Missions in 1998

Current Peacekeeping Operations	Date Started	Date Completed
UNTSO-Middle East	June 1948	Present
UNMOGIP-India/Pakistan	January 1949	Present
UNFICYP-Cyprus	March 1964	Present
UNDOF-Golan Heights	June 1974	Present
UNIFIL-Lebanon	March 1978	Present
MINURSO-Western Sahara	April 1991	Present
UNIKOM-Iraq/Kuwait	April 1991	Present
UNOMIG-Georgia	August 1993	Present
UNMOT-Tajikistan	December 1994	Present
UNPREDEP-Macedonia	March 1995	Being Disbanded
UNMIBH-Bosnia-Herzegovina	December 1995	Present
UNMOP-Croatia	January 1996	Present
MONUA-Angola	July 1997	Being Disbanded
MIPONUH-Haiti	December 1997	Present
MINURCA-Central African Republic	April 1998	Present
UNOMSIL-Sierra Leone	July 1998	Present

Source: United Nations Department of Peacekeeping Operations, 1998.

International Terrorist Incidents, 1977-1998

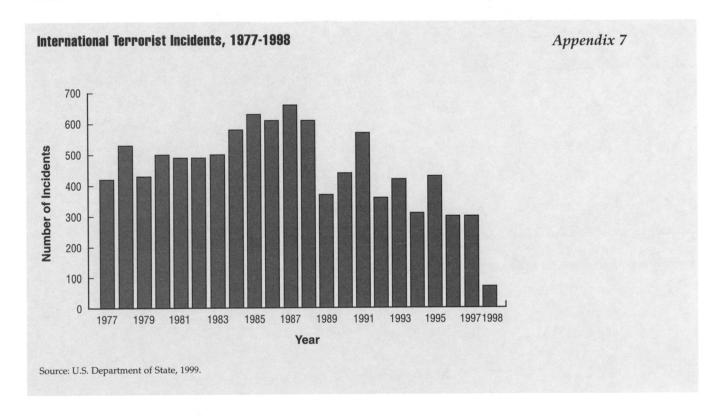

Source: U.S. Department of State, 1999.

Appendix 8   **Casualties Caused by International Terrorism, 1970-1998**

Source: U.S. Department of State, 1999.

REFERENCES

Albright, Secretary of State Madeleine. 1998. "Opening Remarks." Before Senate Foreign Operations Subcommittee, 105th Confress, 2nd Session, (June 11).

Brookings Institutions and Council on Foreign Relations. 1997. *Report of the Brookings Institution and The Council on Foreign Relations Task Force on Resources for International Affairs* (January 13).

"Charter of the United Nations." 1945 (June).

Cohen, Secretary of Defense William. 1998. *Annual Report to the President and the Congress 1998.*

Congressional Budget Office. 1998. *The Economic and Budget Outlook: Fiscal Year 1999-2008* (January).

Cooper, Jeffrey. 1994. "Another View of the Revolution in Military Affairs." United States Army War College, Carlisle Barracks, PA (July).

Durant, Will and Ariel Durant. 1966. *The Story of Civilization, Part II,* "The Life of Greece." New York: Simon and Schuster.

Eisenhower, President Dwight D. 1953. "The Chance for Peace," speech to the American Society of Newspaper Editors, Washington, D.C. (April).

Executive Office of the President. 1999. *Budget of the United States Government Fiscal Year 2000.* Historical Tables 3.2, 5.1, and 10.1 (February).

Gallup News Service. 1999. "Kosovo May Be Causing Americans to Rethink Military Spending" (May 19).

Kay, Alan. 1995. *Americans Talk Issues,* Survey 28 (August 14).

Layne, Christopher. 1998. "Rethinking American Grand Strategy." *World Policy Journal,* Vol. XV, No. 2, pp. 8-28.

Metz, Steven, William Johnsen, Douglas Johnson II, James Kievit, and Douglas Lovelace, Jr. 1996. "The Future of American Landpower: Strategic Challenges for the 21st Century Army." United States Army War College, Carlisle Barracks, PA (March).

National Defense Panel. 1997. *Transforming Defense: National Security in the 21st Century.* (December).

Organization for Security and Cooperation in Europe, web site www.osce.org/indexe-fa.htm.

Roll Call. 1998 (May 7).

Roosevelt, President Franklin Delano. 1941. "Annual Address to the Congress." Senate Document 188, 77th Congress (January 6).

Stockholm International Peace Research Institute Yearbook 1998: Armaments, Disarmament and International Security. 1998. Oxford: Oxford University Press.

Sullivan, General Gordon. 1998. "A Plea for More Defense Spending." *Army Times,* p. 36 (June 22).

Thucydides. 1954. *History of the Peloponnesian War.* VI, Vol. 18, No. 18. Baltimore: Penguin Books.

Tilford, Earl. 1997. "National Defense in the 21st Century." United States Army War College, Carlisle Barracks, PA (June).

United Nations Department of Peacekeeping Operations, web site www.un.org/Depts/dpko.

U.S. Arms Control and Disarmament Agency. 1989, 1996, 1999 *World Military Expenditures and Arms Transfers.*

U.S. Department of Defense. 1994. *Department of Defense Dictionary of Military and Associated Terms, Joint Publication 1-02* (March 23).

U.S. Department of Defense. 1999. "Department of Defense Budget for FY2000." Department of Defense News Release 032-99 (February 1).

U.S. Department of Defense. 1997. *Report of the Quadrennial Defense Review* (May).

U.S. Department of State. 1999. *FY2000 International Affairs Budget Request,* web site www.state.gov/www/budget/2000_table_pg4.html.

U.S. Department of State. 1999. *Patterns of Global Terrorism 1998* (April).

U.S. Department of State. 1998. *Summary and Highlights: FY 1999 International Affairs (Function 150) Budget Request* (February).

U.S. General Accounting Office. 1998. *United Nations: Financial Issues and US Arrears,* GAO/NSIAD-98-201BR (June 18).

University of Maryland. 1997. *The Foreign Policy Gap: How Policymakers Misread the Public.* The Center for International Security Studies, University of Maryland Program on International Policy Attitudes (October).

Vandenberg. 1952. *The Private Papers of Senator Vandenberg.*

The White House. 1997. *A National Security Strategy for a New Century* (May).

The White House. 1998. *A National Security Strategy for a New Century* (October).

Williams, Robert. 1997. "Army's Modernization Strategy Driven by Quest for Info, Physical Dominance." *National Defense Magazine,* Vol. LXXXII, No. 532, pp. 12-13 (November).

Wilson, President Woodrow. 1918. "Annual Address to the Congress." Senate Document 76, 66th Congress (January 8).

Worldwatch Institute. 1998. *Vital Signs 1997.*

Chapter 14

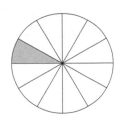

Public Safety Indicator

by Trudy A. Karlson, Ph.D.

I. Introduction

Safety is an important feature of the quality of our lives. We understand it through experiencing its absence. We feel anguish and sorrow at the death of our loved ones and pain and suffering when we or those we love are injured. The anticipation of these events causes additional suffering, fear, and wariness. We protect our infants from harm and train our toddlers and children in safe behaviors – how to conduct themselves in their environments. In this way, humans are like other animals that teach their young to avoid danger.

These actions can be considered dimensions of personal safety. Safety has a public dimension as well. As our culture becomes more complex, the way we conduct our lives becomes further removed from our primitive heritage. New dangers and hazards arise from our increasingly complex human behaviors. To cope, we have developed public institutions to protect us. The term "public safety" is used for some public institutions and their jurisdictions. Public safety commissions in our cities and counties generally are responsible for fire fighting and law enforcement. The public dimension of safety encompasses other aspects of our lives. Federal agencies, for example, reflect this in their titles and roles: Occupational Safety and Health Administration, National Highway Traffic Safety Administration, National Transportation Safety Board, and the Consumer Product Safety Commission.

The Calvert-Henderson Public Safety Indicator examines how effectively our society promotes safety – as measured by those instances when we have failed to prevent outcomes that result in death or injury. While some might expect an indicator on safety to be about crime, the Public Safety Indicator takes a different approach. In the United States, the vast majority of injuries and deaths stem from events that do not fall into the common definition of crime. In this indicator, safety means more than the absence of crime. Also important is a safe physical environment, including safe products, safe roadways, and safe shelters.

We begin with a conceptual model for both the determinants of safety and measures of outcomes. This model is one way of perceiving the complex relationships between personal decisions, public actions, risks, and hazards in the environment that result in deaths and injuries. After briefly describing the Public Safety model, we discuss the measurement of outcomes. Our model has limitations, which are also described. We end with a detailed discussion of the determinants of safety to help us focus on what we can do to reduce hazards.

II. The Public Safety Model

The Public Safety model shows determinants of safety and outcomes. Outcomes are externally caused deaths and injuries, as well as some diseases. The indicator stresses deaths and injuries as a primary measure for several reasons. Externally caused deaths and injuries have easily identifiable causes that are codified in the United Nations World Health Organization International Classification of Diseases, for example, motor vehicle crashes, firearms, poisonings, and falls. They are preventable causes of death yet relatively new to scientific scrutiny (Haddon 1980). Despite the toll they take and enormous potential for prevention, fatal and nonfatal injuries are understudied and often ignored. Injuries have succeeded infectious diseases as the primary killer of children and younger adults.

We are not focusing on deaths and morbidity from chronic and acute illnesses in the Calvert-Henderson Public Safety Indicator, although illness can sometimes result from failures to supply safe and adequate food, water and clean air, industrial pollution, and human behaviors such as smoking. Acute and chronic disease prevention is the focus of environmental and public health indicators, which are more fully addressed in the Calvert-Henderson Environment and Health Indicators in this volume.

Determinants of safety exist in both public and private spheres. Many people are accustomed to think about safety within the private sphere. They believe safety is something to be controlled through individual action. This has cultural support, as evidenced by traditional safety education and its focus on how we should deal with the hazards we face. The model identifies several important features of individual action within the private sphere that affect the probability of being injured. These include the propensity of engaging in risk-taking behaviors; the frequency, quantity, and situations in which alcohol is used; the use of protective equipment; and the availability of training in skills necessary to avoid hazards.

The Public Safety model moves beyond the private sphere to include public actions and environmental factors as important determinants of safety. Daily, we deal with the result of environmental factors and public actions that are beyond individual control yet have enormous impact on our safety and potential for harm. By public actions we mean laws, the design of products and our public spaces, and the financial incentives that drive manufacturers and consumers. As our society has become more complex, an individual may neither be aware of hazards nor have the means to avoid them. To reduce some of these hazards, we need first to identify them then take collective action to reduce them. The latter half of the Public Safety Indicator provides more explanation and examples of the determinants of safety included in the model.

Calvert-Henderson Public Safety Model

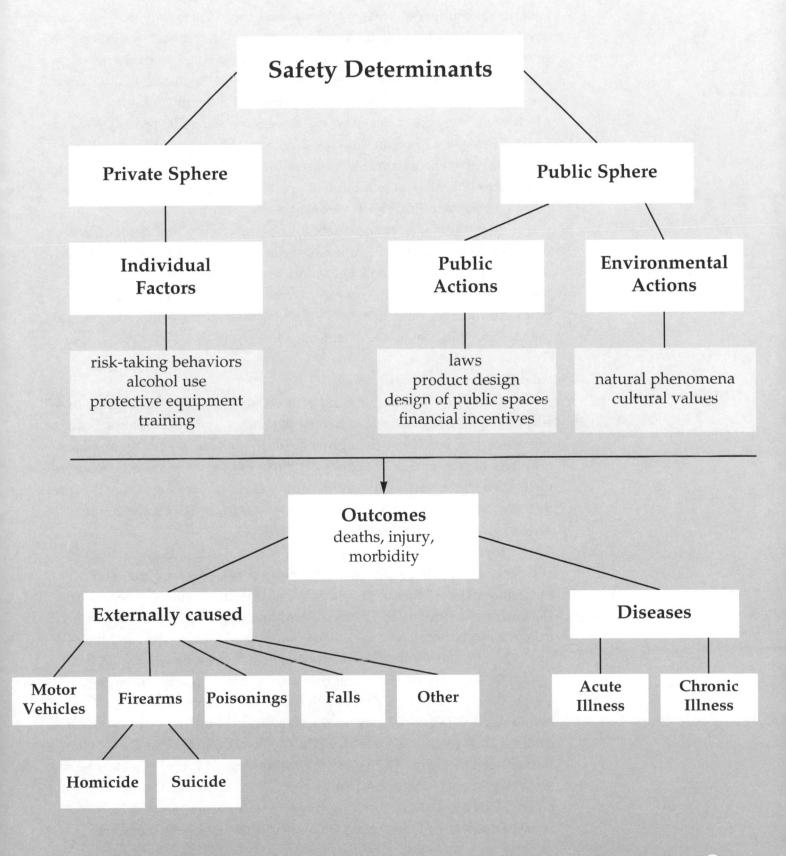

Safety Determinants

Private Sphere

Public Sphere

Individual Factors

Public Actions

Environmental Actions

risk-taking behaviors
alcohol use
protective equipment
training

laws
product design
design of public spaces
financial incentives

natural phenomena
cultural values

Outcomes
deaths, injury,
morbidity

Externally caused

Diseases

Motor Vehicles

Firearms

Poisonings

Falls

Other

Acute Illness

Chronic Illness

Homicide

Suicide

III. How Can We Measure Outcomes Related to Public Safety?

The Calvert-Henderson Public Safety Indicator uses deaths from injuries as a measure of how well our society protects the population because injuries are the leading cause of death for most Americans. At a basic level, injuries occur when humans are exposed to energy that surpasses the body's ability to dissipate it without damage. Mechanical energy, or impact force, is the most common cause of injury death. Mechanical energy injures for example, when the forces engendered in the impact of a car crash are transmitted to the human chest as it strikes the steering wheel. Mechanical energy is involved when the velocity of a bullet propelled from a firearm exceeds the human skull's ability to shield the brain. Electrical energy and thermal energy are also causes of injury: electrocutions, scaldings, and deaths in conflagrations. Drownings and poisonings interfere with the body's necessary cellular energy exchanges.

Identification of energy exchanges as the cause of injury was first described in the scientific literature of the early 1960s (Haddon 1980). While the scientific community no longer considers injuries to be "accidents," the lay community still uses the concept. To the public, the term "accident" connotes unavoidable, random events – perhaps inescapable – and excludes the intentional injuries of homicide and suicide.

Fatal Injuries

While death from injury has been common through the ages, it now surpasses infectious diseases as a cause of death in the United States. Social conditions and public health improvements in housing, water, air, and food resources have combined to reduce the threat of many infectious diseases in the United States since the beginning of the 20th century (Appendix 1). Now, those who die of infectious diseases are likely to be older or have immune systems that have been compromised by HIV.

Injuries are *the* leading cause of death for Americans ages one to 44. For the age group 15-24, deaths from injuries (homicides, suicides, and unintentional) are 5 times as likely as the next leading cause (Appendix 2). Despite this, injuries receive far less attention than heart disease and cancer from the public health and medical community and those who fund their work (Bonnie, Fulco and Liverman 1999).

Deaths from injuries occur disproportionately among the young (Appendix 3). A leading public health indicator, "Years of Potential Life Lost Before Age 65" (YPPL<65), shows the magnitude of the causes of death for children and working age adults. YPPL <65 measures the total years of life lost between the age at death and 65. A death at age 15 from a firearm represents 50 years of potential life lost to an injury compared to the one year of potential life lost to heart disease when a 64-year-old dies from a heart attack. Deaths from unintentional injuries, suicide, and homicide were

Injuries are the leading cause of death for Americans age one to 44.

responsible for more than 3.5 million years of potential life lost in 1995, compared to 1.5 million years of potential life lost to deaths from heart disease.

For injuries, we can easily measure deaths. Each death that occurs is counted and its cause is classified in a manner roughly depicted in the Public Safety model. The taxonomy that ascribes external causes to injury deaths is codified in the International Classification of Diseases of the United Nations World Health Organization and used worldwide in reporting vital statistics. Measures of death in the population are among the most easily accessible and comparable measures of public safety over time and between population groups.

In the United States in 1997, the total number of injury deaths from external causes was almost 150,000 (Appendix 4). Motor vehicle crash-related deaths are the single largest group, accounting for almost 43,000 deaths followed by deaths from firearms, which accounts for nearly 33,000. Suicides account for 18,000 of deaths from firearms (54 percent). Until recent years, the total number of U.S. deaths from firearms was overlooked because firearm suicide, homicide, and unintentional deaths were reported separately by national and state offices of vital statistics. This may also have enforced the common wisdom that the "firearm problem" relates to homicides when the majority of deaths from firearms are suicides among older white male adults (Karlson and Hargarten 1997).

Motor vehicles crashes have been the leading cause of injury death for over 50 years (Appendix 5). Age-adjusted motor vehicle death rates have decreased compared to those from firearms (Appendix 6).[1] Age-adjusted firearm mortality decreased by 11 percent from 1993 to 1995, while motor vehicle fatality rates increased slightly. However, firearms lead motor vehicles as the cause of death in several states and many cities. Firearms and motor vehicles account for more than half of the injury deaths in the United States. Because of their prominence in causing injury deaths, these two types of products are the focus for most of the examples in the Public Safety Indicator.

Nonfatal Injuries

Not all of those who are injured die, so nonfatal injuries are also an important measure. Commonly, hospitalization is considered a measure of severity for nonfatal injuries. In 1995, the last year for which data are available, there were more than 2.5 million hospitalizations for injuries compared to the almost 150,000 deaths (Bonnie, Fulco, and Liverman 1999). Unfortunately, for nonfatal injuries we are not able to measure external causes for hospitalizations as we do for deaths because hospitals report injuries by their anatomic diagnosis (e.g., fracture), rather than their external cause. Not every state has a hospital data system, and even among those that do, not all report external causes (e.g., firearms). From those states that have the information, we know that falls are the most common cause of injuries requiring hospitalization followed by motor vehicle crashes. Firearms cause a much smaller proportion of injury hospitalizations because so many of those who are shot do not survive. This is especially true for suicide attempts.

Not only do we have imprecise information on the causes of nonfatal injuries, but we cannot measure adequately the lifelong outcomes from these injuries. We do know that nonfatal injuries such as spinal cord or brain injuries can be extremely disabling with life-long consequences. Even for injuries that do not threaten loss of life, such as lower leg injuries, rehabilitation can be lengthy and expensive. For example, in one study of working age men with serious lower extremity injuries, half were not able to return to work at six months after the injury (Rice and MacKenzie 1989).

Economic Costs

Estimates of the cost of injury include not only the medical care required for the initial treatment and rehabilitation, but lost wages and the value of "foregone productivity" (i.e., the productivity lost when people die or are injured when they are young). Acute medical costs, additional rehabilitation, and long-term care costs for all injuries are estimated to be $45 billion per annum (in 1985 dollars). When foregone productivity is included, the costs more than double to $160 billion (Rice and MacKenzie 1989).

Putting economic costs to injuries is one way to capture the attention of policy makers. But it is hard to measure the costs of human tragedy and sorrow from injuries or the erosion of community from fear and wariness when people feel they cannot safely lead their lives.

IV. What is Missing in This Approach to Measuring Safety?

Deaths from injuries are the most extreme measure of a safety failure. The statistics are reliably reported, easily measured over time, and indicate the areas in which the quality of our community life needs to be improved. But using this measure of physical injury is limited in its inability to capture the direct and indirect effects of psychic injury, environmental hazards, and crime.

Psychic injury includes both the direct emotional effects of physical injury and indirect effects from the injuries of others. Direct effects might include post-traumatic stress disorders and increased emotional fragility. Psychic injury occurs as well in the abuse or threatened abuse of children, domestic partners, employees, or co-workers. Sexual harassment, abuse, and rape also have emotional after-effects. For an individual these stresses can result in increased health-care costs or diminished human capacity.

Indirect effects of injuries to others are also important. How do fear and wariness that arise from failures of public safety affect our sense of community? They may diminish social support as expressed through willingness to help neighbors or willingness to engage in social action. There is a growing scientific interest in documenting the results of fear, sometimes focusing on families who live in unsafe situations. Indirect effects are important but not easily measured. Our Public Safety Indicator captures the domain of psychic injury and other indirect effects only by association. But just as the failure of public safety diminishes human capacity for individuals, it diminishes the capacity of communities to flourish.

The Calvert-Henderson Public Safety Indicator also does not adequately represent environmental hazards that result in illness. Threats to safety include exposure to pesticides and other chemicals, low doses of ionizing radiation and other energy sources, and bacteria and viruses in food and water supply. Sometimes, with acute exposures, we can identify the cause of ill health, but others have a more complex patho-physiology expressed as chronic health problems ranging from asthma and gastroenteritis to diseases with a longer latency period such as cancer. Generally, these outcomes are addressed in the fields of environment and health, discussed elsewhere in this volume.

We have acknowledged that our measure of safety might differ from one based on criminal justice and law enforcement. While the Public Safety model includes homicides and injuries from assaults, it does not encompass crimes of property, fear of harm, increased vulnerability, and the threats they pose to community life. But models of safety based on the concepts of criminal justice might also be seen as more narrow than ours as they do not include preventable deaths in motor vehicle crashes, suicide, or from hazardous products and their environment. These also threaten the fabric of our community life.

What Determines our Safety?

The Public Safety model depicts the determinants that lead to the injury outcomes discussed above. These determinants can be seen as either promoting safety or, by their absence or failure, promoting unfavorable outcomes. The model indicates that individual decisions and actions make contributions to safety but are not its only determinants. Public actions and environmental factors also play a part. Below we discuss safety determinants and improvements for each of these realms separately. Although not shown in the figure, there are interrelationships among individual factors, public interventions, individual actions, and environmental factors.

Individual Factors

Injury outcomes will vary among individuals and population groups according to: (1) type and quantity of exposure to hazards, (2) ability to perceive and respond to hazards, (3) probability of survival, and (4) injury threshold (extent to which a body can withstand injurious forces).[2]

As children move into their teen-age years, the type and quantity of hazards to which they are exposed increase dramatically in the United States, especially as they begin to drive passenger vehicles. Appendix 7 shows the extremely high death rates for 16-year-old drivers and aptly demonstrates this point. For white children and youth ages 5 to 24, motor vehicle crashes lead all other causes of death including cancers, infectious disease, HIV, and heart disease. Black youth (15 to 24) have hazardous exposure of another kind. For them, death by firearm homicide leads all causes of death.

For middle-age adults, death rates from injuries are lower in part because their exposure to hazards has decreased and they are better able to perceive and respond to their environment. For the elderly, the ability to perceive and respond to hazards decreases with age as reflexes slow, eyesight and hearing ability decreases, and judgment becomes impaired. Among the elderly, the injury threshold also is affected as osteoporosis weakens bones leading to fractures under less impact force. The aged also are less likely than younger people to survive injuries of the same degree of severity. This may be due to diminished capacity of the body to repair tissue or due to underlying respiratory and circulatory health problems.

Finally, for persons at every age, excessive alcohol and other drug use increases the probability of injury by degrading the ability to perceive and respond to hazards and increasing the quality and quantity of exposure to hazards. Emergency department physicians report that excessive alcohol use impedes assessment and treatment for those with severe head injuries (Karlson 1992).

Individuals make decisions that affect their safety. Efforts aimed at promoting safety at the individual level try to counter risk-taking behaviors, encourage the use of protective equipment, provide warning signs, and supply appropriate training.

Risk-taking Behavior

Our society provides mixed messages about risk-taking behavior. We often attach the blame for injuries and deaths to those who are injured: "He must have been drinking." "She was in the wrong neighborhood." "They should never have kept a loaded weapon in the house" or "They should have supervised their toddler better." Yet, we encourage risk-taking through the messages that are sent in advertising, the media, sports, and other entertainment that have enormous cultural value.

Sometimes, individuals do not have adequate information to help them make decisions. Without information it is difficult to know what constitutes "risk-taking." For example, a driver may not know what model automobile will perform better in a head-on collision. Often, individuals assume a level of control and safety that may not be realistic. For many years, the common myth was that it was better to be thrown from a car in a crash than to wear a safety belt. Yet data was readily available to show that ejection in a car crash increased the probability of fatal or severe injuries.

Individuals may have access to appropriate information, but their choices may be constrained by economics; choosing to live in the safest neighborhood may not be feasible if it also has the most expensive housing, as discussed in the Calvert-Henderson Shelter Indicator.

We can endeavor to make the living environments of our population and the products we use as safe as possible so that risk-taking behavior does not necessarily have fatal or severe consequences. These are often actions that need to take place in the public sphere that we will discuss later.

Alcohol Use

Studies of many types of injuries have found overwhelming evidence of association with alcohol. Forty to fifty percent of fatally injured motor vehicle drivers have elevated blood alcohol levels. More than 50 percent of fatally injured pedestrians have elevated blood alcohol, as do adult victims of drowning, fatal burns, hypothermia, and homicide (Karlson 1992). Alcohol ingestion increases the likelihood that individuals will be exposed to hazards and decreases the ability to perceive and respond to hazards. It encourages aggression and also reduces the likelihood of fleeing or turning away from aggressive acts by others. Individuals increase their risk of injury when they combine alcohol use with activities that also carry increased risks of injury – driving, hunting, operating motorcycles, boating, swimming, or other water sports. Public health advocates raise concerns about alcohol advertising messages that show individuals engaged in these pursuits or those that portray alcohol as a beverage rather than a drug.

Use of Protective Equipment

Individuals can protect themselves and others with a wide variety of protective equipment including seatbelts and child passenger restraints in vehicles; helmets when riding motorcycles, bicycles, and horses; flotation devices for water sports; trigger locks on guns; goggles, mouth guards, and face masks in sports; and body armor for law enforcement agents. All of these require action each time they are expected to afford protection, and are considered to be "active" measures of injury control rather than "passive" ones in the jargon of the discipline. Passive measures work to protect with-out requiring action on the part of the individual to be protected. These include air bags that inflate in crashes, automatic sprinklers in high-rise buildings, construction of homes to building codes, design of aircraft to fed-erally administered safety specifications, and other endeavors that are gener-ally a result of public intervention discussed later in this chapter.

Injury control specialists promote "passive" measures whenever pos-sible because they know that "active" measures are not always taken. Often, the population that engages in high-risk activity augmented with alcohol is the same population that disdains appropriate use of protective equipment. The amount of protection afforded a given population will decrease as the frequency of action increases and as the action required becomes more com-plex (Baker 1981).

We can endeavor to make the living environments of our population and the products we use as safe as possible so that risk-taking behavior does not necessarily have fatal or severe consequences.

Training

For many activities, training programs are used to help promote safety and safe behaviors. Swimming is an excellent example of a skill that requires training and can help promote safety around water.

When certain skills are required to ensure that an individual can cope safely with a complex task or a complex environment, training is sometimes mandated. This is the case for airplane pilots, those who operate nuclear reactors, or other highly skilled occupations that involve risk to others. Our society also requires that evidence of skill be demonstrated before individuals can operate motor vehicles. We do not require similar evidence of skill or training in other situations that involve hazardous products such as guns. Training cannot always compensate for hazards in the environment, as demonstrated by our high rates of death in motor vehicle crashes, but should be considered as one of many activities that can contribute to a safer society.

V. The Public Sphere

For much of this century, the concept of safety and safety education focused on the role of the individual and his or her behavior. "Accident prevention" was the goal rather than reducing injuries and their severity should an "accident" occur. Perhaps because avoiding danger is an instinctive and primitive drive, we sometimes forget that although we can maximize our safety, we do not completely control it. In the personal sphere, individual behavior and choices are generally under our control. We are taught how to avoid danger, how to handle ourselves, our tools and our environment to maximize the possibility of survival. But actions in the public sphere and environmental influences have much to do with our safety and influence the quality and quantity of the hazards we face as we lead our lives. These hazards include the behavior of other individuals, the lethal and injury potential of products we use or that surround us, natural phenomena, and the cultural values that help determine human behavior.

Laws and Formal Rules to Regulate Human Behavior

Laws and formal rules to regulate human behavior either proscribe behavior that is deemed socially unacceptable or criminal or require that certain behaviors take place, such as requiring the use of protective equipment. Similarly, agencies such as the Food and Drug Administration, the Federal Trade Commission, and the Environmental Protection Agency oversee the laws relating to corporate behavior.

Proscribed behavior is a matter for law enforcement and the criminal justice system. Crime, its prevention, deterrence, and punishment are important features of public safety, especially for crimes that involve harmful behavior to persons rather than property. A focus on injuries and their prevention allows us to address crime through statistics on deaths and injury.

Laws requiring the use of protective equipment primarily concern

Actions in the public sphere and environmental influences have much to do with our safety and influence the quality and quantity of the hazards we face as we lead our lives.

motor vehicles and reflect their unique role in American life and economy. All states have laws requiring the use of passenger restraints for children in vehicles and most states have laws requiring use of seatbelts, although enforcement provisions vary widely. Motorcycle helmet use laws existed in almost every state because federal dollars for highway construction required states to have helmet use laws. When this federal provision was repealed, many states rescinded their laws, and motorcycle fatalities increased (Karlson 1992).

Passage of laws does not always mean universal use of the desired protective equipment, nor dramatic decreases in death rates. In states that passed seatbelt laws, usage rates increased from around 20 to 55 percent. In part because usage rates did not increase among high-risk drivers, death rates in motor vehicle crashes decreased only 5 to 10 percent (Robertson 1998). In contrast, mandatory motorcycle helmet use laws generally resulted in universal use because enforcement is easy; unhelmeted riders are hard to miss.

Adherents of laws regulating the use of protective equipment usually argue that the general public pays the costs of treating all who are injured, and therefore has the right to impose behaviors on those who put themselves at risk (e.g., motorcycle operators). Those who oppose laws generally argue that the protective equipment does not save money, or when faced with evidence that use of protective equipment would reduce health care and other social costs, argue on the basis of personal liberty. Generally it is easier to get such laws passed when they concern protecting children, as with tobacco and guns.

The spread of seatbelt laws is an interesting case. States were slow to pass seatbelt laws until seatbelt laws became an issue in the federal government's decision about airbags. In the late 1980s, automobile manufacturers were going to be required to install airbags or automatic restraint systems unless two-thirds of the nation's population lived in states with seatbelt laws. Preferring seatbelts to airbags, automotive manufacturers infused money into grassroots organizations that then successfully lobbied for state seatbelt laws. Eventually, however, manufacturers were required to install airbags in all passenger vehicles.

Not all laws that aim to regulate human behavior have a positive effect on safety. For example, Philadelphia officials were reported to be concerned that their city had not experienced the same decrease in firearm homicide rates seen in other urban areas. They ascribed this in part to changes in the state gun laws in 1995 that removed some discretion from law enforcement agencies' ability to deny permits for carrying concealed weapons. As a result Pennsylvania has more licensed gun carriers than any other state (Janofsky 1998).

If we wish to use laws to improve the safety of the population, the public health impact of the laws should be evaluated scientifically and the laws modified for improvement. But laws are influenced by many interest groups with competing goals and the legislative process is not always rational.

Design of Products

As human culture and technology has evolved, tools have become more powerful. Cars and airplanes harness power to move us at higher speeds. Guns replaced bows and arrows as powerful weapons more than five hundred years ago, eventually making suits of armor obsolete. Electrical appliances use electrical energy for multiple tasks of living. One aspect of human ingenuity involves harnessing powerful forces to enrich and ease our lives, developing tools that achieve the desired ends without undue harm. As a society, we have managed through technology and human institutions to design some products that have relatively few harmful outcomes. Others have proven to be more troublesome. In general, where there are many levels of societal control over the product, injurious outcomes are less likely, for example in the case of commercial aviation or electrical power. These are to be contrasted with cars and guns. With cars, there is some societal control over their use and design. For guns, there are societal controls over their use, but few over their design.

Electrical energy has the potential to be deadly. Yet each day, humans use tools powered by electricity without harm. There are multiple societal controls over this energy source. We have entire books of building codes that are continuously upgraded to ensure safe wiring for electrical power. Those who work with electricity have years of training and go through licensing procedures. A national private sector organization, the Underwriters Laboratory, certifies products to guarantee that they can be safely used. Electrocutions and electrical burns are relatively rare in the United States, occurring most commonly as workplace injuries.

Cars also harness energy. When an automobile is in motion, the human body it carries is in motion as well. And if stopped abruptly, as in a crash, the human body is also stopped abruptly in the so-called "second crash." Film clips of crash test dummies are common enough that this point is fairly obvious to consumers today.

But designing cars to improve their crashworthiness is a fairly recent phenomenon. The National Highway Traffic Safety Administration first promulgated Federal Motor Vehicle Safety Standards to improve crashworthiness in the late 1960s. Since then, federal standards have been one of the forces encouraging automobile makers to design their vehicles to move their human cargo more safely. Examples include the provision of seat belts and air bags to spread the impact forces over the bony skeleton, smooth and cushioned dashboards, steering columns that collapse when compressed by a human chest, windshields designed to keep the human body within the car yet not lacerate soft tissue, and door latches that help prevent ejection. All of these features are conscious designs to reduce injury and have been achieved in large part because of governmental requirements. The technology exists to make even greater strides in reducing injuries to passenger car occupants.

Guns are a third example of product design affecting safety. While there are many state laws and local ordinances about gun use, there are relatively few standards about the design of guns, their safety features, or any other performance criteria in the United States.

There is no federal agency with responsibility to regulate the safety of firearm products, set safety standards for manufacturers, or track firearm injuries and deaths from products. There are a collection of regulations based on laws passed over the years in response to public outcry and media attention that address mostly criminal justice concerns – keeping the guns out of the hands of criminals. This ad hoc approach is essentially reactive and cannot respond to changes in technologies or other circumstances without an arduous legislative process (Karlson and Hargarten, 1997).

Although the federal Bureau of Tobacco, Alcohol, and Firearms has jurisdiction over the existing federal firearm laws, it has no specific authority to implement new technologies. The law establishing the Consumer Product Safety Commission to ensure the safe design of other products specifically excludes firearms from its jurisdiction. As a result, there are anomalies such as more stringent design standards for toy guns than for real ones.

Even basic safety devices are not required on guns, so that each year there are many deaths from unintentional shootings. When there are safety devices, they may not always effectively prevent unintentional shootings. For example, guns with safety devices that keep the trigger from being pulled can be accidentally discharged when dropped.

It is possible to design guns so that they are far less likely to be involved in homicides, suicides, and unintentional injuries. One promising design is for a personalized weapon that could not be shot by an unauthorized user. A personalized gun would help prevent adolescent suicides by firearms, which increased by 290 percent from 1962 to 1994 (Ikeda et.al. 1997). It would prevent at least some of the 1,600 deaths from unintentional shootings each year, especially those in which a child pulls the trigger. Firearm manufacturers have developed prototypes and are exploring the production of personalized guns. One method of personalization uses an electromagnetic encoder small enough to fit into a finger ring with an electromagnetic decoder embedded in the grip of the gun. The gun cannot be fired until the electromagnetic lock is unlocked, as would happen when the authorized user wearing the encoder ring grips the gun. Palm print, fingerprint, or voice activated personalization devices have also been suggested and have been used in other settings for security purposes (Karlson and Hargarten 1997).

In sum, injury scientists believe that the safety of populations can be promoted through the attention to design of common products. Changing the product can protect, for example, individuals who forget to buckle their

It is possible to design guns so that they are far less likely to be involved in homicides, suicides, and unintentional injuries.

seatbelts, good drivers who encounter icy roads, as well as angry or depressed teenagers. No one deserves death or injury because they are humanly careless, forgetful, impulsive, acting on wrong information, or otherwise less than perfect. Deaths and injuries from products measure the results of our social choices for safety.

Design of Public Spaces

Public spaces are similar to products in that they can be altered to reduce the risk of injury and death. For motor vehicles, the safe design of an interstate highway is an example that most citizens would recognize. These roads are designed with safety as one consideration. There are very few fixed objects allowed at the roadside, and even bridge abutments are designed to be well away from the edge of the road. The potential for head-on collisions is reduced with multiple lanes for traffic. Medians are wide with few barriers. One result is fewer deaths and injuries on roadways that meet these design standards, despite a higher volume of vehicles travelling at high speeds.

We have mentioned briefly the use of building codes to reduce probability of electrocution. Building codes also address safety from falls and fire. Urban areas sometimes require child-resistant environmental barriers for windows in multiple story buildings as well as safe, nontoxic paints.

Similarly, there are some codes for the design of public spaces around water. Pool drowning in Australia has almost been eliminated because of regulations requiring "isolation fencing" (i.e., four-sided fencing that separates the pool completely from house and yard). This standard is being implemented in a few locales in the United States (Karlson 1992). In some states, revisions in public safety codes around natural bodies of water have reduced drowning by requiring the removal of diving boards and the modification of float lines.

Some types of injury deaths do not involve any products (e.g., falls, drowning, and assault with personal or body weapons). For these injuries especially, attention to the design of public spaces is essential.

There is a growing interest in the area of "universal design," which considers access for persons with disabilities in the design of public spaces and products. This movement could also encompass attention to safety and the prevention of injuries and deaths.

Financial Incentives

In our economy, financial incentives are paramount; profit and economic growth are measured by the Gross Domestic Product. Yet often we make social choices to balance the public good with private motivations of profit. This may be accomplished through government action or by consumers, shareholders, and workers. For example, early in this century we determined that child labor was not good for society and developed governmental regulations and enforcement measures to prevent it. Investment strategies that promote socially responsible business practices are another example.

The power of the government to levy taxes has proved to be an occasional financial disincentive for manufacturers or purchasers of hazardous products. Winchester stopped producing the Black Talon cartridge that expands on impact into a razor-edged starburst when Senator Daniel Moynihan of New York proposed a 10,000 percent excise tax on the product. Coupled with other measures, a $200 transfer tax imposed on automatic machine gun sales in 1934 by Congress was adequate financial disincentive to keep these types of weapons out of the civilian market (Karlson and Hargarten 1997).

If injuries from products were a liability to manufacturers, financial incentives would exist to improve product safety. In our economic accounting system, we do not do a good job of allocating the costs of injuries to those most able to make the necessary changes to prevent them. Generally those who bear the costs of injuries are the injured and their families. Often, these are externalized from manufacturer balance sheets. There are also multiple hidden economic costs to the public, the most obvious of which is medical care for those who are not insured or who are underinsured. An example is captured in a 1994 article that traced all the costs of a 40-cent bullet shot with a twenty-dollar gun in an assault. The title, "The Two Million Dollar Bullet," nicely sums up the findings (Lalli 1994). The adult victim sustained a spinal cord injury and lived only a month. Medical expenses accounted for $65,000, life insurance policy payouts amounted to more than $525,000, annual Social Security and worker's compensation pay were $46,000, the criminal justice expenses were more than $200,000, and the person's lost productivity was estimated to be $1,000,000.

Litigation or its threat also changes the economic incentives that drive manufacturers. When laws and regulation have not successfully protected people from hazardous products, some turn to product liability suits. These are decided by courts, which may be less susceptible to the intense lobbying that usually surrounds legislative and regulatory processes when a product's hazard is under discussion. Product liability suits or their threat have eliminated some injury hazards from many consumer products including passenger cars. These suits were instrumental in the eventual inclusion of air bags and other passive restraint systems in passenger cars. Currently, some are using this approach to change the design and manufacturing of firearms (Christoffel and Teret 1993).

Environmental Factors

Environmental factors can promote or impede safety through forces beyond the control of an individual. Both natural phenomena and cultural values are aspects of the environment that affect safety.

Natural Phenomena

Natural phenomena have always threatened safety and, in turn, humans have developed responses, including warning systems such as lighthouses to warn ships of rocks, fog horns and buoys to guide ships at sea, and sirens for tornadoes and hurricanes. If the warnings are timely, populations can act to prevent or escape damage.

Other responses include those to limit damage from natural phenomena, such as ordinances and insurance policies that discourage people from building in flood plains, and building codes that limit damage from earthquakes. Government sources have also spent significant amounts of money on scientific systems to predict earthquakes. Federal, state, and local governments are usually responsible for these early warnings and damage prevention strategies. Unlike the controversy that sometimes surrounds government regulation of consumer products, there appears to be wide consensus that protecting the public against natural phenomena is a reasonable role for government.

Cultural Values

Lastly, our cultural values influence safety through the determinants identified in the Public Safety Model. Cultural values provide a guide to individuals to determine appropriate risk-taking. Cultural values define the norm and the ends of the spectrum of risk-taking behavior. In our culture, we honor individuals who take risks in the military, the business world, competitive sports, and activities pitting the individual against the elements. We seem to believe that the individual is responsible for outcomes-both the rewards and the damages. This cultural value in turn contributes to the political and social systems that are necessary to effect safety. For safety, we favor strategies involving individual behavior whether it is warning individuals to take action or laws requiring individuals to use protective equipment. We also depend on individuals to moderate use of alcohol.

Individualism and the rights of private property influence our cultural suspicion about government intervention in safety through product design. U.S. culture supports the private property rights and due process of manufacturers over government regulation of products. These manufacturers in turn blame individuals for unsafe actions. As a result, promoting safety through product design or other public intervention is often an arduous and lengthy process.

One illustration of this is found in the reluctance and outright resistance of automobile manufacturers to install airbags in cars despite repeated demonstrations of their life-saving capabilities. Airbags were first patented in 1952. The bags were installed on 10,000 General Motors cars in 1974 and functioned well. The U.S. Department of Transportation first ordered airbags on 1974 model cars, then amended the order to include automatic belts, and rescinded it completely in 1974. The standard was reinstated in 1977, and rescinded again in 1981. Insurers sued the Department of Transportation, and finally, under direction from the Supreme Court, the department reinstated the standard to begin in 1987. Many manufacturers initially chose to meet the standard with automatic seat belts. Dual airbags were required on all passenger cars for the 1998 model year (Karlson and Hargarten 1997).

Cultural values about individuals' access to guns also affect safety. International comparisons show that no other industrialized country has homicide death rates from firearms that even come close to those of the United States (Karlson and Hargarten 1997).

Yet cultural values change. Automobile manufacturers who once resisted product modifications now extol the "safety features" of their vehicles. If safety is now a selling point, market forces may promote the installation of side airbags more quickly than government regulation.

There is also widespread agreement in opinion polls that we need to change our current public policy of almost unrestricted access to handguns. Some public health researchers liken the intensity of the discussion to that which greeted the Surgeon General's Report on Smoking in 1964. Incremental changes in cultural values about smoking ensued so that today both federal and state governments are holding the tobacco industry accountable for their unsafe product.

VI. Conclusion

Safety is intensely personal; humans go to great lengths to protect themselves and their loved ones. But safety cannot be guaranteed through individual action alone. Our collective safety is made up in part by decisions of individuals as they engage in high-risk behaviors, impede judgement and self-control through excessive use of alcohol, decide whether or not to use protective equipment, or avail themselves of training opportunities. Yet our safety is also determined by actions in the public sphere: laws and the design of public spaces and products.

Financial incentives drive safety as well. The decisions of corporations as they balance profit and costs have an enormous effect on our safety. These decisions include how much to spend on improved product design, advertising, litigation as well as presenting their interests to decision- and policymakers.

Governmental actions also determine our collective safety. They influence regulation of the design of public spaces or products, emergency response, disaster preparedness, and the extent and nature of advertising. Tax policies of the government can include financial incentives to improve products or restrict their distribution.

Collectively, our ideas and our actions become our cultural values that influence individual, corporate, and governmental behaviors affecting safety. Supporting safe personal behaviors has always been an important part of improving the safety of our population. But it is also necessary to acknowledge what can be improved in the public sphere. Reducing deaths and injuries – especially from cars and guns, the leading causes of death from injury – will require changes in the public sphere. To do so, in part, we need to foster cultural values that support public action as well as personal behaviors as essential determinants of safety.

ENDNOTES

[1] Age-adjusting is a technique used for phenomena that vary with age, for example, heart disease. A population with an average age of 65 has a higher rate of heart disease than a population with an average age of 40 because heart disease is more common among the elderly. Age adjusting removes the effect of the age structure of populations so that other differences can be examined. It is most commonly done with comparing diseases in populations at different points in time.

[2] For example, very young children cannot appropriately perceive and respond to hazards they encounter when they are first able to move or walk. Caretakers provide the necessary oversight to protect children and train them to protect themselves.

Appendix 1 **Death Rates from Injuries and Infectious Diseases by Year, 1910-1997**

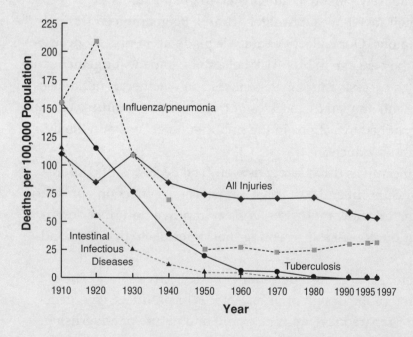

Source: Adapted from The Injury Fact Book and National Center for Disease Control mortality data.

Ten Leading Causes of Death, United States, 1997

Appendix 2

Age Groups

Rank	<1	1-4	5-9	10-14	15-24	25-34	35-44	45-54	55-64	65+	Total
1	Congenital Anomalies 6,178	**Unintentional Inj.& Adv. Effects 2,005**	**Unintentional Inj.& Adv. Effects 1,534**	**Unintentional Inj.& Adv. Effects 1,837**	**Unintentional Inj.& Adv. Effects 13,367**	**Unintentional Inj.& Adv. Effects 12,598**	Malignant Neoplasms 17,099	Malignant Neoplasms 45,429	Malignant Neoplasms 86,314	Heart Disease 606,913	Heart Disease 726,974
2	Short Gestation 3,925	Congenital Anomalies 589	Malignant Neoplasms 547	Malignant Neoplasms 483	**Homicide & Legal Int. 6,146**	**Suicide 5,627**	**Unintentional Inj. & Adv. Effects 14,531**	Heart Disease 35,277	Heart Disease 65,958	Malignant Neoplasms 382,913	Malignant Neoplasms 539,577
3	SIDS 2,991	Malignant Neoplasms 438	Congenital Anomalies 223	**Suicide 303**	**Suicide 4,186**	**Homicide & Legal Int. 5,075**	Heart Disease 13,227	**Unintentional Inj. & Adv. Effects 10,416**	Emphysema Asthma 10,109	Cerebro-vascular 140,366	Cerebro-vascular 159,791
4	Respiratory Distress Synd. 1,301	**Homicide & Legal Int. 375**	**Homicide & Legal Int. 174**	**Homicide & Legal Int. 283**	Malignant Neoplasms 1,645	Malignant Neoplasms 4,607	HIV 7,073	Cerebro-vascular 5,695	Cerebro-vascular 9,676	Bronchitis Emphysema Asthma 94,411	Bronchitis Emphysema Asthma 109,029
5	Maternal Complications 1,244	Heart Disease 212	Heart Disease 128	Congenital Anomalies 224	Heart Disease 1,098	HIV 3,993	**Suicide 6,730**	Liver Disease 5,622	Diabetes 8,370	Pneumonia & Influenza 77,561	**Unintentional Inj. & Adv. Effects 95,644**
6	Placenta Cord Membranes 960	Pneumonia & Influenza 180	Pneumonia & Influenza 76	Heart Disease 185	Congenital Anomalies 420	Heart Disease 3,286	**Homicide & Legal Int. 3,677**	**Suicide 4,948**	**Unintentional Inj. & Adv. Effects 7,105**	Diabetes 47,289	Pneumonia & Influenza 86,449
7	Perinatal Infections 777	Perinatal Period 75	HIV 62	Bronchitis Emphysema Asthma 79	HIV 276	Cerebro-vascular 678	Liver Disease 3,508	Diabetes 4,335	Liver Disease 5,253	**Unintentional Inj. & Adv. Effects 31,386**	Diabetes 62,636
8	**Unintentional Inj. & Adv. Effects 765**	Septicemia 73	Bronchitis Emphysema Asthma 50	Pneumonia & Influenza 65	Pneumonia & Influenza 220	Diabetes 620	Cerebro-vascular 2,787	HIV 3,513	Pneumonia & Influenza 3,759	Alzheimer Disease 22,154	**Suicide 30,535**
9	Intrauterine Hypoxia 452	Benign Neoplasms 65	Anemias 38	Cerebro-vascular 51	Bronchitis Emphysema Asthma 201	Pneumonia & Influenza 534	Diabetes 1,858	Bronchitis Emphysema Asthma 2,838	**Suicide 2,946**	Nephritis 21,787	Nephritis 25,331
10	Pneumonia & Influenza 421	Cerebro-vascular 56	Benign Neoplasms 35	Benign Neoplasms 41	Cerebro-vascular 188	Liver Disease 516	Pneumonia & Influenza 1,394	Pneumonia & Influenza 2,233	Septicemia 1,852	Septicemia 18,079	Liver Disease 25,175

See Appendix 8, page 317, for definition of terms. Deaths from injuries are in boldface type.

Source: National Center for Injury Prevention and Control (http://www.cdc.gov/ncipc).

Appendix 3 **Years of Potential Life Lost Before Age 65 (YPLL) by Cause of Death, 1995**

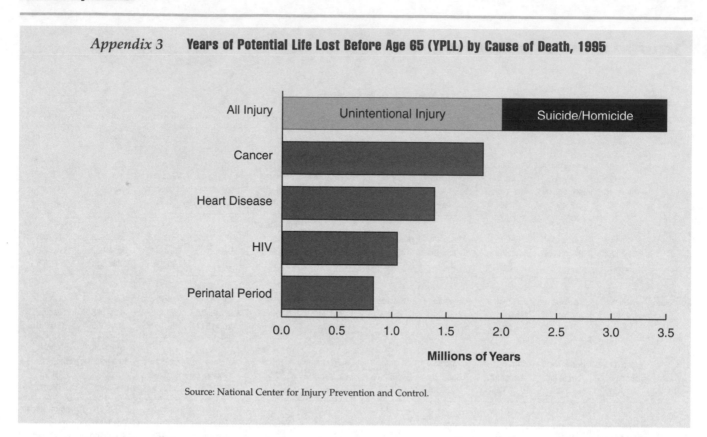

Source: National Center for Injury Prevention and Control.

Appendix 4 **Causes of Deaths from Injuries, 1997**

External Causes of Death	Number of People
All Injuries	146,400
Motor Vehicles	42,500
Firearms	32,400
Suicide by firearm	17,600
Homicide by firearm	13,300
Poisonings from drugs, gases, and other means	17,700
Falls	12,600
Suffocation	10,700
Drowning	4,700
Fire and Burns	4,100
Cutting and piercing instruments	2,900
Other	18,800

Note: "Other" includes injuries from events such as airport crashes, electrocutions, injuries from machinery, boating among others.

Source: National Center for Health Stastistics.

Death Rates from Injury by Year and Cause, 1936-1997　　　　*Appendix 5*

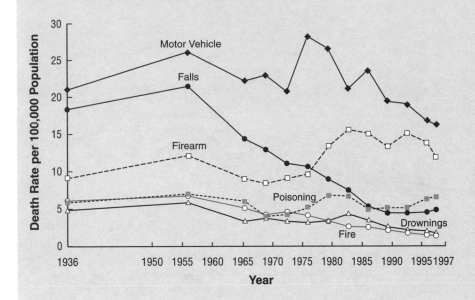

Source: National Center for Injury Prevention and Control and Historical Vital Statistics.

Appendix 6   **Death Rates from Motor Vehicle Crashes and Firearms, 1960-1997**

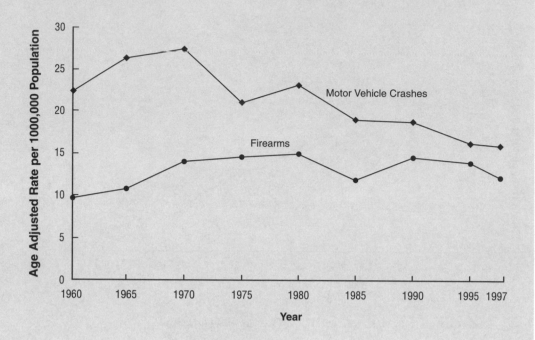

Source: National Center for Injury Prevention and Control.

Driver Deaths in Passenger Vehicles, 1997

Appendix 7

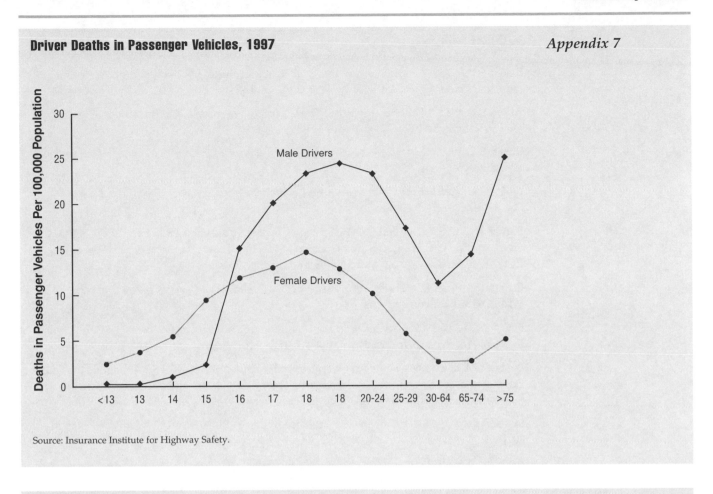

Source: Insurance Institute for Highway Safety.

Definitions of Terms

Appendix 8

Medical Terminology	Common Lay Term
Congenital anomaly	Birth defect
HIV (Human immunosupressive virus)	AIDS (Acquired immunodeficiency syndrome
Malignant neoplasm	Cancer
Cerebrovascular disease	Stroke
Nephritis	Kidney disease
Perinatal	Around the birth
Intrauterine hypoxia	Lack of oxygen for the fetus
Short gestation	Premature birth
Septicemia	Blood infection

REFERENCES

Baker, S.P. 1975. "Determinants of Injury and Opportunities for Intervention." *American Journal of Epidemiology,* Vol. 101, pp. 98-102.

Baker, S.P. 1981. "Childhood Injuries: The Community Approach to Prevention." *Journal of Public Health Policy,* Vol. 2, No. 3, pp. 235-246.

Baker, S.P. 1989. "Injury Science Comes of Age." *Journal of the American Medical Association,* Vol. 262, No. 16, pp. 2284-2285.

Baker, S.P., and B. O'Neill, M. Ginsburg, L. Guohaa. 1992. *The Injury Fact Book.* New York: Oxford University Press.

Bonnie R.J., C.E. Fulco, and C.T. Liverman eds. 1999. *Reducing the Burden of Injury,* Committee on Injury Prevention and Control, Division of Health Promotion and Disease Prevention, Institute of Medicine. New York: National Academy Press.

Christoffel, T. and S.P. Teret. 1993. *Protecting the Public: Legal Issues in Injury Prevention.* New York: Oxford University Press.

Haddon, W., Jr. 1980. "Advances in the Epidemiology of Injuries as a Basis for Public Policy." *Public Health Reports,* Vol. 95, No. 5, pp. 411-421.

Ikeda, R.M. et al. 1997. *Fatal Firearm Injuries in the United States, 1962-1994,* Centers for Disease Control and Prevention, National Center for Injury Prevention and Control, Violence Surveillance Summary Series, No. 3.

Janosfsky, M. 1998. "Decline in Gun Violence Bypasses Philadelphia." *New York Times,* May 20, A14.

Karlson, T.A. 1992. "Injury Control and Public Policy." *Critical Reviews in Environmental Control,* Vol. 22, No. 3/4, pp. 195-241.

Karlson, T. A. and S. Hargarten. 1997. *Reducing Firearm Injury and Death: A Public Health Sourcebook on Guns.* New Brunswick, NJ: Rutgers University Press.

Lalli, F. 1994. "The Cost of One Bullet: $2 Million." *Money,* Vol. 23, pp.7-8.

MacKenzie E.J., B.M. Cushing, and G. J. Jurkovich. 1993. "Physical Impairment and Functional Outcomes Six Months After Severe Lower Extremity Fractures." *Journal of Trauma,* Vol. 34, pp. 528-61.

Rice, D.P. and E.J. MacKenzie. 1989. *Cost of Injury in the United States.* San Francisco: Institute for Health and Aging, University of California and Injury Prevention Center, Johns Hopkins University.

Robertson, L. 1998. *Injury Epidemiology,* 2nd Ed. New York: Oxford University Press.

Chapter 15

Re-Creation Indicator

by Richard A. Peterson, Ph.D. and Carrie Y. Lee

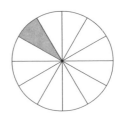

I. Introduction

Recreation involves re-creating oneself, to be revitalized in body and mind and to reestablish social contacts. According to the Oxford English Dictionary recreation also means creating something new of oneself through new experience, education, and travel (1989). Thus, "re-creation" includes all activities that make one able or willing to return to work or engage in family activities again; it is, in effect, recharging batteries. But it can, and often does, involve efforts to improve oneself, change one's social position, or take on an identity separate from those connected to work or family.

On average, American adults now spend upwards of a quarter of their time in recreation (Schor 1991, Robinson and Godbey 1997). According to the Bureau of Economic Analysis, in 1995, spending on recreation amounted to $401 billion and accounted for 8.2 percent of personal consumption budgets; tourism alone now generates 11.3 percent of the gross domestic product (Lipman and Dickinson 1998).

Recreation has been a vital component of the quality of life in this nation since its founding. This is exemplified in the Declaration of Independence in which John Locke's "life, liberty, and property" formulation for the good life (1689) was transformed into the American Revolutionary War call to arms to achieve, "life, liberty, and the pursuit of happiness." In the 1830s, Alexis de Tocqueville, the perceptive French commentator on the American way of life, made clear that what was good for the individual person was also important for the flowering of democracy on this continent (1845). Being a responsible and creative citizen, he argued, requires that all individuals participate in a wide range of activities rather than just a few, no matter how ennobling the few might be considered.

As de Tocqueville recognized, the "pursuit of happiness" in the United States is seen as largely a matter of individual choice rather than as the province of government control or planning. Consequently, unlike the other industrialized nations, we do not have an official "cultural policy" or Ministry of Culture. One unfortunate consequence of the laissez-faire policy in the United States is that there has been little governmental concern with systematically collecting data to track the ebb and flow of the competing types of recreational activities over time.[1]

The purpose of the Calvert-Henderson Re-Creation Indicator is to facilitate a better understanding of the contribution of re-creation to the quality of life in America. To begin this process we identify the range of recreational activities widely available in the United States today and propose a model linking these with the resources that help determine peoples' opportunities for recreation and shape their preferences. True to the historic American commitment to the freedom of expression, we do not evaluate which forms of recreational activity are good or bad for the society or for the individual. As noted by Herbert Gans, in a cultural democracy it is important to assess all kinds of activities, even if they are negatively evaluated by the reader or others, because all activities compete for people's discretionary time, attention, and money (1974). This is not to say that all types of recreation are equally valuable, but that such evaluative judgments are beyond the scope of this project.

There is no agreed upon model that captures a common understanding or framework of re-creation, so we must take a number of steps to create one. We begin by showing why we use the term "re-creation" rather than the related terms "free time" and "leisure." We then discuss the reasons for focusing primarily on the consumption of recreation rather than on the recreation industries that produce recreational activities. To complete the section on defining terms, we explain our reasons for choosing the activity-survey measure of recreation rather than measures based on time or money budgets.

Next we introduce the three elements of the re-creation process model: resources, choice points, and types of re-creation. Recreation in an advanced society like the United States depends on a number of institutional and individual resources, and these are discussed in turn. Four institutional investments that structure recreation include law, technology, facilities, and community diversity. Six individual and population resources that condition recreation are formal education, socialization for recreation, age, gender, discretionary time, and discretionary money.

The second major element of the re-creation process model is the recreation choice point. Here, depending on the institutional investments and their personal resources, individuals select among the welter of recreational opportunities that are available. We suggest that their value choices depend on their assessment of (a) the time and money available, (b) an appropriate occasion, and (c) available companions. Chosen recreation, we argue, also depends on the welter of *attention inducers* that vie in shaping recreational choices.

An inventory of 13 major types of recreation available in the United States comprises the final major element of the re-creation process model. Each is defined, briefly discussed, and illustrated using statistics to suggest the import in society today. Because this enumeration of the types of recreation is one of the major contributions of the Calvert-Henderson Re-Creation Indicator, it is given nearly half of the text.

We conclude by outlining some of the important steps needed to implement the recreation process model. These include taking steps to systematically gather the necessary types of data and a clear articulation of the

Calvert-Henderson Re-Creation Model

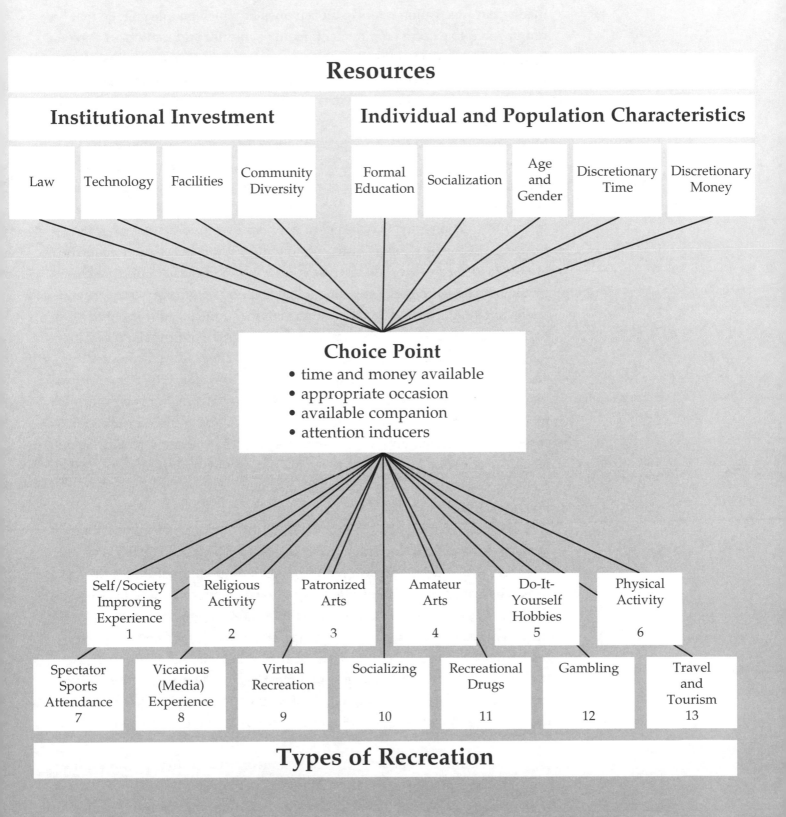

Resources

Institutional Investment

Law | Technology | Facilities | Community Diversity

Individual and Population Characteristics

Formal Education | Socialization | Age and Gender | Discretionary Time | Discretionary Money

Choice Point

- time and money available
- appropriate occasion
- available companion
- attention inducers

Self/Society Improving Experience 1

Religious Activity 2

Patronized Arts 3

Amateur Arts 4

Do-It-Yourself Hobbies 5

Physical Activity 6

Spectator Sports Attendance 7

Vicarious (Media) Experience 8

Virtual Recreation 9

Socializing 10

Recreational Drugs 11

Gambling 12

Travel and Tourism 13

Types of Recreation

research and policy uses to which the model might be applied.

II. Defining Terms

The distinction between "recreation" and "re-creation" needs to be made clear. Recreation refers to all activities in which people engage that are not devoted to gainful employment, family activities and matters of personal hygiene. The thirteen general types of recreation are discussed below. Re-creation, as we use the term, refers to the balance of recreational activities that improve the quality of life for the individual and the society. No activity necessarily adds to or detracts from the quality of life. After all it is possible to get so involved in any activity, be it opera, exercise or gambling, that it detracts from one's quality of life. Since our knowledge of the range and distribution of recreational activities is too scattered, it is necessary first to focus on recreation.

Recreation may be engaged in with family or work associates, but many recreational activities foster intense interactions between people who are not family or co-workers. In many instances, otherwise important distinctions of age, gender, occupation, ethnicity, and income become virtually irrelevant among those who share a recreational interest. All recreational enthusiasms from hot-rod racing (Moorehouse 1991), quilt-making and neighborhood socio-political activity (Halle 1984) to political action groups such as Amnesty International and futurist organizations (Henderson 1996) involve the potential for re-creation. To highlight a distinction, civic and religious participation do not typically fall under the term recreation, though these activities are important elements of our term "re-creation." Since paid labor has received by far the greatest amount of attention from economists, the other aspects of human activity have remained virtually invisible (Waring 1988).

Here, what we call "recreation" is termed "free time" by time-budget analysts such as John Robinson (1984) and Arlie Hochschild (1997). The term free time, is avoided because it seems to mean quite different things to social researchers than it does to people generally. For the former, free time is time that is not "paid work," "household/family care" or "personal time." And yet respondents regularly report having a good deal less "free time" than researchers find they spend in what the researchers define as free time (Robinson 1984). The data suggest that most people do not consider their time is "free" when, for example, they attend a weekly poker game, take part in religious services, or engage in other regularly scheduled recreational activities.

"Leisure" is another term that is sometimes used for the cluster of activities focal in this indicator. Relying on a venerable philosophical tradition, Grazia (1962) differentiates between "free time" and "leisure." For him, leisure is not just time away from work, rather, it consists of time devoted to creative enjoyment. At the same time leisure has come to have much the

Re-creation refers to the balance of recreational activities that improve the quality of life for the individual and the society.

opposite connotation, that of time used unproductively. For example, disparaging references are often made to the "person of leisure" and the "leisure class" (Oxford English Dictionary 1989: 815-816). In line with our commitment to avoid evaluations, we avoid the word leisure because we do not want to presume, a priori, that some time or money is ill spent. Finally, the term "leisure" is avoided because it means much the same thing as "free time" to many empirical researchers, Staffan Linder (1970) and Juliet Schor (1991) among many others.

How to Measure Recreation

Because we are interested in the quality of life experienced by people in the United States today, our primary measures of recreation focus on how people spend their time and money in recreational activities. This focus on consumption has the clear advantage of casting the broadest possible net in the search for recreational activities. Only when the range and frequency of participation is better known, will researchers and policy makers be in a position to target particular industries or products of concern. The terms "consumption" and "participation" have both been used in the literature, and we will use them interchangeably here as the context dictates.

Because what people can do is determined, in part, by what recreational opportunities are available and recognized, measures of production in what is increasingly being called the "culture industry' need to be considered as well.[2] Their importance is recognized in the re-creation model elaborated below. Finally, since many have policy concerns about one or another form of recreation, measures of the symbolic meaning of the increasingly pre-packaged or mass-produced products of the culture industry are important to understand. This approach is exemplified by systematic studies of the content of television programming (Gerbner 1984) as well as content analyses of recreational activities ranging from operas and computer games to horror movies and rap and country music.[3]

Measuring Consumption

There is no one agreed upon way of measuring consumption or collecting detailed information on recreation, so one of the purposes of the Re-Creation Indicator is to lay the groundwork for developing such a system. Several different metrics have been used to measure participation in recreation. Some measure time and others measure money expenditures.[4]

We advocate using the activity-survey method of measuring consumption as the most appropriate for our interest in recreation's contribution to the quality of life (Peterson 1980). This method of data collection is widely used in consumer research because it has proved most economical in successfully capturing participation in a broad array of recreational activities. Two data sources that exemplify activity surveys are the General Social Survey (GSS) and the Survey of Public Participation in the Arts (SPPA).

These surveys ask respondents how many times they have participated in a list of activities in the past week, month, or year. Such surveys have the distinct advantage of covering a long enough reference period so that respondents can report the full range of recreational activities in which they have engaged, even if participation is infrequent and consumes a smaller amount of time than other activities.

The activity-survey method is not without its problems. Given the long reference period, many respondents do not accurately remember the things they actually did in the reference period, or they tend to give answers that suggest more about what they should like to do or what they think is appropriate to do rather than report accurately what they have done. Therefore an activity survey cannot be relied on to accurately reflect rates of participation in specific recreational activities. Nonetheless, the fact that errors of estimate are not random can be seen as an asset rather than as a liability when surveys are replicated over time. Then the focus shifts to the *changes* in reported participation from one survey period to another. Leaving random error aside, changes in estimates are due to two factors. First, they are due to the actual change in the rates of the activity from one survey year to another. Second, they are due to the changing social desirability of the specific kind of activity over time.[5] Thus, while it is not safe to extrapolate from reported survey results an attendance rate for the entire population, *changes* in participation rates are meaningful and we strongly advocate this metric for measuring recreation.

Money-budget accounts that measure how people spend their money is an alternative measure of consumption. Most of a family's budget goes to food, lodging, clothing, and transportation, so it has proved difficult to get detailed data on recreation expenditures. In addition, the amount of money available for recreation varies widely with the level of wealth, and while some forms of recreation are very expensive, others are virtually free (Peterson 1980).

Some researchers – thinking of time, like money, as a scarce resource – have studied time budgets (Schor 1991, Hochschild 1997, Robinson and Godbey 1997). Such accounts of time expenditures have the clear advantage over money budgets in that there is only a fixed period of time for all respondents rich and poor, young and old, to spend in a day or in a week. However, since time cannot in reality be saved, traded, or sold, no elaborate public system of accounting for time analogous to the system of financial accounts has been developed. As a consequence, no regularly replicated set of time accounts has been developed that details the expenditure of nonwork time.

Measures of how people budget their time are available only for the past few decades, and there is a dispute over whether leisure time is increasing or being eroded.[6] The biggest differences in the hours of free time are correlated with hours of gainful employment, gender, marital status, and the presence of children in the home. On average, gainfully employed women experienced two hours less free time per week than their male counterparts, but for the unemployed, the gender difference was over nine hours per week (Robinson and Godbey 1997). Thus, the amount of time for recreation is now determined more by work status, child raising, and gender than by personal preferences or social class position.

Time budgets work well in comparing the gross activity categories such as work, household maintenance, personal time, and free time (which equates roughly with recreation). Although the amount of time devoted to recreation is considerable – occupying slightly more than the time devoted by the average adult to work – television accounts for nearly one half of all free time, and the time devoted to each of the other activities of interest appears trivial. What is more, the wide range of other types of recreation cannot be disaggregated.[7] Thus, it is not possible to meaningfully examine the many other components of recreation or free time by using the time budget technique.

III. The Re-Creation Model

Unlike most of the other topics treated in the Calvert-Henderson Quality of Life Project, such as employment, income, and health, there is no accepted way of conceptualizing a model to help us understand participation in recreation, so it is necessary to start the construction de novo. Following the pattern of the other Calvert-Henderson process models, the re-creation model represents a range of resources as inputs and various types of recreation as outputs. To highlight the volitional nature of choice among types of recreation, the model connects resources with recreation outcomes through the decision point at which recreation choices are made. Thus the model has three classes of elements. In the discussion that follows, the most attention is given to understanding the diverse types of recreation because, until we know what it is that we want to track, it is not possible to fully explicate the resources that are called into play.

Institutional Investments as Resources

We are interested in all the institutional investments that shape patterns of leisure. For example, television, which now accounts for so much of the average American's leisure time, depends on a series of technological innovations. The nature and availability of specific sorts of programming are conditioned by numerous laws and regulations. The left-hand side of the resources line in the model includes four examples of the investments made by governments, organizations, and foundations that facilitate or inhibit specific types of recreation: law, technology, facilities, and community diversity. The current array of recreation would not be possible without these four investments described briefly below.

Law

Diverse types of law help shape recreational resources. For example, copyright and trademark laws are vital in converting creativity into property, making possible the development of the vast entertainment industry. Tax laws relating to inheritance have fostered the development of the fine arts by providing tax incentives to donate art and money to arts institutions. Numerous regulatory laws have shaped the mass media in this country, including the laws relating to pornography.

Technology

Investments in technology – from the printing press, telegraphy, and railroads to the radio, television, personal computer, and the Internet – have greatly expanded recreational opportunities. Each new technology has not only had a direct impact on recreational activities, but has also restructured the use of others. For example, the emergence of phonograph records, the radio, and movies in the second quarter of the 20th century created vastly increased recreational opportunities, but they also profoundly reshaped the uses of earlier technological systems (Ennis 1992, Peterson 1997).

Facilities

Many types of recreation require facilities for participation to take place. Public investments in stadiums, museums, and concert halls make possible the vast array of recreational opportunities unavailable to people in earlier generations. Even wilderness activities such as hiking, hunting, fishing, and camping are made widely available by today's vast systems of state and federal parks and airports. In most instances, the facilities have been built through the lobbying efforts of recreation-oriented organizations that also shape and promote recreation.

Community Diversity

Except for tourist travel, recreation takes place in one's home or no more than a few hours from home. Thus the diversity of activities available within easy distance of the home conditions the rate and range of participation in recreational activities. Generally, the larger the population of the community, the more diverse the recreational opportunities. Comparisons are often made between the isolated small town and the large city, but even among cities there are wide differences. For example, people living in New York, Washington, D.C., and Chicago can choose from among a wider range of films showing in local theaters at any given time than can people living in Green Bay, Nashville, and Tucson. Moreover, the nature of the local industry, ethnic mix, level of education, region, and weather as well as conscious public policy and economic development goals also influences the diversity of available recreation.

Individual and Population Characteristics

Moving from the left to the right side of the Resource line in the model, we find the individual and population characteristics that, in combination with institutional investments, condition recreation. Depending on the focus of the inquiry, either the characteristics of populations or of individuals may be emphasized.

Formal Education

Individuals with at least a college education are most likely to participate in the fine arts (Survey of Public Participation in the Arts 1982, 1992). Even taking into account the effects of income, gender, and age, those with higher education are more likely to engage in the full range of nonelite recreational activities (Peterson and Simkus 1992, Peterson and Kern 1996).

Socialization for Recreation

A great deal of socialization for recreation takes place outside of formal schooling. It occurs informally through family interaction, peer groups, clubs, playgrounds as well as media exposure. Not easily quantified, this socialization to habitus is not well measured in extant activity surveys (Bourdieu 1984).

Age and Gender

Many forms of recreation appeal to one age group more than others because of the content or skills and physical ability necessary to participate. Thus, after education, many studies have found that age is the most potent predictor of participation in selected recreational activities. Many recreational activities are participated in more often by one gender than by the other. Thus, gender also is a good predictor of participation in selected recreational activities.

Time

All recreational activities require time and each activity must compete with gainful employment, family activities, and personal activities – as well as with one another – for the finite time available in a day, week, or year. Spare time, like spare money, can be considered a resource that may be spent in recreation. Discretionary time is not distributed equally in the population, and, like the distribution of discretionary income, it influences the patterns of recreation choices.

Money

Many recreational activities require money and compete with other monetary demands, including food, shelter, apparel, utilities, furniture, transportation, health, and education. As Dora Costa shows, the least well-off segment of working American families had virtually no money to spend on recreation in 1888 (1997). But wages have since risen, and the cost of recreation has dropped sufficiently that it has now become more democratized and has become what she calls an "affordable luxury" available to virtually all. The shift has been great enough that the share of the average family's budget going to recreation has nearly tripled since 1888.

The Recreation Choice Point

In the middle of the input-output model is a box designated as the Recreation Choice Point. Placing this box at the midpoint of the model signals that participation in particular forms of recreation does not flow automatically from institutional investments and individual characteristics; there are vastly more recreational opportunities than time/money available. Thus choices must be made. The elements in this box are decision-making criteria used by individuals or populations to choose the types of recreations in which to engage.

Decisions to participate in particular forms of recreation rather than others are influenced by (1) the perception that one has the time and money available to engage in a recreation, (2) the knowledge that there is an appropriate occasion for a particular recreation, (3) the availability of appropriate companions, and (4) the operation of attention inducers.

The concept of "attention inducers" suggested by Hazel Henderson (1996) conveniently bundles together a number of factors that bring particular forms of recreation to people's attention and shape their views of time, money, and availability of companions. Advertisements and news stories, for example, bring to people's attention the availability of particular kinds of recreational activities. Attention inducers are disseminated largely via the mass media to increase consumption and shape people's views of the kinds of activities that are appropriate, prestige-bringing, and declassé. Often in competition with each other, attention inducers attempt to teach what combinations of recreational occasions, companions, time, and money are appropriate in maximizing one's quality of life.

Creating a Taxonomy of Recreation

In the lower portion of the model is an array of recreational activities that show the diverse forms of recreation, not just those that some might judge as healthy, beneficial, or appropriate. The aim is to get a picture of what people actually do with their free time.

There is no agreed upon taxonomy of recreation, and even if we established a taxonomy, some activities might be placed in several places. The appropriate placement of religious activities illustrates the problem of forming categories. Most religious activities are participated in as self- and society-improving, but some are not, and the link to the supernatural makes them somewhat different from secular activity. Moreover, since religious participation is so frequent in this country, it seems appropriate to designate it as a separate category.

Travel and tourism poses a different set of considerations. Some of the most unlikely places have become tourist destinations. For example, Antarctica was visited by 1,500 eco-tourists in 1997 (*Economist* 1998a). According to the World Travel and Tourism Council, travel and tourism now account for 11.3 percent of the gross domestic product of the United States and 10.6 percent worldwide (*Economist* 1998b). But tourism and travel are not distinct in the way going to the movies or to a lecture are, because virtually the entire range of forms of recreation represented in the other categories may involve extensive travel. People in large numbers travel a good distance from their homes to get horizon-expanding education, attend a cultural festival, procure sex, visit a theme park, gamble, commune with nature, attend a major football game, take a religious pilgrimage, or visit a special museum exhibit.

To bundle tourism with other recreational activities obscures the fact that engaging in leisure activities as part of vacation travel is usually qualitatively different than engaging in them in one's home town; recreational activity that involves overnight travel is more meaningful than the same activity at home. Professional sports fans, amateur contradance club members, opera goers, or quilt-makers who attend a game/contest/performance away from home make a much bigger commitment of time and money than when they attend similar events near home. What is more, they are going into the home territory of others and are expected to dress and deport themselves accordingly. They are likely to affiliate more closely with co-recreation enthusiasts.

Our resolution of the overlap problem is to factor the recreative value of tourist activity into two parts. The usual recreative value of the activity is counted with the appropriate type of nontravel activity, and the considerable quality-of-life gains of recreational activity away from home are recognized in a separate category in the re-creation model designated travel and tourism.

Sexual activity also poses a problem for classification. Time-budget analysts either ignore it or quietly include it in "household time" along with housework, shopping, and child care. This is to implicitly classify sex as procreation, but clearly, even for married couples with fewer than a dozen children, most sexual activity is justified as, and engaged in, as recreation. Not only is sexual intercourse a significant recreation, but the wide range of activities that go into trying to make oneself an attractive partner permeates most other forms of recreation in America today. We advocate classifying recreational sexual intercourse as physical activity and putting the rest of sex-related or motivated activity in the appropriate substantive categories of recreation.

IV. Data on Types of Recreation

Below we explicate thirteen types of recreation and present data that illustrate their variety and extent. The intention is not to judge the relative importance of these activities, but rather to provide a snapshot indicating their prevalence.

Data on recreation have unfortunately not been collected systematically over time. Available statistics are wide-ranging, but they come from studies made at various times, for widely different purposes, and using differing measures of recreation so that accurate comparisons between the 13 types are not possible. Most of the figures cited below come from one of two reliable sources. The first is the General Social Survey (GSS) conducted periodically by the National Opinion Research Center of the University of Chicago under contract from the National Science Foundation. The second is the *Statistical Abstract of the United States,* published annually by the U.S. Bureau of the Census with data from both government and private sources. Unless otherwise noted, all quoted figures refer to samples of the adult population 18 years of age or older.

1. Self/Society Improving Experience

People engage in a wide range of recreational activities to improve themselves, their communities, and their world. This can be seen as re-creation in its purest sense. Examples include self-improvement classes, reading and videos, political activity, volunteering, visits to museums, zoos and aquaria, and searching Internet information sources. The extent of self-society improving activity is suggested by the following findings:

- In 1994, 10 percent of the adults surveyed participated in literary, art, discussion, or study groups in the last year (GSS 1994).
- In the same year, 5 percent of adults said they belonged to a political club, 8 percent said they belonged to a veteran's group, 4 percent were members of nationality groups, and 12 percent were members of a labor union. In 1996, 5 percent of adult respondents reported they had participated in more than one public meeting concerning government actions (GSS 1996).
- In 1996, 49 percent of adults and 59 percent of teenagers engaged in volunteer activities (Independent Sector 1996).
- An estimated $958 million was spent on microcomputer software for home education in 1996, and $337 million was invested in software for amateur artistic activity (U.S. Bureau of the Census 1997).[8]

2. Religious Activities

Although people engage in religious activity to be closer to higher powers, much of it is also intended to improve oneself or society. The United States is unique among the advanced nations in its rates of religious activity. The level of activity is suggested by the following figures on the range of religious activities:

- In 1996, 29 percent of adult respondents said they attended religious services at least once a week, and an additional 16 percent attended at least once a month (GSS 1996).

- Twenty percent of adults said that they contributed more than $250 to religious organizations, excluding money for student tuition and fees (GSS 1996).
- In 1995, 3,324 books on religious subjects were published, which represents 6 percent of all nonfiction books published that year (U.S. Bureau of the Census 1997).
- Asked if they were members of a religious organization in 1994, 33 percent of adults responded yes; 24 percent said that they had volunteered time to religious organizations in the prior year (GSS 1996).

3. Patronized Arts

Connoisseurship of the fine arts has long been seen as ennobling the individual and civilizing the society (Arnold 1875). More than any other recreational activity, the fine arts have been financially subsidized by kings and queens, governments, foundations, and other wealthy individuals. None of these art forms would exist in their present form without substantial amounts of unearned income. Because we do not want to stigmatize, a priori, any other recreational activities as not being "fine," forms are grouped together here based on their financial patronage by governments, corporations, foundations, and individuals.[9]

As the following clearly shows, the patronized forms comprise a substantial part of recreation:

- The 1992 Survey of Public Participation in the Arts (SPPA) found that 13 percent of respondents attended at least one classical music performance in the prior year. For opera, the corresponding figure was 3 percent, 17 percent for musical theater, 14 percent for legitimate theater, 11 percent for jazz, 5 percent for ballet, and 25 percent for museums.
- In 1995, the paid attendance at professional theater companies was 19 million people, 6.5 million for opera companies, and 23 million for symphony orchestras (U.S. Bureau of the Census 1997).
- According to the National Income and Product Accounts, $9 billion was spent in 1995 to attend "legitimate theaters and operas, and entertainments of non-profit institutions (not including athletics) of the total recreation expenditure of $401 billion, or 2.2 percent of the money spent on recreation (U.S. Bureau of the Census 1997).
- In 1996, 3.4 percent of the $12.5 billion spent on recorded music went to classical music recordings (U.S. Bureau of the Census 1997).

4. Amateur Arts

Most people create things that they invest with aesthetic meaning. The amateur arts cover much the same range of activities as the patronized arts but also include a number of activities other than those that receive patron-age. For example, such things as meals, flower arrangements, a display gar-den, a renovated classic car, slight-of-hand displays, Internet homepage art, or a bluegrass banjo solo are regularly invested with aesthetic meaning.

- In 1992, 4 percent of surveyed adults said they had played classical music in the past 12 months, 8 percent had taken part in modern dance, 10 percent had painted, and 7 percent said they had engaged in creative writing (SPPA 1992).
- In 1993, 23 percent of adults played a musical instrument in the past year; 10 percent had taken part in music, dance, or theatrical perfor-mances; and 40 percent had made art or craft objects such as pot-tery, woodworking, quilts, or paintings in the past year (GSS 1993).

5. Do-It-Yourself Hobbies

A great deal of time, effort, and pride is invested in repairing, reno-vating, and beautifying one's house, apartment, or car. Keeping plants and gardens is also widely practiced, and the range of hobbies from needlework to model building, from food preparation to conservation activities, from birdwatching to astronomy, from preserving food to wine making, from Barbie doll to sports memorabilia collecting, from model train layouts to bootleg concert tape trading is vast. A number of activities now pursued as hobbies were once a part of work activities.

Most hobbies bring people together who share the same interests. Even in the case of those hobbies that are usually solitary pursuits, serious enthusiasts meet together in clubs, meets, the Internet, and the like to cele-brate their shared enthusiasm and to show off their work. They also exchange information, techniques, and hobby items, and recruit new enthu-siasts. Along the way, they also make friends with like-minded people.

There are no clear records of the number of people seriously involved in most recreational hobbies, but the following figures suggest the impor-tance of this domain for understanding the contribution of recreation to the quality of life:

- In 1993, 60 percent of the adults reported having planted flowers, vegetables, or shrubs in their garden or apartment in the past year (GSS 1993). In the year before, retail purchases of flowers, grass seed, and potted plants amounted to $12.3 billion (U.S. Bureau of the Census 1997).
- Twenty-five percent of the respondents to the 1992 SPPA survey reported that they had engaged in needlework during the prior year, 8 percent in pottery-making, and 12 percent in amateur photo, video, or movie-making as an artistic activity.
- In 1994, 9 percent of all adults were members of hobby or garden clubs (GSS 1994).
- In 1998, $100 million was spent by those participating in or observ-

ing reenactments of historical events, and 20,000 people took part in the reenactment of the Civil War battle of Gettysburg (CBS Evening Report July 2, 1998).

6. Physical Activity

At least since the late nineteenth century, physical activity has been considered an essential part of recreation. It was viewed then as a way for people living sedentary urban lives to regain the virtues of what was romantically seen as a more natural existence on the land. The sense of self-reliance was at the center of this set of ideas. Physical activity was also seen as a way to preoccupy young men, keeping them away from the temptations of urban vices and giving them the discipline and strength to be good soldiers. Today these reasons for promoting physical activity are still expressed, but health, weight control, and good looks are now more widely seen as the benefits of physical activity. The important place of physical activity in recreation is suggested by the following statistics:

- There are 79 million bowlers, 42 million softball players, 25 million golfers, 17.8 million tennis players, and 1.4 million sailboat enthusiasts 12 years of age or older who participated in the activity at least once during the year (U.S. Bureau of the Census 1997). A 1992 survey found that 5.4 million runners trained at least 150 days a year (Brown and Henderson 1994).
- The facilities of the National Park System had 269 million visitors in 1995, and the National Forest Recreation Service had 172 million visitors in the same year (U.S. Bureau of the Census 1997).
- A 1991 summary of state data showed that 35.5 million fishing licenses and 14 million hunting licenses had been issued (U.S. Bureau of the Census 1997). In 1996, 16 percent of those with licenses said that they had hunted game in the prior year (GSS 1996).
- Seven million people have taken a bungee plunge since the late 1980s and 150,000 skydive yearly (Henderson 1997).

7. Spectator Sports Attendance

Spectator attendance at sports events has been a major form of leisure in all societies. In the United States, it began to take on its present form in the middle of the nineteenth century with the development of organized horse racing, boxing, baseball, and school athletics. The rapid expansion of professional athletics has occurred since World War I. Now affiliation with a particular team is a major source of personal and civic identity for many.

- In 1993, 53 percent of adults said they had attended at least one amateur or professional sports event in the prior year; 15 percent had attended an auto, stock car, or motorcycle race (GSS 1993).
- The 1995 attendance figures at selected National Collegiate Athletic Association sports are as follows: women's basketball, 5 million;

men's basketball, 28 million; and men's football, 36 million (U.S. Bureau of the Census 1997).

- The 1995 attendance figures for selected professional sports are as follows: 51 million for major league baseball, 20 million for the National Basketball Association, 18 million for the National Football League, and 16 million for the National Hockey League (U.S. Bureau of the Census 1997).

There are numerous other sports that are a significant element of recreation for a large number of people. For example, in 1995 there were 2,217 sanctioned rodeo competitions (U.S. Bureau of the Census). Unfortunately there are no comparable figures for other sports.

8. Vicarious (Media) Experience

At least since the invention of language, our species has been able to experience worlds unknown from personal observation, and, until recently, story-telling was the prime mode of vicarious experience. The printing of books brought the first form of mass-produced vicarious experience. Since the World War I, it has become ever easier to experience sports events, travel, nature, spectacle, theater, music, dance, the cultural practices of groups unknown from personal experience, and many other forms of recreation by way of mechanical reproduction. The primary media of communication, in the order of their appearance, are printing (books, magazines, comics), the movies, phonograph recordings, radio, television, and the Internet.

While the mass media can greatly enrich peoples lives by bringing the world of recreation into the home, their mechanical form necessarily provides quite a different experience from that provided by live participation. Numerous critics have condemned television for violent, sexist, and escapist programming. Others have been dismayed by the pervasiveness of commercial advertising on television and radio. The 1995 advertising revenues to radio was $8.8 billion and for television $25 billion (U.S. Bureau of the Census 1997). As the mass media have expanded, they have reshaped the other recreational activities to fit the limits and advantages of the media of vicarious experience. As Neil Postman argues in *Technopoly*, the commercial interests that largely control the media are able to dictate its content and in the process shape consumer preference and political beliefs (1992; see also Mander 1978).

However one may evaluate it, vicarious experience available via the mass media is vast as reported by the Census Bureau in the *Abstract of the United States:*

- In 1995, the media consumed 3,401 hours of the average person's time, and the average person spent $485 out of pocket per year to access the media.
- In 1993, 70 percent of the adults had attended a theater to see movies in the prior year. In 1995, motion picture attendance was 1.2 billion.

- In 1996, just over one billion cassettes and CDs were sold in the United States with sales amounting to $12.5 billion.
- As of 1995, 99 percent of all U.S. households had at least one radio set, 98 percent had television, 63 percent had cable TV, and 81 percent had VCRs.

9. Virtual Recreation

If vicarious experience began to grow in the late nineteenth century and blossomed in the twentieth, virtual recreation promises to do the same a century later. Going one step beyond vicarious experience, virtual recreation is interactive. It employs computers, sophisticated software, and electronic communication systems to allow individuals and groups to interact with each other in an environment that collapses the conventional constraints of space/time/corporeality. Communication on the Internet is the simplest and currently the most widespread form of virtual recreation.

In more sophisticated applications, the conventional constraints of the physical world are minimized and a virtual world is created. Here the technology not only delivers a recreational experience but also provides the opportunity for the person to enter into and interact with the media-constructed world. This may involve simply navigating at will through an environment generated by the computer software, as, for example, in a program that allows one to walk through the rooms of the Louvre inspecting the paintings and sculptures. It can also be a program for piloting a specific type of aircraft from any airport in the United States to any other airport, using the dozens of controls, experiencing the weather, and seeing the landscape as one flies along.

Programs also allow a set of players to interact with a virtual environment in ways that alter the environment and continually modify the parameters of the virtual social-cultural system. The logical progression of these developments is to create virtual realities in which the human merges into and interacts on a par with virtual players in this newly constructed world. The potential for virtual recreation to increase the quality of life, and even to change the way it is conceptualized, seems enormous. At the same time, virtual recreation is not without its dangers as Theodore Roszak (1972), Clifford Stoll (1995), and others have cautioned.

Virtual recreation is in its infancy, but the few available measures collected by the Census Bureau suggest that it is not a trivial part of recreation:

- In 1997, 15 percent of adults had accessed the Internet in the past 30 days. It is interesting to note that the level of education is a better predictor of Internet use than is family income.
- In 1996, $862 million was spent on microcomputer software for entertainment.
- By 1996, a good proportion of all school children were learning the computer skills necessary to engage in virtual recreation, up dra-

matically from just a decade earlier. In 1985, schools with computers had an average of 62.7 pupils per computer, by 1996 this number had drooped to 7.4 pupils per computer.
- In 1993, 65 percent of students used computers in school, and 15
  percent were using computers at home for school work. But the differences between ethnic groups and across family income were dramatic: only 5 percent of students from homes with less than $15,000
  in family income used computers for home work as compared with
  48 percent of students from families with incomes over $50,000.

10. Socializing

Sharing food, drink, talk, and experiences with others in mutual
affect has always been the most ubiquitous form of recreation and may
involve the celebration of an individual or group achievement. Because it is
done informally or in conjunction with other kinds of recreation and non-
recreation, this activity is not well-measured. Lodges, fraternities, religious
groups, interest clubs, and groups of all sorts serve, in part, as a context for
socializing. The family is the most frequent context for social interaction not
only in the process of daily interaction but also in seasonable celebrations
like Christmas, Thanksgiving, family reunions, and special events like birth-
days, graduations, marriages, and funerals.

The following statistics suggest the importance of socializing with
others as a part of recreation:
- In 1996, 33 percent of adults reported spending a social evening
  with neighborhood friends at least several times a month, 35 percent spent time with friends outside the neighborhood, and 53 percent visited with relatives (GSS 1996).
- In 1996, 18 percent of adults said they went to a bar or tavern more
  than once a month. Sales for food and drink in bars and taverns
  amounted to $11.2 billion, or 4 percent of the money spent on food
  and drink outside the home (U.S. Bureau of Census 1997).
- It is conventional to think of socializing as interaction with other
  human beings, but pets are often treated as part of the family in the
  ways they are cared for, fed, doctored, talked to, loved, and griev-
  ed. Clearly pets are companions for many people and make a major
  contribution towards their quality of life. The Census Bureau
  reports in a 1996 survey that 32 million households had dogs, 27
  million had cats, 5 million had a pet bird, and 1.5 million households had one or more horses.

11. Recreational Drugs

Naturally occurring chemical means of altering consciousness have
been known since time immemorial. Two centuries ago derivatives of the
poppy joined alcohol and tobacco as widely used ways of altering conscious-

ness in the United States. Only since the 1950s have synthetic drugs been used by large numbers of Americans as part of recreation.

At one time or another all recreational drugs have been viewed as unhealthy, addictive, if not illegal. Consequently, the statistics on their use in recreation are spotty at best. Although information is scant, the following data from the U.S. Bureau of Justice Statistics suggests the prevelance of drugs in recreation.

- Of the average annual United States household expenditures of $32,277 in 1995, $277 went to alcohol and $269 went to tobacco.
- In 1994, 1.1 million arrests were made for drug possession in the United States. This amounts to almost one arrest for every two thousand adults in the population.
- The estimated total value of domestic cannabis plants eradicated in 1995 was $42 million.
- In 1995, the United States Customs Service seized 220,000 pounds of heroin, 17,000 pounds of hashish, 158,000 pounds of cocaine, and 642,000 pounds of marijuana. Over half this amount of each drug was seized by local police departments in the United States. In that same year, 5.7 million dosage units of illegal artificial drugs were seized by the United States Customs Service.

12. Gambling

Gambling permeates our recreation. When individuals or groups compete in activities, from baking contests to playing chess, they are staking their personal reputation on the outcome of the event. Competition becomes gambling when money or some other valued object or service is wagered on the outcome of the activity. Time-budget studies and activity questionnaires have not asked about gambling, so it is difficult to make any estimates of the amount of informal wagering on sports events and card games. However, the pervasiveness of such activity is suggested by the fact that the point spread for amateur and professional teams is regularly announced in TV, newspaper, and radio sports commentaries. Gambling is increasingly an accepted part of recreation. In 1994, only 15,845 gambling arrests were reported to federal authorities by 10,654 police departments (U.S. Bureau of Justice Statistics 1995). Native American reservations, once bereft of economic assets, have become sites of major gambling casinos since a 1988 change in the laws. For example, the Pequot tribe of Connecticut has opened two casinos on tribal land. The $1 billion annual revenues generated by this activity have compensated the area for the tax revenues lost with the closing of the war factories at the end of the Cold War (*Economist* 1998b).

While the amount of money spent in legal and illegal gambling is huge, the only official Census Bureau statistics on the amount of money spent gambling are for the government-sanctioned lotteries and pari-mutuel betting:

- The 1996 ticket sales on state lotteries aggregated to $34 billion.
- The money wagered in officially sanctioned pari-mutual betting in 1994 was $14 billion on horse racing, $2.9 billion on greyhound racing, and $331 million on jai alai.
- $34 billion was collected through state lotteries in 1966.

13. Travel and Tourism

According to the 1988 figures generated by the World Travel and Tourism Council, travel accounts for 10 percent of the gross domestic product worldwide (Lipman and Dickinson 1998). But travel is a major component of most other forms of recreation, so that a considerable portion is already counted in the twelve types of recreation discussed above. The part of travel and tourism recognized here as cell 13 in the re-creation model is the considerable value added to recreation by traveling away from one's home and negotiating social interaction in an unfamiliar environment with distinctive customs, whether it be a New Yorker going to Nashville for the country music or sightseeing in Taipei while on a business trip.

Although it clearly should be done, the currently available statistics do not separate out the quality-of-life contributions of touristic travel. The following figures suggest that its contribution is immense:

- In 1992, 35 percent of adults reported having visited a historic park in the prior year (SPPA 1992).
- In 1995, Americans took 51 million trips outside the United States, 19 million of which went to places other than Mexico and Canada (U.S. Bureau of the Census 1997). That same year, expenditures abroad by United States travelers was estimated at $45 billion.
- In the Caribbean, tourism accounts for 70 percent of the regional economy. The Bahamas, with a local population of 300,000, welcomed more than one million visitors in 1996. The 30 million visitors to Las Vegas in 1997 spent a total of $22 billion (*Economist* 1998b).
- Eco-tourism is the fastest growing segment of tourism, expanding annually by 25 to 30 percent (Henderson 1996).

V. Implementation

To better understand the process of re-creation and begin to assess its contribution to quality of life, the Calvert-Henderson Re-Creation Indicator reviewed definitions of the concept of recreation. We showed why participation is the best way to measure recreation. We discussed the three classes of elements in the model of recreation, specifically resources, choice points, and types of re-creation. We then provided figures showing the importance of each of the 13 identified components of recreation. We conclude by suggesting two lines along which research might proceed to learn more about this topic, followed by four distinct ways to use the data generated by such research.

Next Steps to Systematically Gather Information

The re-creation model presented here should be considered a tentative first step in the process to more systematically chart recreation's contribution to the quality of life. A good deal of effort is needed both to provide a rigorous basis for the selection of elements of recreation and to search for types of recreation beyond the initial 13.

Much work is required to develop ways to systematically collect participation data on each of the types of recreation and to measure the various components in a comparable manner. Not only must the data cover all aspects of recreation, but the data must also be collected regularly every five to ten years. The development of time-series data on recreation that is comparable to those available for the population and economic indicators is vital if we want to trace changes in the patterns of recreational choices in the United States.

Ideally, a government (or private) agency not directly involved with promoting any one element of recreation should be given the mandate and the resources to regularly gather information on recreational participation. If it is not possible to establish such an agency, some other coordination mechanism is needed to more completely measure the component elements of recreation.

Five Ways to Use the Data To Be Generated

Improved and expanded data that speak directly to a better understanding of the quality of life in the United States could be used in numerous ways. The first use is to trace the links between the three levels of the model (i.e., resources, choice points, and types of recreation). We know that there are close links between participation in the patronized arts and level of education, but education is not a good predictor of most other elements of recreation. Age and gender are often important, but so are a number of the other components of institutional and individual resources. There is suggestive evidence that factors at the recreational choice point are influenced by resources and, in turn, influence choices among the elements of recreation. However, at this time we have no systematic understanding of this process aside from what has been done by commercial market research firms.

The second use of improved data is to track changes in the 13 components of recreation and to illuminate changes in the amount of participation in recreation relative to other activities. According to the available data, the time and money invested in recreation has increased dramatically over the 20th century for most groups of Americans. But these gains have not spread evenly over all types of recreation. It is commonly believed that travel, vicarious experience, and recreational drugs have been the big gainers. Is this true? Have investments in other forms of recreation also grown? It will be interesting to watch changes in component participation rates in the decades to come. It will also be interesting to track changes in virtual recreation and to see how this activity enhances or takes away from participation in other components of recreation.

Third, the data could be used to follow changes in the diversity of recreation enjoyed by individuals, the society at large, and segments therein. Presently, people with more than average education and income are engaged in a far greater diversity of recreation than other people. Diversity of experience leads to a greater ability to problem-solve, adapt to change, and move in widely differing circles of people. Civic leaders, whatever their political stripe, tend to be more eclectic in their tastes than the politically inert (Peterson and Kern 1996, Bryson 1996). This information is important for policy purposes, because in line with the ideas of de Tocqueville, the diversity of recreation is vital. Diversity is important to the quality of life of the individual and also to the development of a democratic society.

Linking closely with the focus on the diversity of recreational opportunities, the fourth use of enhanced recreational data is to trace changes in patterns of recreational choices. The patterns of recreational activities that mark high, intermediate, and low social status continually change. Beyond the ebb and flow of particular fashions and fads, there are important secular changes over time. In the century spanning roughly the years between 1870 and 1950, members of the elite in America were expected to participate actively in the patronized arts and, as importantly, to shun all the other components of recreation that were not considered elevating (Levine 1988, Bourdieu 1984, Peterson 1997). In recent decades what has been identified as "cosmopolitan omnivorousness" has come to be the mark of high status in the United States and to redefine the meaning of quality of life (Peterson and Simkus 1992, Peterson and Kern 1996). Studies suggest that the patronized arts are still appreciated, but for people of today to move in a wide range of different circles across the world in this age of cultural tolerance and aesthetic pluralism, at least some participation in a wide range of recreational activities is necessary.

At the outset we drew a distinction between recreation and re-creation but left open the relationship between the two. The fifth and by far the most important use of the data streams called for in the Calvert-Henderson Re-Creation Indicator is to make it possible to empirically access the contribution of each type of recreation to re-creation and the quality of life. With this data in hand, it will be possible to assess the premise that it is more desirable for the American way of life that all people enjoy the widest possible range of recreations. It will be possible to seek out the most time- and most cost-effective means of attaining the greatest re-creation. It will be possible to find the most socially productive and ecologically responsible routes to greater re-creation. Finally, it will be possible to test for the possibility that there are several patterns of recreation that make possible equally great re-creation.

In sum, to more accurately assess the contribution of re-creation to the quality of life in the United States, there needs to be a more systematic understanding of the types of recreation. The Calvert-Henderson Re-Creation Indicator identifies 13 types of recreation. If regularly collected, data on these activities will make it possible to trace the links between recreational types, resources, and choice points; to better understand the choices people make when deciding between alternate recreational activities; to track over time changes in each of the 13 components of recreation; to illuminate changes in the amount of participation relative to nonrecreational activities; to follow changes over time in the diversity of the components of recreation enjoyed by individuals and by society at large; and to trace changes in patterns of recreation choices.

ENDNOTES

[1] To note that recreation is not systematically measured in this country is not to say that it has been an unimportant activity. In the early years of the republic, the United States was largely a nation of farmers, fishers, and loggers, whose rhythm of activities were determined by changes in the seasons. Some of the time the work was very heavy, but in winter and other fallow seasons there was a great deal of time for recreative activities. Even in the towns and cities of the era, the rhythm of activity was influenced by the extractive seasons of the surrounding region. What is more, many activities that are now engaged in as recreation, from hunting, horse riding and gardening to food preservation, animal tending, and needle work comprised a major part of the annual round of work activities in earlier times.

[2] Production is conventionally captured by looking at the size of the various components of what is coming to be called the "culture industry." This can be measured in terms of gross revenues, units sold, or levels of employment in the production process. Such production measures typically focus on the increasingly large organizations that manufacture recreational opportunities, ranging from television networks to eco-tourist agencies, from fine arts organizations to computer game makers and professional sports organizations (Peterson 1994). In looking at classical music, for example, one would find the number and average size of orchestras, their total budgets, earned income, wages paid, ticket prices, and numbers of performances (Peterson 1980: 3.2-3.17).

[3] A fourth emerging approach to the analysis of recreation involves an observation of how people combine, reinterpret, and transform the largely mass-produced available symbolic cultural elements to express who they are and to give meaning to their lives. This approach has been called the study of "urban folklore," "subcultures," or "lifestyles," but is perhaps best termed the "auto-production of culture" since this term highlights the active role that individuals and groups take in shaping patterns of recreation for themselves (Peterson 1994). The auto-production approach is best applied to the study of delimited groups, organizations, and communities and is therefore not appropriate in this search for patterns of recreation, broadly conceived.

[4] Measures of how people spend discretionary income have distinct advantages over those based on time, because a great deal of empirical data has been accumulated on money flows, which has been developed into elaborate systems of accounts. For example, in order to periodically recalibrate the cost of living index, the U. S. Bureau of Labor Statistics has asked respondents to keep diaries of their expenditure of money over a three-month period to learn the allocation of money to a range of goods and services.

While dollar expenditures are easily quantifiable, the money metric has several drawbacks. First, many recreational activities are free or virtually so, while others are quite expensive. Consequently, the first group of activities would be invisible or nearly so in measures of consumption based on money spent, and the contribution of the second group to the actual quality of life would be overestimated (Costa 1997). Second, the cost of specific items varies over time, so that fluctuation in the expenditures for a particular service may be as much a function of the changing costs of the item as a measure of changing preferences. Third, the state of the economy may dramatically affect the level of expenditures, particularly on discretionary goods and services.

[5] For example, the SPPA survey data clearly show that the frequency of classical music attendance dropped from 1982 to 1992 (Robinson 1993). To some degree this means that the rate of attendance dropped, and perhaps to some degree it also means that the social desirability of classical music concert attendance declined. The same is true for comparing the reported participation rates for different demographic segments such as women vs. men, college educated vs. others. In all these cases, the reported absolute levels are suspect but the differences between segments of the population is readily interpretable. Whatever the circumstances, a detailed analysis of the aging of the classical music audiences in recent decades clearly shows the efficacy of activity surveys (Peterson and Sherkat 1995; Peterson, Sherkat, Balfe, and Meyersohn 1996).

[6] The dispute is primarily between Juliet Schor (1991) and Arlie Hochschild (1997), who say leisure time is shrinking, and John Robinson and Geoffrey Godbey (1997), who say it is expanding. The large substantive differences they find in the amount of time devoted to leisure seem to depend on the characteristics of the samples they have drawn and on the way they measure time use.

[7] For example Robinson and Godbey bundle together attendance at sports events, movies, amusement parks, museums, and concerts of all sorts as "cultural events" (1997: 174). Even with the melding of such diverse elements of recreation, "cultural events" so defined account for just five minutes a week of the time budget of the average adult American. And since it is expensive to collect time-budget data, the samples are generally small. Consequently the standard errors estimates are too large for disaggregating types of recreation beyond television.

[8] While the use of computers for self-improvement in school and in the home has many advocates, other critics warn against the wholesale use of computers in education. See Roszak (1972) for example.

[9] Today, many aspects of the fine arts in America operate without patronage, most particularly the visual arts and theater. At the same time, several other commercial forms receive subsidies for some of their activities, most notably musical theater and jazz.

REFERENCES

Argyle, Michael. 1996. "Subjective Well-being." In *In Pursuit of the Quality of Life*, edited by Avner Offer. Oxford: Oxford University Press.

Arnold, Matthew. 1875. *Culture and Anarchy.* New York: Smith and Elder.

Bourdieu, Pierre. 1984. *Distinction: A Social Critique of the Judgment of Taste.* Translated by Richard Nice. Cambridge, MA: Harvard University Press.

Brown, Richard L. and Joe Henderson. 1994. *Fitness Running.* Champaign, IL: Human Kinetic Publishers, Inc.

Bryson, Bethany. 1996. "Anything But Heavy Metal: Symbolic Exclusion and Musical Dislikes." *American Sociological Review.* Vol. 61, No. 1, pp. 884-899.

Costa, Dora. 1997. "Less of a Luxury: The Rise of Recreation Since 1888." Working Paper No. 6054. Cambridge, MA: National Bureau of Economic Research.

Economist. 1998a. "Travel and Tourism Survey." (January 10).

Economist. 1998b. "Foxworth Resort Casino." (June 13).

Ennis, Philip H. 1992. *Seventh Stream: The Emergency of Rock n Roll.* Hanover, NH: Wesleyan University Press.

Gans, Herbert. 1974. *Popular Culture and High Culture.* New York: Basic Books.

General Social Surveys, 1972-1996. *Cumulative Codebook.* Chicago, IL: National Opinion Research Center, as part of the National Data Program for the Social Sciences.

Gerbner, George. 1984. "Political Functions of Television Viewing: A Cultivation Analysis." In *Cultural Indicators: An International Symposium*, edited by G. Melischek, K.E. Rosengren and J. Strappers. Vienna: Institute for Audience Research, Austrian Academy of Sciences.

Gershuny, Jonathan and Brendan Halpin. 1996. "Time Use, Quality of Life, and Process Benefits." In *In Pursuit of the Quality of Life*, edited by Avner Offer. Oxford: Oxford University Press.

Grazia, Sebastian de. 1962. *Of Time, Work and Leisure.* New York: The Twentieth Century Fund.

Halle, David. 1984. *America's Working Man.* Chicago: University of Chicago Press.

Henderson, Hazel. 1996. *Building a Win-Win World: Life Beyond Global Economic Warfare.* San Francisco: Berrett-Koehler Publishers.

Henderson, Hazel. 1997. "Extreme Times, Part II: Risks and the Search for Balance." *Briefing International Focus.*

Hochschild, Arlie Russell. 1997. *The Time Bind: When Work Becomes Home and Home Becomes Work.* New York: Metropolitan.

Hochschild, Arlie Russell. 1983. *The Managed Heart: Commercialization of Human Feeling.* Berkeley: University of California Press.

Independent Sector. 1996. *Giving and Volunteering in the United States.* Washington, D.C.

Levine, Lawrence W. 1988. *Highbrow/Lowbrow: The Emergence of Cultural Hierarchy in America.* Cambridge, MA: Harvard University Press.

Linder, Staffan. 1970. *The Harried Leisure Class.* New York: Columbia University Press.

Lipman, Geoffrey and Richard Dickinson. 1998. "Travel & Tourism Can Create 12 Million New Jobs in the Americas by 2010." *World Travel & Tourism Council* (April 17).

Licke, John. 1689. (1960 edition). *Two Treatises of Government.* Cambridge: Blackwell.

Mander, Jerry. 1978. *Four Arguments for the Elimination of Television.* New York: Morrow.

Moorehouse, H.F. 1991. *Driving Ambitions: An Analysis of the American Hot Rod Enthusiasm.* Manchester: Manchester University Press.

Offer, Avner, editor. 1996. *In Pursuit of the Quality of Life.* New York: Oxford University Press.

Oxford English Dictionary, 2nd edition. 1989. Compiled by J.A. Simpson and E.S.C. Weiner. Oxford: Clarendon Press.

Peterson, Richard A. 1997. *Creating Country Music: Fabricating Authenticity.* Chicago: The University of Chicago Press.

Peterson, Richard A. 1994. "Culture Studies Through the Production Perspective: Progress and Prospects." in *The Sociology of Culture,* edited by Diane Crane. Cambridge: Blackwell.

Peterson, Richard A. 1980. *Arts Audience Statistics and Cultural Indicators: A Review of Complementary Approaches.* Washington, D.C.: National Endowment of the Arts.

Peterson, Richard A. and Roger M. Kern. 1996. "Changing Highbrow Taste: From Snob to Omnivore." *American Sociological Review.* Vol. 61, No. 5, pp. 900-907.

Peterson, Richard A. and Darren E. Sherkat. 1995. *Age Factors in Arts Participation: 1982-1992 (RFQ 93-17).* Washington, D.C.: National Endowment for the Arts.

Peterson, Richard A., Darren E. Sherkat, Judith Huggins Balfe, and Rolf Meyersohn. 1996. *Age and Arts Participation: With a Focus on the Baby Boom Cohort (Research Report No. 34).* Washington, DC: National Endowment for the Arts.

Peterson, Richard A. and Albert Simkus. 1992. "How Musical Tastes Mark Occupational Status Groups." In *Cultivating Differences: Symbolic Boundaries and the Making of Inequality,* edited by M. Lamont and M. Fournier. Chicago, IL: Chicago University Press.

Postman, Neil. 1992. *Technopoly.* New York: Knopf.

Robinson, John P. 1984. "Work, Free Time, and Quality of Life." In *Management of Work and Personal Life,* edited by M. Lee and R. Kanungro. New York: Praeger.

Robinson, John P. 1993. *Arts Participation in America, 1982-1992 (Research Report No. 27).* Washington, DC: National Endowment for the Arts.

Robinson, John P. and Geoffrey Godbey. 1997. *Time for Life: The Surprising Ways Americans Use Their Time.* University Park, PA: The Pennsylvania State University Press.

Roszak, Theodore. 1972. *Where the Wasteland Ends: Politics and Transcendence in Post-Industrial Society.* Garden City, NJ: Doubleday.

Schor, Juliet B. 1991. *The Overworked American: The Unexpected Decline of Leisure.* New York: Basic Books.

Stoll, Clifford. 1995. *Silicon Snake Oil: Second Thoughts on the Information Highway.* New York: Doubleday.

Tocqueville, Alexis de. 1845 (1990 edition). *Democracy in America.* New York: Vintage Books.

U.S. Bureau of Justice Statistics. 1995. *Sourcebook of Criminal Justice Statistics.* Washington, D.C.

U.S. Bureau of the Census. 1997. *Abstract of the United States (117th edition).* Washington, D.C.

Waring, Marilyn. 1988. *If Women Counted.* San Francisco: Harper Collins.

Chapter 16

Shelter Indicator

by Patrick A. Simmons, Ph.D.

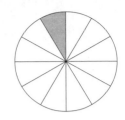

I. Introduction

The United States is in the midst of a major housing boom. In 1998, the national homeownership rate reached an all-time annual high of 66.3 percent. The net addition of 4 million homeowners between 1994 and 1997 exceeded homeownership growth during any previous three-year period (Joint Center for Housing Studies of Harvard University 1998). Home sales were at record levels in 1998, and new homes were produced at the fastest pace in 12 years.

Current housing market conditions, although atypical in their strength, are consistent with the long-term trend in U.S. housing progress during the post-World War II period. The trend has left the majority of Americans well-housed, with over two-thirds of households living in dwellings that are affordable, physically adequate, and uncrowded (U.S. Department of Housing and Urban Development [HUD] 1998).

Despite this progress, considerable shelter deprivation persists. The economic expansion and housing boom of the 1990s have not reduced worst-case housing needs. In 1995, 5.3 million very low-income renters experienced acute housing distress (HUD 1998).[1] An additional half to three-quarters of a million people are homeless at any given moment.

Housing progress has also been distributed unequally across population groups. Inequalities occur across multiple demographic dimensions, including income, gender, and household type. Inequality is nowhere more evident, however, than in the persistent disparities across racial and ethnic groups. Hispanics and African Americans, for example, have substantially lower homeownership rates (44.7 percent and 45.6 percent, respectively, in 1998) than non-Hispanic white households (72.6 percent) (U.S. Bureau of the Census 1999a). Furthermore, Hispanic and African American renters are respectively 60 percent and 34 percent more likely to experience worst-case housing needs than are non-Hispanic white renters (U.S. Bureau of the Census and HUD 1997).

Such inequalities have significance beyond the housing sector. Housing is a complex good that encompasses much more than shelter from the elements. It has physical, economic, consumption, and locational dimensions, with each having implications for the socioeconomic prospects of its occupants (Shlay 1995). Socioeconomic mobility is especially influenced by the economic dimension, which includes tenure, affordability, and locational attributes, such as workplace proximity and public service availability and quality. Intergroup differences in these housing outcomes contribute to broader patterns of socioeconomic inequality in the United States.

The Calvert-Henderson Shelter Indicator begins with a conceptual model that disaggregates the U.S. resident population by shelter status and describes different types of housing indicators. It then discusses housing standards and the multidimensional indicators included in the Calvert-Henderson Shelter model. Next, these indicators are used to describe aggregate national shelter trends, which show substantial progress in overall housing conditions in America. By comparing housing outcomes for whites and African Americans, the findings demonstrate that housing progress has not been shared equally. The next section reviews the literature on the relationships between housing outcomes and socioeconomic opportunity. It focuses on how housing inequalities affect the economic prospects of African Americans. The chapter concludes by assessing some recent federal housing policy developments in light of their potential to redress disparities in housing outcomes and possibly decrease broader socioeconomic inequalities.

Although shelter is only one element in the array of indicators that comprise the Calvert-Henderson Quality of Life Indicators, it has a broader significance for quality of life as it relates to employment, income, and wealth. The Shelter Indicator goes beyond describing housing outcomes to explore some of the links between shelter and other dimensions of quality of life.

II. Shelter Model

The U.S. resident population can be divided into three major categories based on shelter status: the population living in housing units, the population residing in group quarters, and the population that is homeless. By far the largest segment of the population resides in housing units, which are defined as houses, apartments, mobile homes, groups of rooms, or single rooms occupied or intended for occupancy as separate living quarters.[2] The population living in housing units, alternatively referred to as the household population, included 242 million persons in 1990, or 97 percent of the total U.S. resident population (U.S. Bureau of the Census 1992). Sixty-seven percent of the household population, or 162 million persons, resided in owner-occupied dwellings. The remaining 33 percent of the household population, comprising some 80 million persons, lived in rented units.

The 3 percent of the population that does not live in housing units either resides in group quarters or is homeless. The former category consists of residents of institutions, such as prisons or psychiatric hospitals, and those living in noninstitutional group quarters such as college dormitories and military barracks.[3] In 1990, the group quarters population included 6.5 million persons, or about 2.5 percent of the total U.S. resident population (U.S. Bureau of the Census 1992).[4]

Calvert-Henderson Shelter Model

U.S. Resident Population
(249 million or 100%)

Homeless Population
(500,000-750,000 or 0.5%)

(e.g., living on the streets or in emergency shelters)

Population in Housing Units
(242 million or 97%)

Housing Outcomes

Quality (plumbing)

Crowding (persons per room)

Affordability (rent as % of income)

1
2
3

Location (neighborhood poverty)

Tenure (homeownership rate)

Group Quarters Population
(6.5 million or 2.5%)

(e.g., living in college dormitories, nursing homes, prisons)

Note: All statistics as of 1990.

The final shelter status category consists of persons who are homeless. Because members of this population lack traditional places of residence, the extent of homelessness is very difficult to estimate. The "Shelter-and Street-Night" ("S-night") operation conducted as part of the 1990 Census counted just under 230,000 persons at emergency shelters for homeless persons and in street locations (U.S. Bureau of the Census 1992). However, the Census Bureau acknowledged that the S-night operation undercounted the homeless population. Other estimates of the size of the homeless population vary from several hundred thousand to several million (Kondratas 1991), with 500,000 to 750,000 likely representing a reasonable estimate for a given point in time. Based on the latter range of estimates, the homeless population comprises less than one-half of one percent of the total resident population. It should be noted, however, that a much larger number of persons might experience homelessness over periods of a year or more, as research by Culhane, Dejowski, Ibanez, Needham, and Macchia (1994) in Philadelphia and New York City has shown.

III. Selection of Housing Standards and Indicators

Baer (1976: 362) provides useful definitions of the concepts of "standard" and "indicator." The former is "...an established criterion or recognized level of excellence [measured by an indicator] used as a determinant of achievement," while the latter is "...a measure [usually a time series] that permits comparison in the item measured at different points in time so as to detect fluctuation in rates of change and long-term trends." Housing standards and indicators have changed considerably over time, complicating assessment of national housing progress.

Measuring housing progress is further complicated by the fact that change can be assessed from several different perspectives, including those of housing consumers, producers, or marketers; housing finance institutions; and local, state, and central governments (Priemus 1998). Each perspective adopts different performance standards and uses different indicators to measure progress towards these standards. The analysis contained herein derives from a consumer perspective and examines indicators that describe the housing status of the household population. The middle panel of the model depicts the broad categories of indicators that are typically used to describe the housing circumstances of the household population. The discussion to follow introduces the specific indicators within each of these categories that will be used in the Calvert-Henderson Shelter Indicator. The data sources for each indicator are described in the appendix.

Tenure

Tenure refers to whether an occupied housing unit is owned or rented by the household living there. A housing unit is owner-occupied if the owner or co-owner lives in the unit, even if it is mortgaged or not fully paid for. All occupied housing units that are not owner-occupied are classified as renter-occupied. Renter-occupied units include dwellings rented for cash and those occupied without payment of cash rent.

The homeownership rate, which is the percentage of all occupied housing units that are owner-occupied, is the specific measure of tenure used in the Shelter Indicator. Increases in the homeownership rate are frequently cited as indicating national housing progress. For example, the current administration cites the recent record homeownership rate as evidence that its economic and housing policies are succeeding (HUD 1999).

Crowding

Like tenure, crowding is generally measured by a single indicator: the number of persons per room in occupied housing units. Although persons per room has long been used as a crowding indicator, the standard for overcrowding has changed several times. Whereas a standard of more than 2.0 persons per room was commonly used earlier this century, by the 1960s housing experts frequently employed a standard of more than 1.0 persons per room. Units with more than 1.0 persons per room are considered overcrowded and those with more than 1.5 persons per room are deemed severely overcrowded (Myers, Baer, and Choi 1996).[5] The Shelter Indicator adopts the current standards, recognizing that the measured extent of overcrowding would be considerably lower were the earlier standards used.

Unit Physical Quality

In contrast to indicators of tenure and crowding, there is no widely accepted and consistently used indicator of the physical condition of housing units. Baer (1976: 368) writes that, "…the history of national measures of structural quality has been one of continuing change. The indicators have been constantly altered [making a time series difficult] in search of better ones."

The indicator that is the most consistent over time is the presence of complete plumbing facilities in the housing unit. A housing unit has complete plumbing facilities if it has hot and cold piped water, a flush toilet, and a bathtub or shower. All three facilities must be located inside the housing unit, but not necessarily in the same room. Housing units are classified as lacking complete plumbing facilities when any of the three facilities are not present.

Affordability

Indicators of housing affordability are numerous, and the selection of an appropriate measure depends in large part on which segment of the household population is being studied. For example, most indicators of homeownership affordability assess the ability of all renters, or alternatively a "typical" renter, to purchase a home given prevailing house prices, interest rates, and mortgage terms. Homeownership affordability indices are designed to measure the ability of renter households to change their tenure status from renting to owning.

In contrast, housing cost-to-income ratios are typically used to assess the affordability of the housing unit currently occupied by a household, and are applied to both renters and owners. Renter housing costs include rent plus payments for utilities and fuels. Property insurance, mobile home land rent, and garbage and trash collection are also included if these items are paid by the renter (or paid by someone else, such as a relative, welfare agency, or friend) in addition to rent.

The Shelter Indicator is restricted to renters because they constitute the majority of households that experience high housing cost-to-income ratios. This is particularly true at lower income levels.[6] In addition to examining the prevalence of housing cost burdens among all renters, the indicator analyzes separately households with very low incomes. These lower income renters deserve special attention because high cost burdens are more likely to compromise their abilities to pay for other life necessities and because they are the focus of federal low-income rental housing programs.

The standard for excessive housing cost burden has changed over time. Originally, housing costs consuming more than 25 percent of gross household income were deemed excessive. This standard derived from the adage, "a month's rent should not exceed a week's pay" (Baer 1976: 381). For federal low-income rental housing programs, this standard of affordability was in place until 1982, at which time it was increased to 30 percent (Mitchell 1985). Increasingly, federal low-income housing policy has focused on assisting very low-income renters facing severe housing cost burdens, defined as housing costs in excess of 50 percent of income. The Shelter Indicator analyzes changes in rent burdens using both the 30 percent and 50 percent standards.

Location

The final category, location, is the most variable in terms of measurement and standard. The broad concept of "location" can refer to a range of characteristics, including the quality of the built environment surrounding the housing unit, the socioeconomic characteristics of neighborhood residents, the availability and quality of local services, and the proximity of the housing unit to places of employment.

The indicator examines the socioeconomic characteristics of nearby residents as an indicator of neighborhood condition. Specifically, the proportion of neighborhood residents with incomes below the poverty level is analyzed. As will be discussed in greater detail below, the poverty rate is an important neighborhood characteristic because there is mounting evidence that spatial concentrations of poverty affect neighborhood residents' prospects for socioeconomic mobility (Ellen and Turner 1997; Galster and

Killen 1995). The spatial concentration of poverty is also a growing concern of federal low-income housing policy. The concern is reflected in the design of HUD's Moving to Opportunity Demonstration, which assesses the effects of moving public- and assisted-housing residents away from areas with very high concentrations of poverty (Turner 1998).

A neighborhood poverty rate of more than 40 percent will be used here to indicate an excessive concentration of poverty. Neighborhoods that exhibit such high rates of economic deprivation are referred to as *extreme poverty neighborhoods* or *extremely poor neighborhoods*.

Unit of Analysis and Geographic Coverage

The household will be the unit of analysis for all indicators except those related to neighborhood condition. The neighborhood condition indicator is calculated on a population base; that is, it reflects the proportion of all persons in a neighborhood – regardless of shelter status – who are living in poverty.

All indicators included in the Shelter Indicator are measured at the national level. However, housing conditions vary considerably across regions, states, and metropolitan areas, and even across jurisdictions within a given metropolitan area. For example, the incidence of renter overcrowding is greater in metropolitan areas with high proportions of recent immigrants and Latino renters (Myers, Baer, and Choi 1996). As another illustration, homeownership rates in central cities (50 percent in 1998) are considerably lower than in suburbs (73 percent) or nonmetropolitan areas (75 percent) (U.S. Bureau of the Census 1999b). An analysis of geographic variations in housing conditions is beyond the scope of the Shelter Indicator.

IV. U.S. Housing Progress in the Post-World War II Period

Using the indicators described above, this section examines aggregate national housing trends for all U.S. households, without differentiation by demographic characteristic. The nation has experienced considerable progress in the areas of homeownership, crowding, and unit physical quality. As problems related to overcrowding and physical inadequacy have eased, rental housing affordability and spatial concentration of poverty have emerged as major concerns of national housing policymakers. Trends for each of these indicators are described in greater detail below. Appendices 1-6 contain detailed data tables for the indicators.

Homeownership

Perhaps the nation's greatest housing achievement in the post-World War II era has been expanded homeownership. In 1940, only 43.6 percent of households owned their homes (Appendix 1). The homeownership rate increased by more than 20 percentage points during the next four decades, reaching 64.4 percent in 1980. Growth was particularly strong in the 1940s and 1950s. The expansion of homeownership was supported by strong post-World War II economic growth and federal housing policies that encouraged homeownership through tax incentives and support of the mortgage finance system.

After increasing for four decades, the homeownership rate stalled during the 1980s and was actually slightly lower at the time of the 1990 Census than it was ten years earlier. Rapid house price appreciation during the 1970s, combined with declining real household incomes and double-digit mortgage rates during the early 1980s, decreased homeownership affordability for prospective homebuyers and helped to halt the advance in the homeownership rate. The National Association of Realtors® Housing Affordability Index, which measures the ability of a household with median income to purchase the median priced home given prevailing mortgage interest rates and mortgage underwriting standards, fell to a record low in 1981 (Simmons 1997).

Since 1991, low mortgage interest rates, job growth, the continued advance of baby boomers into middle age, and new affordable lending products have supported renewed homeownership progress. In 1998, the homeownership rate reached an all-time annual high of 66.3 percent, up two percentage points from the 1990 rate. Since 1994, all income, age, household type, and major racial/ethnic groups have experienced increasing homeownership rates (Joint Center for Housing Studies of Harvard University 1999).

The 23 percentage point increase in the national homeownership rate in the post- World War II period might seem an abstract achievement, at least until it is translated into numbers of homeowners. If the homeownership rate had remained at the level recorded in the 1940 Census, there would be 23.5 million fewer homeowners in the United States today.

Crowding

The nation has also experienced considerable success in eradicating overcrowding, which was a major concern of housing reformers at the turn of the century. In 1940, 20 percent of households reported living in overcrowded units (more than 1.0 persons per room) and 9 percent reported living in severely overcrowded units (more than 1.5 persons per room). By 1980, these rates had fallen to 4.5 and 1.4 percent, respectively (Appendix 2).

The long-term trend of declining overcrowding ended in the 1980s. Between 1980 and 1990, the proportion of overcrowded units increased from 4.5 to 4.9 percent, and the share of severely overcrowded units increased from 1.4 to 2.1 percent. These slight increases are likely associated with rapid growth in population groups, such as Latinos and recent immigrants, who tend to experience greater rates of overcrowding (Myers, Baer, and Choi 1996). Between 1980 and 1990, the proportion of the nation's population represented by Latinos and recent immigrants increased by 2.5 and 1.1 percentage points, respectively.

Still, the level and rate of overcrowding in the United States today are very low by historical standards. In 1990, the number of severely over-crowded households was one-third less than it was in 1940, despite the fact that the total number of households was nearly three times greater.

Reduced overcrowding reflects rapid growth in the housing stock, smaller households, and increasing sizes of newly constructed homes. Between 1940 and 1998, the population of the United States increased by 104 percent, but the number of housing units increased by 214 percent. Concomitantly, the average household size decreased from 3.6 to 2.6 persons per household between 1947 and 1997. Finally, the median square footage of newly constructed single-family homes increased by 43 percent between 1970 and 1997, growing from 1,385 square feet to 1,975 square feet.[7]

Plumbing Facilities

In the early part of this century, the nation's housing problems were defined not only in terms of overcrowding but also in terms of the physical adequacy of housing units (Shlay 1995). Physical inadequacy, at least as mea-sured by the complete plumbing facilities indicator, has been largely eradi-cated (Appendix 3). In 1940, almost one-half of all housing units lacked com-plete plumbing. As the post-World War II building boom took off in the 1950s, the share of housing units with inadequate plumbing facilities dropped dramatically, falling by more than one-half between 1950 and 1960. By the 1990 Census, just over one percent of housing units lacked complete plumbing facilities, although a change in definition slightly suppressed the proportion of units categorized as having inadequate plumbing.[8] The 1995 American Housing Survey (AHS), which used a definition consistent with that used in censuses prior to 1990, indicate that only 2 percent of housing units lacked complete plumbing facilities.

A more comprehensive composite indicator of housing quality, avail-able from the AHS, provides additional evidence that problems related to physical inadequacy are rare. The AHS defines moderately and severely inadequate housing units based on problems related to plumbing, heating, electricity, upkeep, kitchen facilities, and the condition of public hallways.[9] In 1995, only 2 percent and 4 percent of all occupied housing units exhibited severe or moderate physical problems, respectively. Even among renters the incidence of physical housing problems is quite low, with the corresponding rates measured at 2 percent and 7 percent (U.S. Bureau of the Census and HUD 1997).

The decline of physical inadequacy has been facilitated by rapid con-struction of new, high-quality units. Between 1970 and 1995, 48 million new housing units were produced in the United States, a quantity greater than the size of the entire U.S. housing stock as of 1950. The vast majority of these newly produced units had complete plumbing facilities.

Rental Affordability

As physical inadequacy and overcrowding have become less prevalent, federal housing policy has increasingly focused on problems related to housing affordability (Baer 1976, Myers and Wolch 1995, Hartman 1998). The magnitude of housing affordability problems, relative to other housing ills, is illustrated by the fact that 79 percent of the very low-income renters who experienced a priority housing problem in 1995 had a severe rent burden but no other housing problem.[10]

Longitudinal data from the AHS indicate that the number of renters with affordability problems has increased during the last 20 years and has yet to decrease during the current economic expansion. Between 1978 and 1995, the number of renters with housing cost burdens over 30 percent of income increased by 61 percent, from 8.4 million to 13.6 million (HUD 1998). The proportion of renters experiencing a rent burden increased from 32 percent to 40 percent (Appendix 4a). During the same period, the number of renters experiencing rent burdens of over 50 percent increased by 69 percent, and the incidence of severe rent burdens among renters increased from 14 to 18 percent. Both the number and proportion of renters experiencing rent burdens increased slightly between 1991 and 1995.

The level and incidence of affordability problems have also increased among very low-income renters. Between 1978 and 1995, the number of very low-income renters with rent burdens increased by 57 percent, from 3.2 million to 5.1 million households. The proportion of such households with severe rent burdens grew from 30 percent to 35 percent during the period (Appendix 4b).

Increasing inequality in the income distribution is an important factor contributing to growing affordability problems (Linneman and Megbolugbe 1992). In addition, the supply of affordable rental housing has decreased, with unsubsidized units affordable to renters earning 30 percent or less of area median income declining by about 337,000 units between 1991 and 1995 (Joint Center for Housing Studies of Harvard University 1999). Finally, the number of renters receiving federal rental housing assistance has stagnated in recent years (U.S. House of Representatives, Committee on Ways and Means 1998).

Neighborhood Poverty

Growth of concentrated poverty in inner cities is one of the most pressing urban problems now facing the nation (Turner 1998, Massey 1996). Much of the academic work on this issue stems from William Julius Wilson's (1987) *The Truly Disadvantaged*, which points to the deleterious effects of living in urban neighborhoods with high rates of poverty and joblessness. According to Wilson, the decreasing presence of working- and middle-class households in poor inner-city neighborhoods contributes to the social and economic isolation of the urban poor. This isolation deprives inner-city neighborhoods of material resources, conventional role models, and cultural learning from mainstream social networks, thereby exacerbating the problems associated with living in poverty.

Concerns over the detrimental effects of concentrated urban poverty take on added weight given the rapid growth of extremely poor neighborhoods during the last two decades. Analysis of 1970-1990 Census data by John Kasarda (1993) indicates that the number of persons in the nation's largest 100 cities living in neighborhoods with poverty rates of at least 40 percent grew from 2.7 million in 1970 to 5.5 million in 1990. Because the overall population of these cities increased at a much slower rate, the proportion of their total population living in extremely poor neighborhoods grew from 5.2 percent in 1970 to 10.7 percent in 1990 (Appendix 5).

The proportion of these cities' *poverty* population living in extremely poor neighborhoods increased at an even faster rate, from 16.5 percent in 1970 to 28.2 percent in 1990. These statistics are even more worrisome than those for the total population, in that poor persons do not possess the financial resources to buffer themselves from the detrimental effects of living in concentrated poverty areas. For example, middle-income families who live in poor neighborhoods often can afford to send their children to private schools or pay for supplemental instruction if local public schools are inadequate (Ellen and Turner 1997).

As with recent increases in rental affordability problems, the growth of concentrated urban poverty is related to growing income inequality (Massey 1996). Racial segregation in the housing market also contributes to the spatial concentration of poverty by constraining the housing choices of poor minorities to relatively few inner-city locations. The relatively high cost of housing in suburban locations, abetted by exclusionary land use practices and fewer older, low-cost units, also constrains the housing choices of poor persons to inner-city locations.

V. Uneven Progress: The African American-White Divide in Housing Outcomes

The indicators described in the preceding section reflect two major national housing trends: substantial progress towards the federal housing policy goal of expanding homeownership and a major shift in the nature of the nation's housing problems, from physical inadequacy and overcrowding to rental affordability and spatially concentrated poverty.

This section demonstrates that the nation's considerable housing progress has not been distributed equally across population groups, using a comparison of housing outcomes of African Americans and whites as an illustration. Disparities in housing outcomes have also been demonstrated for other population characteristics, such as income (HUD 1998), gender (Smith and Thomson 1987), and Hispanic origin (Carr 1998). A focus on the relative housing deprivation of African Americans is not intended to mini-

The Shelter Indicator reflects two major national housing trends: substantial progress towards the federal housing policy goal of expanding homeownership and a major shift in the nature of the nation's housing problems.

mize the high incidence of housing problems experienced by other groups. Rather, it permits a more in-depth analysis of how outcomes compare across multiple housing indicators. It also allows discussion of the relationship between unequal housing outcomes and other socioeconomic disparities.

For the most part, African Americans and whites have shared improvements related to housing quality and crowding, although the latter group still fairs somewhat better according to both indicators. Nonetheless, the incidence of severe physical inadequacy and overcrowding among African Americans is very low in absolute terms. The 1995 AHS shows that only 4 percent of African American households reside in units with severe physical problems and that the same percentage experiences overcrowding.

Very low-income African American renters are somewhat less likely than their white counterparts to experience severe housing affordability problems. In 1995, 36 percent of very low-income white renters had housing cost burdens of 50 percent or more, compared with 30 percent of African Americans. This difference is partly a reflection of the fact that lower-income African Americans are more likely than other groups to participate in federal rental housing assistance programs, most of which cap the proportion of income that can be devoted to rent. In 1993, 38 percent of income-eligible African American renters received federal low-income housing assistance. In comparison, only 22 percent of eligible non-Hispanic whites and 18 percent of eligible Hispanics received federal assistance (McGough 1997).

The remainder of this section will focus on homeownership and neighborhood poverty, indicators that reveal major differences in the housing circumstances of African Americans and whites.

Homeownership

The African American homeownership rate reached the highest level on record in the first quarter of 1999 (HUD 1999). A chasm remains, however, between the homeownership attainment of whites and African Americans (Appendix 6). According to the Housing Vacancy Survey (HVS), the homeownership rate of African Americans was 46.1 percent in 1998, compared with 72.6 percent for non-Hispanic whites.

The absolute size of the homeownership rate gap between whites and African Americans has remained relatively stable over time. The current gap of 26.5 percentage points compares to a difference of 23.5 percentage points when the HVS began tabulating rates by race 15 years ago. In the 1940 Census of Population and Housing (CPH), the gap was 22.9 percentage points.[11]

The ratio of African American and white homeownership rates has fallen somewhat over time, however. In 1940, the homeownership rate of African American households was only 50 percent of white households. By 1998, the homeownership rate of African Americans had increased to 63 percent that of white households.

Not only is there an interracial difference in homeownership rates, but there are also important differences in the homeownership experiences of African Americans and whites. Most notably, homes owned by whites and African Americans differ considerably in value. In 1990, the median value of homes owned by African Americans was $50,700, only 63 percent of the value of homes owned by non-Hispanic whites (Appendix 6).

Neighborhood Poverty

Urban African Americans are much more likely than urban whites to live in areas of concentrated poverty. In 1990, 850,000 non-Hispanic whites, or about 3.2 percent of the non-Hispanic white population of the nation's 100 largest cities, lived in neighborhoods with poverty rates of more than 40 percent (Kasarda 1993). In contrast, 3.1 million African Americans, or almost one-quarter (24.2 percent) of non-Hispanic African Americans in these cities, lived in extreme poverty neighborhoods (Appendix 6).

In fact, a stunningly high proportion of the *total* U.S. African American population lives in these neighborhoods. In 1990, one out of every nine African Americans in the nation lived in an extreme poverty tract in a large city. By comparison, less than 1 in 200 of the nation's whites lived in such neighborhoods.

The situation of poor African Americans in these cities is even bleaker, with 42 percent of this population living in extreme poverty areas. The corresponding figure for poor whites is only 11 percent.

Equally troublesome is the rapid increase in the concentration of poor African Americans in extremely poor neighborhoods. During the 1970s, the proportion of poor African Americans in extremely poor areas increased by 6 percentage points; in the 1980s, this proportion increased by another 8 percentage points.

VI. Factors Contributing to African American-White Housing Inequalities

A variety of factors contribute to the large inequalities in tenure and neighborhood quality described above (see Appendix 7, Prism A). Interracial differences in average household socioeconomic characteristics contribute to the poorer housing outcomes experienced by African Americans. Median income of African American households was $25,050 in 1997, compared with $40,577 for non-Hispanic whites (U.S. Bureau of the Census 1998). As of March 1998, 76.0 percent of African Americans who were age 25 and older had at least a high school education. The corresponding figure for whites was 83.7 percent (Day and Curry 1998).[12] These characteristics prove to be significant factors in determining homeownership attainment (Wachter and Megbolugbe 1993, Gyourko and Linneman 1997), the attainment of suburban residence (Alba and Logan 1991), and neighborhood quality (Rosenbaum, Friedman, Schill, and Buddelmeyer 1999).

However, intergroup differences in socioeconomic characteristics only partially explain housing inequalities. For example, Wachter and Megbolugbe (1993) find that differences in household socioeconomic characteristics fail to explain all of the difference in homeownership rates between whites and nonwhites. African American-white gaps in neighborhood quality also persist after controlling for socioeconomic status (Rosenbaum, Friedman, Schill, and Buddelmeyer 1999).

The persistence of housing inequalities after controlling for intergroup differences in socioeconomic status suggests that housing and mortgage market discrimination constrain the housing options of African Americans. The most rigorous evidence of housing market discrimination, furnished by 3,800 matched-paired audits of real estate transactions conducted in 25 metropolitan areas during the spring and summer of 1989, indicated that African Americans experience discrimination over 50 percent of the time in their interactions with rental and sales agents (HUD 1991).[13] Studies have also found that African Americans are substantially more likely to be denied home mortgage loans, even after controlling for virtually all of the risk factors that are evaluated by lenders in the underwriting process (Munnell, Browne, McEneaney, and Tootell 1996, 1992; Carr and Megbolugbe 1993). Considerable debate persists, however, about whether discrimination in mortgage lending causes differences in the probability of loan denial (LaCour-Little 1999). Furthermore, matched-paired audits of lenders' behavior prior to the submission of a loan application have found that African Americans and Hispanics experience less favorable treatment than whites (Yinger 1999). For example, white testers were required to obtain a pre-appointment credit check less frequently than minority testers, were quoted more lenient loan qualification standards, and were offered more advice on how to qualify for a loan.

In addition, federal housing policy has played no small role in creating racially disparate housing outcomes. The early underwriting policies of the Federal Housing Administration officially sanctioned racial redlining, cautioning lenders that, "…if a neighborhood is to retain stability, it is necessary that properties shall continue to be occupied by the same social and racial classes" (Oliver and Shapiro 1997: 18). The public housing program, which let local officials segregate African American residents of public housing through site selection and tenant assignment policies (Chandler 1993), helped concentrate African Americans in urban areas with high poverty rates (Newman and Schnare 1997; Turner 1998).

Intergroup differences in housing and neighborhood preferences also contribute to disparities in housing outcomes. Farley, Fielding, and Krysan (1997) found, for example, that African Americans and whites in four metropolitan areas had different preferences for neighborhood racial composition, although there was sufficient overlap to permit more integration than currently exists. In addition, members of recent immigrant groups often select neighborhoods occupied by coethnics because of cultural similarities, even if it means sacrificing some neighborhood or housing quality.

VII. Unequal Housing Outcomes and Socioeconomic Inequality

As discussed in the preceding section, interracial differences in average socioeconomic characteristics such as income and education contribute to unequal housing outcomes for African Americans and whites. For example, the lower average income and wealth of African Americans means that fewer African Americans are able to meet mortgage qualification requirements, purchase high-valued homes, and reside in neighborhoods with low poverty rates. Housing discrimination, public policies, and consumer preferences also are likely to contribute to intergroup differences in housing outcomes.

There is also considerable evidence that differences in housing outcomes, in turn, perpetuate socioeconomic disparities between the races (Appendix 7, Prism B). As will be discussed in greater detail below, home equity plays an important role in wealth accumulation and can be used in various ways to promote socioeconomic mobility. Location also plays a key role in shaping opportunity. The discussion to follow will examine the relationship between living in high poverty neighborhoods and adverse socioeconomic outcomes such as joblessness and sub-par educational attainment.

Homeownership

Home equity is by far the largest asset held by most households and, on average, is even more important to the asset portfolio of African American households than white households. In 1987, home equity accounted for 63 percent of all African American net worth, versus 43 percent for white households (Oliver and Shapiro 1997).

The greater relative importance of homeownership to African Americans' net worth is more a reflection of an inability to accumulate other financial assets than an indicator of greater benefits from homeownership afforded to African Americans (Oliver and Shapiro 1997). In fact, both the homeownership rate and the value of homes owned by African Americans are less than two-thirds the corresponding statistics for whites. Because of these disparities in homeownership rates and home values, African Americans held only about 5.4 percent of the nation's combined home equity in 1984, despite receiving 7.6 percent of total money earned that year and accounting for 11 percent of households (Brimmer 1988).

Interracial differences in home equity not only perpetuate interracial wealth disparities, but they also contribute to unequal opportunities for social and economic advancement. African Americans are less able than whites to tap housing nest eggs for a variety of mobility enhancing activities:

> Blocked from low-interest government-backed loans, redlined out by financial institutions, or barred from home ownership by banks, African American families have been denied the benefits of housing inflation and the subsequent vast increase in home equity assets.

Interracial differences in average socioeconomic characteristics such as income and education contribute to unequal housing outcomes across racial groups. There is also considerable evidence that differences in housing outcomes, in turn, perpetuate socioeconomic disparities.

African Americans who failed to secure this economic base were much less likely to be able to provide education access for their children, secure the necessary financial resources for self-employment, or participate effectively in the political process (Oliver and Shapiro 1997: 22-23).

As this quote suggests, homeownership can facilitate socioeconomic mobility in several ways. Home equity growth can contribute directly to increases in household wealth. In turn, this accumulated home equity can be used to finance economic opportunities for homeowners and their children. About 20 percent of drawdowns on home equity lines of credit, which are held by about 8 percent of all homeowners, are used for educational or business expenses (Canner, Durkin, and Lucken 1998). Nonwhite and Hispanic homeowners, however, are only half as likely as all homeowners to have a home equity line of credit.

Besides the direct financial role that home equity can play in financing a child's education, there is also some evidence that growing up in an owner-occupied home might enhance a child's educational attainment. A study by Green and White (1996) found that the 17-year-old children of low-income owners were more likely to be enrolled in school than were similar children of renters. Although the study could not conclude that homeownership, rather than unmeasured characteristic of families that own, caused this difference, it provides provocative preliminary evidence that growing up in an owned home contributes to better outcomes for youth.

Neighborhood Poverty

Like homeownership, location also offers access to various resources that shape opportunity:

Because it determines access to goods and services, location is a key ingredient for human capital development. Although it is difficult to distinguish the effects of place from the effects of people (e.g., the impact of living in a poor neighborhood compared with the impact of living in a poor family), the unequal distribution of resources across space makes location an important concern for housing policy.... [H]ousing, through location, affects social and economic mobility and future income streams. For this reason, location exacerbates inequality.... (Shlay 1995: 701)

Mounting research suggests that the socioeconomic characteristics of neighborhood residents is an important aspect of housing location. The "neighborhood effects" literature has linked high concentrations of neighborhood poverty, joblessness and single-parent families to detrimental socioeconomic outcomes for both youth and adults, and especially teenagers (Galster and Killen 1995, Ellen and Turner 1997). Studies provide preliminary evidence that growing up in such disadvantaged neighborhoods is associated with poorer cognitive development and greater behavioral problems in children and lower educational attainment, higher probabilities of single parenthood, and higher unemployment for adolescents and young adults.

The Gautreaux Program provides some direct quasi-experimental evidence that moving out of poor neighborhoods has a positive impact on employment of adults (Rosenbaum 1995). In this program, African American residents of public housing developments in distressed Chicago neighborhoods were given rental housing certificates that permitted them to move to suburban locations or other locations in the city. The study showed that adults who chose to move to suburban locations experienced higher employment rates than those who chose other city locations. Compared with their city-mover counterparts, the children of suburban movers were more likely to be in school, in college-track classes, in four-year colleges, employed, and employed in jobs with benefits and better pay.

VIII. Implications for Federal Housing Policy

The link between housing and socioeconomic mobility, when paired with substantial inequality in housing outcomes across racial groups, suggests that federal housing policy can play a significant role in ameliorating interracial socioeconomic disparities. Indeed, federal housing policy has increasingly recognized the broader, non-shelter role of housing. The discussion below focuses on recent policies that reflect this new perspective.

Federal Homeownership and Fair Lending Policies

Federal housing and tax policies have long promoted homeownership (Krueckeberg 1999, Mitchell 1985, HUD1995a). Recently, federal homeownership policy has incorporated an explicit emphasis on expanding homeownership for groups with low homeownership rates, including minorities and low-income households. This emphasis is evident in the following excerpt from the National Homeownership Strategy, announced by President Clinton and former HUD Secretary Henry Cisneros in 1995:

> Across all income levels, African-American and Hispanic-American households have lower homeownership rates compared to other groups with comparable incomes. At the same time, low- and moderate-income households are much less likely than higher income households to own homes. Breaking down racial and ethnic barriers and increasing access for other underserved households will extend homeownership opportunities to millions of families and enable minority households to own homes in a much wider range of communities (HUD 1995b).

This new policy orientation has not been implemented through new federal subsidies. Rather, the foci of federal policies have been increased legislative and regulatory efforts to promote fair housing and lending and, to a lesser extent, outreach and education efforts to prospective minority and lower-income homebuyers. Legislative changes included significant revisions to the Home Mortgage Disclosure, Community Reinvestment, and Fair Housing Acts. Legislation was also recently passed encouraging Fannie Mae and Freddie Mac to increase their purchases of loans in low- and moderate-income and minority communities. Federal regulatory agencies have also increased their enforcement efforts, as evidenced by the fact that referrals to the Department of Justice for violations of fair lending laws increased from one in fiscal year 1991 to 35 in fiscal year 1995 (U.S. General Accounting Office 1996).

It is difficult to isolate the effects of these legislative and regulatory changes, but lending to African Americans has increased substantially in recent years. Between 1993 and 1997, the number of home purchase loans to African Americans increased by 58 percent, compared with an increase of 16 percent for white homebuyers (Federal Financial Institutions Examination Council 1998).

Although recent data suggest that African Americans' access to homeownership is improving, the quality of homeownership attained remains an outstanding issue. As Oliver and Shapiro (1997) point out, minority homeowners typically pay more for mortgage credit and purchase homes that fail to appreciate as much as those owned by whites. The push to expand minority homeownership will not significantly affect interracial wealth imbalances if new minority owners face higher borrowing costs that put them at greater risk of default. Similarly, the lower average price appreciation experienced by minority homebuyers reduces the wealth-accumulating potential of homeownership.

New Attention to Location: Shifts in the Form of Low-Income Rental Housing Assistance

Recent federal efforts to promote homeownership have not been accompanied by increased assistance to low-income renters. Between 1977 and 1997, net new additions to the number of assisted low-income renters fell by nearly 90 percent (U.S. House of Representatives, Committee on Ways and Means 1998). A virtual cessation in the expansion of federal rental assistance is one reason why worst-case housing needs have not diminished during the 1990s, despite strong economic growth.

Although the total number of assisted renters stagnated in recent years, there has been a major shift in the way that subsidies are provided. Tenant-based forms of assistance, which tie subsidies to households rather than housing units and include the Section 8 certificate and voucher programs, increased their share of federally assisted renters from 18 percent in 1980 to 29 percent in 1997 (U.S. House of Representatives, Committee on Ways and Means 1998). As tenant-based forms of assistance have grown in popularity, the proportion of assisted renters who live in public housing and other subsidized housing developments has declined.

This federal policy shift reflects, at least in part, growing recognition of the importance of location. The Housing Act of 1949 established the goal of "a decent home and *suitable living environment* for every American [emphasis added]." Until recently, however, federal housing programs have focused on producing assisted units, with little concern for neighborhood quality. Now tenant-based forms of assistance provide low-income households with more locational options and are generally associated with better neighborhood quality than project-based forms of assistance:

> ...[P]roject-based assistance programs appear to do little to improve the quality of recipients' neighborhoods relative to those of welfare households and, in the case of public housing, appear to make things significantly worse. Public housing is disproportionately located in neighborhoods where incomes are low, unemployment and poverty rates are high, and the quality of the surrounding housing stock is poor.... [Conversely,] certificate and voucher programs...appear to reduce the probability that families will live in the most economically and socially distressed areas.... [C]ertificate and voucher units are rarely found in areas with extremely low incomes, high unemployment rates, or high concentrations of minority households (Newman and Schnare 1997).

Despite the fact that voucher and certificate recipients tend to live in better quality neighborhoods, simply receiving tenant-based assistance does not guarantee access to lower poverty neighborhoods, particularly for minority renters (Turner 1998). Recognition that poor households might need additional help to improve their neighborhood circumstances drives HUD's Moving To Opportunity Demonstration (MTO). In addition to receiving housing vouchers, the treatment group in MTO also receives counseling and search assistance to help them locate suitable low-poverty neighborhoods. The demonstration will provide additional evidence on the effects of concentrated poverty on socioeconomic mobility.

IX. Summary

The conclusions one draws from an assessment of post-World War II shelter progress depend largely on the lens used to view change. Under low magnification, and viewed from the perspective of housing reformers of early this century, the nation has made phenomenal progress. The two major shelter problems that concerned reformers, overcrowding and physical inadequacy, have largely been eradicated. The nation has also made considerable advances towards the long-standing policy goal of expanding homeownership.

However, with shelter conditions, as with other socioeconomic indicators, the devil is in the details, or more precisely the disaggregation.

African Americans and other groups have not shared equally in the nation's overall housing prosperity. In fact, African Americans lag substantially behind whites on two shelter indicators, homeownership and neighborhood quality, which have profound implications for socioeconomic mobility. Given the slow progress of African Americans towards full economic, social, and political parity, the patterns and relationships described here should raise sufficient concerns to induce a more comprehensive and thorough investigation of how shelter helps to structure and perpetuate interracial inequality in the United States.

If one completely changes the lenses – the indicators and standards – by which housing progress is judged, the view of U.S. housing achievement is blurred even further. Far too many Americans of all demographic groups are still beset by problems of homelessness, excessive housing costs, or stifling neighborhood distress to declare complete victory in the shelter sector.

ENDNOTES

[1] Households with worst-case housing needs are renters with incomes below 50 percent of area median who do not receive federal housing assistance and pay more than half of income for rent or live in severely substandard housing. Because the above statistics are based on the American Housing Survey, which is a housing-unit-based survey, they do not include homeless persons.

[2] Separate living quarters are those in which the occupants do not live and eat with other persons in the structure and that have direct access from the outside of the building or through a common hall. Recreational vehicles, boats, vans, tents, railroad cars, and other nontraditional forms of shelter are counted as housing units if they are occupied by households as usual places of residence.

[3] In general, institutionalized persons are restricted to the buildings and grounds of the institution, or must have passes or escorts to leave, and thus have limited interaction with the surrounding community. They are generally under the care of trained staff who have responsibility for their safekeeping and supervision. The noninstitutional group quarters category includes all persons who live in group quarters other than institutions. Noninstitutional group quarters include living quarters occupied by 10 or more unrelated persons in arrangements such as rooming houses and community-based group homes.

[4] This estimate excludes 230,000 homeless persons enumerated at emergency shelters for homeless persons and in street locations in the 1990 Census. The Census Bureau includes these persons in official estimates of the noninstitutional group quarters population. Here, these persons are included in the third shelter status category, persons who are homeless.

[5] The fact that the standard has shifted over time is one sign of the nation's progress in providing households with dramatically more living space.

[6] In 1995, renters accounted for 51 percent of *all* households with housing cost burdens over 30 percent of income, but they accounted for 62 percent of *very low-income* households with such cost burdens (HUD 1998). Very low-income households are those with incomes at or below 50 percent of the median income for their area of residence.

[7] To put these numbers in longer historical context, the "Levittown" home, which has come to symbolize the wave of suburban tract housing built after World War II, typically had approximately 800 square feet of living space (Hughes and Sternlieb 1987).

[8] See Appendix A for an explanation of this definitional change.

[9] For a complete definition, see U.S. Bureau of the Census and U.S. Department of Housing and Urban Development (1997).

[10] Priority housing problems include paying more than half of household income for housing, living in severely inadequate housing, or being involuntarily displaced.

[11] The gap in 1940 was probably slightly larger in that the rate for whites includes some persons of Hispanic origin. The HVS rates for whites are for non-Hispanics only.

[12] See the Calvert-Henderson Income and Education Indicators for additional discussion of these interracial disparities.

[13] In a matched-paired audit, a minority and a white home seeker are sent to a sales or rental agent or to a loan officer to inquire about an advertised housing unit or about a mortgage loan. The auditors approach the agent or officer separately, but within a short time of each other. The minority and white auditors are matched on key characteristics, such as income, to make them equally qualified for renting or buying housing.

Data Sources

This appendix describes the principal data sources used in the Calvert-Henderson Shelter Indicator. The publications and other sources from which these descriptions are taken or adapted are cited at the end of each source description. For additional discussion of housing data sources, see Simmons (1998).

Indicators and Data Sources

Tenure (homeownership rate). Data on tenure and the homeownership rate come from various sources, including the decennial Census of Population and Housing (CPH), the American Housing Survey (AHS), and the Current Population Survey/Housing Vacancy Survey (HVS). The last source provides data on an annual and quarterly basis and is closely monitored by the government and the housing industry for signs of progress in homeownership attainment.

Crowding. Data for the persons per room indicator are taken from the CPH and the AHS. Although other indicators of crowding, such as floor area per person or families per housing unit, have occasionally been used in the United States and even more frequently in other countries, the Shelter Indicator utilizes the traditional persons per room indicator.

Unit physical quality (plumbing facilities). Data for the plumbing facilities indicator are available dating back to 1940 from the CPH, with more current data provided by the AHS. The plumbing facilities item in the CPH was altered slightly in 1990. In preceding censuses, units with complete plumbing included only those that had facilities for exclusive use of their occupants. Units in which occupants shared plumbing facilities with residents of other units were counted as "lacking complete plumbing." In 1990, the exclusivity requirement was dropped and units having complete plumbing facilities that were not for the exclusive use of their inhabitants were counted as having complete plumbing. Of the 2.3 million year-round housing units classified in 1980 as lacking complete plumbing, approximately 25 percent of these units had complete plumbing equipment, but the facilities were also used by members of another household (U.S. Bureau of the Census 1993).

Affordability (housing cost-to-income ratio for renters). The Shelter Indicator uses data from the AHS to track trends in housing cost-to-income ratios for renters. HUD's Office of Policy Development and Research has analyzed AHS data extensively to measure trends in rental cost burdens by characteristics such as household income, household type, and race and Hispanic origin of the householder (HUD 1998).

Location (neighborhood poverty rate). Analysis of trends in neighborhood poverty rates is taken from Kasarda (1993), who used CPH data to examine changes between 1970 and 1990 in neighborhood poverty in the nation's 100 largest cities.

Data Source Descriptions

American Housing Survey. The American Housing Survey is conducted by the U.S. Bureau of the Census for the U.S. Department of Housing and Urban Development. The main objective of the AHS is to provide current, consistent, comprehensive, and accurate information on housing conditions and housing markets in the United States. With its inception in 1973, the AHS filled a significant gap in the federal statistical program by providing detailed housing statistics between the decennial censuses of housing. The AHS includes a variety of information on the size and composition of the housing stock and on housing and household characteristics. These statistics include age, sex, and race of householders; household composition; income; tenure; housing and neighborhood quality; housing costs and value; structural and equipment characteristics; and size and age of housing units. The AHS also collects data on homeowners' repairs and mortgages, rent control, rent subsidies, previous unit of recent movers, and reasons for moving. In 1995, questions were added regarding rooms used only for business; telecommuting; remodeling, alterations, and repairs; and home equity loans.

The AHS is actually two separate and independent data collection efforts consisting of a national sample (AHS-N) and a metropolitan sample (AHS-MS). The AHS-N, which is the source for all of the AHS data contained in this book, was conducted by the Census Bureau each year from 1973 to 1981, during which time it was called the Annual Housing Survey. Since 1981 the Census Bureau has been conducting the AHS-N only in odd-numbered years. The name was changed to the American Housing Survey in 1985.

In 1995, the AHS-N included an original sample of approximately 60,000 housing units. About 3,600 of these units were ineligible because the unit no longer existed or because the unit did not qualify as a housing unit. Approximately 4,200 of the remaining units (both occupied and vacant) were not interviewed because no one was at home after repeated visits, the respondent refused to be interviewed, or the interviewer was unable to find the unit.

The AHS-MS has been conducted every year since 1974. Originally, the Census Bureau surveyed 20 metropolitan areas each year over a three-year cycle, for a total of 60 metropolitan areas in the AHS-MS. In 1977, the survey cycle was extended to four years to reduce costs. Beginning in 1984, the sample was reduced to 44 metropolitan areas over a four-year cycle, with 11 areas surveyed each year. Currently, there are 47 metropolitan areas included in the AHS-MS.

Beginning in 1995, the Census Bureau began conducting the New York, Northern New Jersey, Philadelphia, Chicago, Los Angeles, and Detroit metropolitan surveys in conjunction with the AHS-N. Supplemental interviews for these six areas will be conducted with every other AHS-N, resulting in a four-year release cycle for the data for these metropolitan areas. As in the past, the results from these metropolitan surveys will be published separately from the results of the national survey.

A new plan for conducting surveys in the remainder of the AHS-MS metropolitan areas was introduced in 1996. With the exception of the six areas that will be surveyed with the AHS-N, all AHS-MS surveys are now being conducted only in even numbered years to spread out interviewing costs. With 13 or 14 metropolitan surveys conducted in each even-numbered year, this will produce a six-year release cycle for these metropolitan areas.

The AHS is currently conducted by three different interviewing methods: personal visit, decentralized telephone interviewing, and computer-assisted telephone interviewing (CATI). Prior to 1983 and in 1985 all interviews were collected through personal visits. (In 1983, an experiment was conducted using decentralized telephone interviewing.) The introduction of CATI interviewing beginning with the 1987 AHS-N affects longitudinal comparability of the AHS data; experiments conducted by the Census Bureau on the effects of telephone interviewing produced evidence that differences exist in data collected from CATI and non-CATI interviewing methods. Although studies of the CATI and non-CATI interviewing methods were inconclusive regarding effects on data quality, it is believed that CATI improves income estimates because the computer ensures that all income questions are asked.

One of the unique features of the AHS is its longitudinal sample design. The same addresses generally remain in the AHS sample from year to year, thereby permitting analyses of changes in the characteristics and occupancy of housing units over time. Because a new sample for the AHS-N based on the 1980 Census was selected in 1985, longitudinal links are not available between 1983 and 1985; however, such links are available prior to 1983 and from 1985 to later years.

Beginning in 1995, new samples based on the 1990 Census are being introduced for the metropolitan areas in the AHS-MS. Only the eight metropolitan areas surveyed in 1994 (Anaheim, Buffalo, Dallas, Fort Worth, Milwaukee, Phoenix, Riverside, and San Diego) still retain a 1970 Census-based sample design.

The primary user of the AHS is the Department of Housing and Urban Development (HUD), which sponsors the survey and employs the data for a wide variety of policy and program uses. The AHS data are essential for evaluating trends in housing supply, costs, and affordability and for identifying where and for whom federal housing assistance may be most needed. For example, the AHS is the basis for an annual report to Congress on "worst-case" housing needs prepared by HUD's Office of Policy Development and Research. HUD also uses the AHS data to develop and evaluate the Fair Market Rents for the Section 8 rental certificate and voucher programs. The AHS is also widely used by academic and industry researchers to conduct a variety of housing research.

Sources:

1. U.S. Bureau of the Census and U.S. Department of Housing and Urban Development. *American Housing Survey for the United States in 1995.* Current Housing Reports H150/95RV, issued July 1997.

2. Personal communication with Barbara Williams, U.S. Bureau of the Census, Housing and Household Economics Statistics Division, May 12, 1997.

3. Fannie Mae Office of Housing Policy Research. *Proceedings: Roundtable Discussion on 1990 Census, Ongoing Survey Work, and Analysis Plans.* April 5, 1991.

Census of Population and Housing

U.S. Bureau of the Census

The decennial population census, mandated by Article I, Section 2, of the United States Constitution, has been conducted since 1790. Early censuses were limited to simple counts of persons by age, sex, and race and did not include any housing information. The census first collected information on housing in 1850, when enumerators counted "dwelling houses occupied by free inhabitants." In addition to housing units, dwelling houses included "hotels, poorhouses, garrisons, hospitals, asylums, jails, penitentiaries, and other similar institutions." In 1890, the census also began collecting information on tenure.

The first extensive battery of housing questions was asked in the 1940 Census for the purpose of assessing the general condition of the nation's housing stock and determining the need for public housing programs. In every decennial census since then, information has been collected on a variety of housing characteristics such as tenure, structure type, plumbing and kitchen facilities, value, rent, fuels, and heating equipment.

The types of housing questions asked in the decennial census have varied in response to the perceived needs of data users and to the changing characteristics of the nation's housing stock. Questions have been added or subtracted and others have been modified. For example, in 1990 a single question asked if the plumbing facilities of a housing unit were either complete or not complete. As recently as 1970, information on plumbing was compiled in three separate categories related to water supply, toilet facilities, and bathing facilities.

The concept of a housing unit has undergone only relatively minor changes between 1940 and 1990. Although the term "dwelling unit" was used originally, the concept that a housing unit is a living quarters where the occupants live and eat separately from the occupants of other living quarters has varied little from census to census. Perhaps the most significant changes occurred in 1980 when the requirement of separate kitchen facilities was dropped from the definition. Additionally, vacant mobile homes were counted as housing units provided that they were located where they were intended for occupancy.

Since 1970, the decennial census has been conducted principally through a mailed questionnaire rather than field enumeration. There are two types of census questionnaires, the short form and the long form. In 1990, the short-form questionnaire was sent to about 83 percent of households and collected information on six housing-related items:

- structure type/number of units in structure
- number of rooms in unit
- tenure (owned or rented)
- acreage and the presence of a commercial establishment on the property
- value of owner-occupied units
- contract rent and inclusion of meals in rent for renter-occupied units

In 1990, the long-form questionnaire was used to collect more detailed demographic, economic, and housing information from about one in six households. In addition to the short-form information, the long-form questionnaire collected additional data on the following housing-related items:

- year householder moved into unit
- number of bedrooms
- presence of complete plumbing facilities
- presence of complete kitchen facilities
- presence of telephone in unit
- vehicles available
- house heating fuel
- source of water
- sewage disposal
- year structure built
- condominium status
- farm/nonfarm status
- cost of utilities and fuels
- selected shelter costs for owner-occupied units
- real estate taxes
- insurance
- mortgage status and mortgage payments
- condominium fee (for condominium units)
- mobile home costs (for mobile home owners)

By combining various questions from the population and housing censuses, the following items were calculated by the Census Bureau from 1990 Census data:

- gross rent
- gross rent as a percentage of household income in 1989
- persons per unit

- persons per room
- selected monthly owner costs
- selected monthly owner costs as a percentage of household income in 1989

Census enumerators also collect information for vacant units, such as vacancy status, duration of vacancy, and boarded-up status.

The Census Bureau's proposal for the Census 2000 questionnaire calls for dropping three housing related subjects: source of water, sewage disposal, and condominium status. In addition, the proposal would move questions on units in structure, home value, monthly rent, and rooms from the short form to the long form. Tenure would be the only housing item retained on the short form.

Congress, the U.S. Department of Housing and Urban Development (HUD), and the private sector use information from the decennial census in a variety of ways. For example, Community Development Block Grant funds are allocated based on a formula that uses data from the census. For much of the country, the census of housing is also the only source of information on rents from which HUD calculates Fair Market Rents used in its Section 8 Rental Certificate and Voucher programs and several other low-income rental housing programs. The decennial census is also the primary source of information on housing characteristics and housing market conditions in small geographic areas used by the private industry, researchers, and local planning and housing officials. In addition, national and regional estimates of households and housing units are often benchmarked to the decennial census of population and housing.

Sources:

1. U.S. Bureau of the Census, *1990 Census of Population and Housing: Guide, Part A. Text.* 1990 CPH-R-1A. September 1992.

2. U.S. Bureau of the Census, *200 Years of U.S. Census Taking: Population and Housing Questions, 1790-1990.* November 1989.

3. Fannie Mae Office of Housing Policy Research. *Proceedings: Roundtable Discussion on 1990 Census, Ongoing Survey Work, and Analysis Plans.* April 5, 1991.

4. Weicher, John. *Statement before the House Subcommittee on Policy Research and Insurance of the Committee on Banking, Finance and Urban Affairs.* May 22, 1990.

5. U.S. Bureau of the Census, "Census Bureau Submits Subjects for Census 2000 to Congress," press release CB97-C.04, March 31, 1997.

Current Population Survey/Housing Vacancy Survey
U.S. Bureau of the Census

Estimates from the Current Population Survey/Housing Vacancy Survey (CPS/HVS) are based on data obtained from two surveys conducted by the Census Bureau. Data concerning vacancy rates and tenure of occupied housing units are from the monthly sample of the CPS, which has the primary purpose of collecting labor force data on the civilian noninstitutional population, but is also a source of a variety of household demographic and economic information. Characteristics of occupied housing units for some tabulations are from the American Housing Survey (the AHS-N, described above).

Each month, about one-half of the vacant housing units from the basic CPS are interviewed for the HVS. In addition to producing quarterly estimates of the housing inventory and homeownership rates, the CPS/HVS also collects and reports data on vacancy rates by tenure and other housing unit characteristics, asking prices and rents for vacant-for-sale and vacant-for-rent units, and duration of vacancy.

The HVS estimation procedure for vacant units is similar to that used for occupied units. Weighted sample results are adjusted at the state level using 1990 Census vacant counts. A second adjustment inflates these results based on the CPS coverage of occupied units by geographic areas.

Quarterly data on vacancy rates and tenure of occupied units are averaged for 3 months. Data concerning the distribution of characteristics for occupied housing units, such as rooms in unit, structure type, and age of structure, are obtained primarily from the AHS-N sample. Distributions of characteristics of occupied housing units from the AHS-N estimates are applied to CPS current housing inventory independent estimates to obtain the characteristics of occupied housing units. The Survey of Construction and the Consumer Price Index also are used to improve estimates of the rent distribution.

Sources:

1. U.S. Bureaus of the Census; "Housing Vacancy Survey: Description;"
   http://www.census.gov/ftp/pub/hhes/www/housing/hvstext.html. and
   "Housing Vacancy Survey: Source and Accuracy of Estimates;"
   http://www.census.gov/ftp/pub/hhes/www/hvs.html.

Homeownership Rate, 1940-1998

Appendix 1

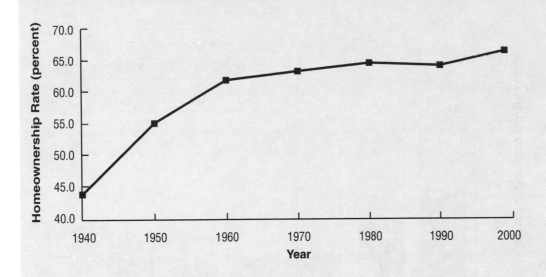

Year	Total Occupied Units (thousands)	Owner-Occupied Units (thousands)	Homeownership Rate
1940	34,855	15,197	43.6
1950	42,826	23,554	55.0
1960	53,024	32,822	61.9
1970	63,450	39,910	62.9
1980	80,390	51,771	64.4
1990	91,947	59,030	64.2
1998	103,534	68,638	66.3

Source: Data for 1940-1990 are from the Census of Housing. Data for 1998 are from the Current Population
  Survey/Housing Vacancy Survey.

Appendix 2   **Overcrowding, 1940-1995**

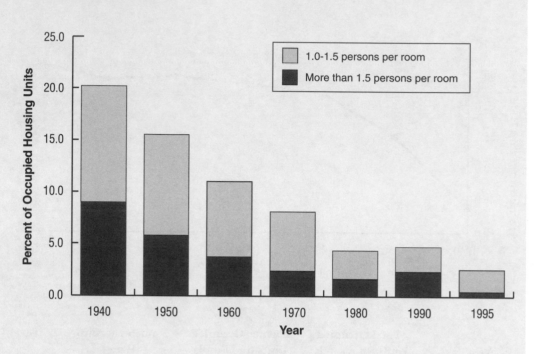

Combined height of both bars represents rate of overcrowding. Bottom bar alone shows rate of severe overcrowding.

Year	Total Occupied Housing Units[1] (thousands)	Number of Overcrowded Units (thousands)		Proportion of Occupied Units (percent)	
		More than 1.0 Persons per Room	More than 1.5 Persons per Room	More than 1.0 Persons per Room	More than 1.5 Persons per Room
1940	34,855	6,965	3,086	20.2	9.0
1950	42,826	6,628	2,608	15.7	6.2
1960	53,024	6,113	1,903	11.5	3.6
1970	63,450	5,211	1,408	8.2	2.2
1980	80,390	3,648	1,135	4.5	1.4
1990	91,947	4,549	1,912	4.9	2.1
1995	97,693	2,554	495	2.6	0.5

[1] For 1940 and 1950, occupied units reporting persons per room. For other years, all occupied housing units.

Source: Data for 1940-1990 are from the Census of Housing. Data for 1995 are from the American Housing Survey.

Units Lacking Complete Plumbing Facilities, 1940-1995   *Appendix 3*

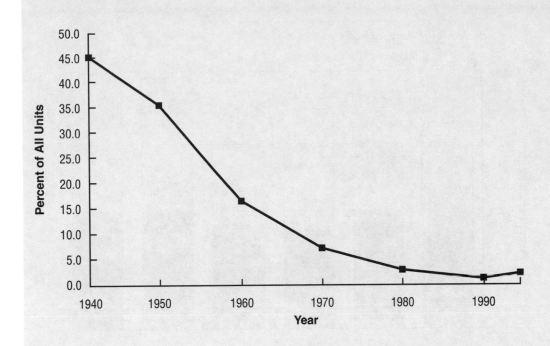

Year	Total Occupied Units[1] (thousands)	Units Lacking Complete Plumbing Facilities	
		Number	Percent
1940	35,026	15,852	45.3
1950	44,502	15,773	35.5
1960	58,315	9,778	16.8
1970	67,657	4,672	6.9
1980	86,693	2,334	2.7
1990	102,264	1,102	1.1
1995	109,457	2,515	2.3

[1] In 1940 and 1950, housing units reporting plumbing facilities. In 1960, 1990, and 1995, all housing units. In 1970 and 1980, year-round housing units.

Source: Data for 1940-1990 are from the Census of Housing. Data for 1995 are from the American Housing Survey.

Appendix 4a   **Rental Cost Burdens, All Renters, 1978-1995**

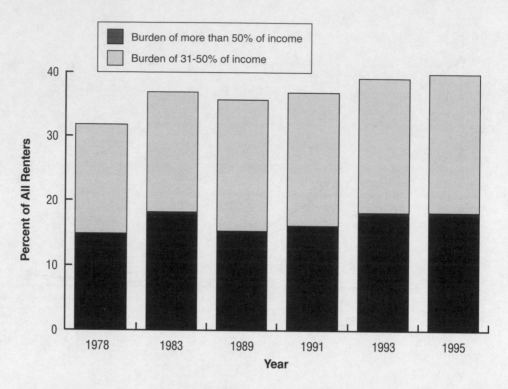

Source: Tabulations of American Housing Survey Data in U.S. Department of Housing and Urban Development, 1998.
Combined height of both bars shows percent with cost burden. Bottom bar shows percent with severe cost burden.

	Percent of All Renters With		Percent of Very Low-Income Renters With	
Year	Burden of 31-50% of Income	Burden of More than 50% of Income	Burden of 31-50% of Income	Burden of More than 50% of Income
1978	18	14	23	30
1983	19	18	19	38
1989	21	15	21	33
1991	21	16	22	33
1993	21	18	22	34
1995	22	18	21	35

Source: American Housing Survey.

Rental Cost Burdens, Very Low-Income Renters, 1978-1995

Appendix 4b

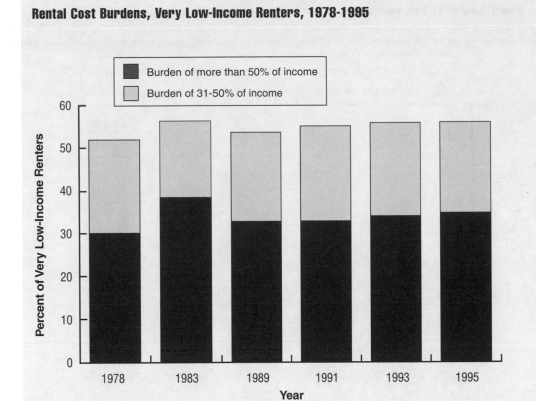

Source: Tabulations of American Housing Survey Data in U.S. Department of Housing and Urban Development, 1998.

Combined height of both bars shows percent with cost burden. Bottom bar shows percent with severe cost burden.

Appendix 5   Population of 100 Largest Cities Living in Extreme Poverty Neighborhoods, 1970-1990

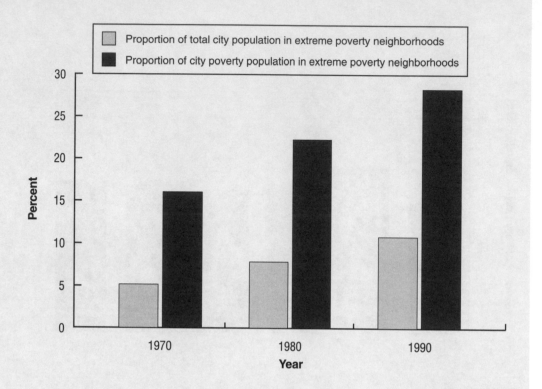

Year	Total City Population Living in Extreme Poverty Neighborhoods		Poverty Population Living in Extreme Poverty Neighborhoods	
	Number	Proportion of Total City Population	Number	Proportion of City Poverty Population
1970	2,690,970	5.2	1,240,855	16.5
1980	3,833,288	7.9	1,828,576	22.5
1990	5,495,852	10.7	2,650,142	28.2

Source: Tabulations of Census of Population by Kasarda, 1993.

African American–White Differences in Housing Conditions

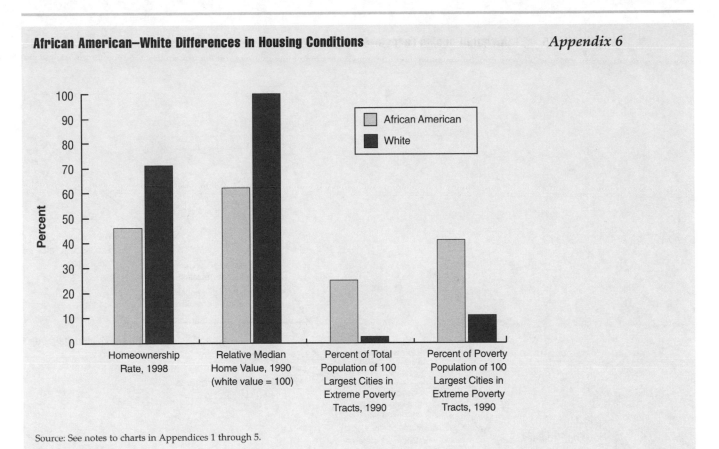

Source: See notes to charts in Appendices 1 through 5.

Appendix 7   **Unequal Housing Outcomes Perpetuate Socioeconomic Inequality**

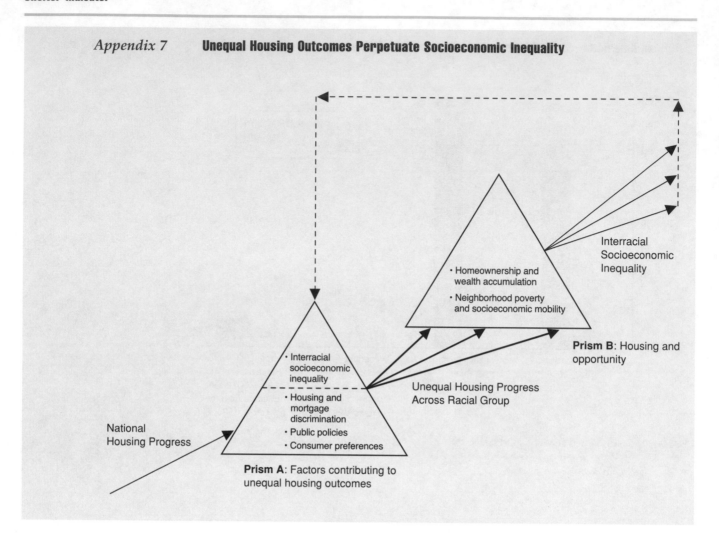

REFERENCES

Alba, Richard D., and John R. Logan. 1991. "Variations on Two Themes: Racial and Ethnic Patterns in the Attainment of Suburban Residence." *Demography*, Vol. 28, No. 3, pp. 431-453.

Baer, William C. 1976. "The Evolution of Housing Indicators and Housing Standards." *Public Policy*, Vol. 24, No. 3, pp. 361-393.

Brimmer, Andrew F. 1988. "Income, Wealth, and Investment Behavior in the Black Community." *American Economic Review Papers and Proceedings* (May), pp. 151-5.

Canner, Glenn B., Thomas A. Durkin, and Charles A. Lucken. 1998. "Recent Developments in Home Equity Lending." *Federal Reserve Bulletin* (April), pp. 241-251.

Carr, James H. 1998. *Toward an Hispanic Housing Agenda: Identifying Baseline Issues.* Washington, D.C.: Fannie Mae Foundation. Paper presented before the National Association of Latino Elected Officials (November).

Carr, James H. and Isaac F. Megbolugbe. 1993. "The Federal Reserve Bank of Boston Study on Mortgage Lending Revisited." *Journal of Housing Research*, Vol. 4, No. 2, pp. 277-313.

Chandler, Mittie Olion. 1993. "Public Housing Desegregation: What Are the Options?" *Housing Policy Debate*, Vol. 3, No. 2, pp. 509-534.

Culhane, Dennis P., Edmund F. Dejowski, Julie Ibanez, Elizabeth Needham, and Irene Macchia. 1994. "Public Shelter Admission Rates in Philadelphia and New York City: The Implications of Turnover for Sheltered Population Counts." *Housing Policy Debate*, Vol. 5, No. 2, pp. 267-287.

Day, Jennifer C. and Andrea E. Curry. 1998. *Educational Attainment in the United States: March 1998 (Update).* Current Population Reports, P20-513.

Ellen, Ingrid Gould and Margery Austin Turner. 1997. "Does Neighborhood Matter? Assessing Recent Evidence." *Housing Policy Debate*, Vol. 8, No. 4, pp. 833-866.

Eller, T.J., and Wallace Fraser. 1995. *Asset Ownership of Households: 1993.* U.S. Bureau of the Census. Current Population Reports, P70-47. U.S. Government Printing Office, Washington, D.C.

Farley, Reynolds, Elaine L. Fielding, and Maria Krysan. 1997. "The Residential Preferences of Blacks and Whites: A Four-Metropolis Analysis." *Housing Policy Debate*, Vol. 8, No. 4, pp. 763-800.

Federal Financial Institutions Examination Council. 1998. Press Release. August 6, 1998.

Galster, George C. and Sean P. Killen. 1995. "The Geography of Metropolitan Opportunity: A Reconnaissance and Conceptual Framework." *Housing Policy Debate*, Vol. 6, No. 1, pp. 7-43.

Green, Richard K. and Michelle J. White. 1996. "Measuring the Benefits of Homeowning: Effects on Children." *Journal of Urban Economics*, Vol. 41, pp. 441-461.

Gyourko, Joseph and Peter Linneman. 1997. "The Changing Influences of Education, Income, Family Structure, and Race on Homeownership by Age over Time." *Journal of Housing Research*, Vol. 8, No. 1, pp. 1-25.

Hartman, Chester. 1998. "The Case for a Right to Housing." *Housing Policy Debate*, Vol. 9, No. 2, pp. 223-246.

Hughes, James W. and George Sternlieb. 1987. *The Dynamics of America's Housing.* New Brunswick: Rutgers University Center for Urban Policy Research.

Joint Center for Housing Studies of Harvard University. 1998. *State of the Nation's Housing 1998.* Cambridge: MA.

Joint Center for Housing Studies of Harvard University. 1999. *State of the Nation's Housing 1999.* Cambridge: MA.

Kasarda, John D. 1993. "Inner-City Concentrated Poverty and Neighborhood Distress: 1970 to 1990." *Housing Policy Debate,* Vol. 4, No. 3, pp. 253-302.

Kondratas, Anna. 1991. "Estimates and Public Policy: The Politics of Numbers." *Housing Policy Debate,* Vol. 2, No.3, pp. 631-647.

Krueckeberg, Donald A. "The Grapes of Rent: A History of Renting in a Country of Owners." *Housing Policy Debate,* Vol. 10, No. 3, pp. 9-30.

LaCour-Little, Michael. 1999. "Discrimination in Mortgage Lending: A Critical Review of the Literature." *Journal of Real Estate Literature,* Vol. 7, pp. 15-49.

Linneman, Peter D., and Isaac F. Megbolugbe. 1992. "Housing Affordability: Myth or Reality?" *Urban Studies,* Vol. 29, No. 3/4, pp. 369-392.

Massey, Douglas S. 1996. "The Age of Extremes: Concentrated Affluence and Poverty in the Twenty-First Century." *Demography,* Vol. 33, No. 4, pp. 395-412.

McGough, Duane T. 1997. *Characteristics of HUD-Assisted Renters and Their Units in 1993.* U.S. Department of Housing and Urban Development, Office of Policy Development and Research (May).

Mitchell, J. Paul. 1985. "Historical Overview of Direct Federal Housing Assistance." In *Federal Housing Policy and Programs,* J. Paul Mitchell, ed. . New Brunswick, NJ, Rutgers University Center for Urban Policy Research.

Mitchell, J. Paul. 1985. "Historical Overview of Federal Policy: Encouraging Homeownership." In *Federal Housing Policy and Programs,* J. Paul Mitchell, ed. New Brunswick, NJ, Rutgers University Center for Urban Policy Research.

Munnell, Alicia H., Lynn E. Browne, James McEneaney, and Geoffrey M. B. Tootell. 1996. "Mortgage Lending in Boston: Interpreting HMDA Data." *American Economic Review,* Vol. 86, No. 1, pp. 25-54.

Munnell, Alicia H., Lynn E. Browne, James McEneaney, and Geoffrey M. B. Tootell. 1992. "Mortgage Lending in Boston: Interpreting HMDA Data." Working Paper 92-7. Federal Reserve Bank of Boston.

Myers, Dowell and Jennifer R. Wolch. 1995. "The Polarization of Housing Status." Chapter 6 in *State of the Union: America in the 1990s,* Reynolds Farley, ed. New York: Russell Sage Foundation.

Myers, Dowell, William C., Baer, and Seong-Youn Choi. 1996. "The Changing Problem of Overcrowded Housing." *Journal of the American Planning Association,* Vol. 62, No. 1, pp. 66-84.

Newman, Sandra J. and Ann B. Schnare. 1997. "...And a Suitable Living Environment: The Failure of Housing Programs to Deliver on Neighborhood Quality." *Housing Policy Debate,* Vol. 8, No. 4, pp. 703-741.

Oliver, Melvin L. and Thomas M. Shapiro. 1997. *Black Wealth/White Wealth: A New Perspective on Racial Inequality.* New York: Rutledge.

Priemus, Hugo. 1998. Housing Indicators. In *The Encyclopedia of Housing,* Willem van Vliet, ed. Thousand Oaks, CA: Sage Publications.

Rosenbaum, Emily, Samantha Friedman, Michael H. Schill, and Hielke Buddelmeyer. 1999. "Nativity Differences in Neighborhood Quality Among New York City Households, 1996." *Housing Policy Debate.*

Rosenbaum, James E. 1995. "Changing the Geography of Opportunity by Expanding Residential Choice: Lessons from the Gautreaux Program." *Housing Policy Debate,* Vol. 6, No. 1, pp. 231-269.

Shlay, Anne B. 1995. "Housing in the Broader Context in the United States." *Housing Policy Debate,* Vol. 6, No. 3, pp. 695-720.

Simmons, Patrick A., ed. 1998. *Housing Statistics of the United States.* Second Edition. Lanham, MD: Bernan Press.

Simmons, Patrick A. 1997. "U.S. Housing Conditions, 1970 to 1995." In *Housing Statistics of the United States,* Patrick A. Simmons, ed. First Edition. Lanham, MD: Bernan Press.

Smith, Rebecca L. and C. Lee Thomson. 1987. "Restricted Housing Markets for Female-Headed Households in U.S. Metropolitan Areas." In *Housing and Neighborhoods,* van Vliet, Willem, Harvey Choldin, William Michelson, and David Popenoe, eds. New York: Greenwood Press.

Turner, Margery Austin. 1998. "Moving Out of Poverty: Expanding Mobility and Choice Through Tenant-Based Housing Assistance." *Housing Policy Debate,* Vol. 9, No. 2, pp.373-394.

U.S. Bureau of the Census. 1999a. *Housing Vacancies and Homeownership Annual Statistics: 1998.* "Table 20. Homeownership Rates by Race and Ethnicity of Householder: 1994 to 1998."

U.S. Bureau of the Census. 1999b. *Housing Vacancies and Homeownership Annual Statistics: 1998.* "Table 12. Homeownership Rates by Area."

U.S. Bureau of the Census. 1998. *Money Income in the United States: 1997.* Current Population Reports P60-200. U.S. Government Printing Office, Washington, D.C.

U.S. Bureau of the Census. 1993. 1990 Census of Housing: *Detailed Housing Characteristics – United States.* 1990 CH-2-1 (December).

U.S. Bureau of the Census. 1992. *1990 Census of Population and Housing Summary Tape File 1C.*

U.S. Bureau of the Census and U.S. Department of Housing and Urban Development. 1997. *American Housing Survey for the United States in 1995.* Current Housing Reports H150/95RV (July).

U.S. Department of Housing and Urban Development. 1999. *America's Homeownership Rate Rises to 66.7 Percent Including Record Numbers of Black and Hispanic Families.* Press release no. 99-69 (April 21).

U.S. Department of Housing and Urban Development. 1998. *Rental Housing Assistance – The Crisis Continues: The 1997 Report to Congress on Worst Case Housing Needs.* Office of Policy Development and Research (April).

U.S. Department of Housing and Urban Development. 1995a. *Homeownership and Its Benefits.* Urban Policy Brief Number 2 (August).

U.S. Department of Housing and Urban Development. 1995b. *The National Homeownership Strategy: Partners in the American Dream.*

U.S. Department of Housing and Urban Development. 1991. *Housing Discrimination Study: Synthesis* (August).

U.S. General Accounting Office. 1996. *Fair Lending: Federal Oversight and Enforcement Improved but Some Challenges Remain.* GAO/GGD-96-145.

U.S. House of Representatives, Committee on Ways and Means. 1998. *1998 Green Book: Background Material and Data on Programs Within the Jurisdiction of the Committee on Ways and Means.* Ways and Means Committee Print WMCP: 105-7.

Yinger, John. 1999. "Testing for Discrimination in Housing and Related Markets." In *A National Report Card on Discrimination in America: The Role of Testing,* Michael Fix and Margery Austin Turner, eds. Washington, D.C.: The Urban Institute.

Wachter, Susan M., and Isaac F. Megbolugbe. 1993. "Racial and Ethnic Disparities in Homeownership." *Housing Policy Debate,* Vol. 3, No. 2, pp. 333-370.

Wilson, William Julius. 1987. *The Truly Disadvantaged: The Inner City, The Underclass, and Public Policy.* Chicago: University of Chicago Press.

Index

Pages followed by "t" refer to tables or graphs.

Pages followed by "f" refer to figures.